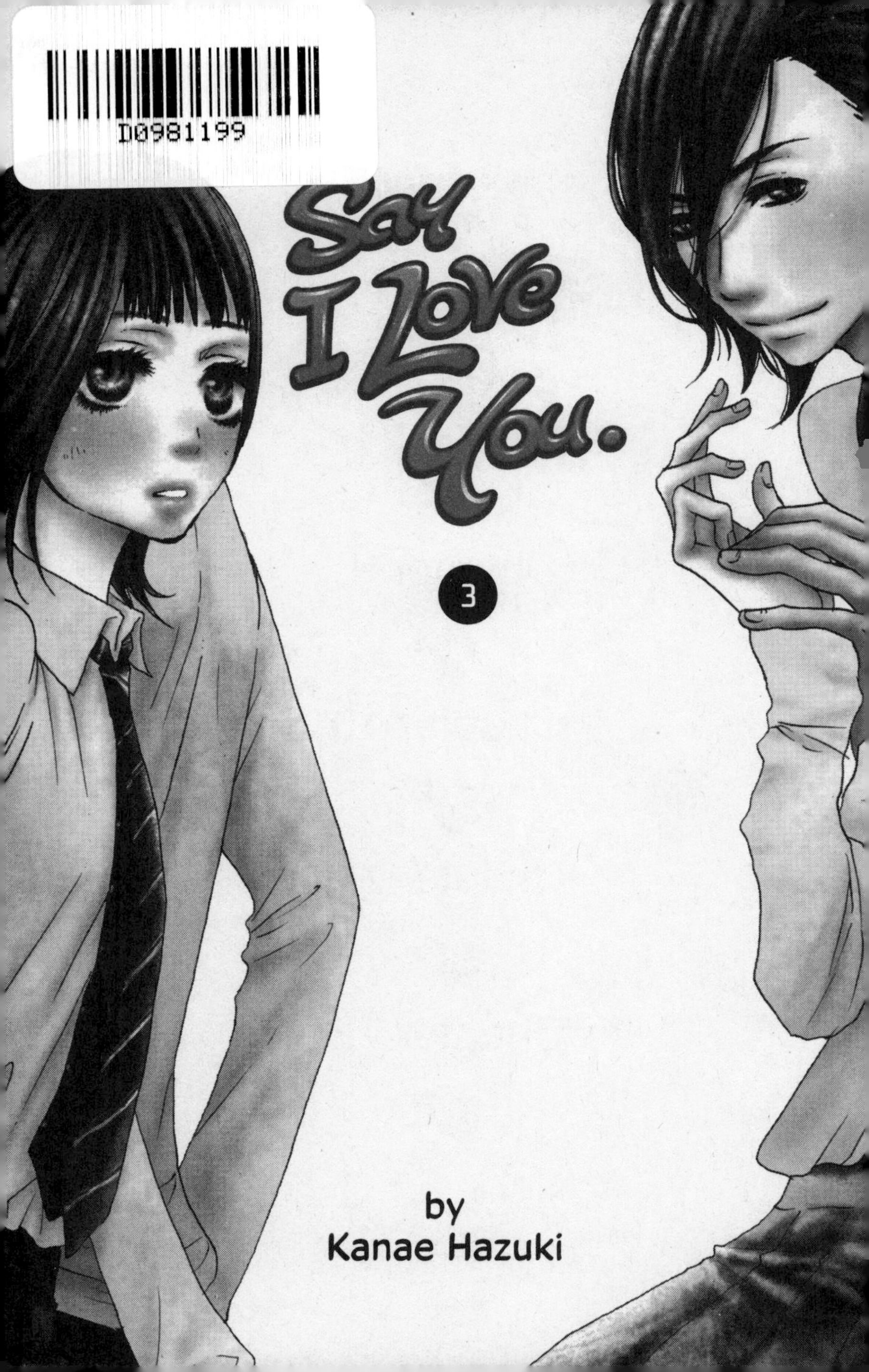
Say I Love You.
3
by
Kanae Hazuki

Kanae Hazuki
presents

Chapter 9

CHARACTERS

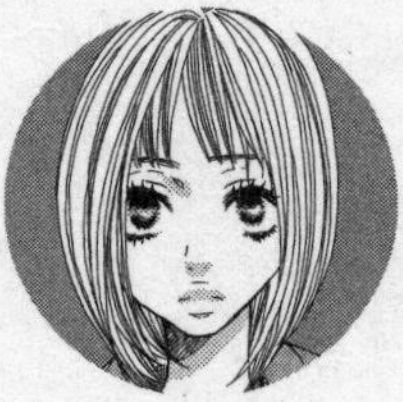

Mei Tachibana

A girl who hasn't had a single friend, let alone a boyfriend, in sixteen years, and has lived her life trusting no one. She finds herself attracted to Yamato, who, for some reason, just won't leave her alone.

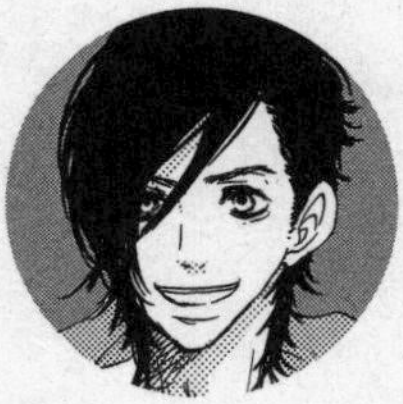

Yamato Kurosawa

The most popular boy at Mei's school. He has the love of many girls, yet for some reason, he is obsessed with Mei, the brooding weirdo girl from another class.

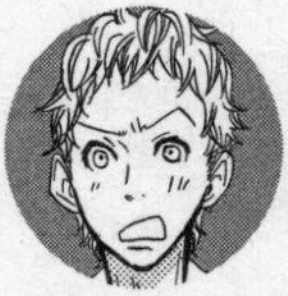

Nakanishi

Yamato's friend and Mei's classmate. He used to harass Mei, which is how Mei and Yamato met.

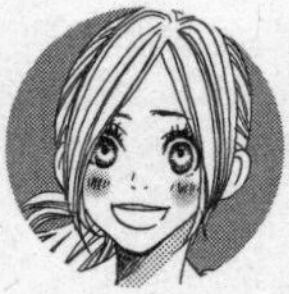

Asami

A girl in Mei's class who admires Yamato. Unlike her other classmates, she interacts with Mei just as she interacts with everyone else. She has started dating Yamato's friend Nakanishi.

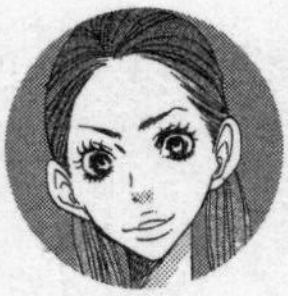

Aiko

A girl who is jealous of Mei. Apparently she is the only person Yamato has slept with, and she still likes him, but she has a few FWBs.

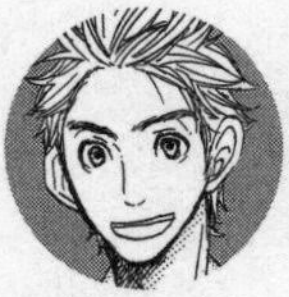

Masashi

Yamato's friend. He has a crush on Aiko and can often be seen following her around, but Aiko only has eyes for Yamato.

STORY

Mei Tachibana spent sixteen years without a single friend or boyfriend. One day, she accidentally injures Yamato Kurosawa, the most popular boy in her school—ironically, that makes him like her, and he unilaterally decides that they are friends. He even kisses her like he means it. Mei has a very difficult time opening her heart, but she is gradually drawn in by Yamato's kindness and sincerity, and they start dating. As she experiences various firsts with Yamato, Mei starts to realize that she is in love, and she begins to awaken to her femininity. But Aiko, who makes no effort to hide her affection for Yamato, keeps provoking her, possibly to her first love battle...

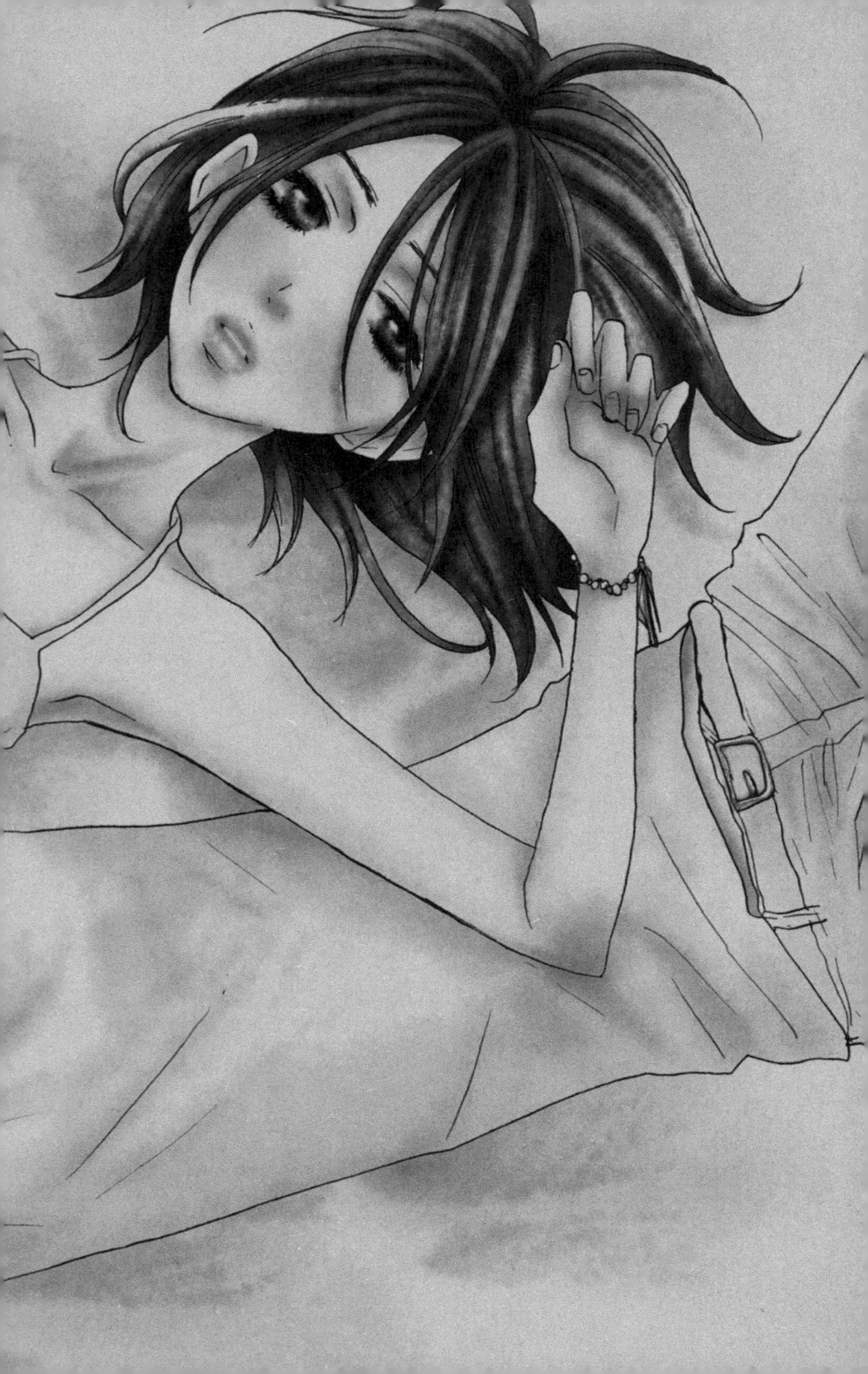

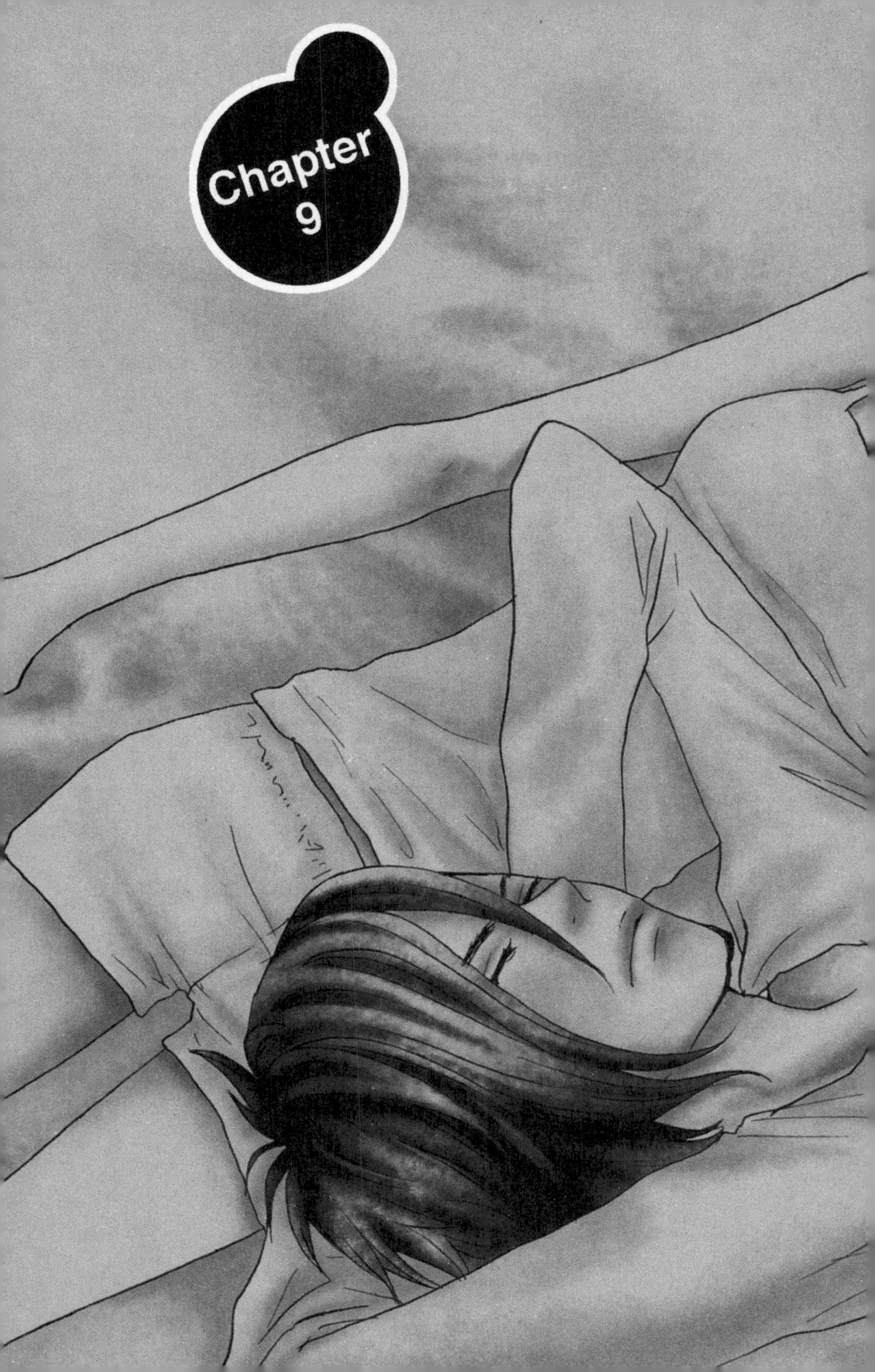
Chapter
9

I said it!
AAAHHH!

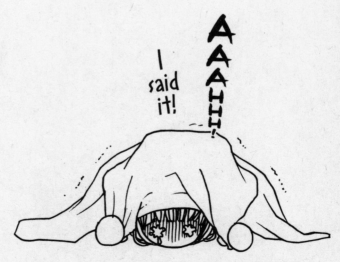

See the end of Volume 2.

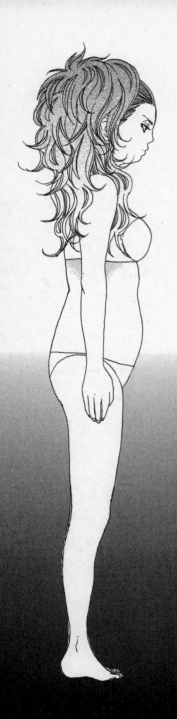

I
THREW
MYSELF
AWAY FOR
THE MAN
I LOVE.

I
REFUSE TO
TOLERATE
ANYONE
WHO TRIES
TO GET
SOMETHING
WITHOUT
WORKING
FOR IT.

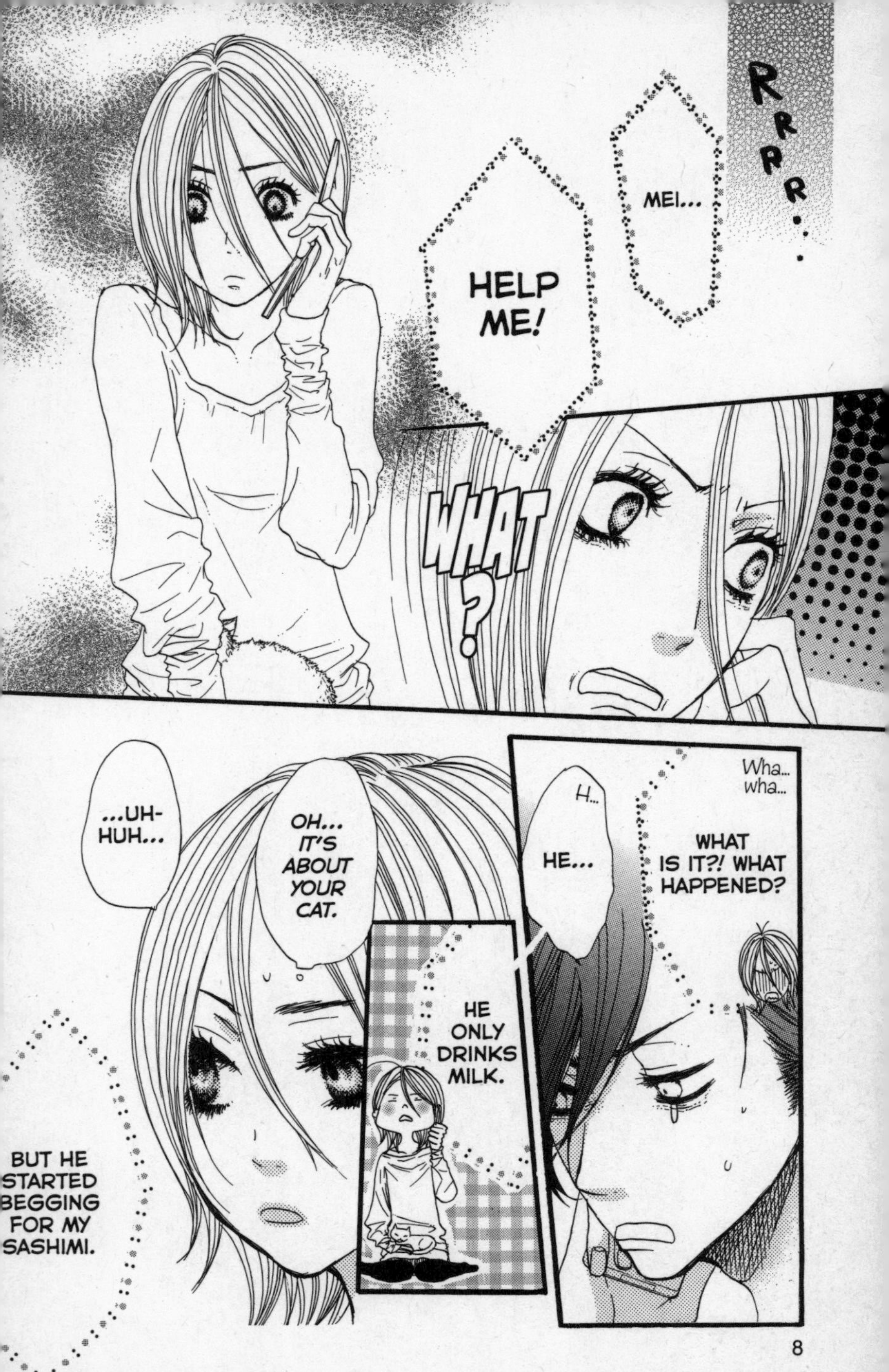
RRRR...
MEI...
HELP ME!
WHAT?
Wha... wha...
WHAT IS IT?! WHAT HAPPENED?
H...
HE...
HE ONLY DRINKS MILK.
OH... IT'S ABOUT YOUR CAT.
...UH-HUH...
BUT HE STARTED BEGGING FOR MY SASHIMI.

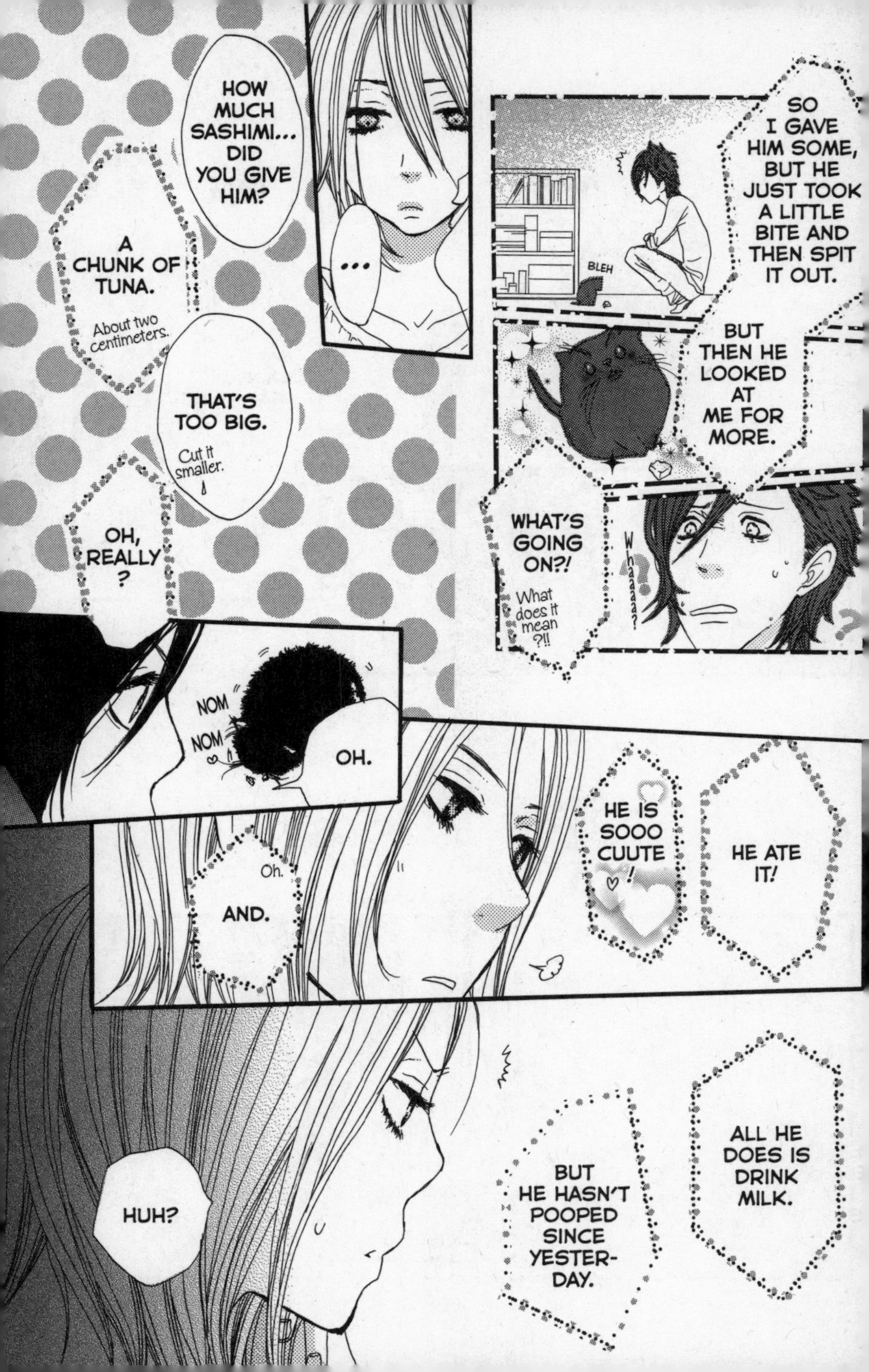
SO I GAVE HIM SOME, BUT HE JUST TOOK A LITTLE BITE AND THEN SPIT IT OUT.
BLEH
BUT THEN HE LOOKED AT ME FOR MORE.
WHAT'S GOING ON?!
What does it mean?!!
Whaaaa?
HOW MUCH SASHIMI... DID YOU GIVE HIM?
...
A CHUNK OF TUNA.
About two centimeters.
THAT'S TOO BIG.
Cut it smaller.
OH, REALLY?
NOM
NOM
OH.
HE ATE IT!
HE IS SOOO CUUTE!
Oh.
AND.
ALL HE DOES IS DRINK MILK.
BUT HE HASN'T POOPED SINCE YESTER-DAY.
HUH?

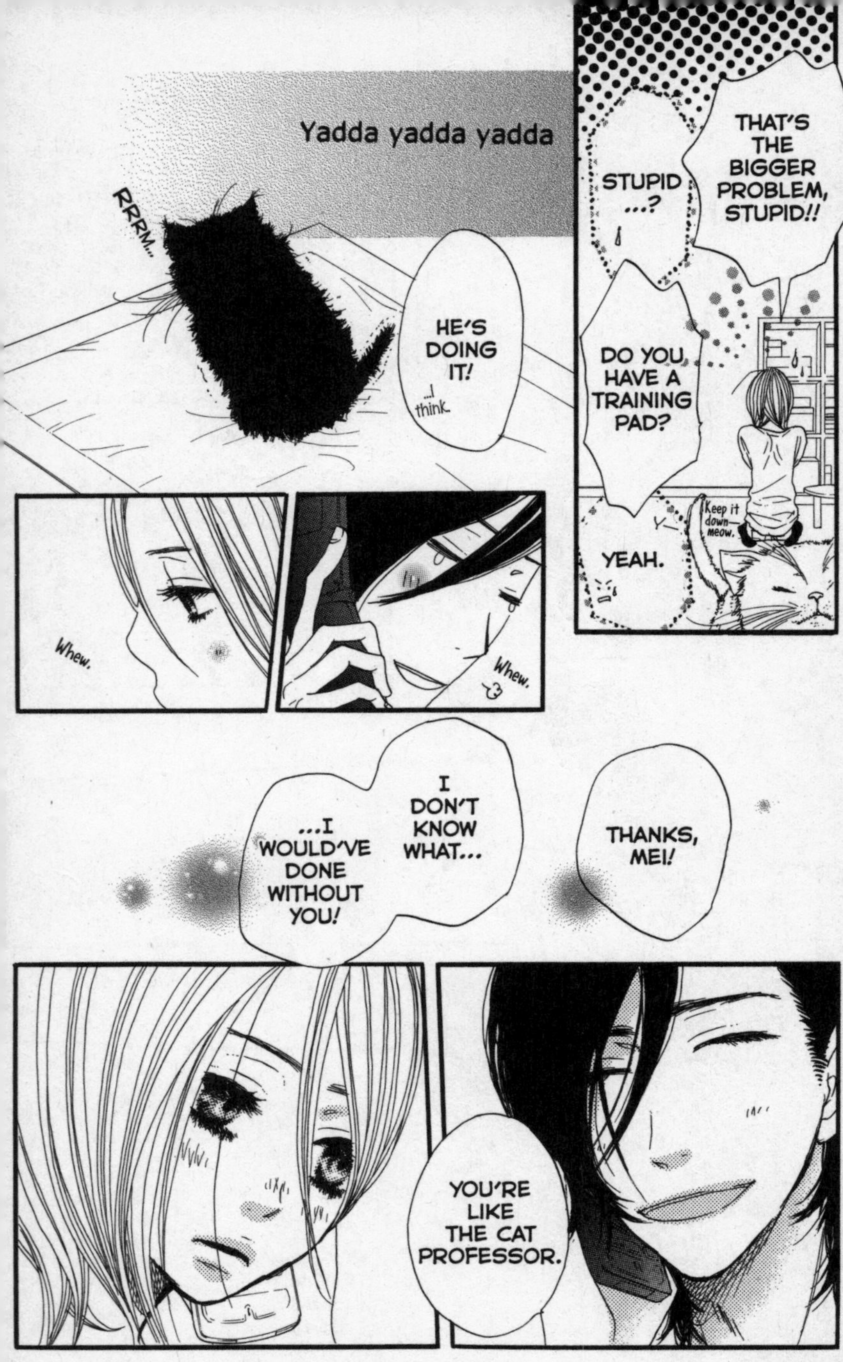
THAT'S THE BIGGER PROBLEM, STUPID!!
STUPID ...?
DO YOU HAVE A TRAINING PAD?
Keep it down—meow.
YEAH.
Yadda yadda yadda
HE'S DOING IT!
...I think.
RRRM...
Whew.
Whew.
THANKS, MEI!
I DON'T KNOW WHAT...
...I WOULD'VE DONE WITHOUT YOU!
YOU'RE LIKE THE CAT PROFESSOR.

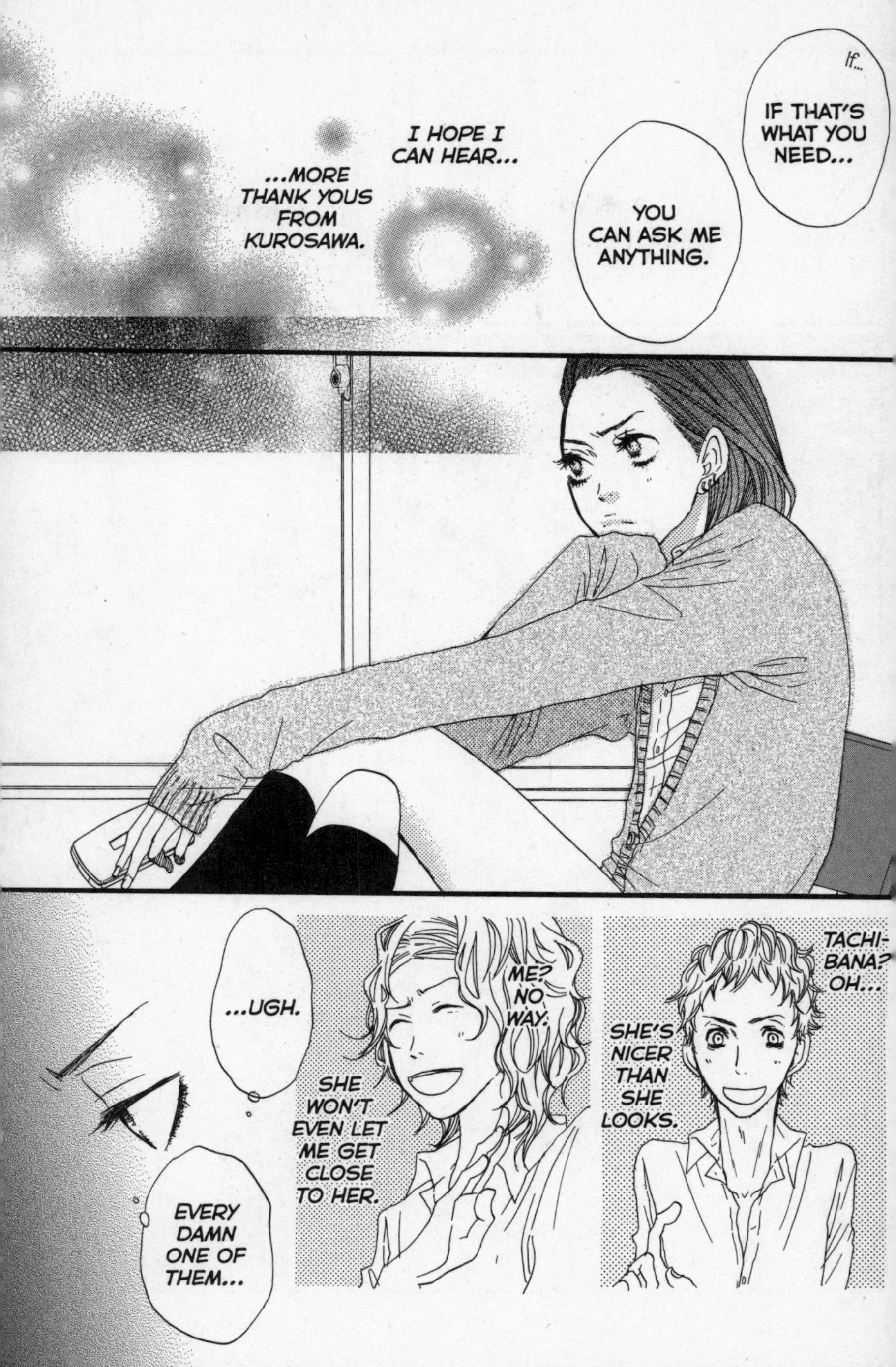
If...
IF THAT'S WHAT YOU NEED...
YOU CAN ASK ME ANYTHING.
I HOPE I CAN HEAR...
...MORE THANK YOUS FROM KUROSAWA.
TACHIBANA? OH...
SHE'S NICER THAN SHE LOOKS.
ME? NO WAY.
SHE WON'T EVEN LET ME GET CLOSE TO HER.
...UGH.
EVERY DAMN ONE OF THEM...

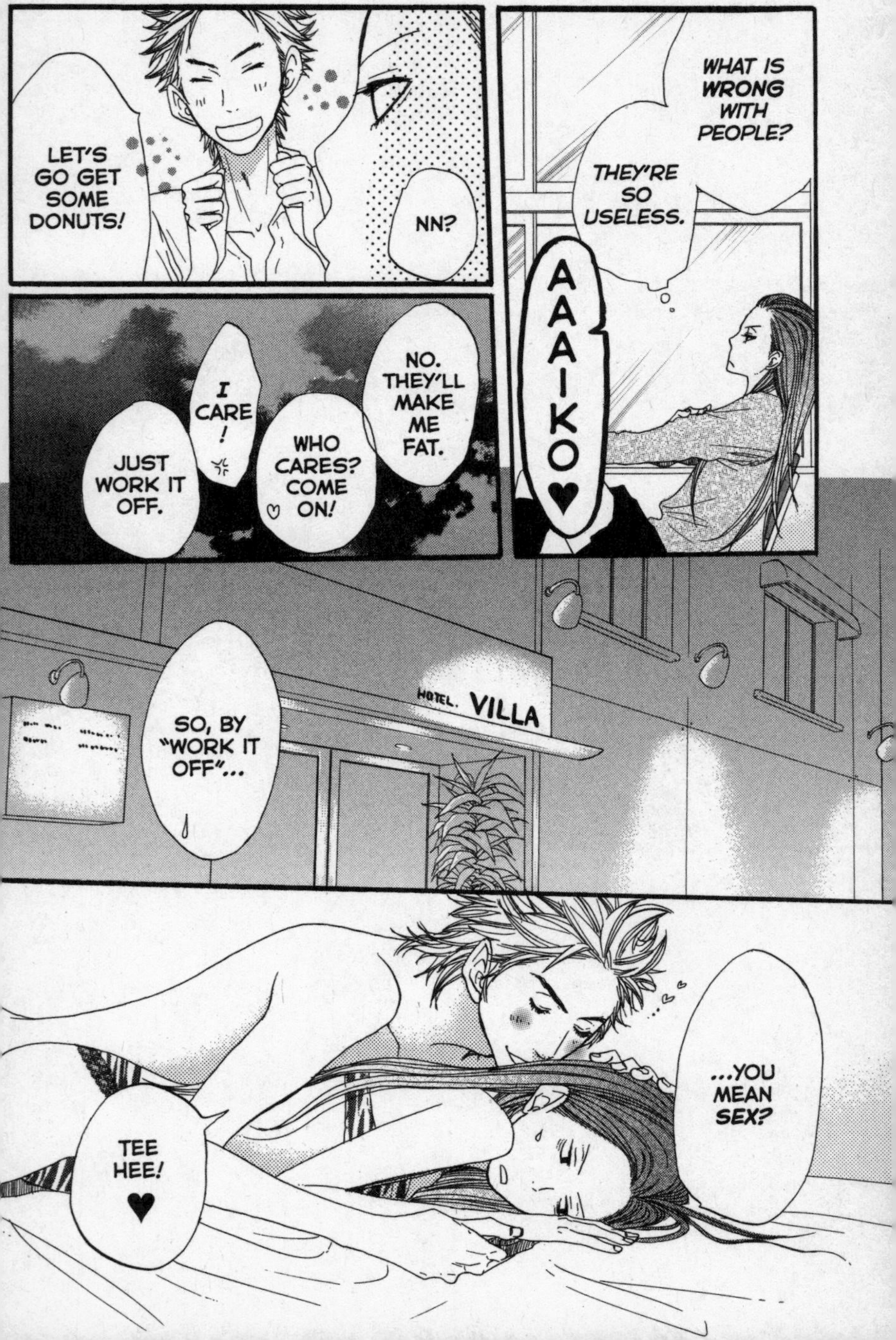
WHAT IS WRONG WITH PEOPLE?
THEY'RE SO USELESS.
AAAIKO♥
NN?
LET'S GO GET SOME DONUTS!
NO. THEY'LL MAKE ME FAT.
WHO CARES? COME ON! ♡
I CARE!
JUST WORK IT OFF.
HOTEL. VILLA
SO, BY "WORK IT OFF"...
...YOU MEAN SEX?
TEE HEE! ♥

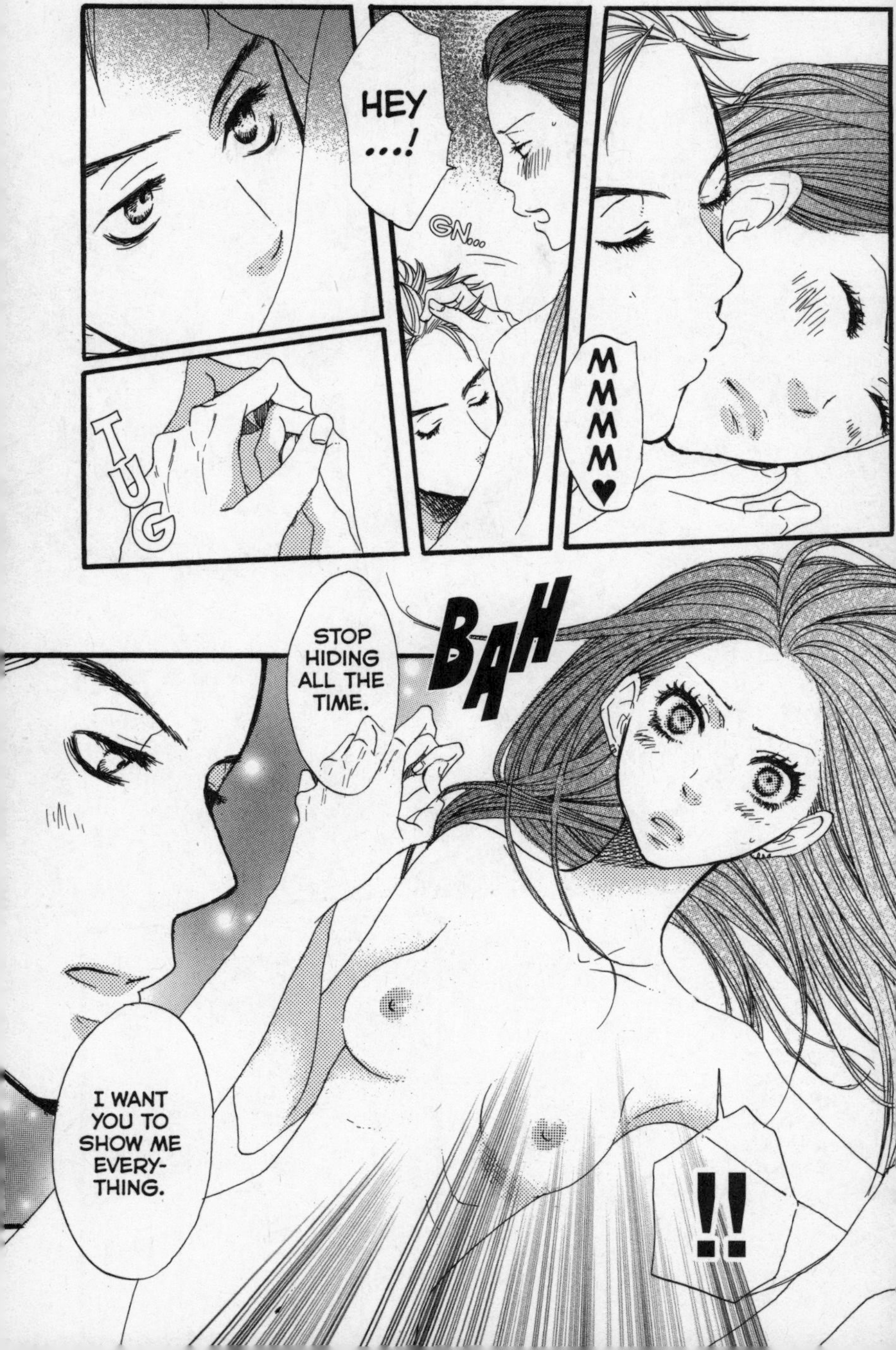
MMMM♥
HEY ...!
GN...
TUG
BAH
STOP HIDING ALL THE TIME.
I WANT YOU TO SHOW ME EVERY-THING.
!!

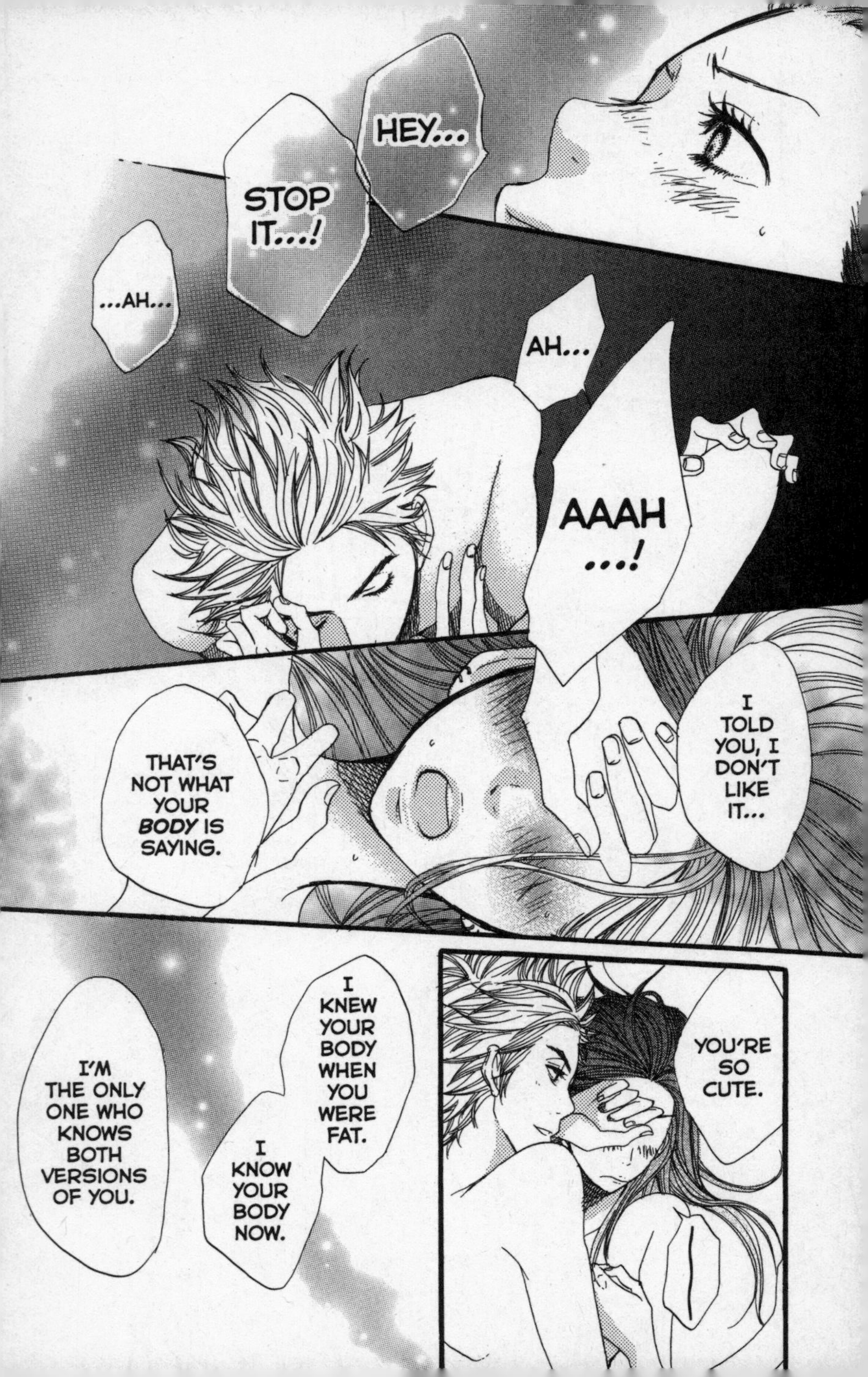
HEY...
STOP IT...!
...AH...
AH...
AAAH ...!
I TOLD YOU, I DON'T LIKE IT...
THAT'S NOT WHAT YOUR *BODY* IS SAYING.
YOU'RE SO CUTE.
I KNEW YOUR BODY WHEN YOU WERE FAT.
I KNOW YOUR BODY NOW.
I'M THE ONLY ONE WHO KNOWS BOTH VERSIONS OF YOU.

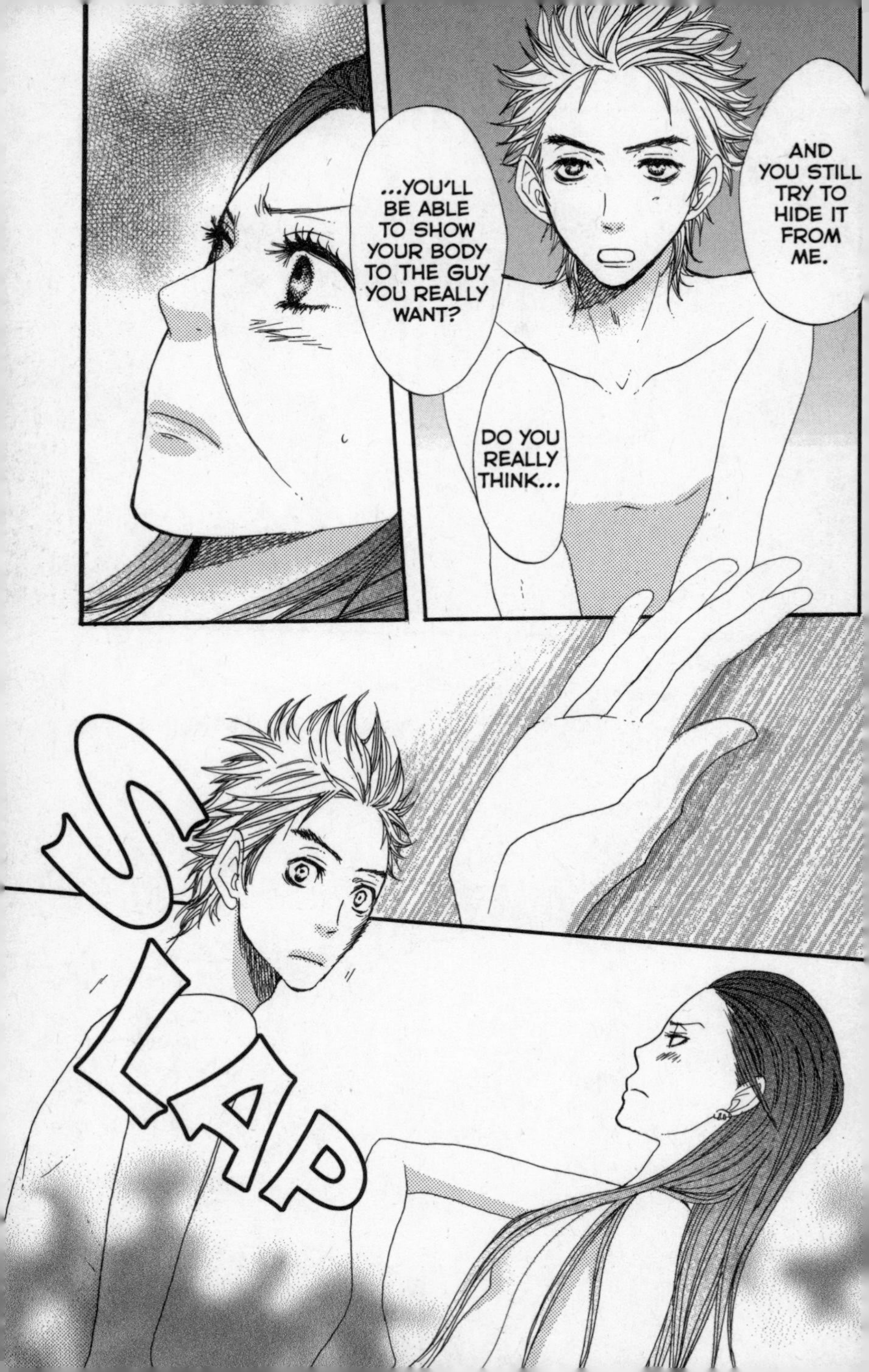
AND YOU STILL TRY TO HIDE IT FROM ME.
DO YOU REALLY THINK...
...YOU'LL BE ABLE TO SHOW YOUR BODY TO THE GUY YOU REALLY WANT?
SLAP

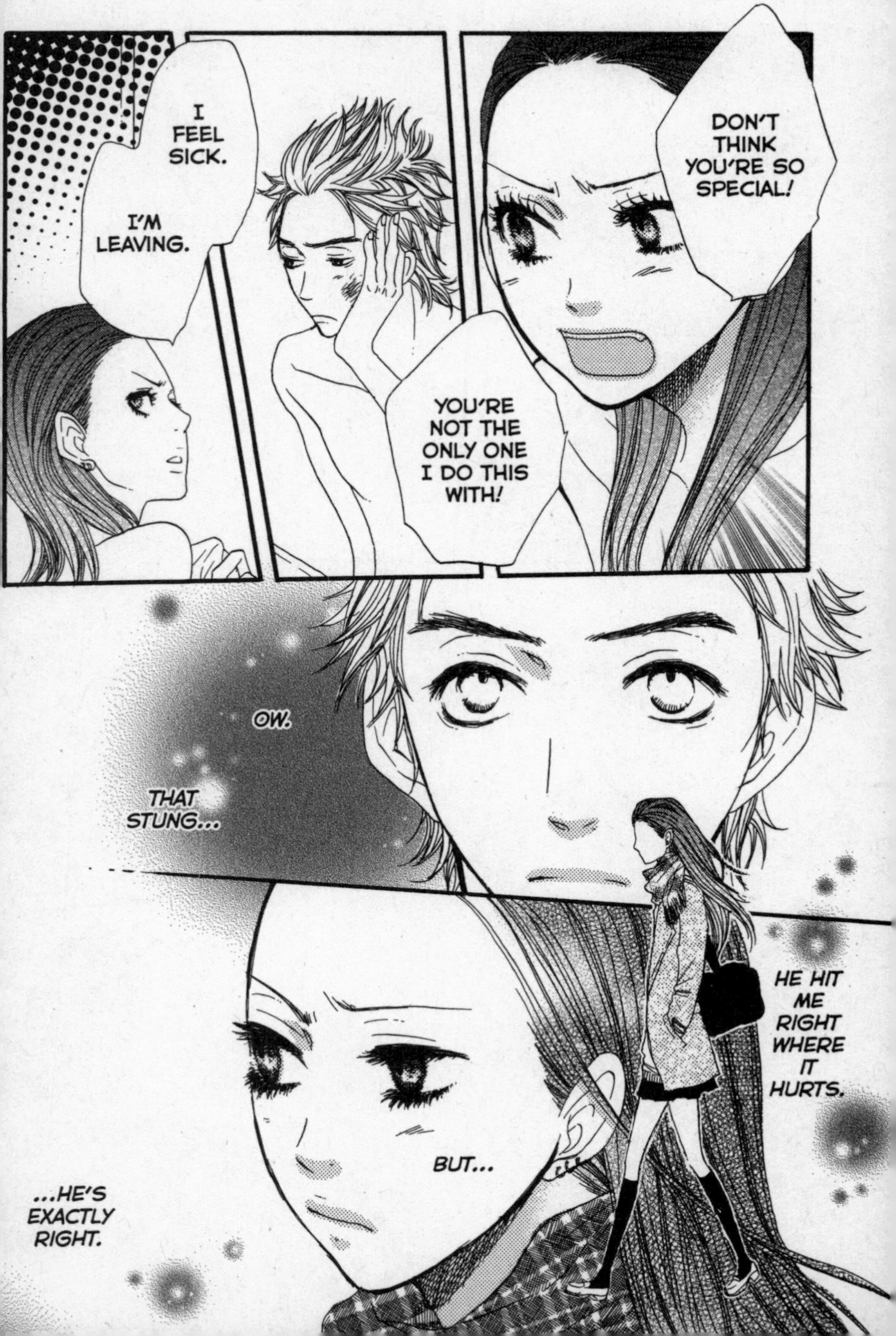
DON'T THINK YOU'RE SO SPECIAL!
YOU'RE NOT THE ONLY ONE I DO THIS WITH!
I FEEL SICK.
I'M LEAVING.
OW.
THAT STUNG...
HE HIT ME RIGHT WHERE IT HURTS.
BUT...
...HE'S EXACTLY RIGHT.

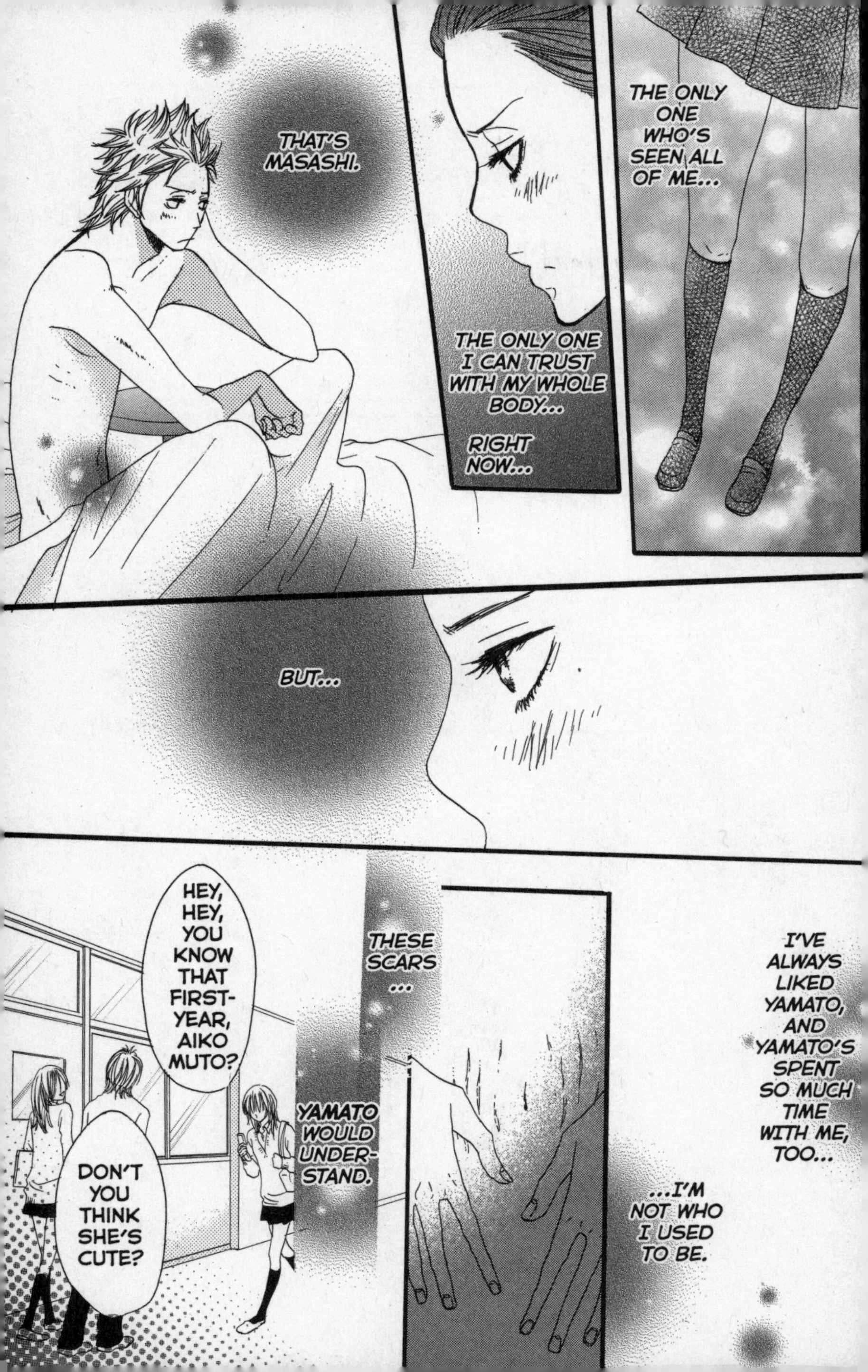
THE ONLY ONE WHO'S SEEN ALL OF ME...
THE ONLY ONE I CAN TRUST WITH MY WHOLE BODY...
RIGHT NOW...
THAT'S MASASHI.
BUT...
I'VE ALWAYS LIKED YAMATO, AND YAMATO'S SPENT SO MUCH TIME WITH ME, TOO...
...I'M NOT WHO I USED TO BE.
THESE SCARS...
YAMATO WOULD UNDER-STAND.
HEY, HEY, YOU KNOW THAT FIRST-YEAR, AIKO MUTO?
DON'T YOU THINK SHE'S CUTE?

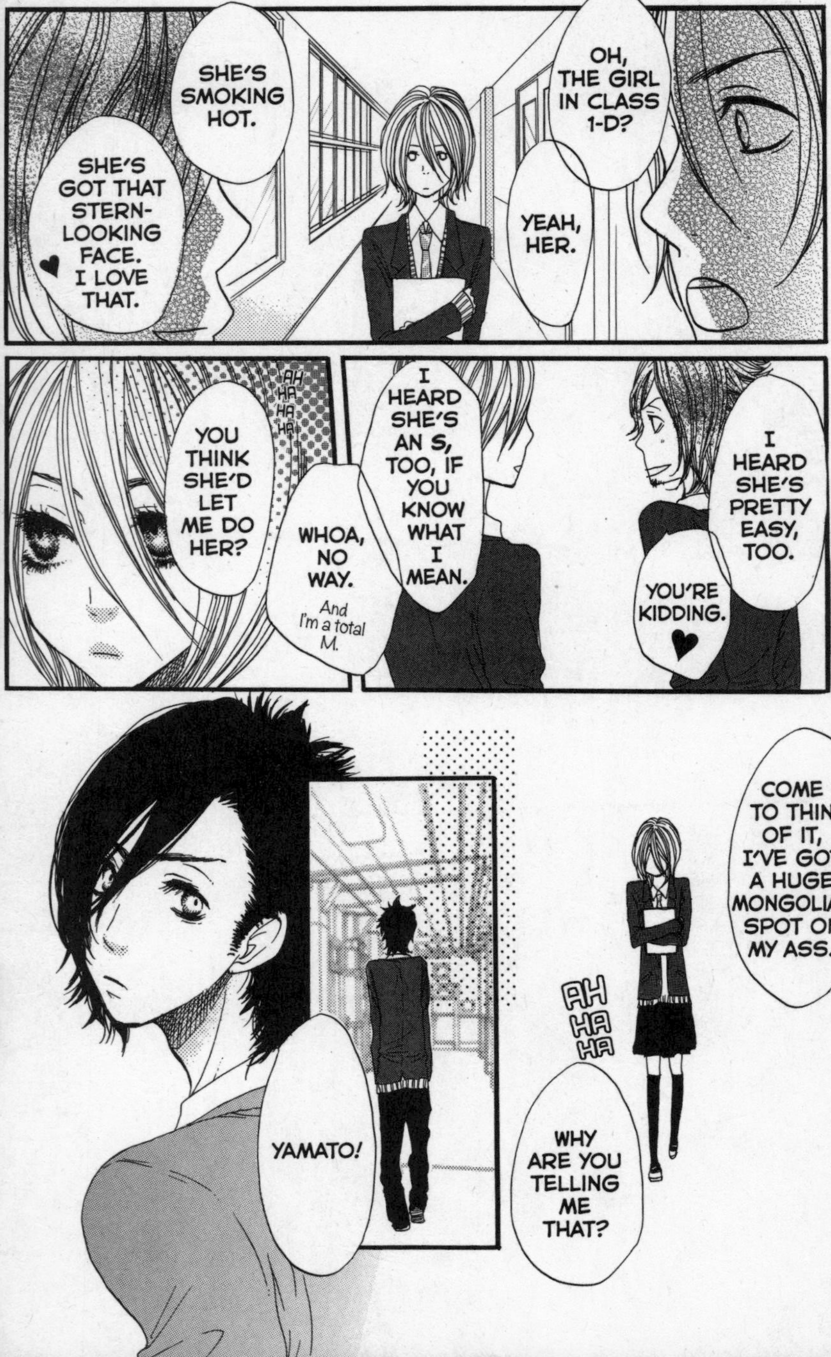
OH, THE GIRL IN CLASS 1-D?
YEAH, HER.
SHE'S SMOKING HOT.
SHE'S GOT THAT STERN-LOOKING FACE. ♥ I LOVE THAT.
I HEARD SHE'S PRETTY EASY, TOO.
YOU'RE KIDDING. ♥
I HEARD SHE'S AN S, TOO, IF YOU KNOW WHAT I MEAN.
WHOA, NO WAY.
And I'm a total M.
AH HA HA HA
YOU THINK SHE'D LET ME DO HER?
COME TO THINK OF IT, I'VE GOT A HUGE MONGOLIAN SPOT ON MY ASS.
AH HA HA
WHY ARE YOU TELLING ME THAT?
YAMATO!

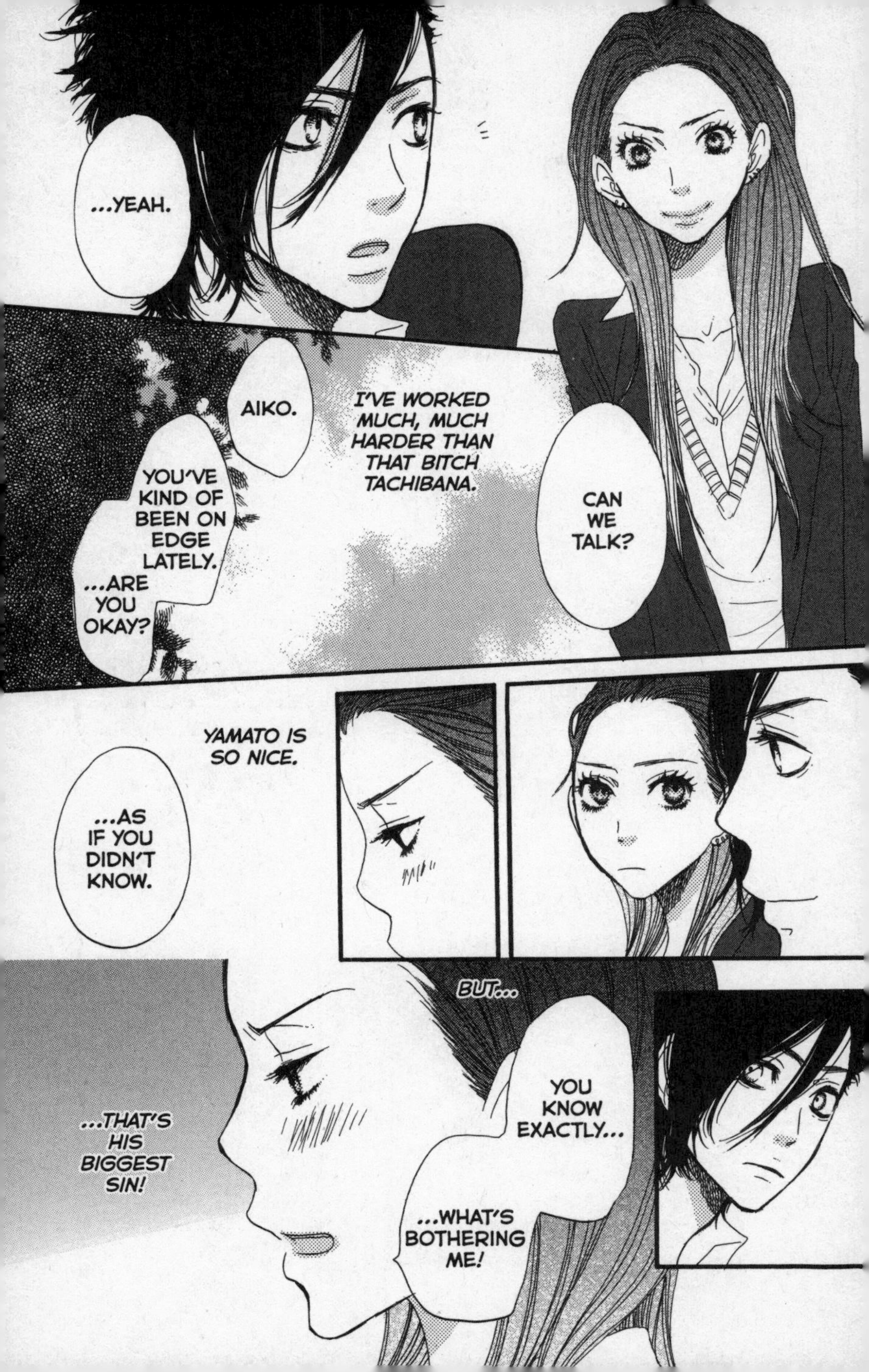
CAN WE TALK?
...YEAH.
AIKO.
YOU'VE KIND OF BEEN ON EDGE LATELY. ...ARE YOU OKAY?
I'VE WORKED MUCH, MUCH HARDER THAN THAT BITCH TACHIBANA.
YAMATO IS SO NICE.
...AS IF YOU DIDN'T KNOW.
BUT...
YOU KNOW EXACTLY...
...WHAT'S BOTHERING ME!
...THAT'S HIS BIGGEST SIN!

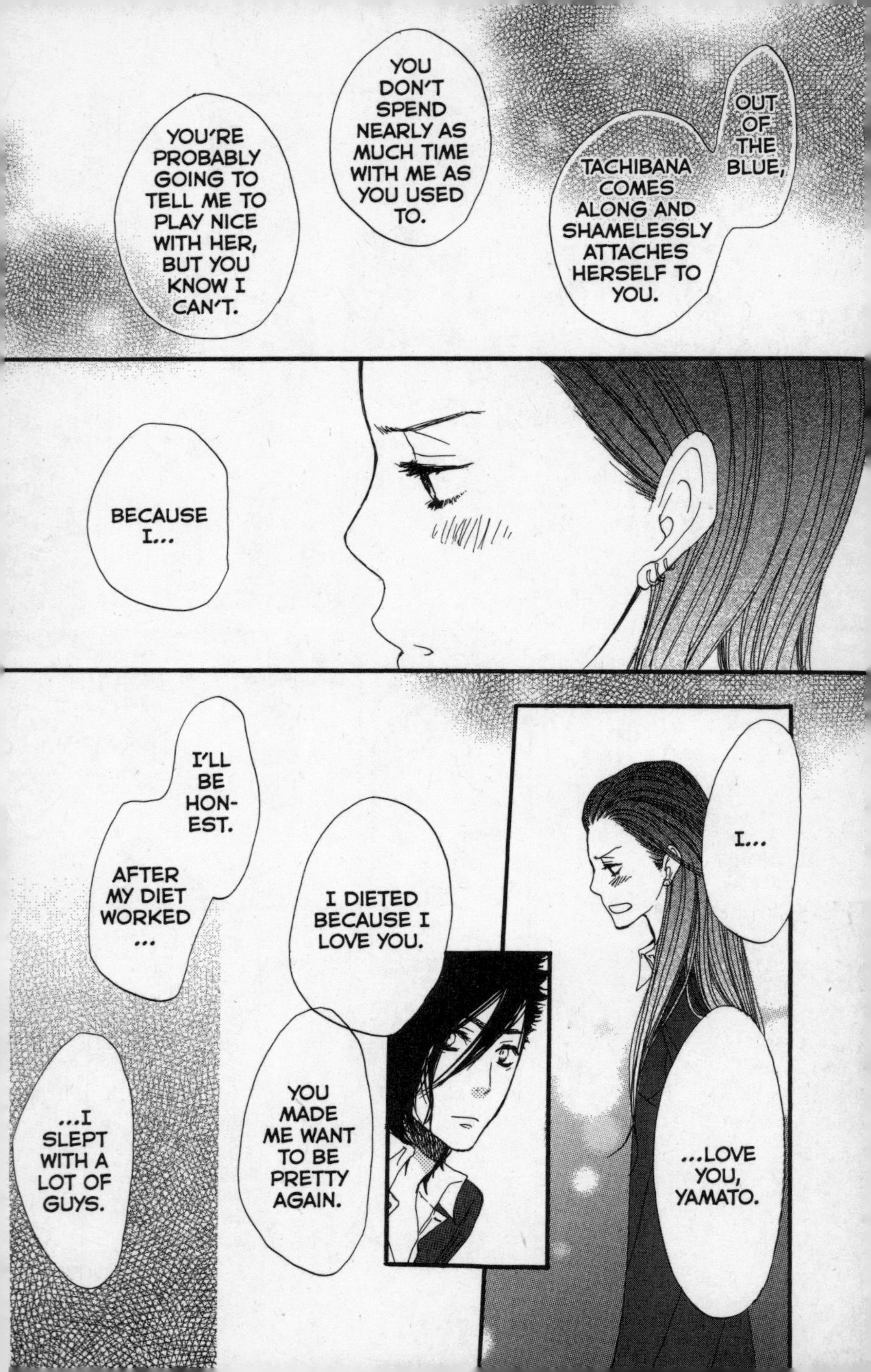
OUT OF THE BLUE, TACHIBANA COMES ALONG AND SHAMELESSLY ATTACHES HERSELF TO YOU.
YOU DON'T SPEND NEARLY AS MUCH TIME WITH ME AS YOU USED TO.
YOU'RE PROBABLY GOING TO TELL ME TO PLAY NICE WITH HER, BUT YOU KNOW I CAN'T.
BECAUSE I...
I...
...LOVE YOU, YAMATO.
I DIETED BECAUSE I LOVE YOU.
YOU MADE ME WANT TO BE PRETTY AGAIN.
I'LL BE HON-EST.
AFTER MY DIET WORKED ...
...I SLEPT WITH A LOT OF GUYS.

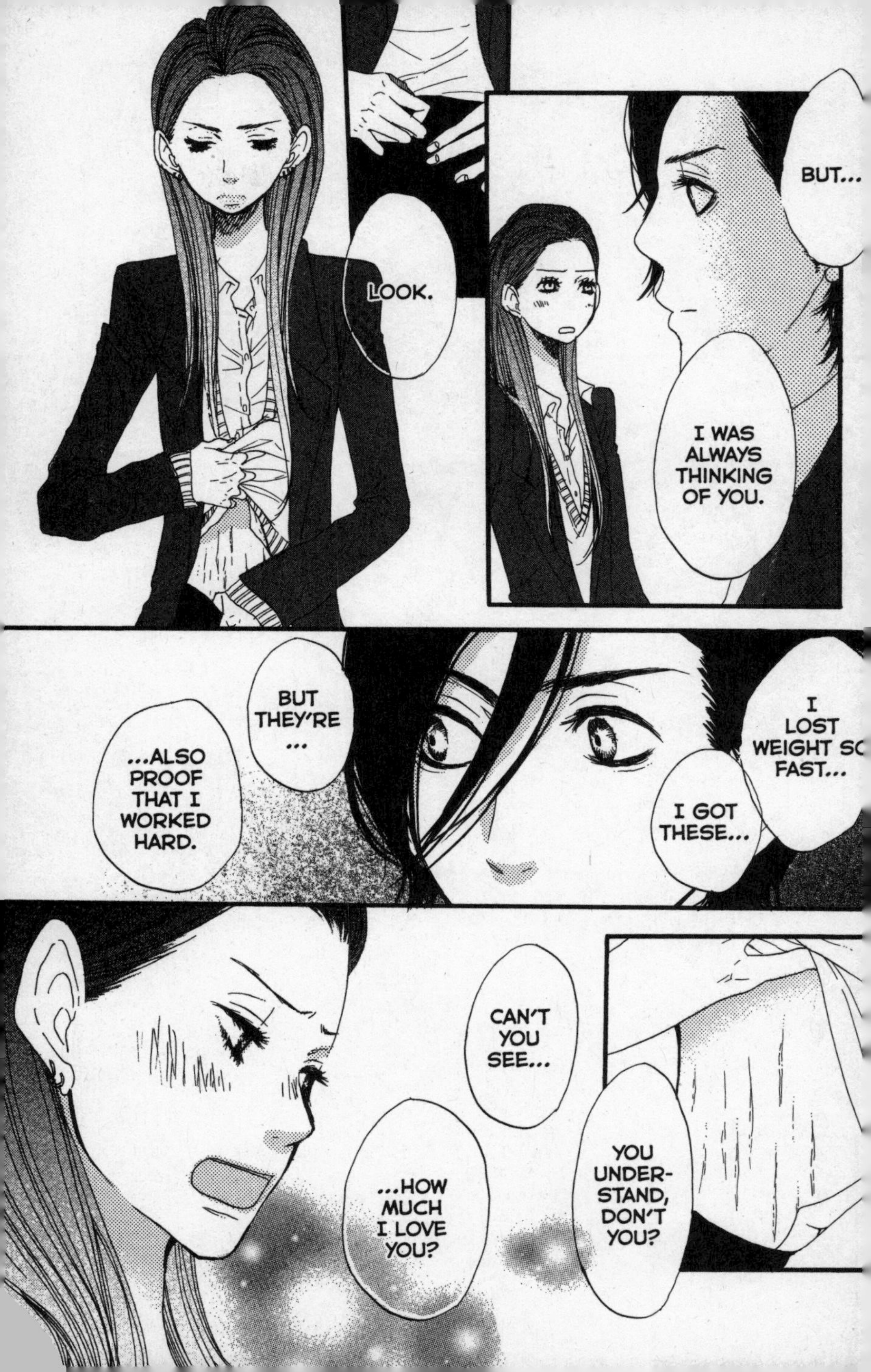
BUT...
I WAS ALWAYS THINKING OF YOU.
LOOK.
I LOST WEIGHT SO FAST...
I GOT THESE...
BUT THEY'RE ...
...ALSO PROOF THAT I WORKED HARD.
YOU UNDER-STAND, DON'T YOU?
CAN'T YOU SEE...
...HOW MUCH I LOVE YOU?

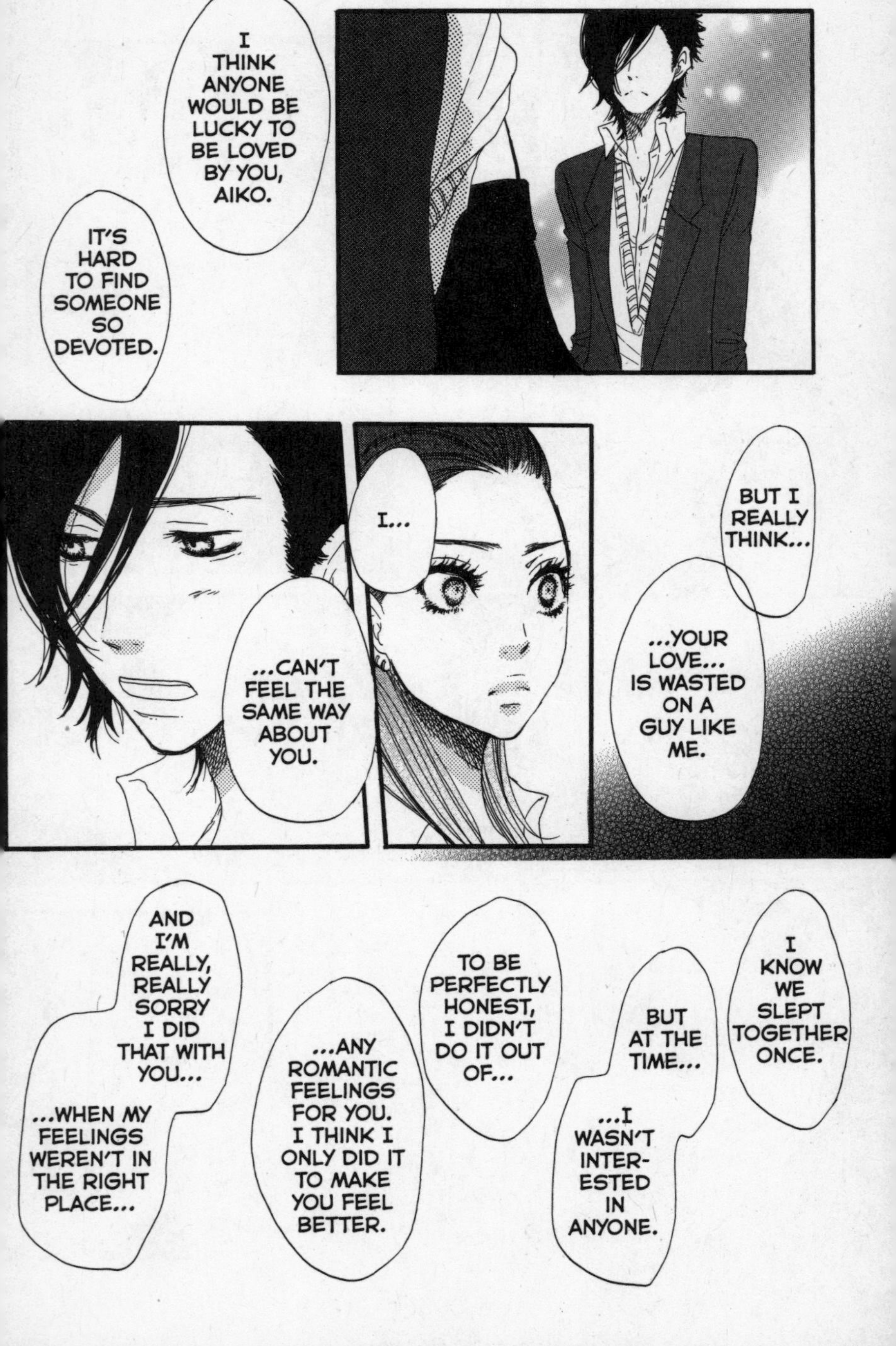
I THINK ANYONE WOULD BE LUCKY TO BE LOVED BY YOU, AIKO.
IT'S HARD TO FIND SOMEONE SO DEVOTED.
BUT I REALLY THINK...
...YOUR LOVE... IS WASTED ON A GUY LIKE ME.
I...
...CAN'T FEEL THE SAME WAY ABOUT YOU.
I KNOW WE SLEPT TOGETHER ONCE.
BUT AT THE TIME...
...I WASN'T INTER-ESTED IN ANYONE.
TO BE PERFECTLY HONEST, I DIDN'T DO IT OUT OF...
...ANY ROMANTIC FEELINGS FOR YOU. I THINK I ONLY DID IT TO MAKE YOU FEEL BETTER.
AND I'M REALLY, REALLY SORRY I DID THAT WITH YOU...
...WHEN MY FEELINGS WEREN'T IN THE RIGHT PLACE...

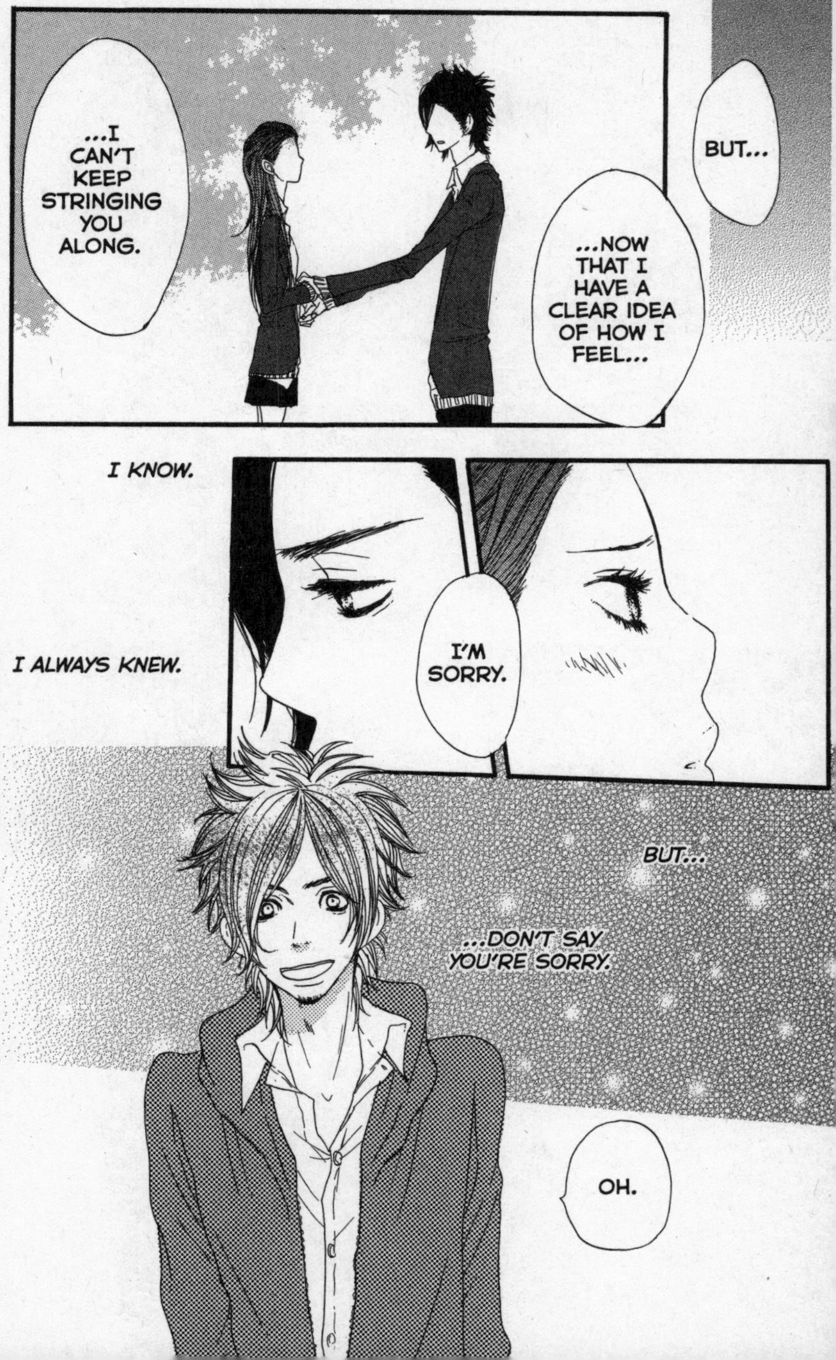
BUT...
...NOW THAT I HAVE A CLEAR IDEA OF HOW I FEEL...
...I CAN'T KEEP STRINGING YOU ALONG.
I'M SORRY.
I KNOW.
I ALWAYS KNEW.
BUT...
...DON'T SAY YOU'RE SORRY.
OH.

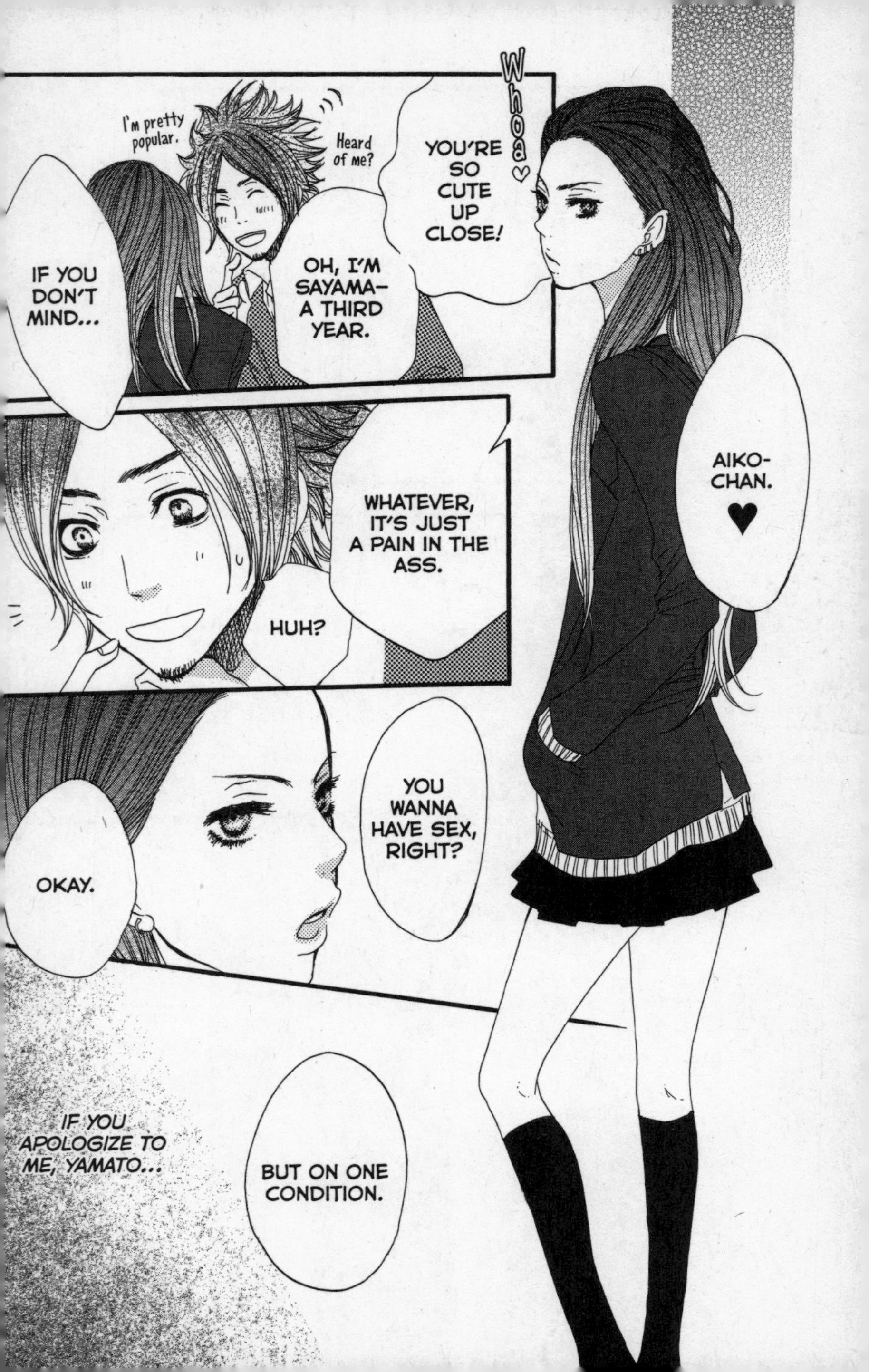
AIKO-CHAN. ♥
Whoa ♡
YOU'RE SO CUTE UP CLOSE!
Heard of me?
OH, I'M SAYAMA—A THIRD YEAR.
I'm pretty popular.
IF YOU DON'T MIND...
WHATEVER, IT'S JUST A PAIN IN THE ASS.
HUH?
YOU WANNA HAVE SEX, RIGHT?
OKAY.
BUT ON ONE CONDITION.
IF YOU APOLOGIZE TO ME, YAMATO...

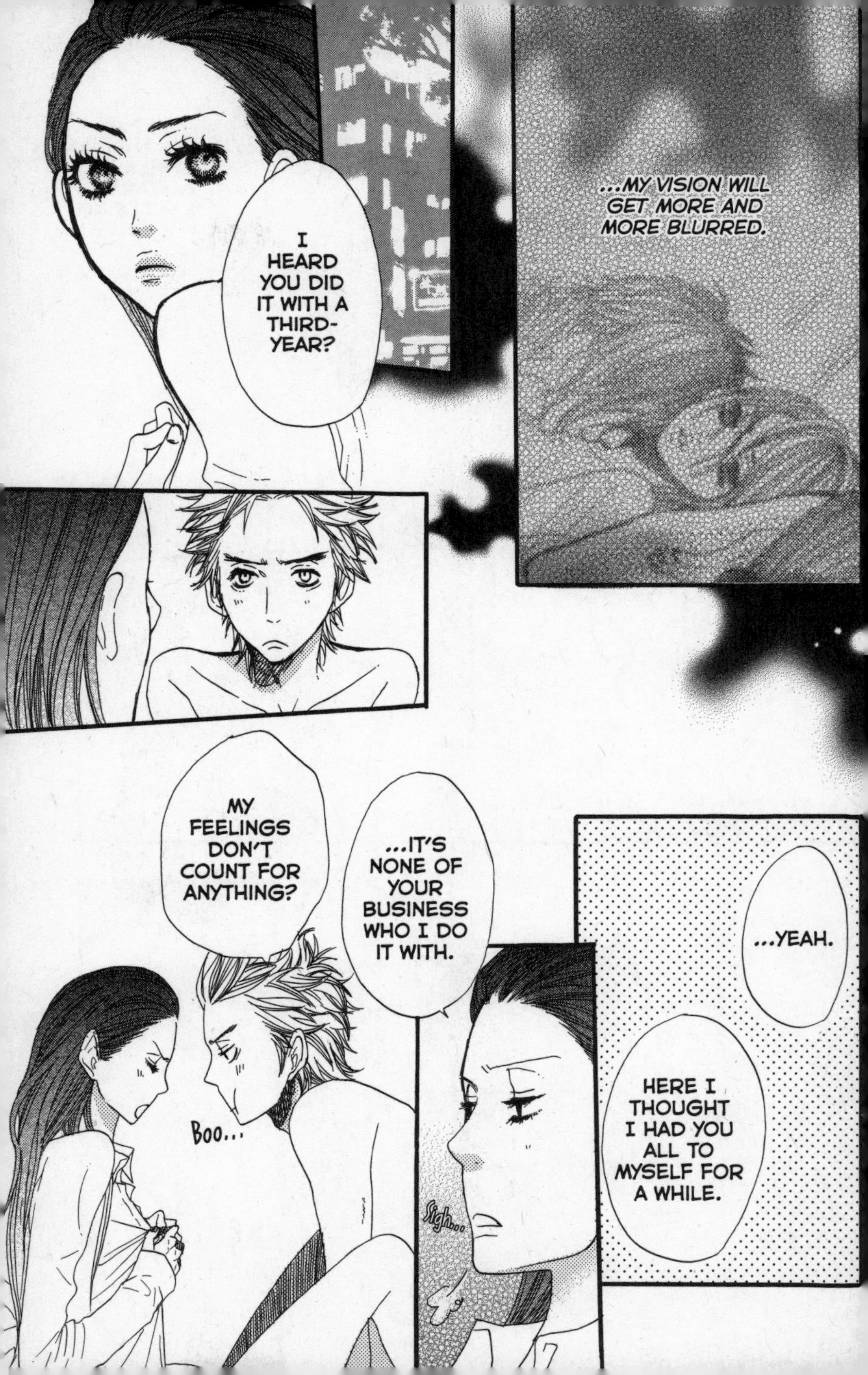
...MY VISION WILL GET MORE AND MORE BLURRED.
I HEARD YOU DID IT WITH A THIRD-YEAR?
...YEAH.
HERE I THOUGHT I HAD YOU ALL TO MYSELF FOR A WHILE.
Sigh...
...IT'S NONE OF YOUR BUSINESS WHO I DO IT WITH.
MY FEELINGS DON'T COUNT FOR ANYTHING?
Boo...

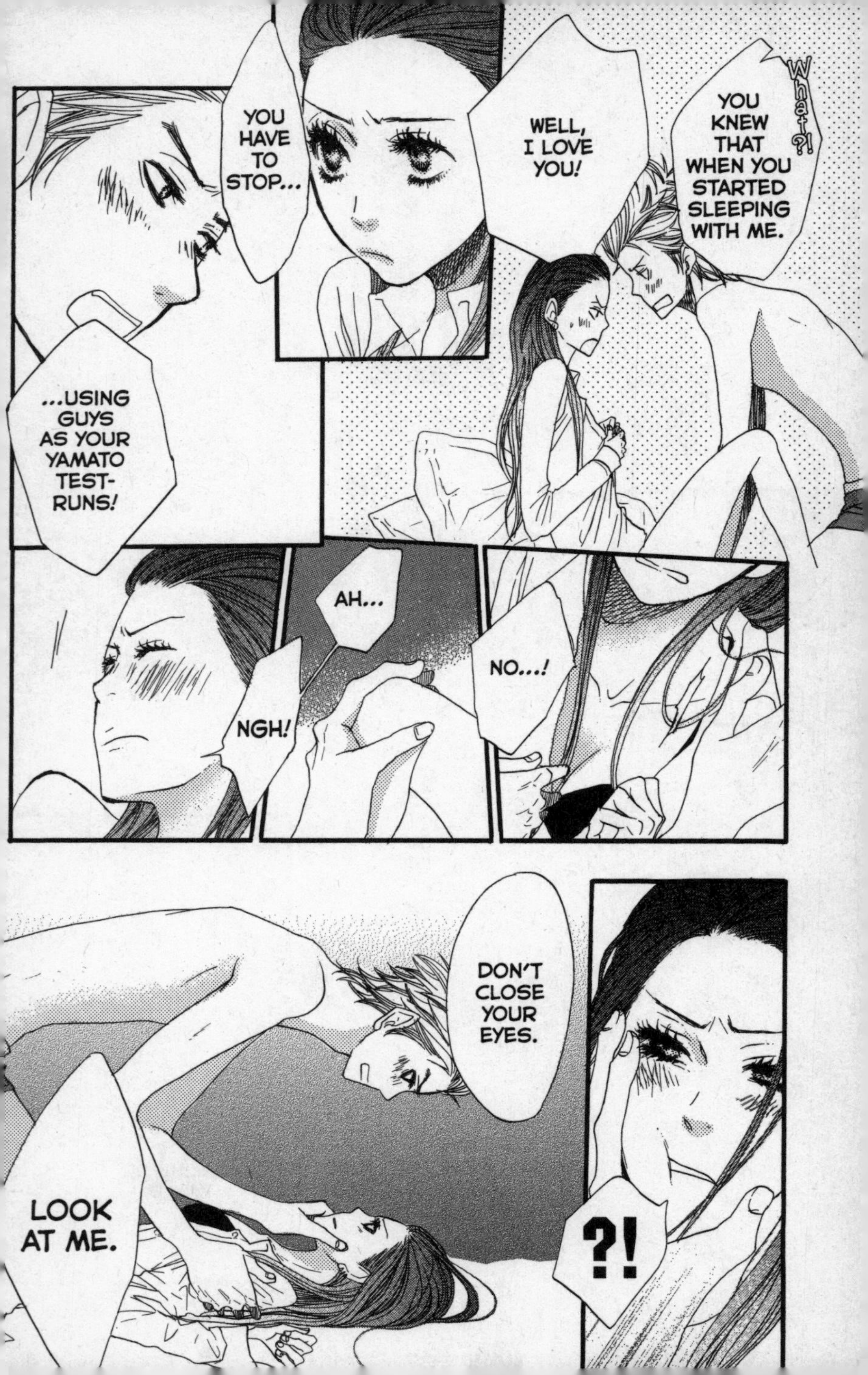
YOU HAVE TO STOP...
...USING GUYS AS YOUR YAMATO TEST-RUNS!
WELL, I LOVE YOU!
What?!
YOU KNEW THAT WHEN YOU STARTED SLEEPING WITH ME.
NO...!
AH...
NGH!
?!
DON'T CLOSE YOUR EYES.
LOOK AT ME.

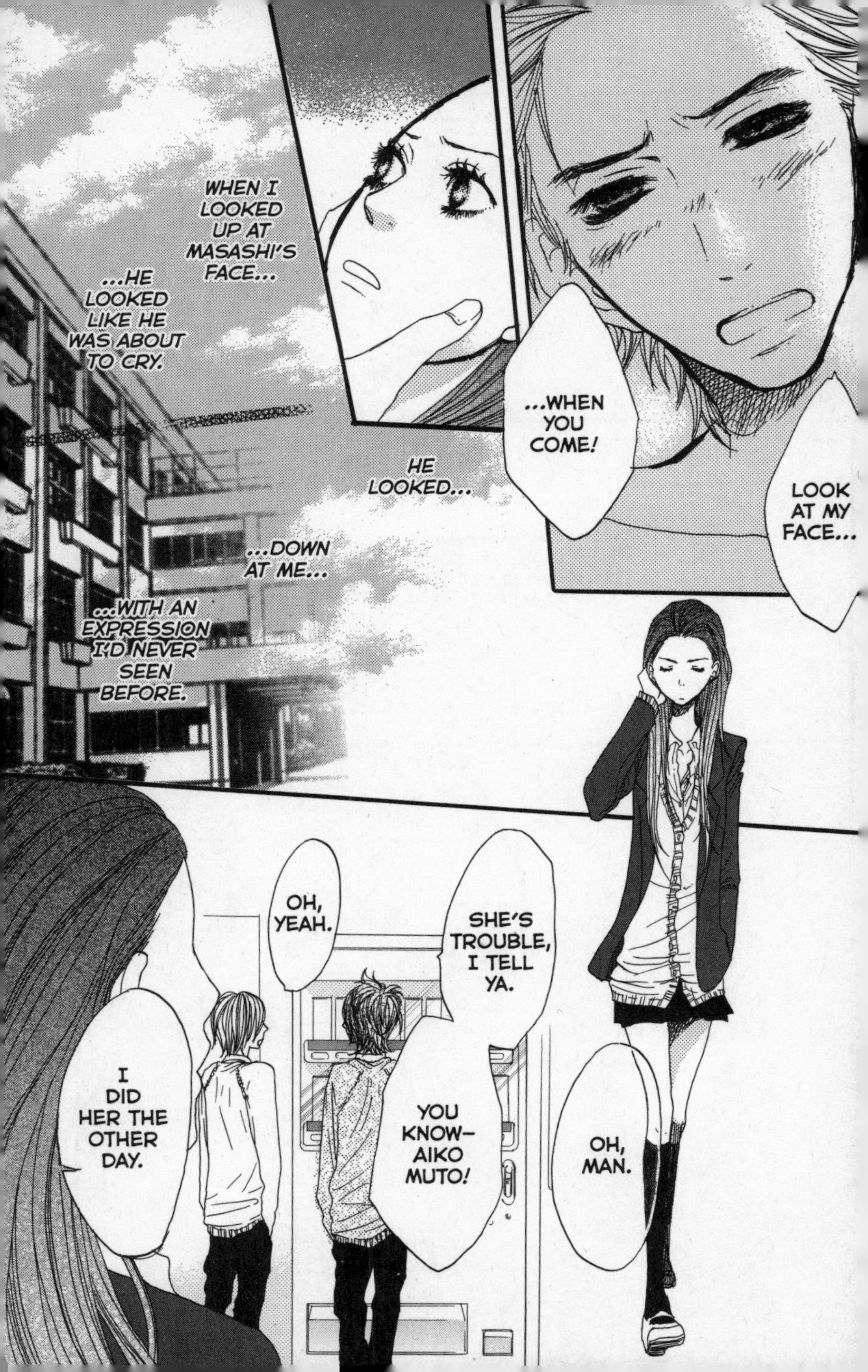
LOOK AT MY FACE...
...WHEN YOU COME!
HE LOOKED...
...DOWN AT ME...
...WITH AN EXPRESSION I'D NEVER SEEN BEFORE.
WHEN I LOOKED UP AT MASASHI'S FACE...
...HE LOOKED LIKE HE WAS ABOUT TO CRY.
OH, MAN.
SHE'S TROUBLE, I TELL YA.
YOU KNOW—AIKO MUTO!
OH, YEAH.
I DID HER THE OTHER DAY.

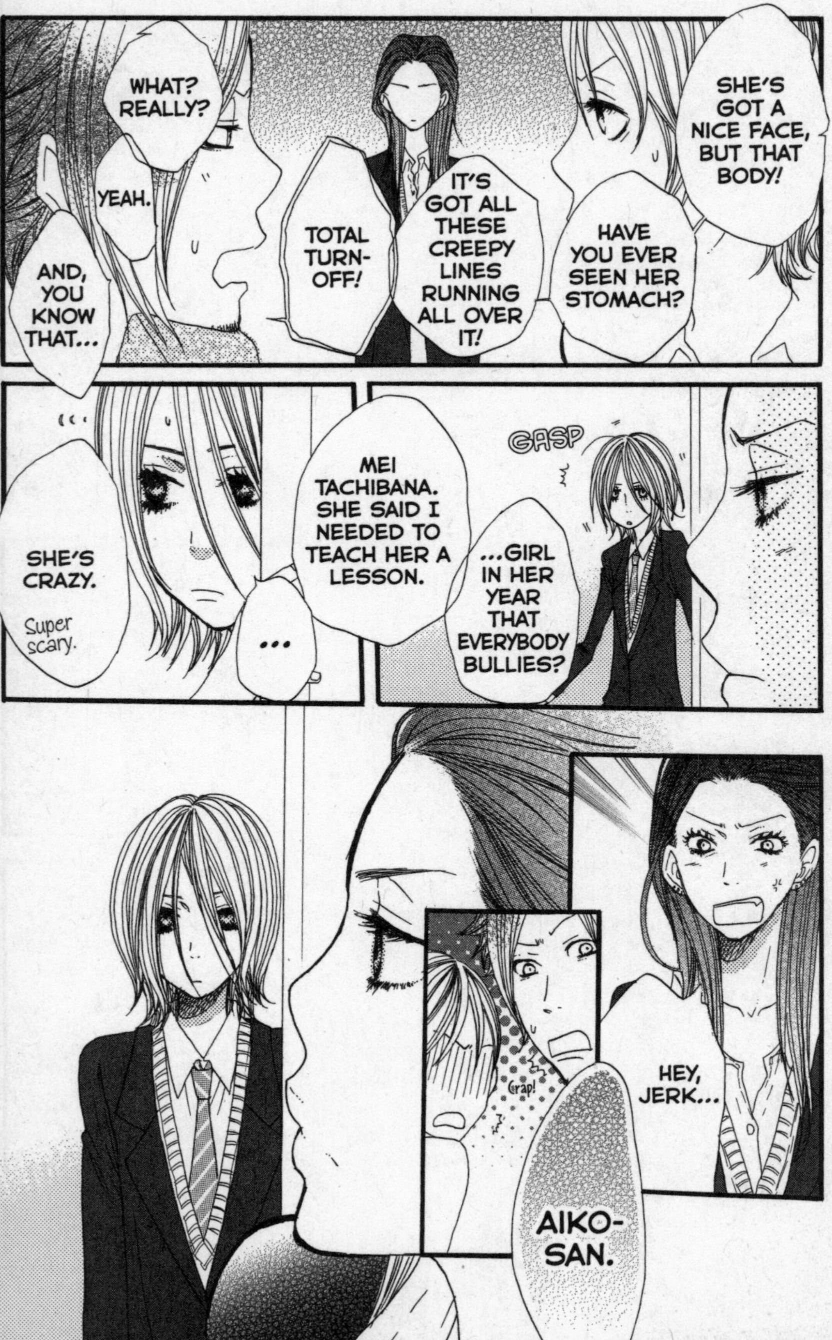

SHE'S GOT A NICE FACE, BUT THAT BODY!
HAVE YOU EVER SEEN HER STOMACH?
IT'S GOT ALL THESE CREEPY LINES RUNNING ALL OVER IT!
TOTAL TURN-OFF!
WHAT? REALLY?
YEAH.
AND, YOU KNOW THAT...
GASP
...GIRL IN HER YEAR THAT EVERYBODY BULLIES?
MEI TACHIBANA. SHE SAID I NEEDED TO TEACH HER A LESSON.
...
SHE'S CRAZY.
Super scary.
HEY, JERK...
Crap!
AIKO-SAN.

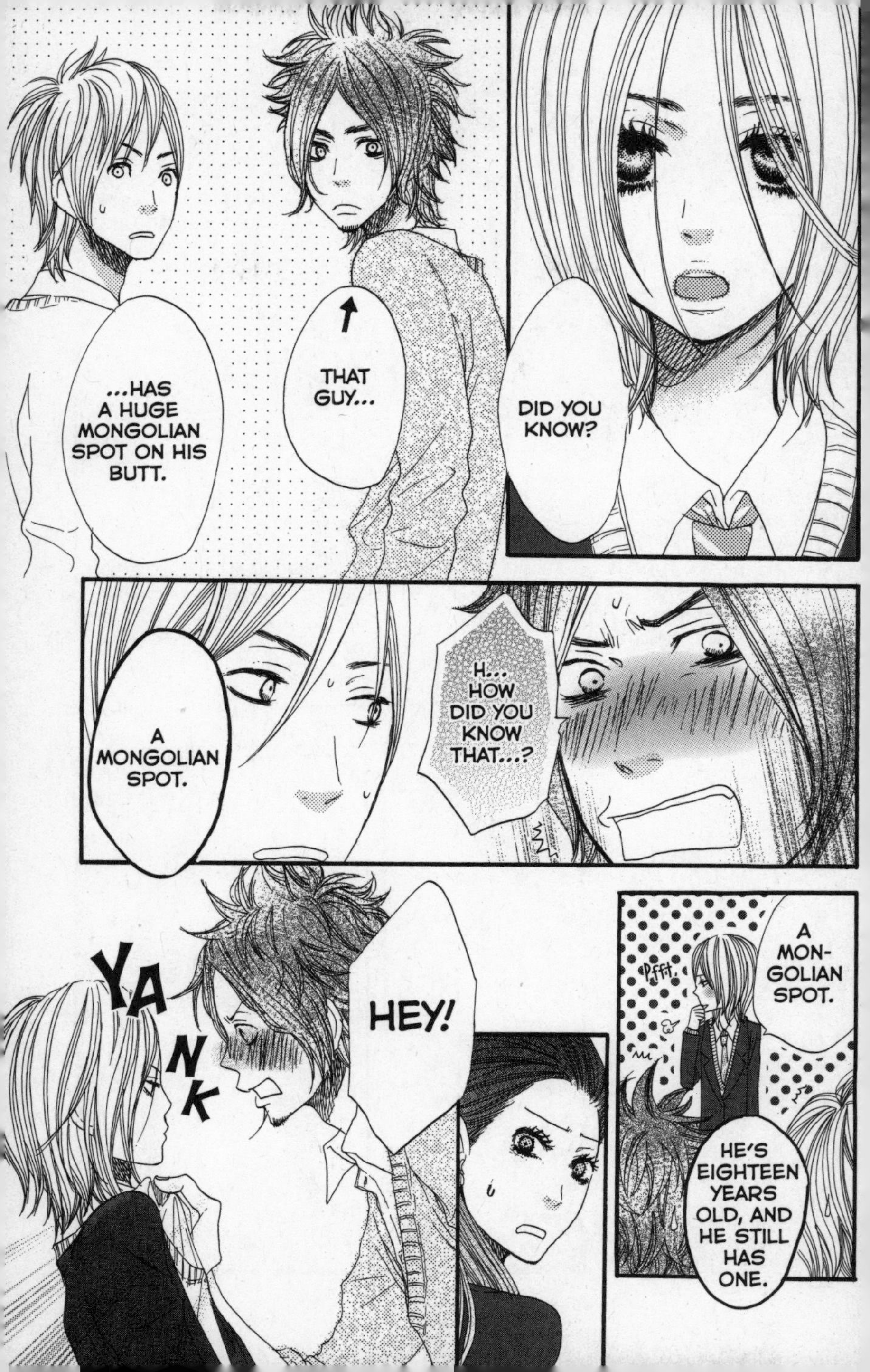
DID YOU KNOW?
THAT GUY...
...HAS A HUGE MONGOLIAN SPOT ON HIS BUTT.
H... HOW DID YOU KNOW THAT...?
A MONGOLIAN SPOT.
A MON-GOLIAN SPOT.
Pffft.
HE'S EIGHTEEN YEARS OLD, AND HE STILL HAS ONE.
HEY!
YANK

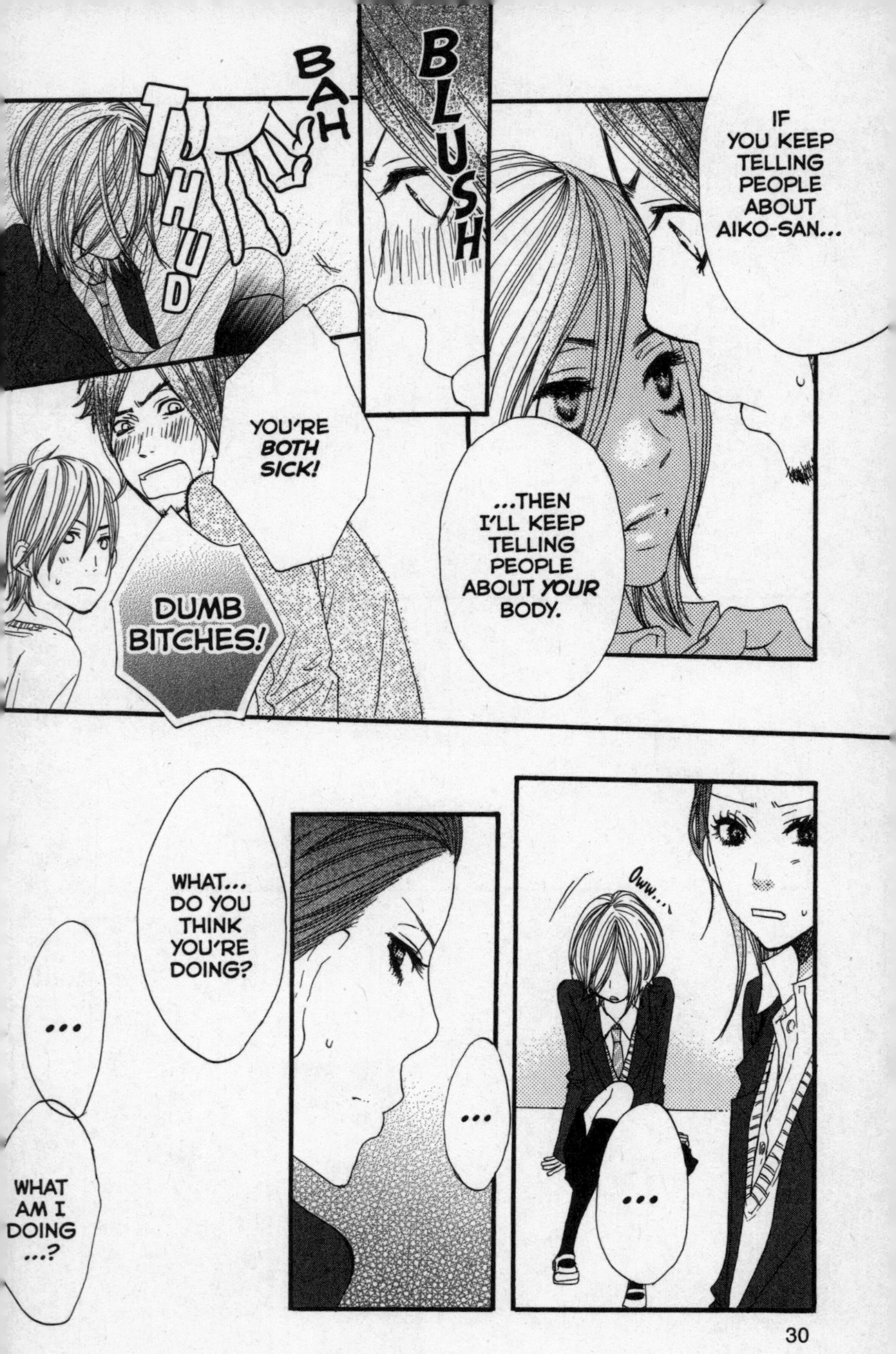
IF YOU KEEP TELLING PEOPLE ABOUT AIKO-SAN...
...THEN I'LL KEEP TELLING PEOPLE ABOUT *YOUR* BODY.
BLUSH
BAH
THUD
YOU'RE *BOTH* SICK!
DUMB BITCHES!
Oww...
...
...
WHAT... DO YOU THINK YOU'RE DOING?
...
WHAT AM I DOING ...?

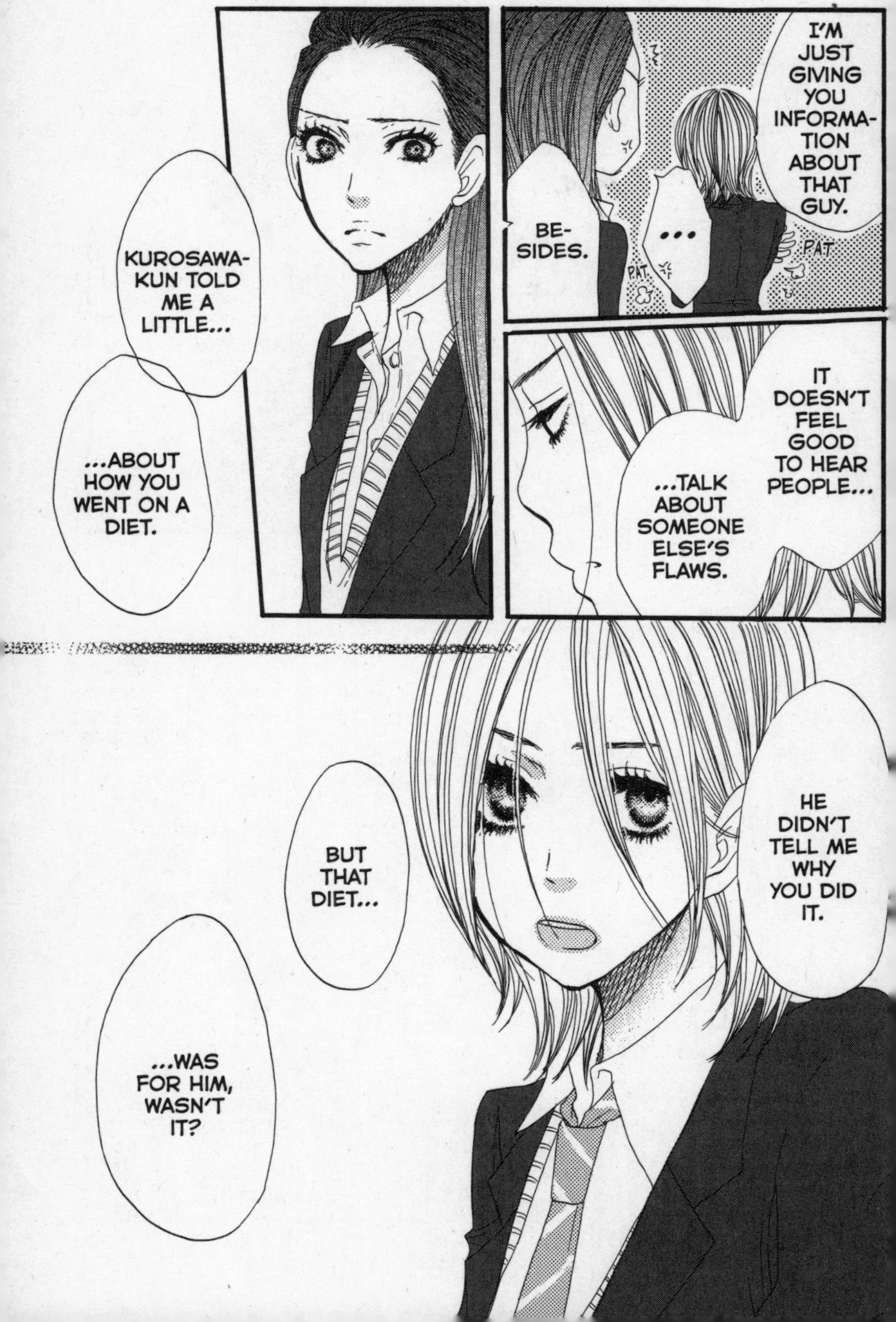
I'M JUST GIVING YOU INFORMATION ABOUT THAT GUY.
PAT
...
BE-SIDES.
P.AT.
IT DOESN'T FEEL GOOD TO HEAR PEOPLE...
...TALK ABOUT SOMEONE ELSE'S FLAWS.
KUROSAWA-KUN TOLD ME A LITTLE...
...ABOUT HOW YOU WENT ON A DIET.
HE DIDN'T TELL ME WHY YOU DID IT.
BUT THAT DIET...
...WAS FOR HIM, WASN'T IT?

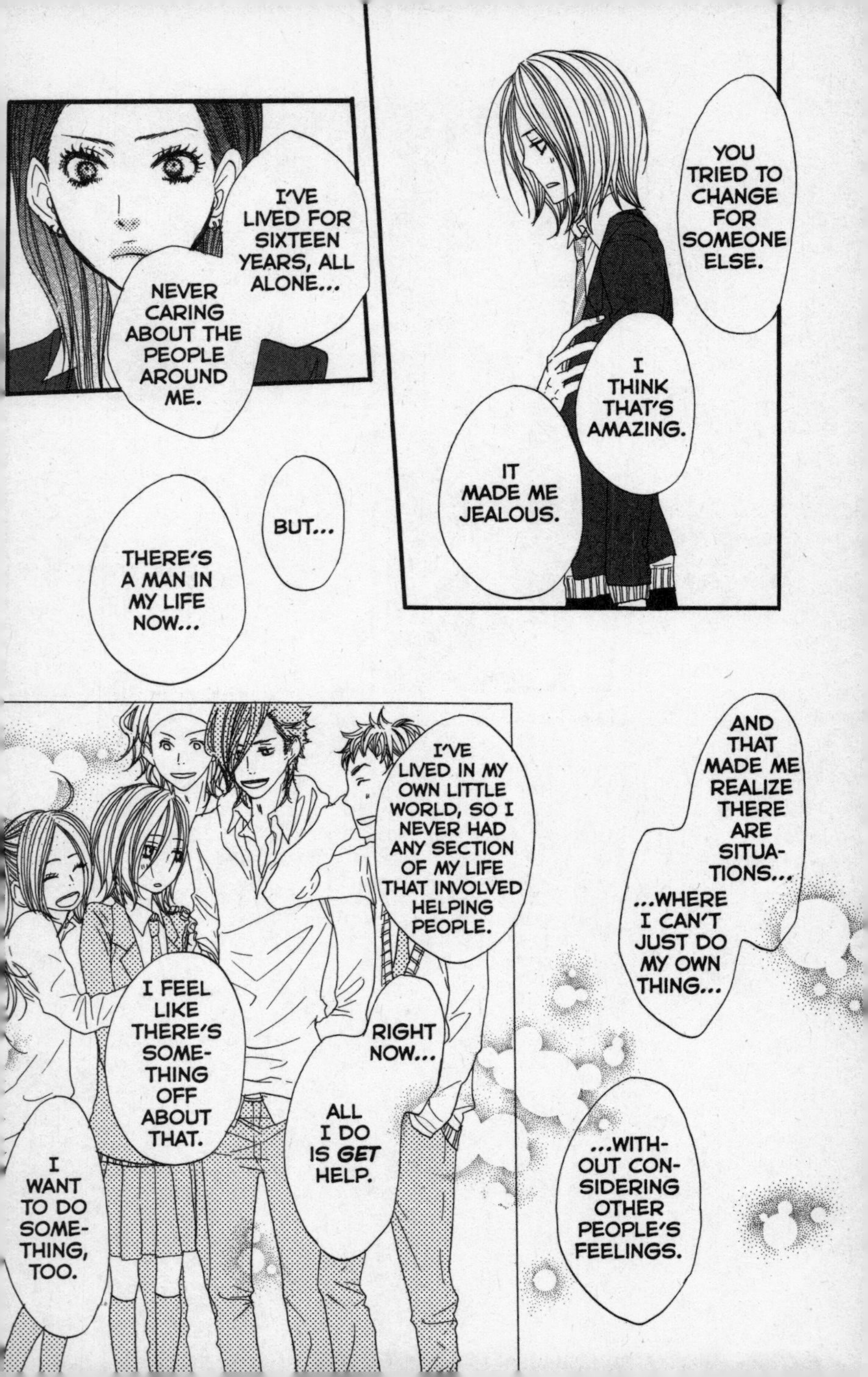
YOU TRIED TO CHANGE FOR SOMEONE ELSE.
I THINK THAT'S AMAZING.
IT MADE ME JEALOUS.
I'VE LIVED FOR SIXTEEN YEARS, ALL ALONE...
NEVER CARING ABOUT THE PEOPLE AROUND ME.
BUT...
THERE'S A MAN IN MY LIFE NOW...
AND THAT MADE ME REALIZE THERE ARE SITUATIONS...
...WHERE I CAN'T JUST DO MY OWN THING...
...WITHOUT CONSIDERING OTHER PEOPLE'S FEELINGS.
I'VE LIVED IN MY OWN LITTLE WORLD, SO I NEVER HAD ANY SECTION OF MY LIFE THAT INVOLVED HELPING PEOPLE.
RIGHT NOW...
ALL I DO IS *GET* HELP.
I FEEL LIKE THERE'S SOMETHING OFF ABOUT THAT.
I WANT TO DO SOMETHING, TOO.

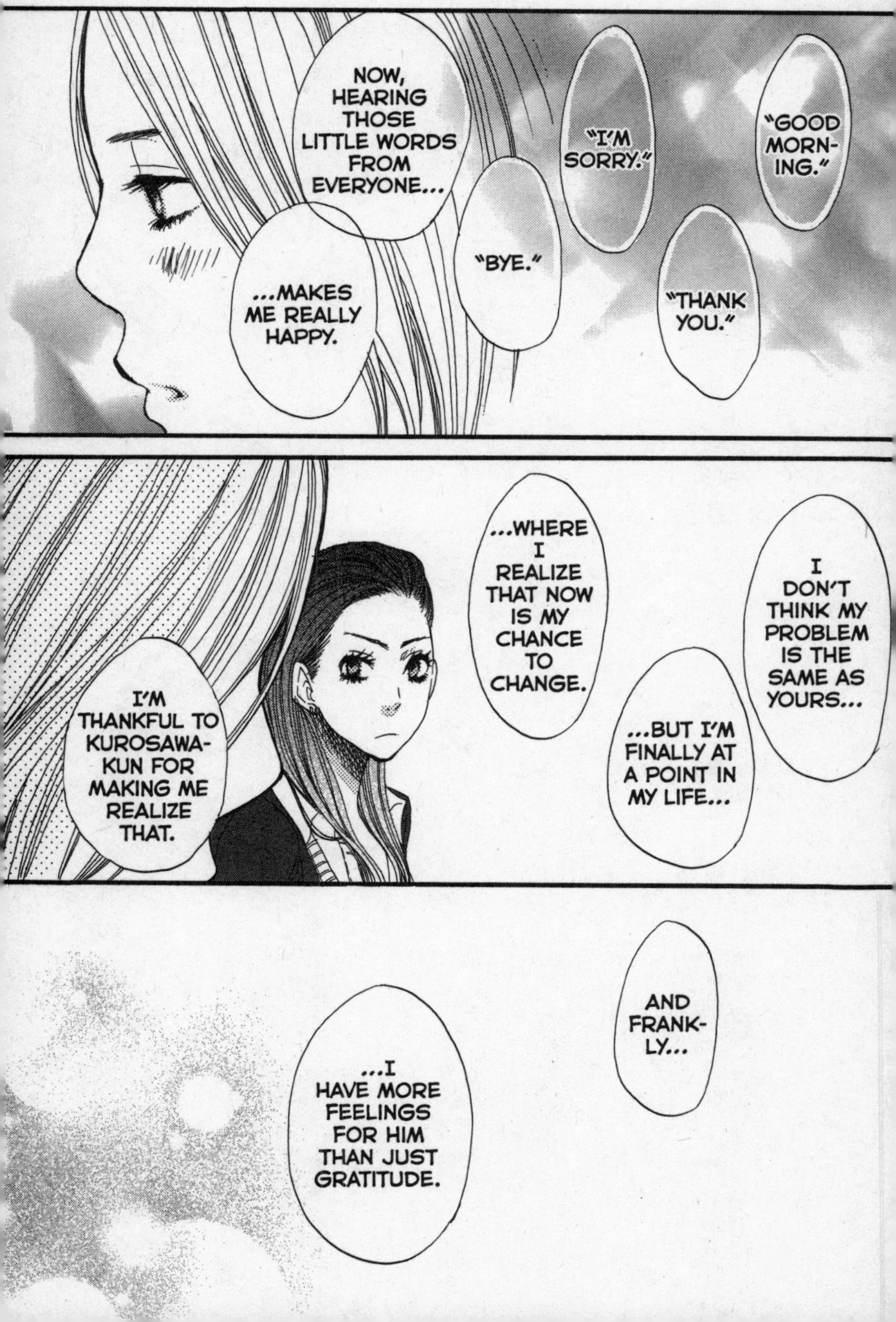
"GOOD MORNING."
"I'M SORRY."
"THANK YOU."
"BYE."
NOW, HEARING THOSE LITTLE WORDS FROM EVERYONE...
...MAKES ME REALLY HAPPY.
I DON'T THINK MY PROBLEM IS THE SAME AS YOURS...
...BUT I'M FINALLY AT A POINT IN MY LIFE...
...WHERE I REALIZE THAT NOW IS MY CHANCE TO CHANGE.
I'M THANKFUL TO KUROSAWA-KUN FOR MAKING ME REALIZE THAT.
AND FRANKLY...
...I HAVE MORE FEELINGS FOR HIM THAN JUST GRATITUDE.

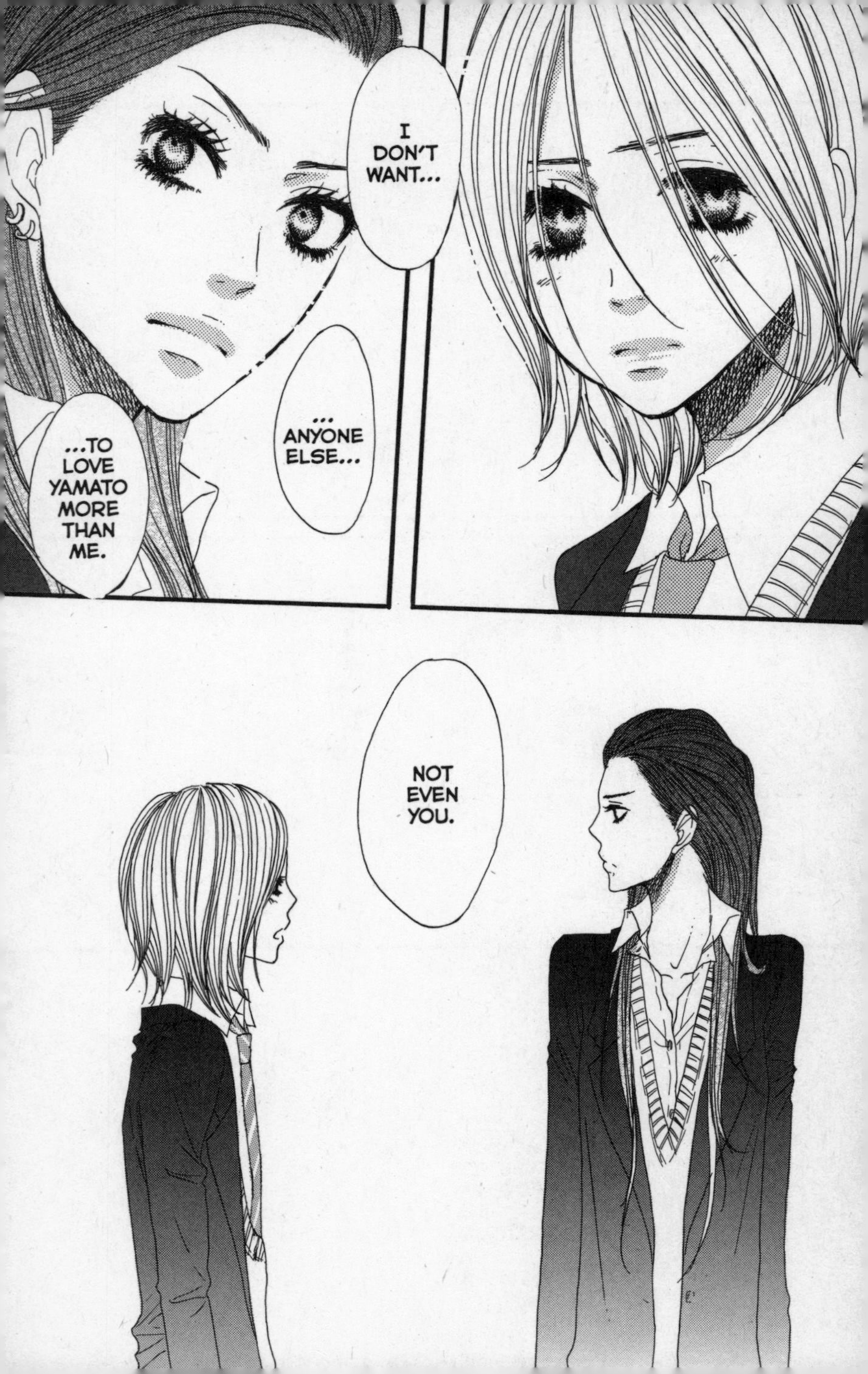
I DON'T WANT...
...ANYONE ELSE...
...TO LOVE YAMATO MORE THAN ME.
NOT EVEN YOU.

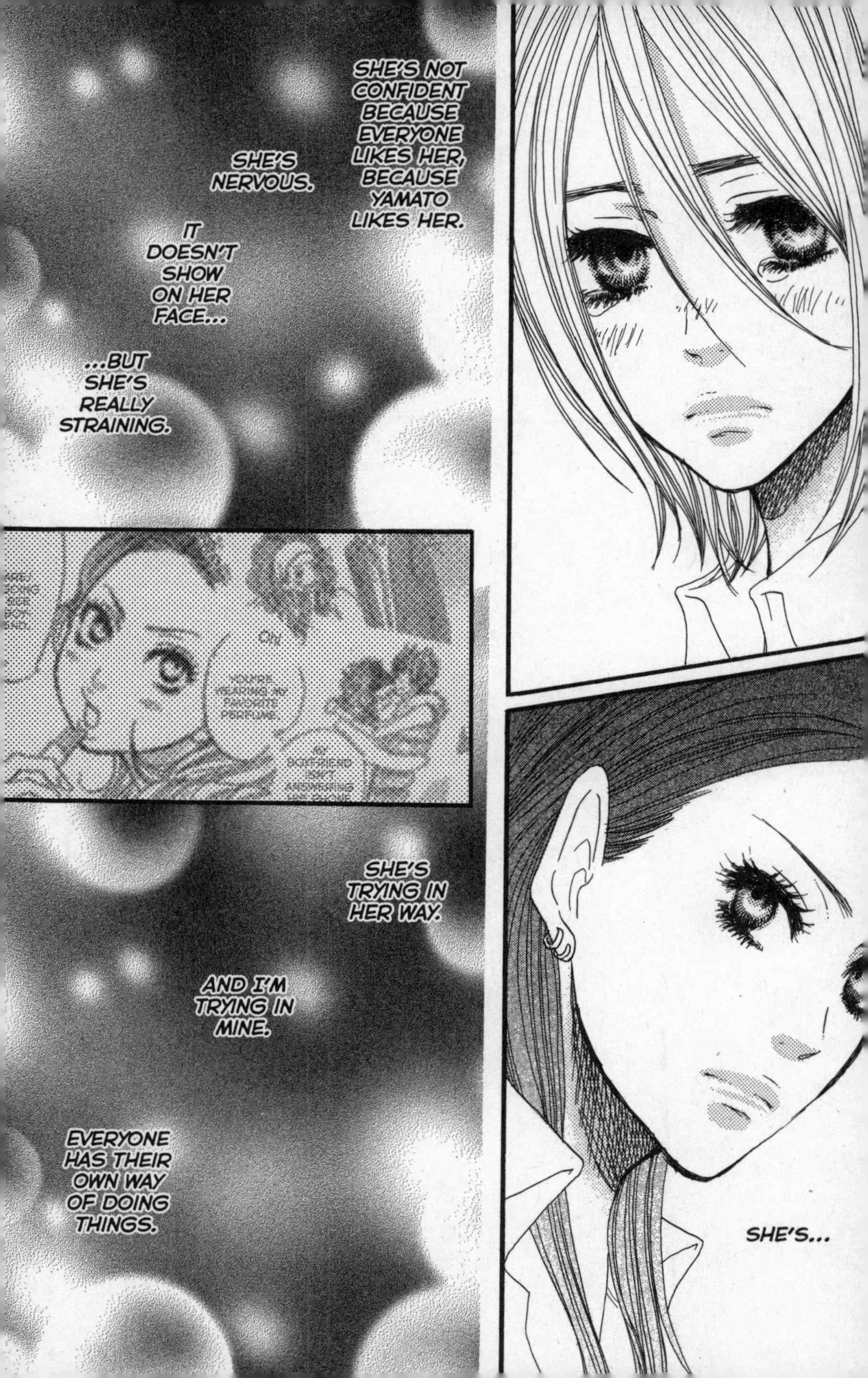
SHE'S...
SHE'S NOT CONFIDENT BECAUSE EVERYONE LIKES HER, BECAUSE YAMATO LIKES HER.
SHE'S NERVOUS.
IT DOESN'T SHOW ON HER FACE...
...BUT SHE'S REALLY STRAINING.
SHE'S TRYING IN HER WAY.
AND I'M TRYING IN MINE.
EVERYONE HAS THEIR OWN WAY OF DOING THINGS.

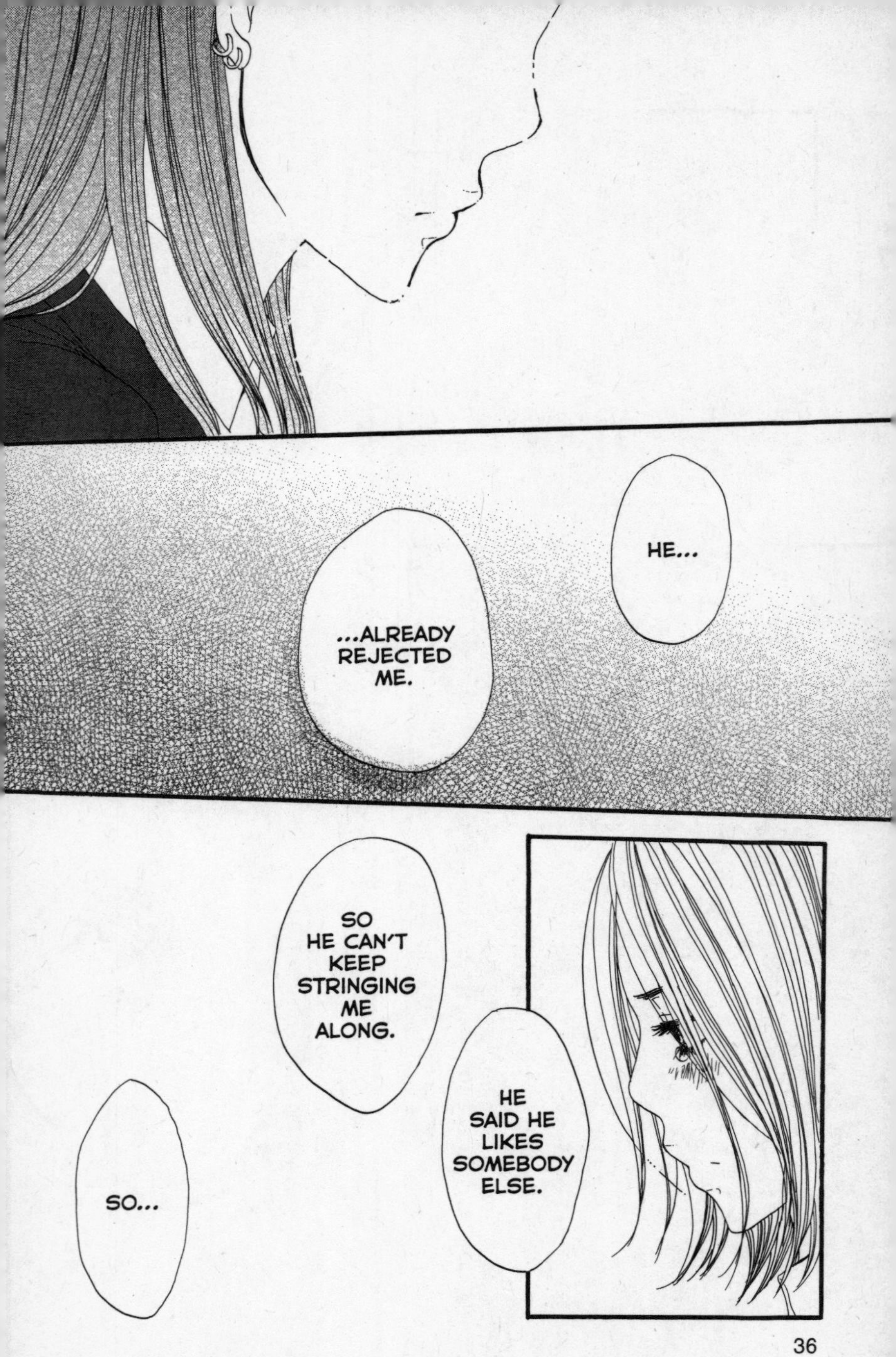
HE...
...ALREADY REJECTED ME.
HE SAID HE LIKES SOMEBODY ELSE.
SO HE CAN'T KEEP STRINGING ME ALONG.
SO...

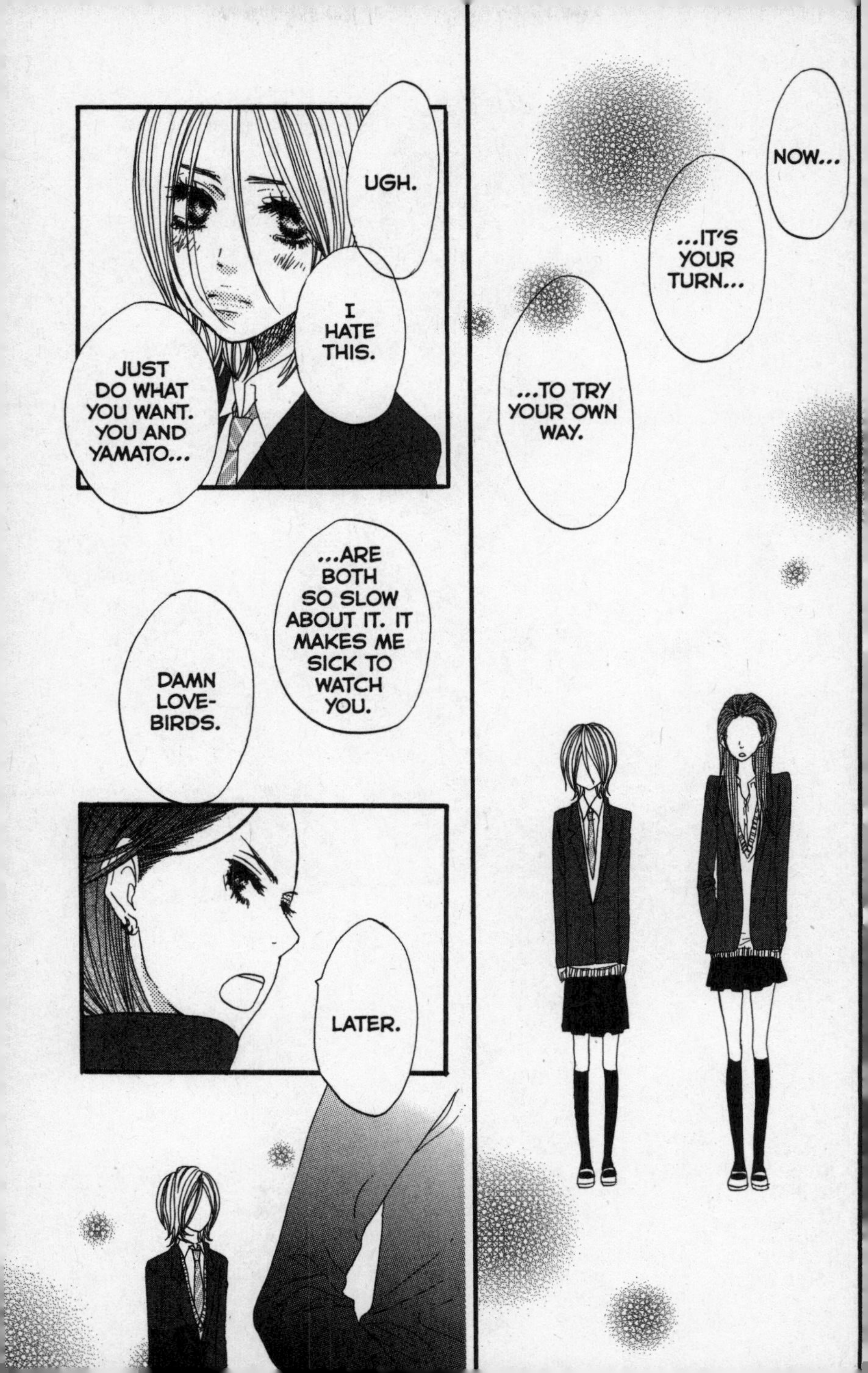
NOW...
...IT'S YOUR TURN...
...TO TRY YOUR OWN WAY.
UGH.
I HATE THIS.
JUST DO WHAT YOU WANT. YOU AND YAMATO...
...ARE BOTH SO SLOW ABOUT IT. IT MAKES ME SICK TO WATCH YOU.
DAMN LOVE-BIRDS.
LATER.

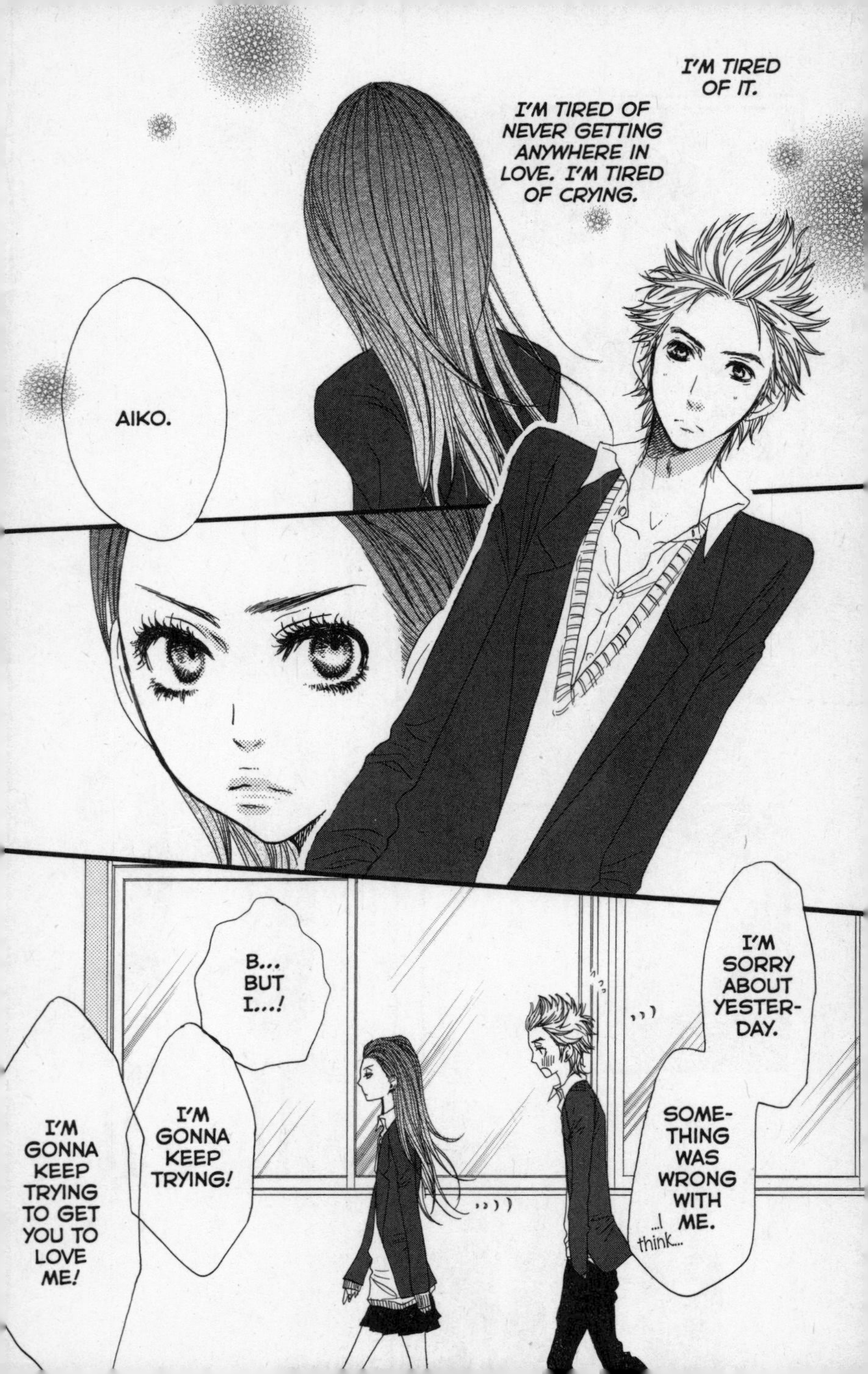
I'M TIRED OF IT.
I'M TIRED OF NEVER GETTING ANYWHERE IN LOVE. I'M TIRED OF CRYING.
AIKO.
I'M SORRY ABOUT YESTER-DAY.
SOME-THING WAS WRONG WITH ME.
...I think...
B... BUT I...!
I'M GONNA KEEP TRYING!
I'M GONNA KEEP TRYING TO GET YOU TO LOVE ME!

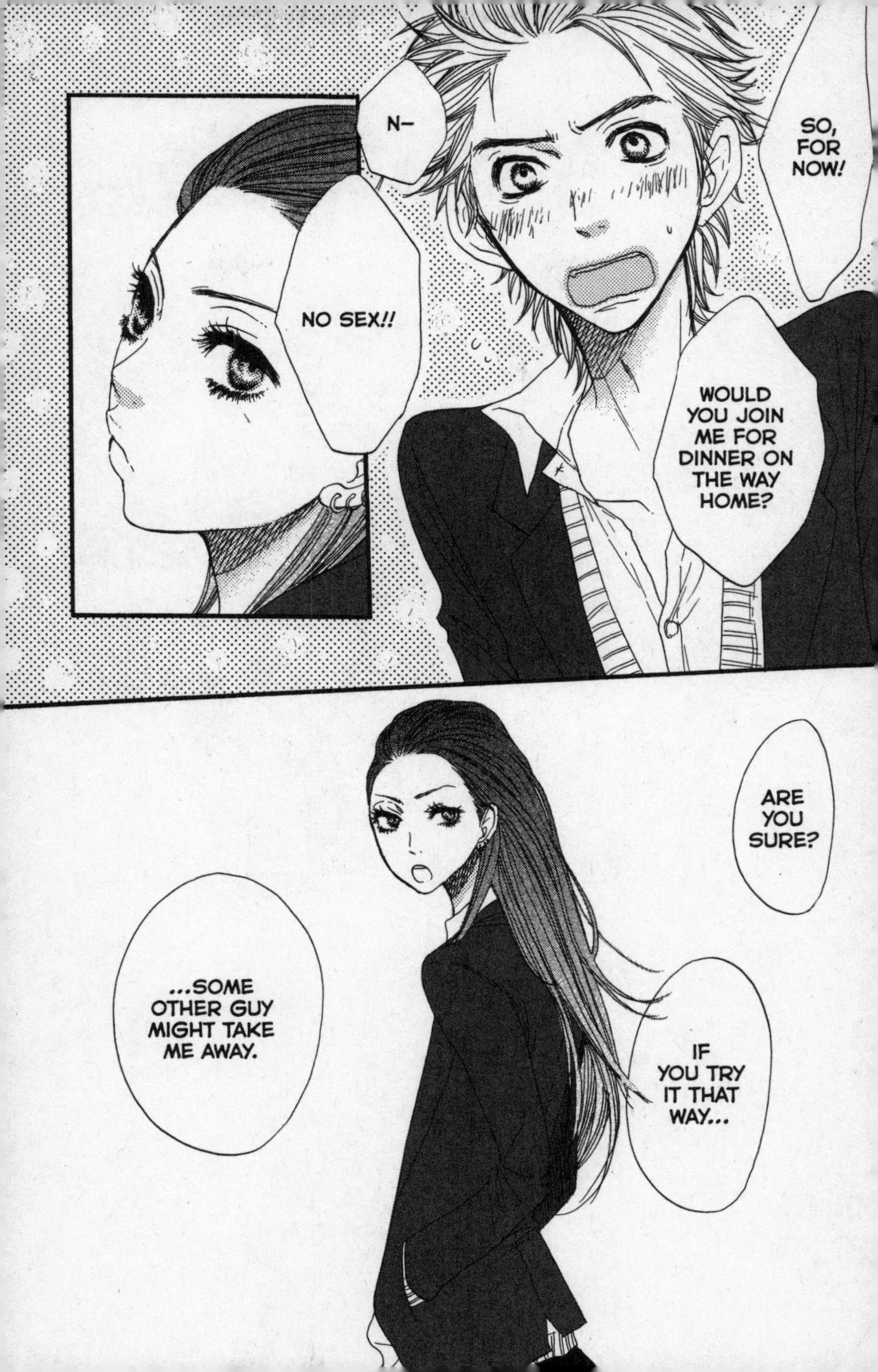
SO, FOR NOW!
N–
NO SEX!!
WOULD YOU JOIN ME FOR DINNER ON THE WAY HOME?
ARE YOU SURE?
IF YOU TRY IT THAT WAY...
...SOME OTHER GUY MIGHT TAKE ME AWAY.

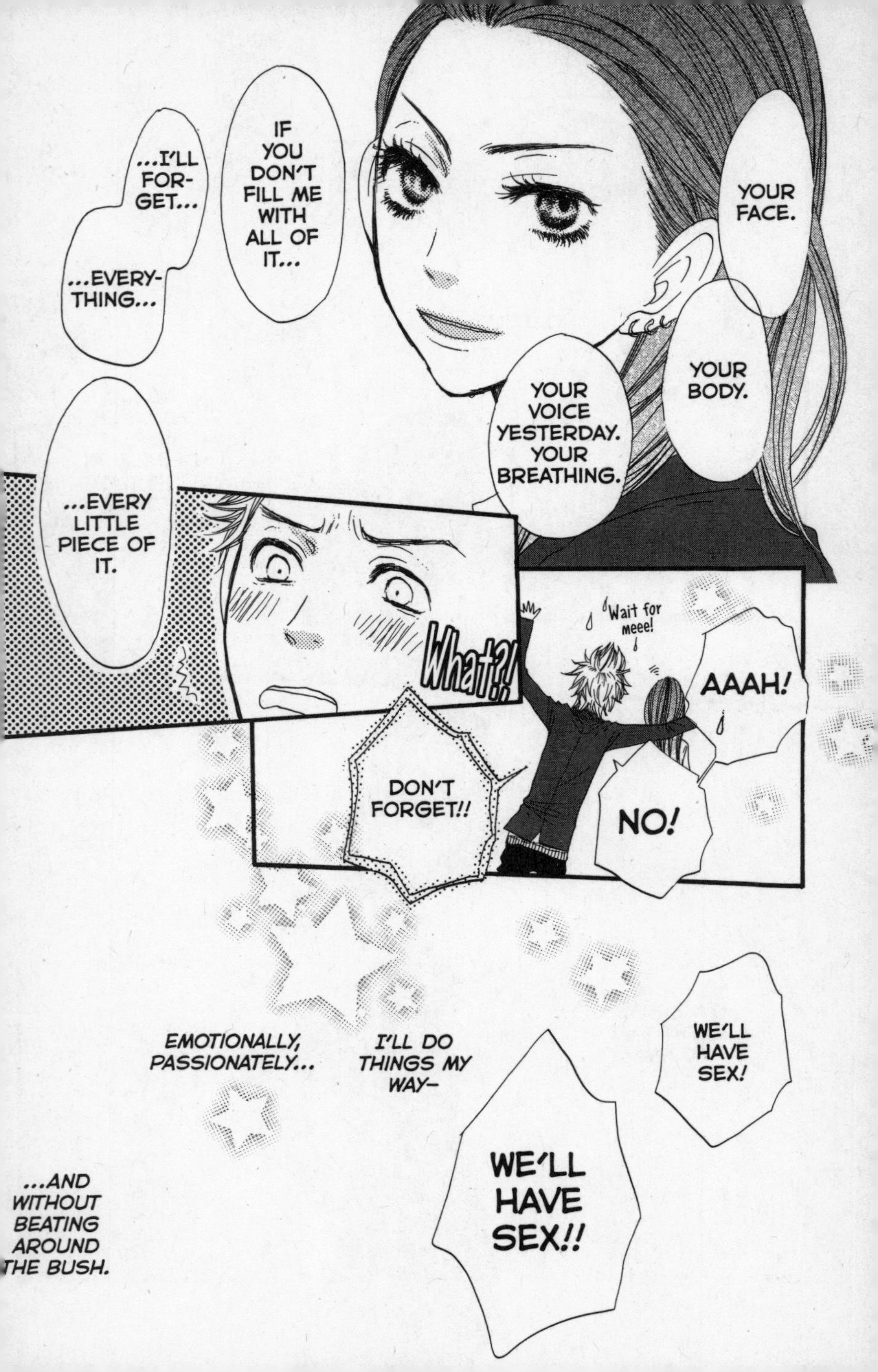
YOUR FACE.
YOUR BODY.
YOUR VOICE YESTERDAY. YOUR BREATHING.
IF YOU DON'T FILL ME WITH ALL OF IT...
...I'LL FOR-GET...
...EVERY-THING...
...EVERY LITTLE PIECE OF IT.
What?!
Wait for meee!
AAAH!
NO!
DON'T FORGET!!
WE'LL HAVE SEX!
WE'LL HAVE SEX!!
I'LL DO THINGS MY WAY–
EMOTIONALLY, PASSIONATELY...
...AND WITHOUT BEATING AROUND THE BUSH.

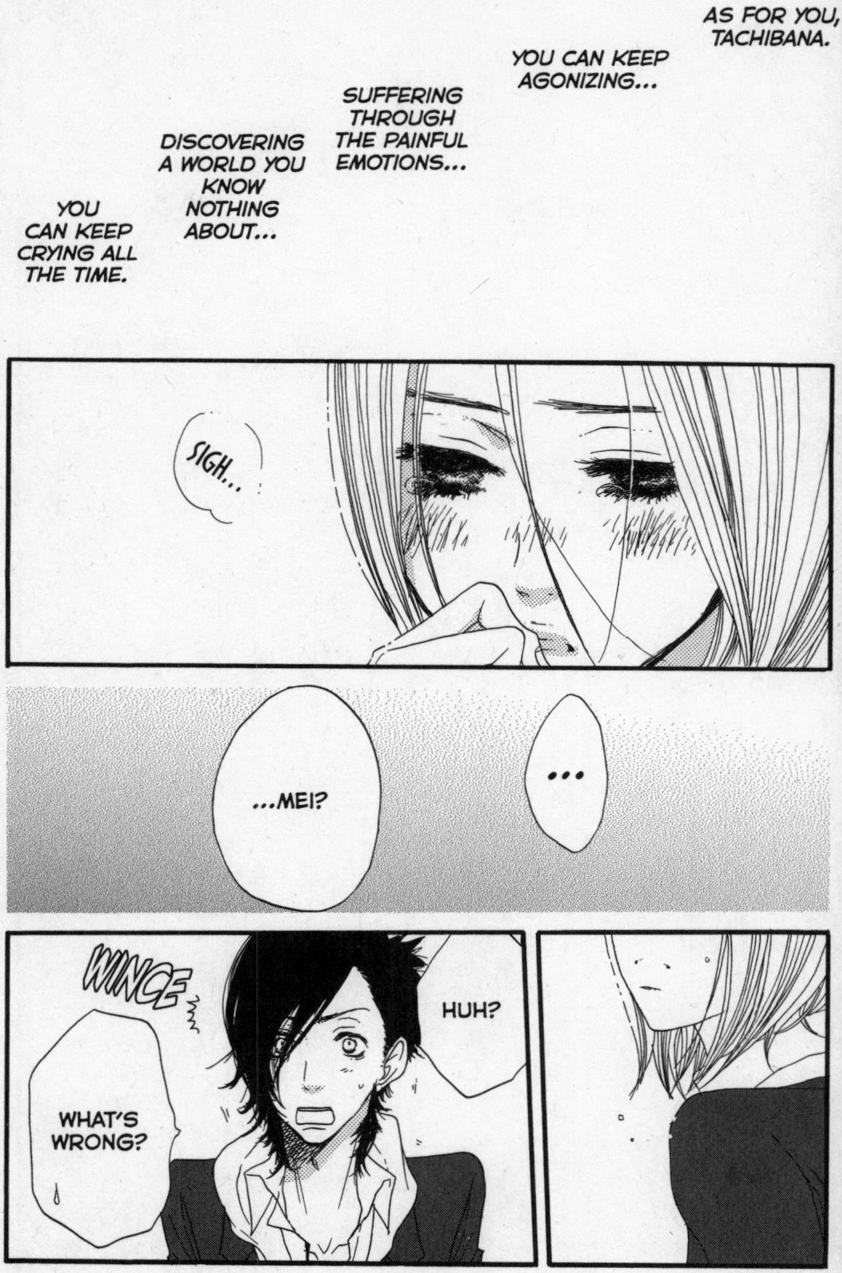
AS FOR YOU, TACHIBANA.
YOU CAN KEEP AGONIZING...
SUFFERING THROUGH THE PAINFUL EMOTIONS...
DISCOVERING A WORLD YOU KNOW NOTHING ABOUT...
YOU CAN KEEP CRYING ALL THE TIME.
SIGH...
...
...MEI?
HUH?
WINCE
WHAT'S WRONG?

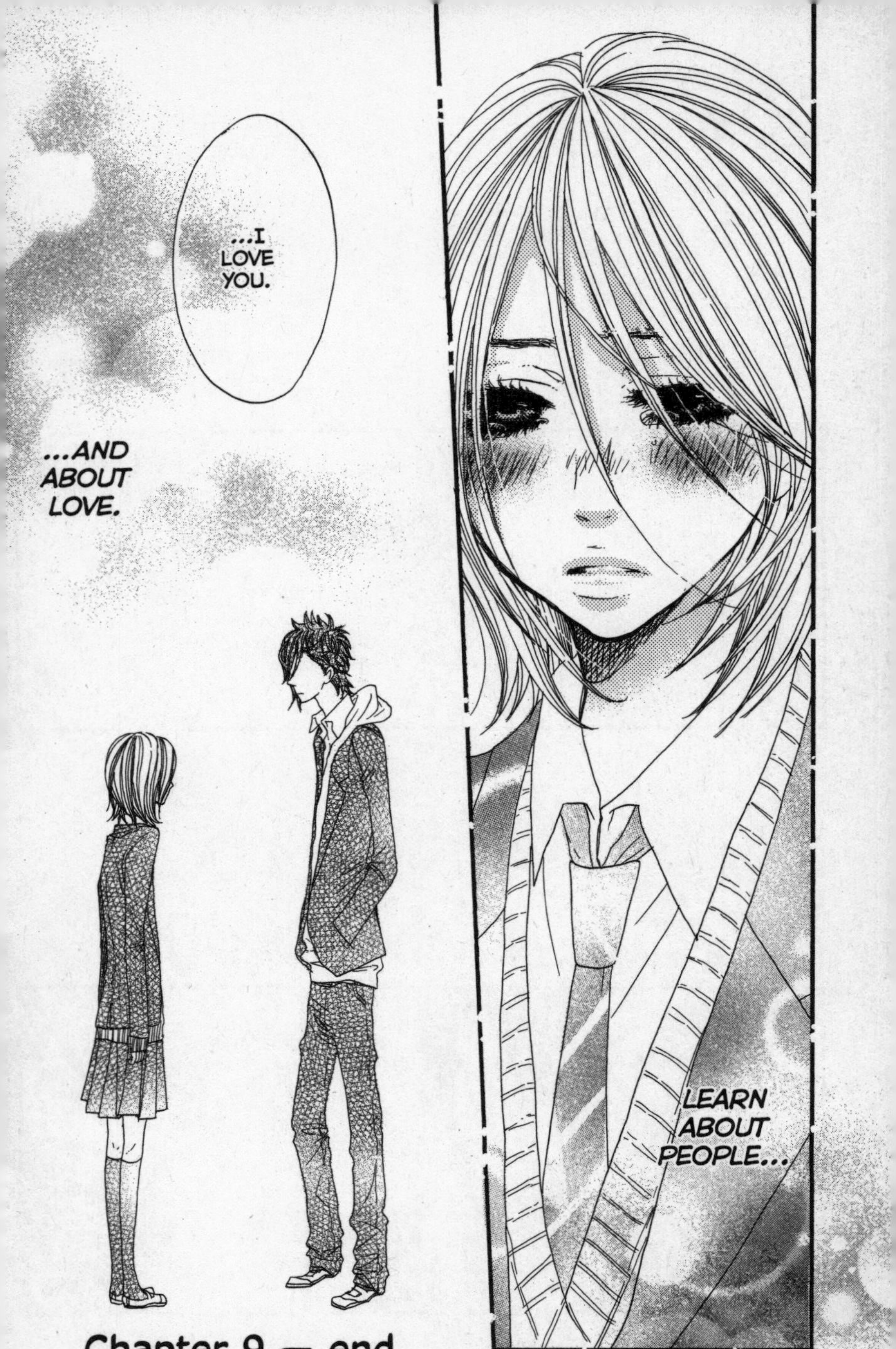
LEARN ABOUT PEOPLE...
...AND ABOUT LOVE.
...I LOVE YOU.

Chapter 9 — end

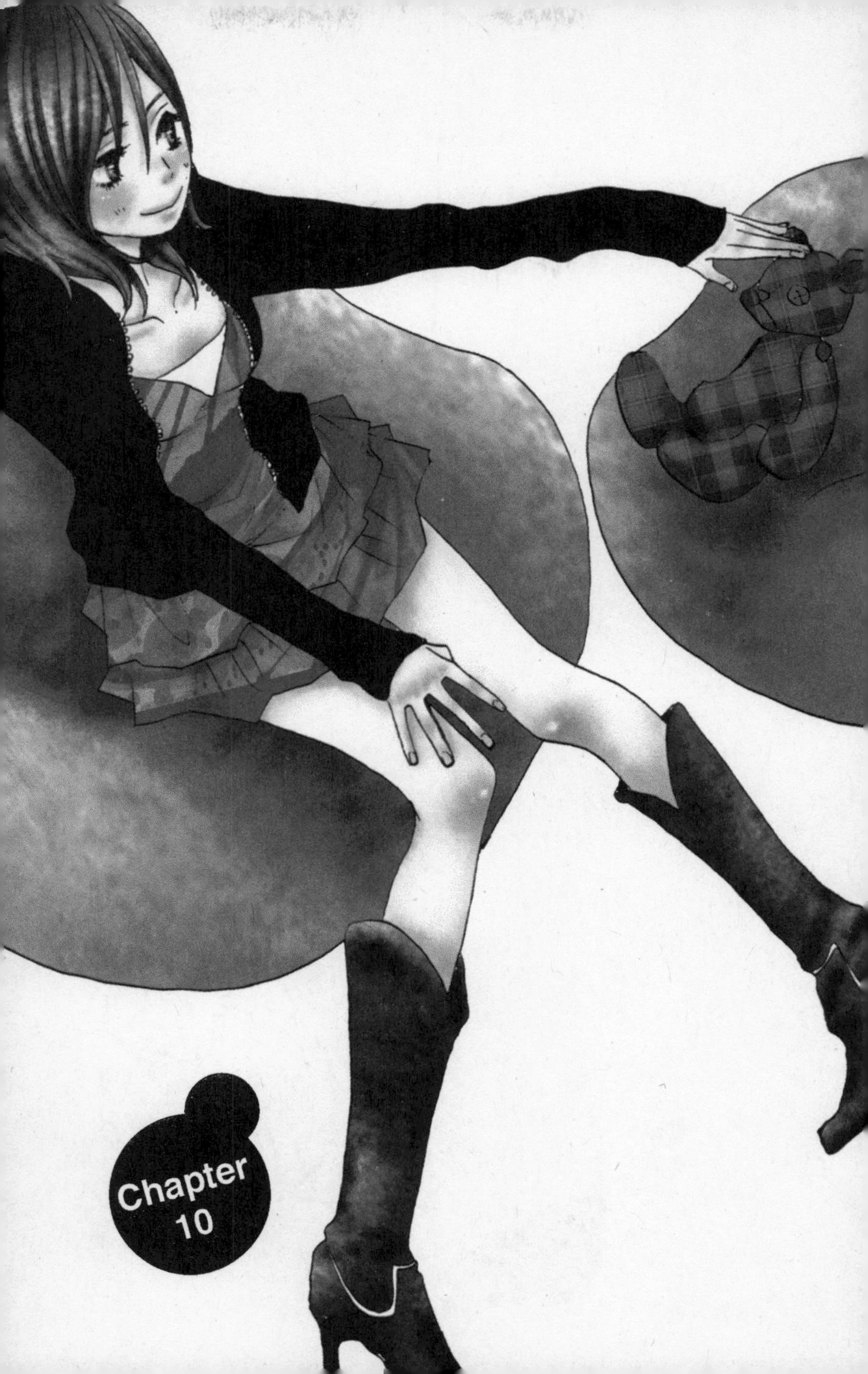
Chapter
10

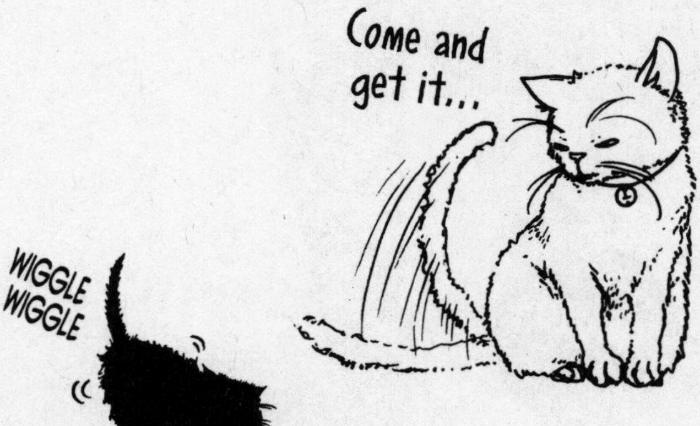
Come and get it...
WIGGLE WIGGLE

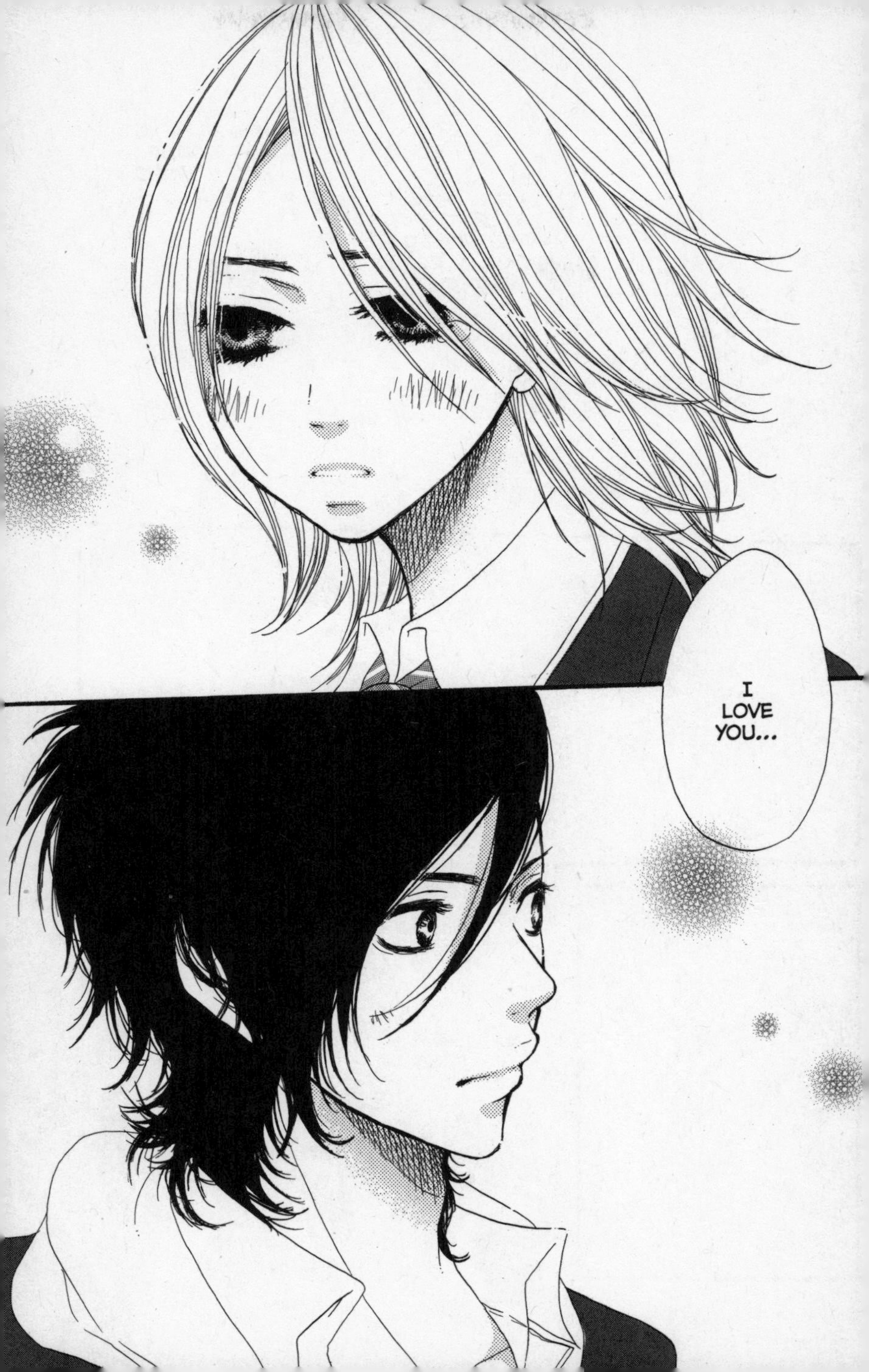
I LOVE YOU...

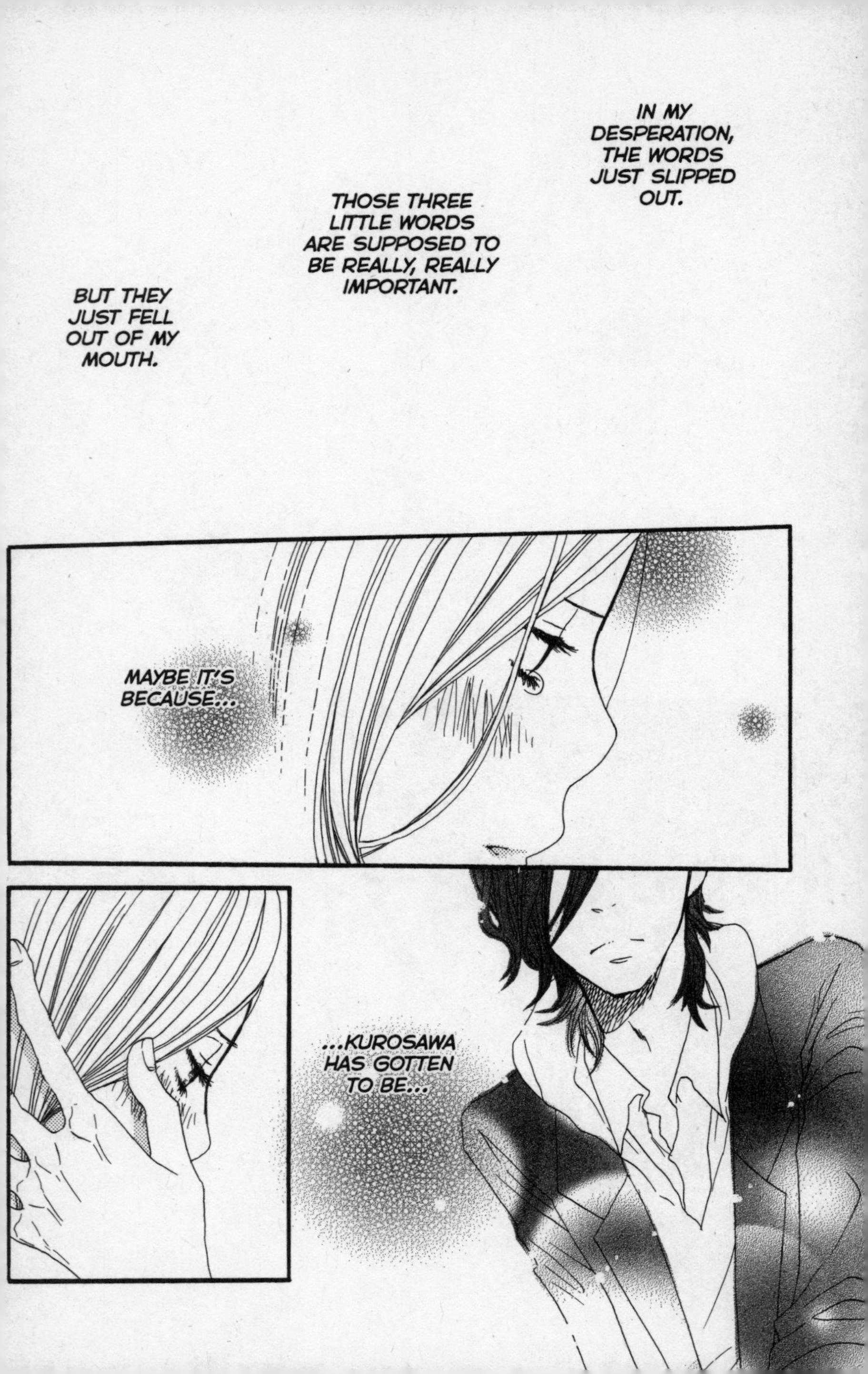
IN MY DESPERATION, THE WORDS JUST SLIPPED OUT.
THOSE THREE LITTLE WORDS ARE SUPPOSED TO BE REALLY, REALLY IMPORTANT.
BUT THEY JUST FELL OUT OF MY MOUTH.
MAYBE IT'S BECAUSE...
...KUROSAWA HAS GOTTEN TO BE...

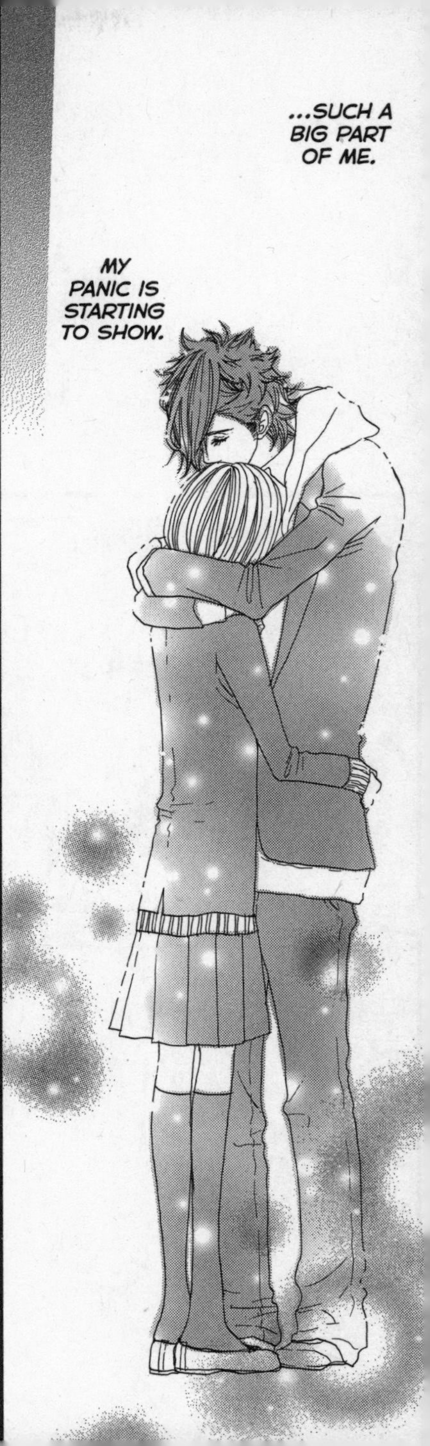
...SUCH A BIG PART OF ME.
MY PANIC IS STARTING TO SHOW.

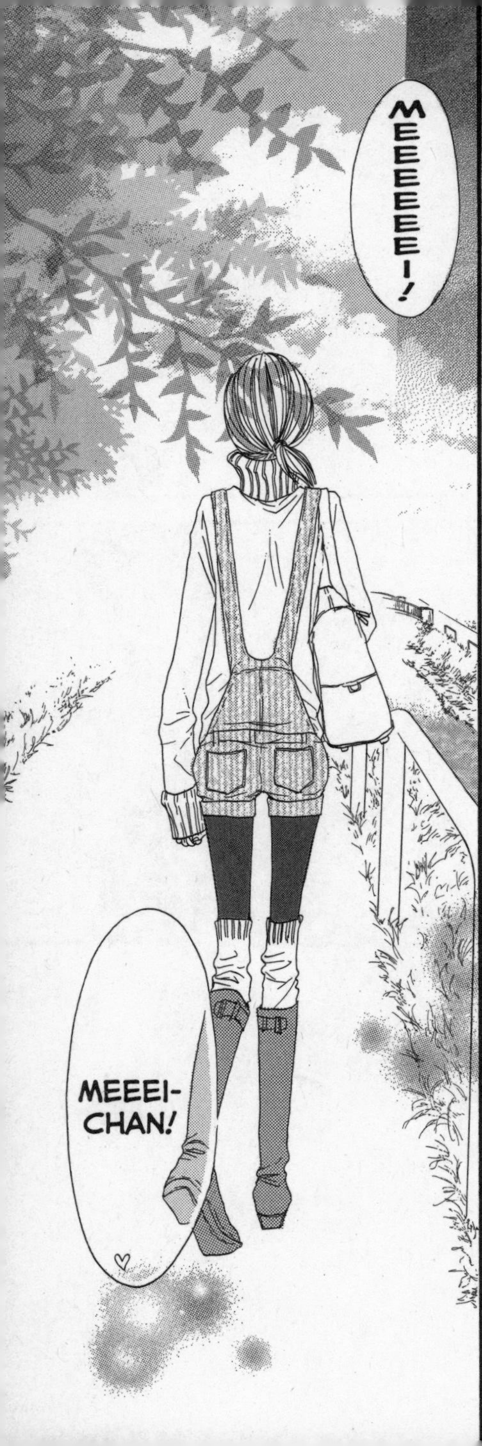
MEEEEEEI!
MEEEI-CHAN!

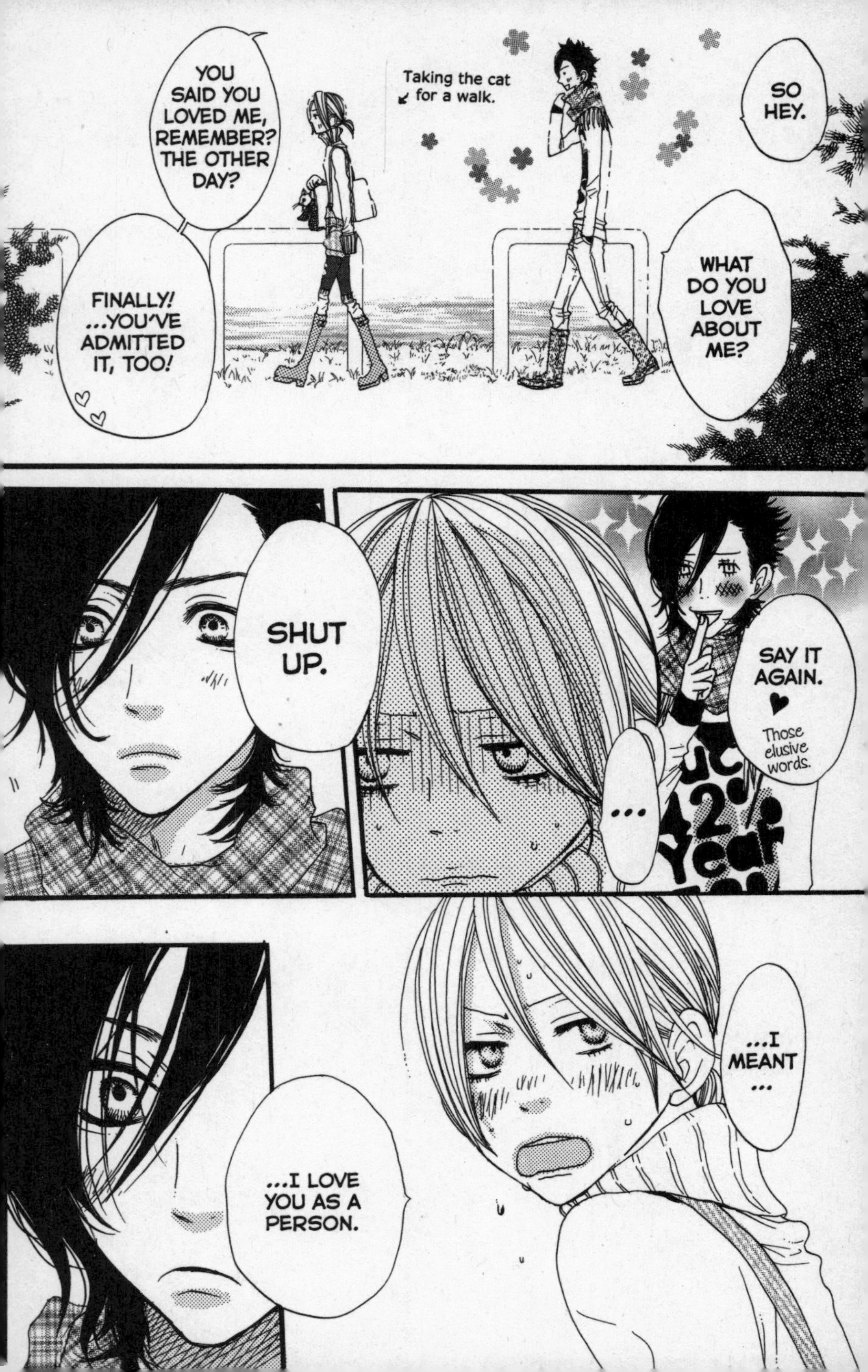
SO HEY.
WHAT DO YOU LOVE ABOUT ME?
Taking the cat for a walk.
YOU SAID YOU LOVED ME, REMEMBER? THE OTHER DAY?
FINALLY! ...YOU'VE ADMITTED IT, TOO! ♡ ♡
SAY IT AGAIN. ♥
Those elusive words.
...
SHUT UP.
...I MEANT ...
...I LOVE YOU AS A PERSON.

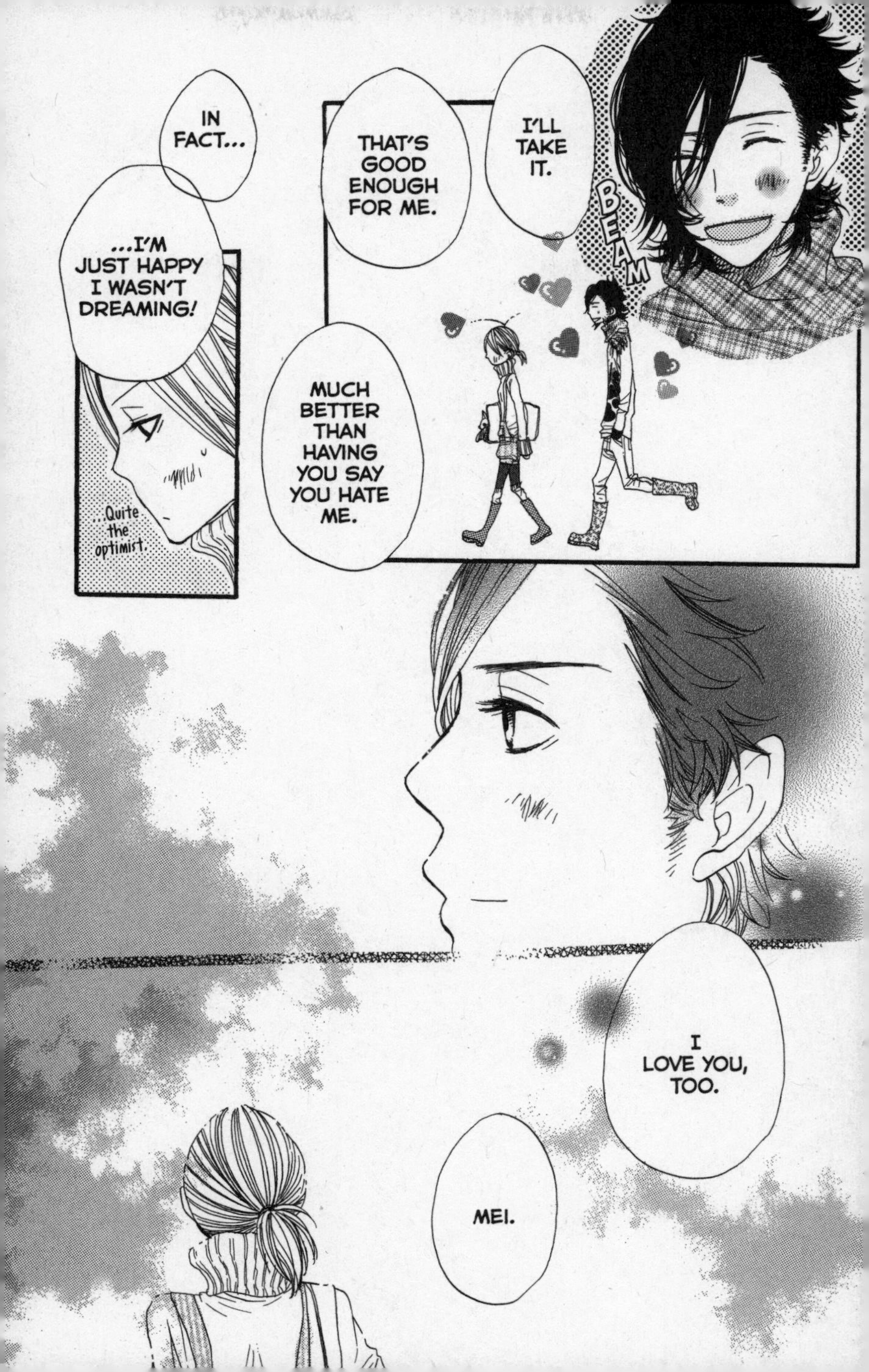
I'LL TAKE IT.
BEAM
THAT'S GOOD ENOUGH FOR ME.
MUCH BETTER THAN HAVING YOU SAY YOU HATE ME.
IN FACT...
...I'M JUST HAPPY I WASN'T DREAMING!
...Quite the optimist.
I LOVE YOU, TOO.
MEI.

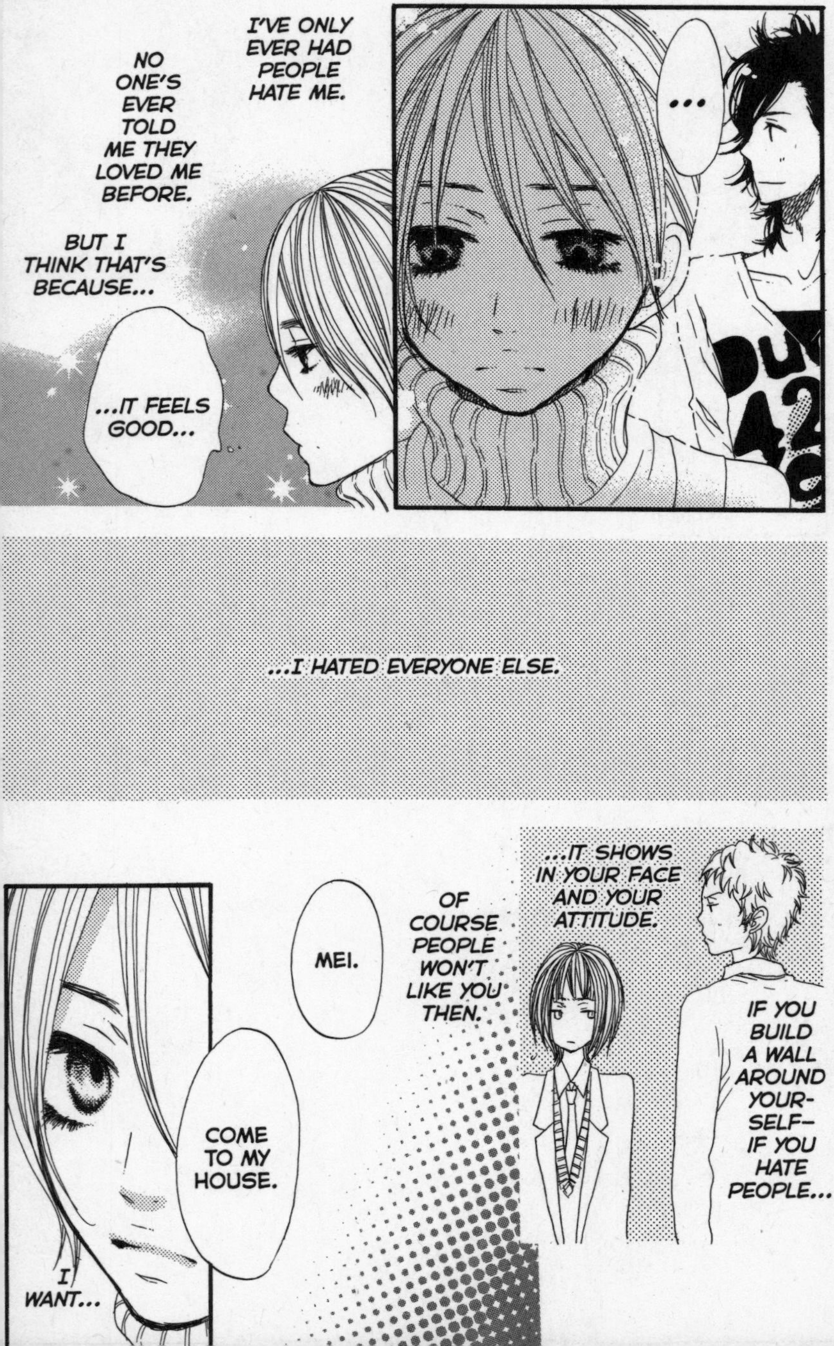
...
I'VE ONLY EVER HAD PEOPLE HATE ME.
NO ONE'S EVER TOLD ME THEY LOVED ME BEFORE.
BUT I THINK THAT'S BECAUSE...
...IT FEELS GOOD...
...I HATED EVERYONE ELSE.
IF YOU BUILD A WALL AROUND YOUR-SELF– IF YOU HATE PEOPLE...
...IT SHOWS IN YOUR FACE AND YOUR ATTITUDE.
OF COURSE PEOPLE WON'T LIKE YOU THEN.
MEI.
COME TO MY HOUSE.
I WANT...

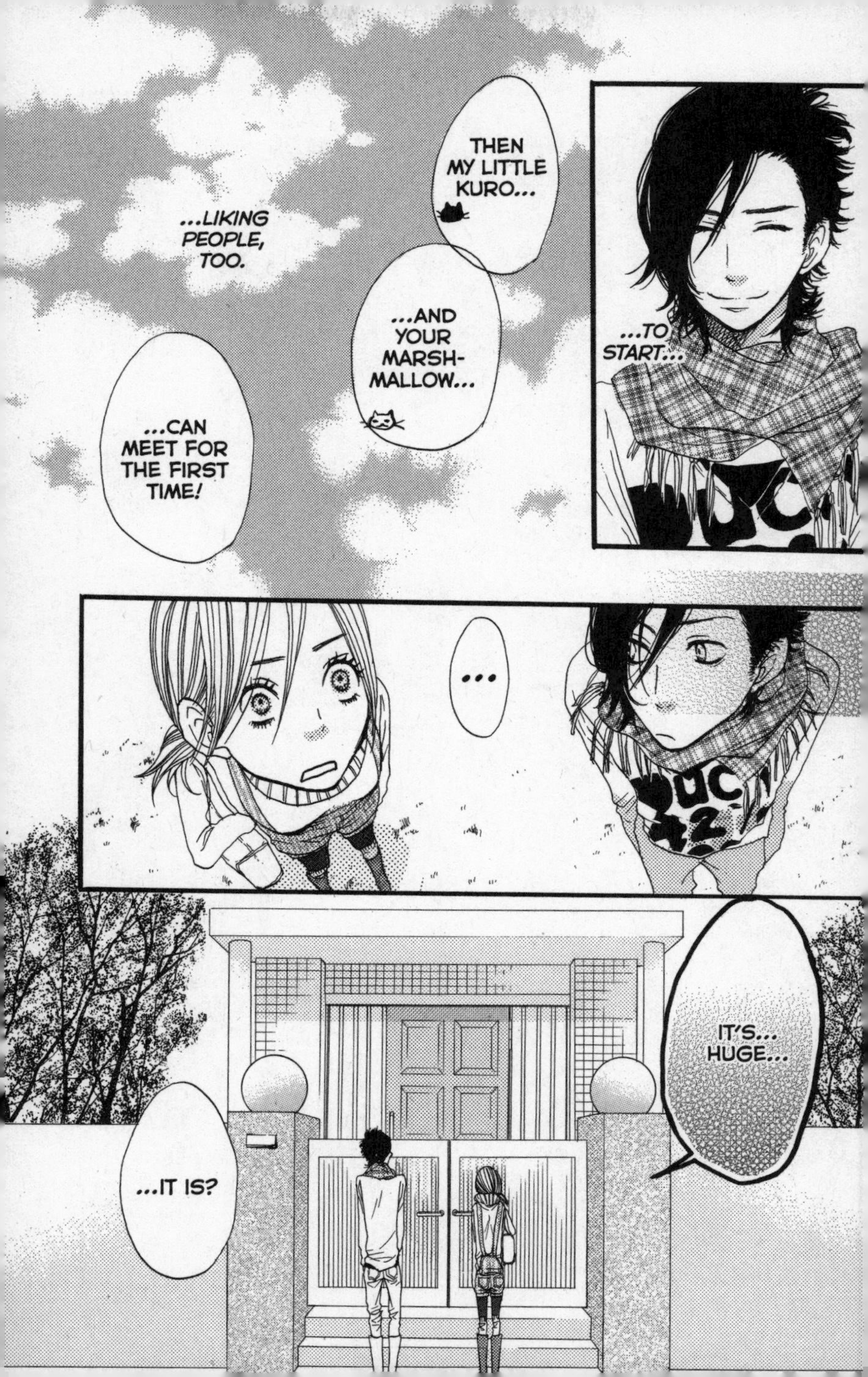
...LIKING PEOPLE, TOO.
...TO START...
THEN MY LITTLE KURO...
...AND YOUR MARSH-MALLOW...
...CAN MEET FOR THE FIRST TIME!
...
IT'S... HUGE...
...IT IS?

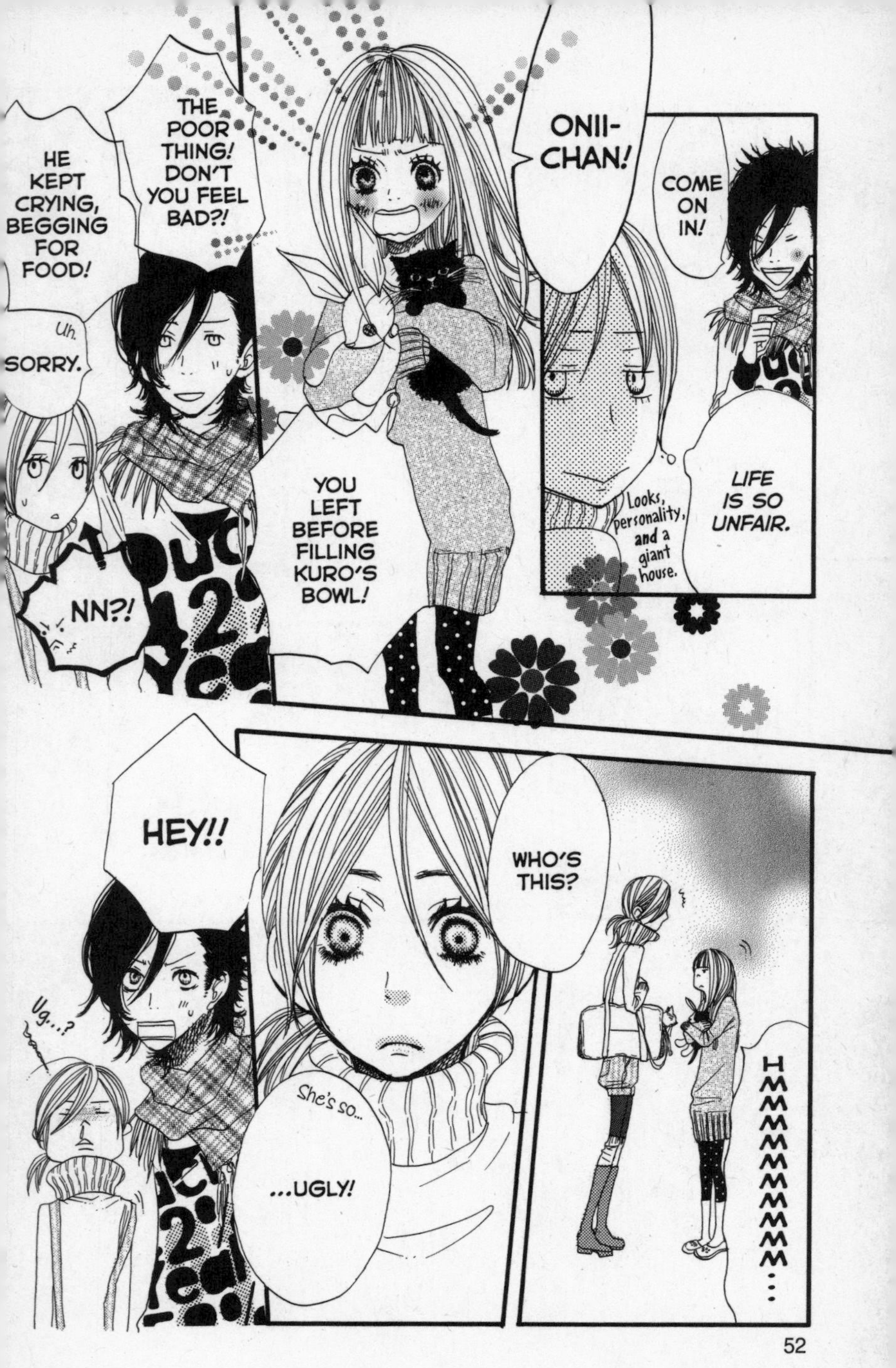
COME ON IN!
LIFE IS SO UNFAIR.
Looks, personality, and a giant house.
ONII-CHAN!
YOU LEFT BEFORE FILLING KURO'S BOWL!
THE POOR THING! DON'T YOU FEEL BAD?!
HE KEPT CRYING, BEGGING FOR FOOD!
Uh.
SORRY.
NN?!
HMMMMMMMMMM...
WHO'S THIS?
She's so...
...UGLY!
HEY!!
Ug...?

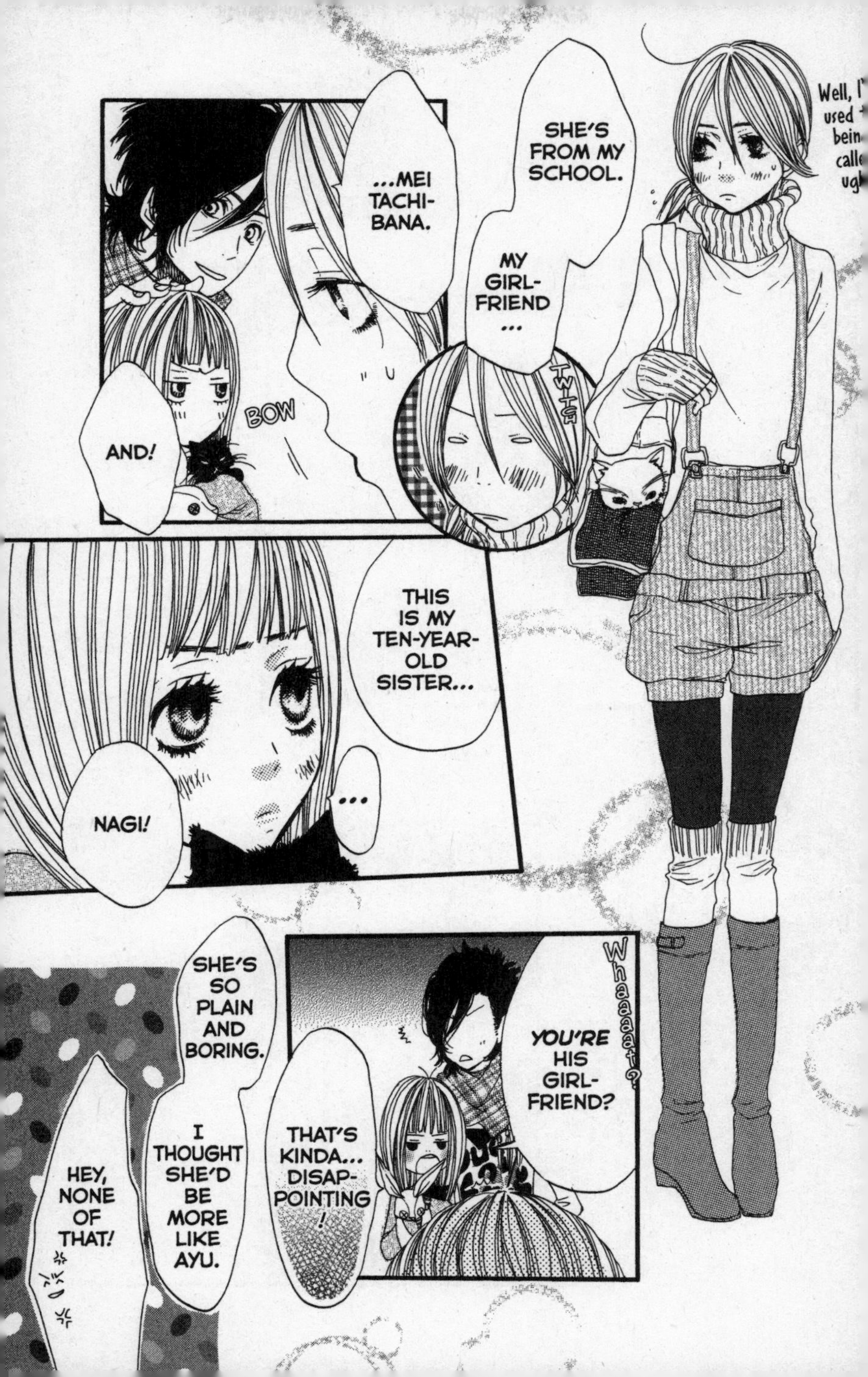
Well, I'
used t
bein
calle
ugl
SHE'S FROM MY SCHOOL.
MY GIRL-FRIEND...
...MEI TACHI-BANA.
TWITCH
BOW
AND!
THIS IS MY TEN-YEAR-OLD SISTER...
...
NAGI!
Whaaaaat?
YOU'RE HIS GIRL-FRIEND?
THAT'S KINDA... DISAP-POINTING!
SHE'S SO PLAIN AND BORING.
I THOUGHT SHE'D BE MORE LIKE AYU.
HEY, NONE OF THAT!

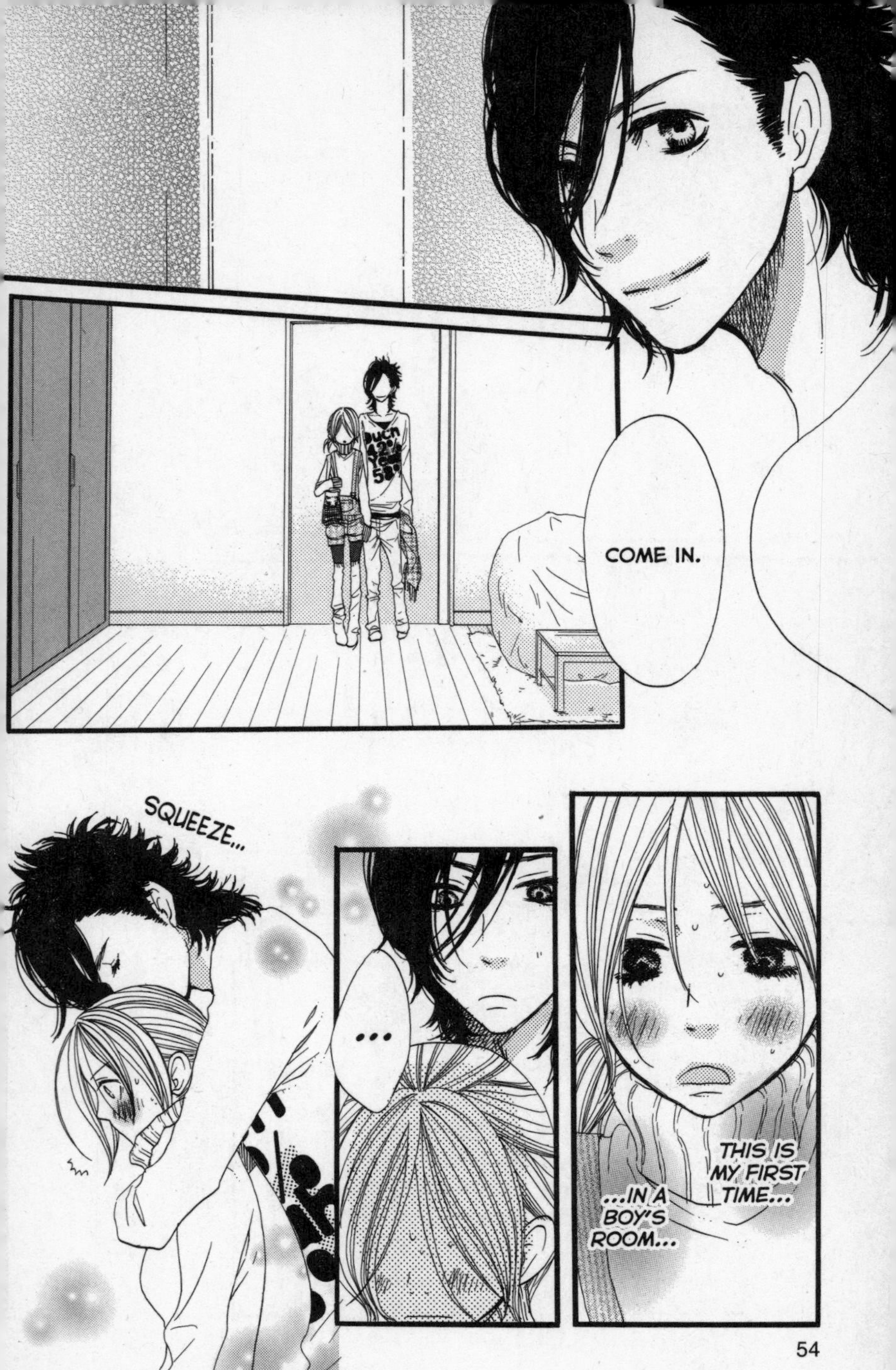
COME IN.
THIS IS MY FIRST TIME...
...IN A BOY'S ROOM...
...
SQUEEZE...

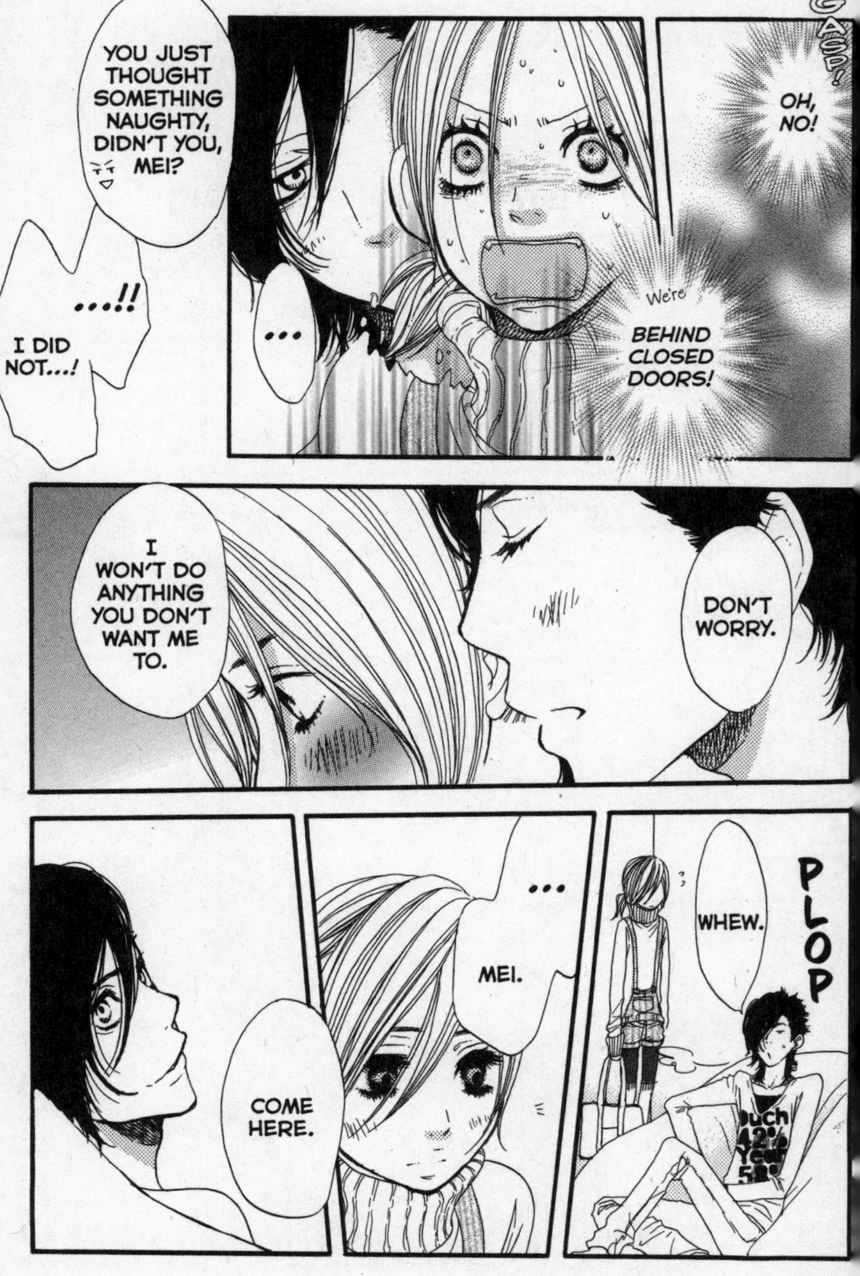
GASP!
OH, NO!
We're BEHIND CLOSED DOORS!
YOU JUST THOUGHT SOMETHING NAUGHTY, DIDN'T YOU, MEI?
...
...!!
I DID NOT...!
DON'T WORRY.
I WON'T DO ANYTHING YOU DON'T WANT ME TO.
PLOP
WHEW.
...
MEI.
COME HERE.

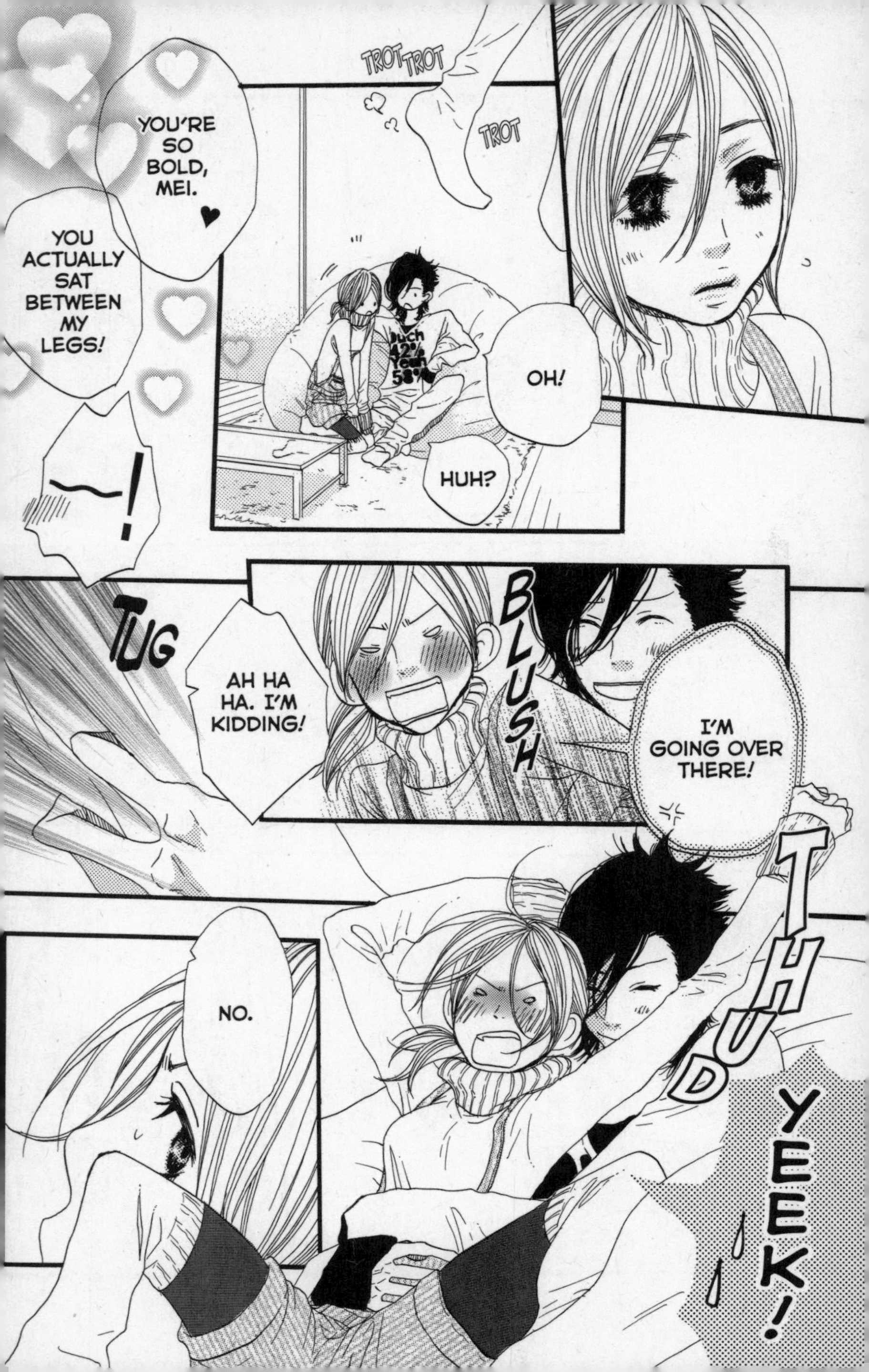
TROT TROT
TROT
OH!
HUH?
YOU'RE SO BOLD, MEI. ♥
YOU ACTUALLY SAT BETWEEN MY LEGS!
~~!
BLUSH
I'M GOING OVER THERE!
AH HA HA. I'M KIDDING!
TUG
THUD
YEEK!
NO.

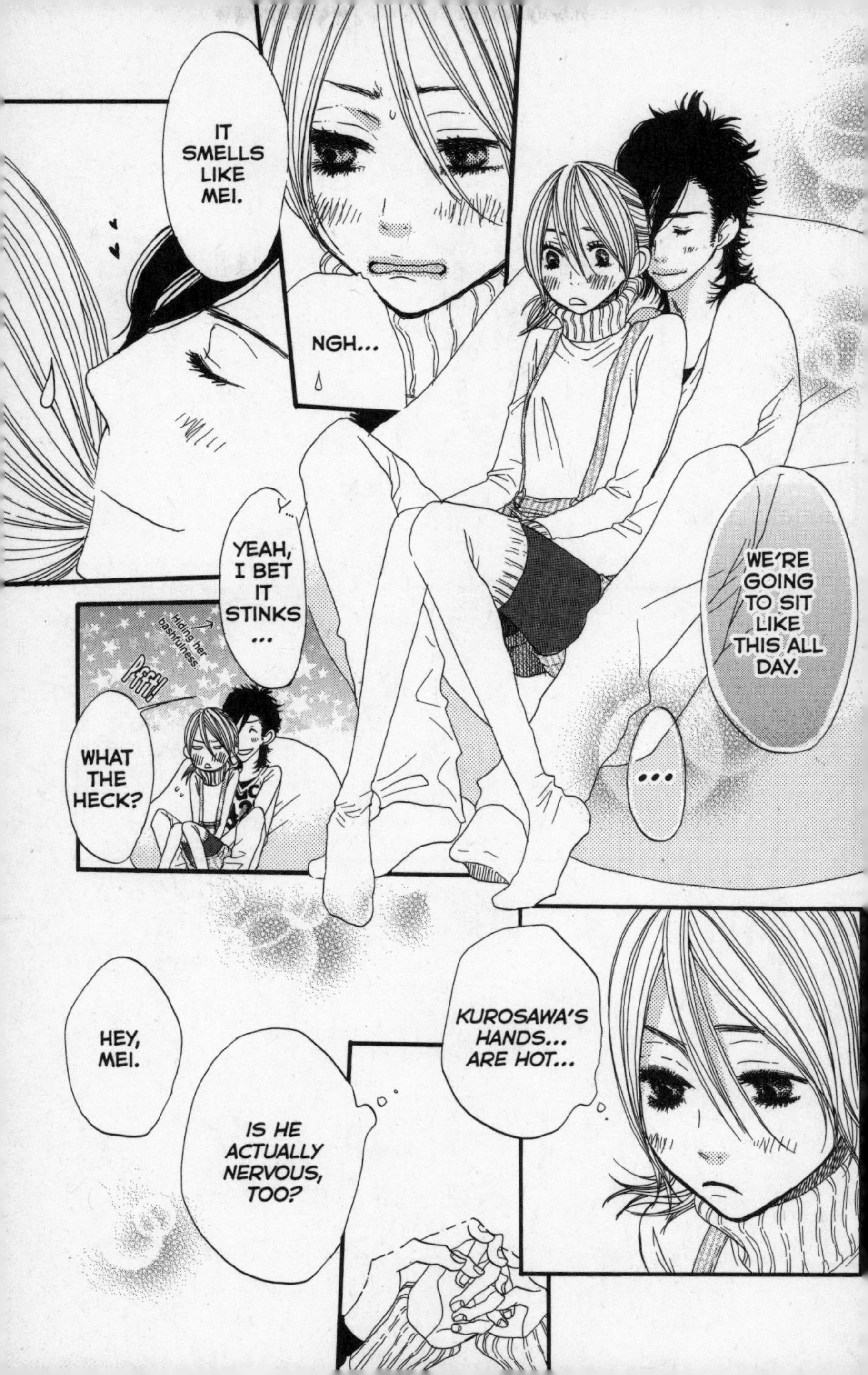
WE'RE GOING TO SIT LIKE THIS ALL DAY.
...
IT SMELLS LIKE MEI.
NGH...
Y... YEAH, I BET IT STINKS...
Pfft!
Hiding her bashfulness.
WHAT THE HECK?
KUROSAWA'S HANDS... ARE HOT...
IS HE ACTUALLY NERVOUS, TOO?
HEY, MEI.

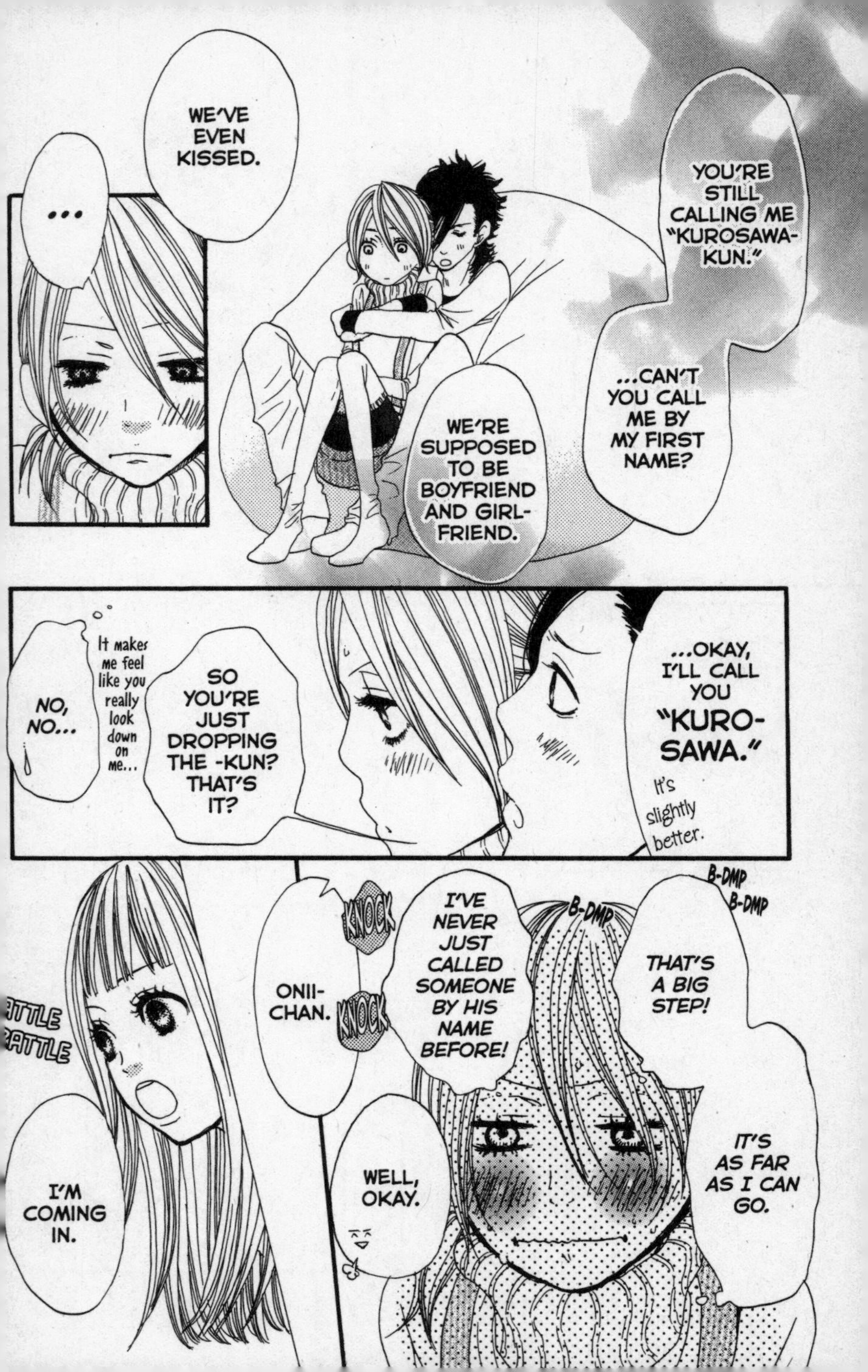
YOU'RE STILL CALLING ME "KUROSAWA-KUN."
...CAN'T YOU CALL ME BY MY FIRST NAME?
WE'RE SUPPOSED TO BE BOYFRIEND AND GIRL-FRIEND.
WE'VE EVEN KISSED.
...
...OKAY, I'LL CALL YOU "KURO-SAWA."
It's slightly better.
SO YOU'RE JUST DROPPING THE -KUN? THAT'S IT?
It makes me feel like you really look down on me...
NO, NO...
B-DMP
B-DMP
THAT'S A BIG STEP!
IT'S AS FAR AS I CAN GO.
B-DMP
I'VE NEVER JUST CALLED SOMEONE BY HIS NAME BEFORE!
WELL, OKAY.
KNOCK
KNOCK
ONII-CHAN.
ATTLE
ATTLE
I'M COMING IN.

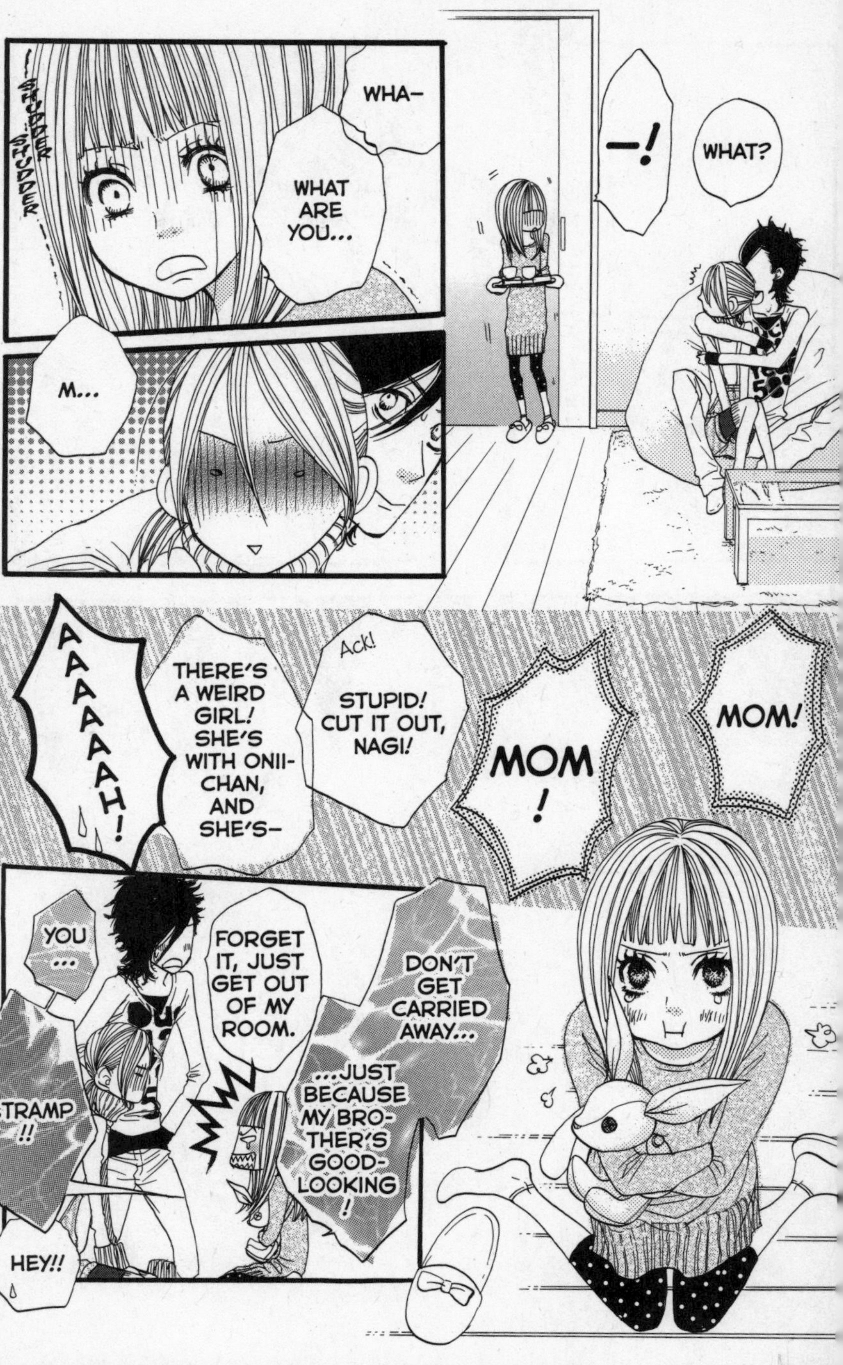
WHAT?
—!
WHA-
WHAT ARE YOU...
SHUDDER SHUDDER
M...
MOM!
MOM!
Ack!
STUPID! CUT IT OUT, NAGI!
THERE'S A WEIRD GIRL! SHE'S WITH ONII-CHAN, AND SHE'S—
AAAAAAH!
DON'T GET CARRIED AWAY...
...JUST BECAUSE MY BROTHER'S GOOD-LOOKING!
FORGET IT, JUST GET OUT OF MY ROOM.
YOU...
...TRAMP!!
HEY!!

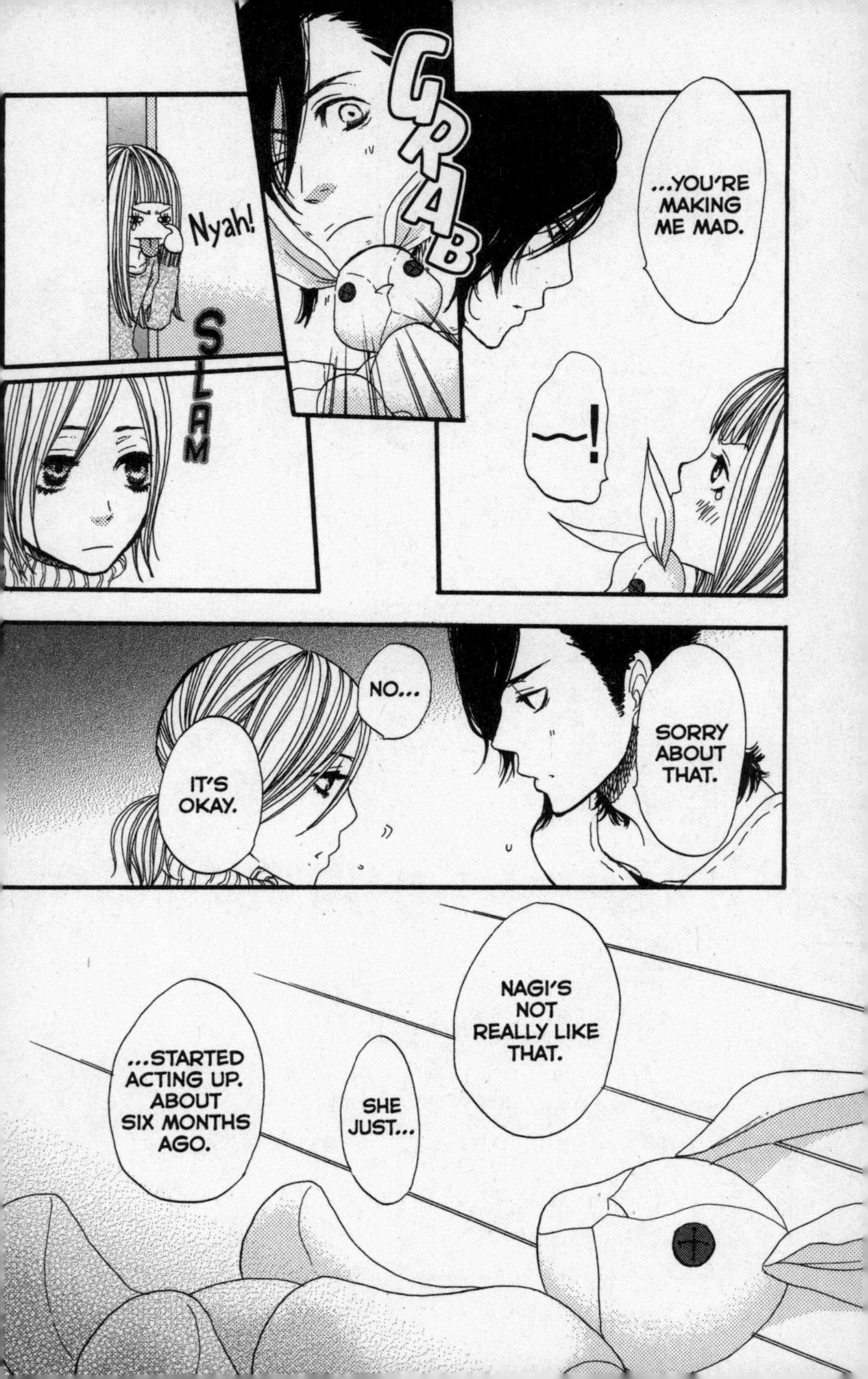
...YOU'RE MAKING ME MAD.
GRAB
~!
Nyah!
SLAM
SORRY ABOUT THAT.
NO...
IT'S OKAY.
NAGI'S NOT REALLY LIKE THAT.
SHE JUST...
...STARTED ACTING UP. ABOUT SIX MONTHS AGO.

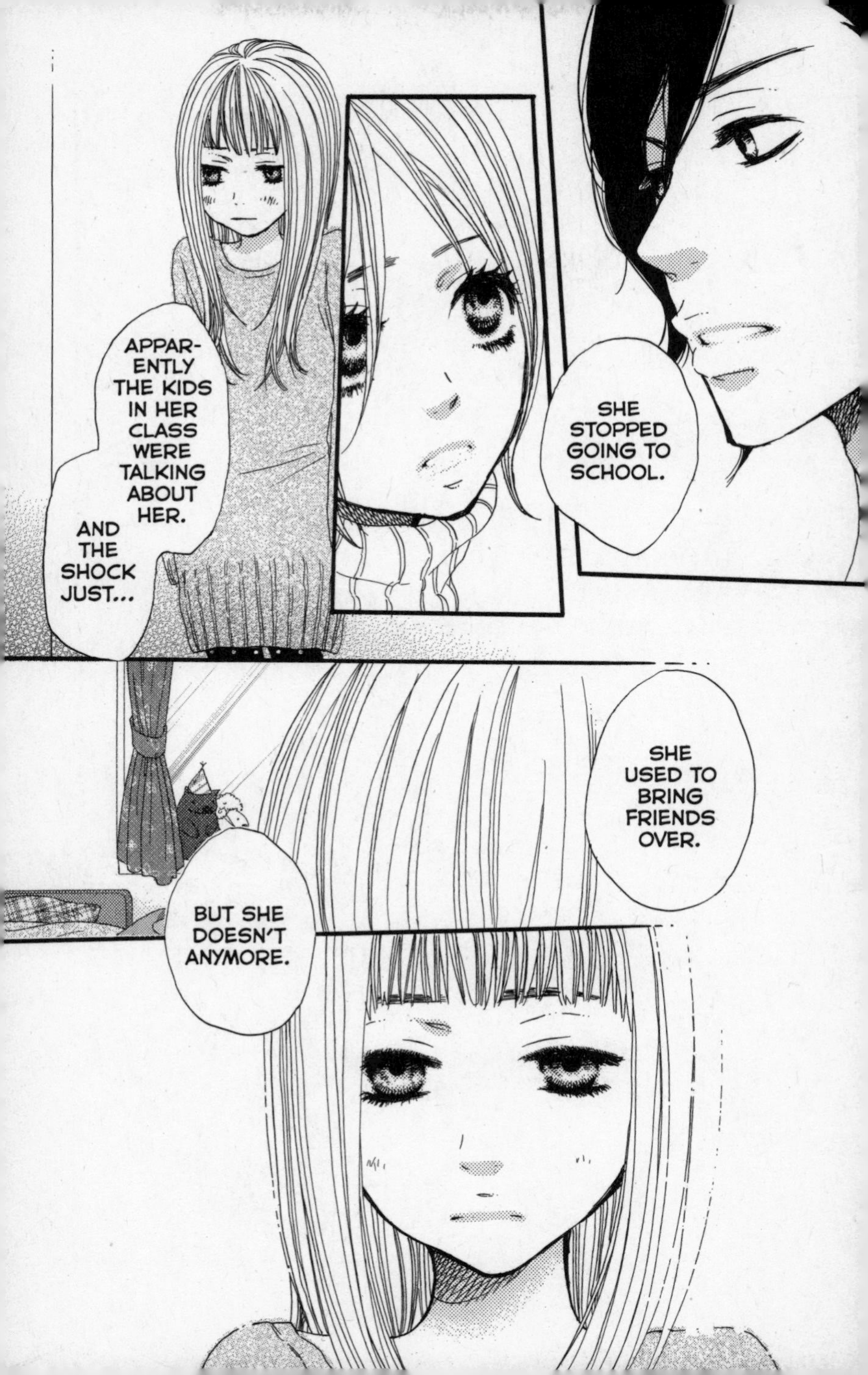
SHE STOPPED GOING TO SCHOOL.
APPARENTLY THE KIDS IN HER CLASS WERE TALKING ABOUT HER.
AND THE SHOCK JUST...
SHE USED TO BRING FRIENDS OVER.
BUT SHE DOESN'T ANYMORE.

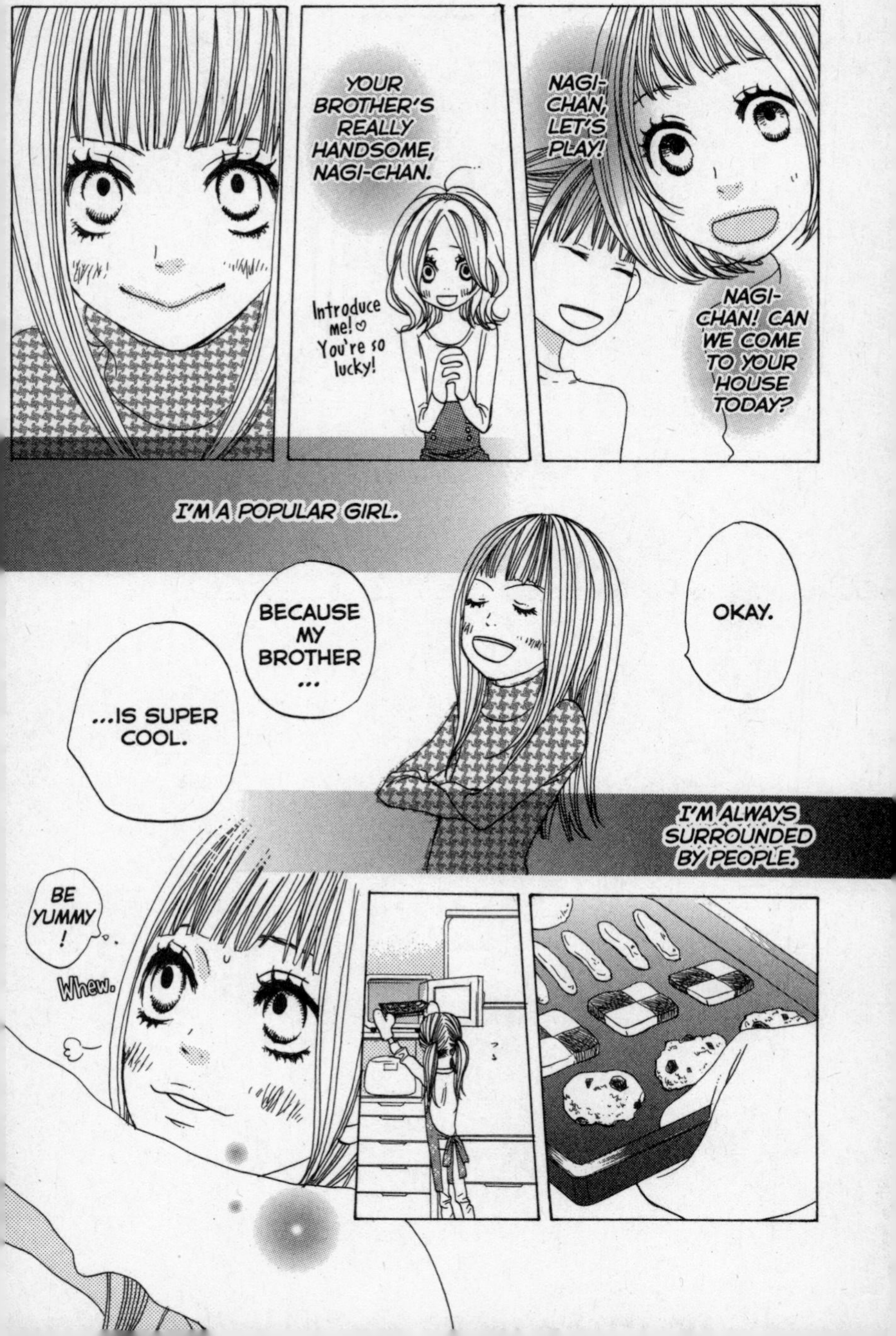
NAGI-CHAN, LET'S PLAY!
NAGI-CHAN! CAN WE COME TO YOUR HOUSE TODAY?
YOUR BROTHER'S REALLY HANDSOME, NAGI-CHAN.
Introduce me! ♡ You're so lucky!
I'M A POPULAR GIRL.
OKAY.
BECAUSE MY BROTHER...
...IS SUPER COOL.
I'M ALWAYS SURROUNDED BY PEOPLE.
BE YUMMY!
Whew.

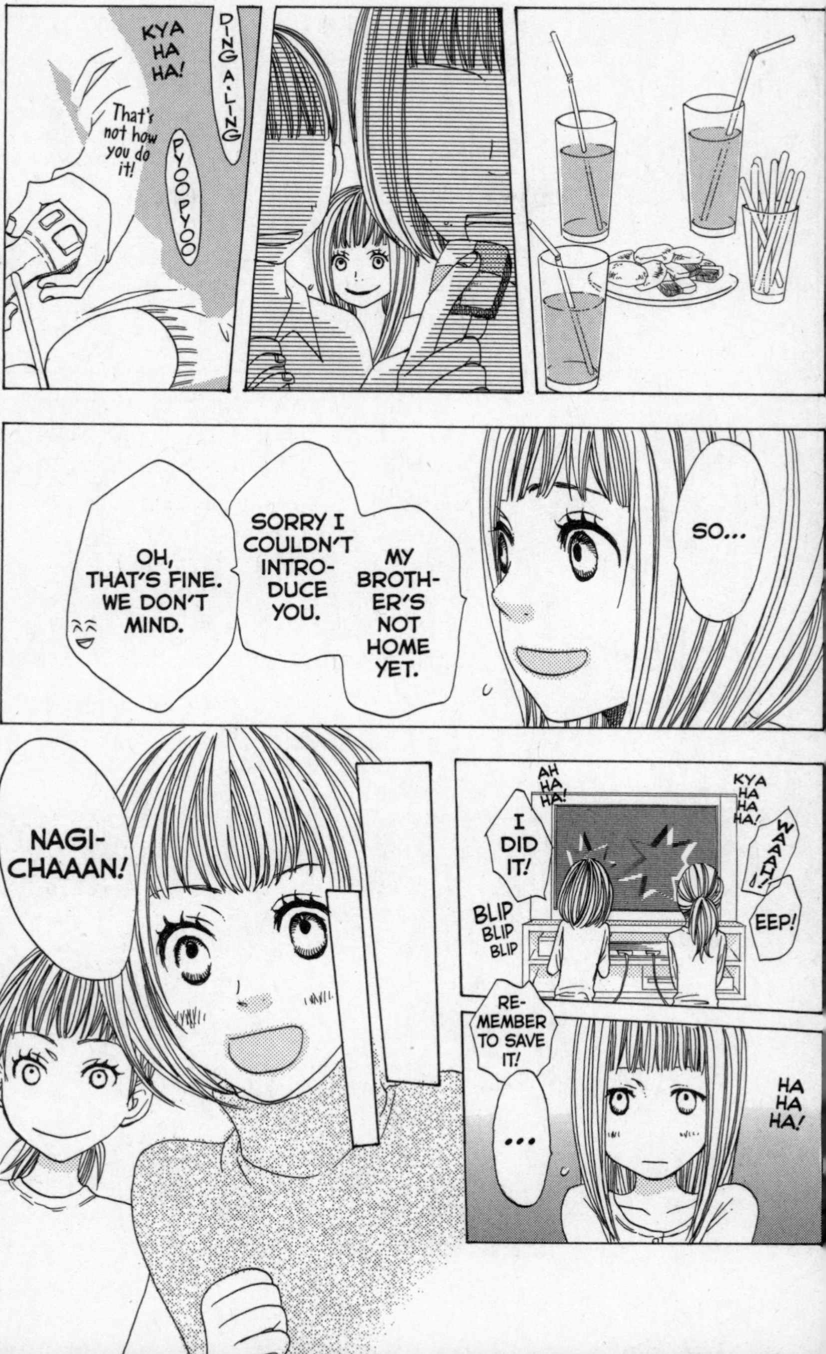
DING A-LING
KYA HA HA!
PYOOPYOO
That's not how you do it!
SO...
MY BROTHER'S NOT HOME YET.
SORRY I COULDN'T INTRODUCE YOU.
OH, THAT'S FINE. WE DON'T MIND.
KYA HA HA HA!
WAAAH!
EEP!
AH HA HA!
I DID IT!
BLIP BLIP BLIP
HA HA HA!
REMEMBER TO SAVE IT!
...
NAGI-CHAAAN!

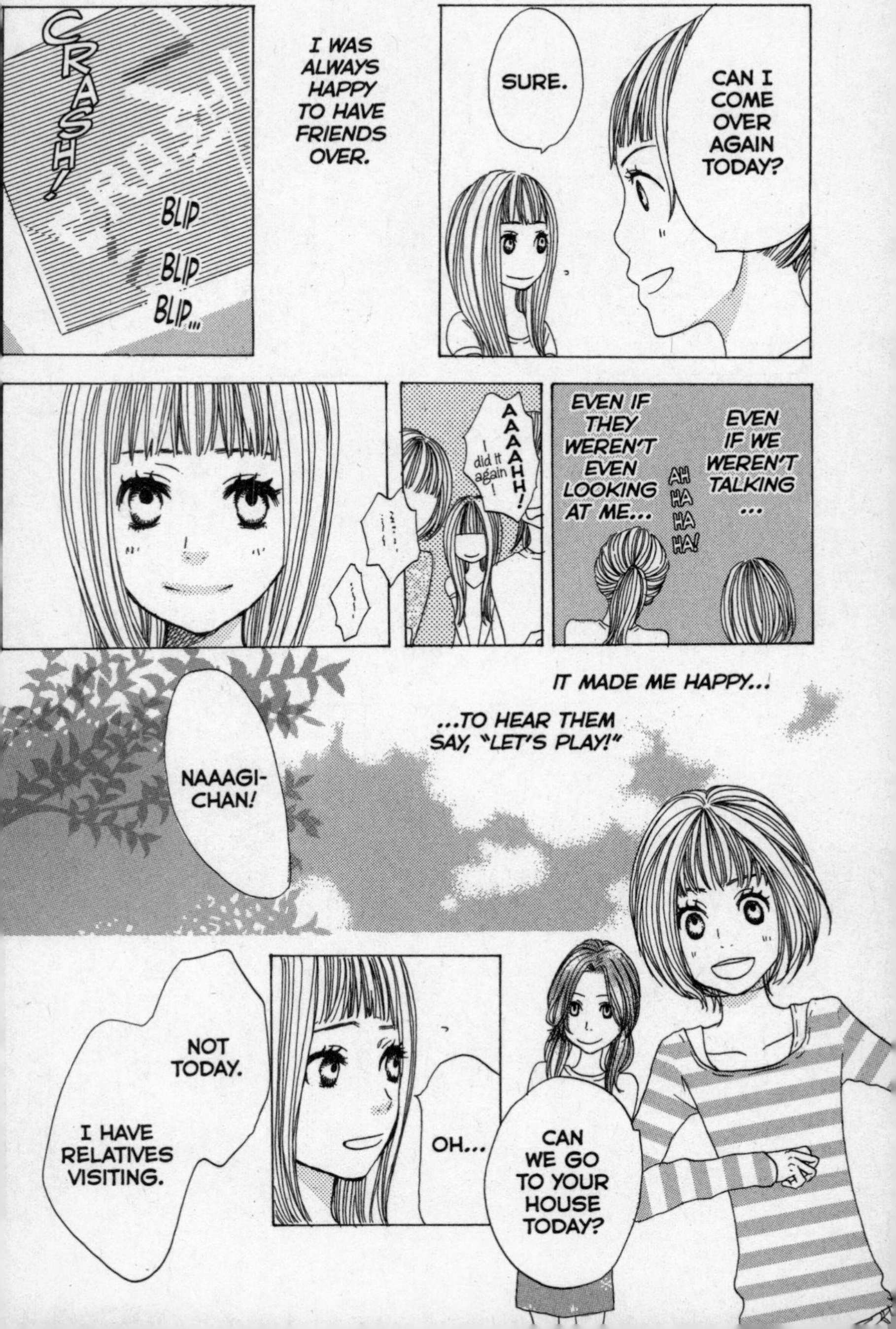
CAN I COME OVER AGAIN TODAY?
SURE.
I WAS ALWAYS HAPPY TO HAVE FRIENDS OVER.
CRASH!
CRUSH!
BLIP
BLIP
BLIP...
EVEN IF WE WEREN'T TALKING...
EVEN IF THEY WEREN'T EVEN LOOKING AT ME...
AH HA HA HA!
AAAAHH!
I did it again!
IT MADE ME HAPPY..!
...TO HEAR THEM SAY, "LET'S PLAY!"
NAAAGI-CHAN!
CAN WE GO TO YOUR HOUSE TODAY?
OH...
NOT TODAY.
I HAVE RELATIVES VISITING.

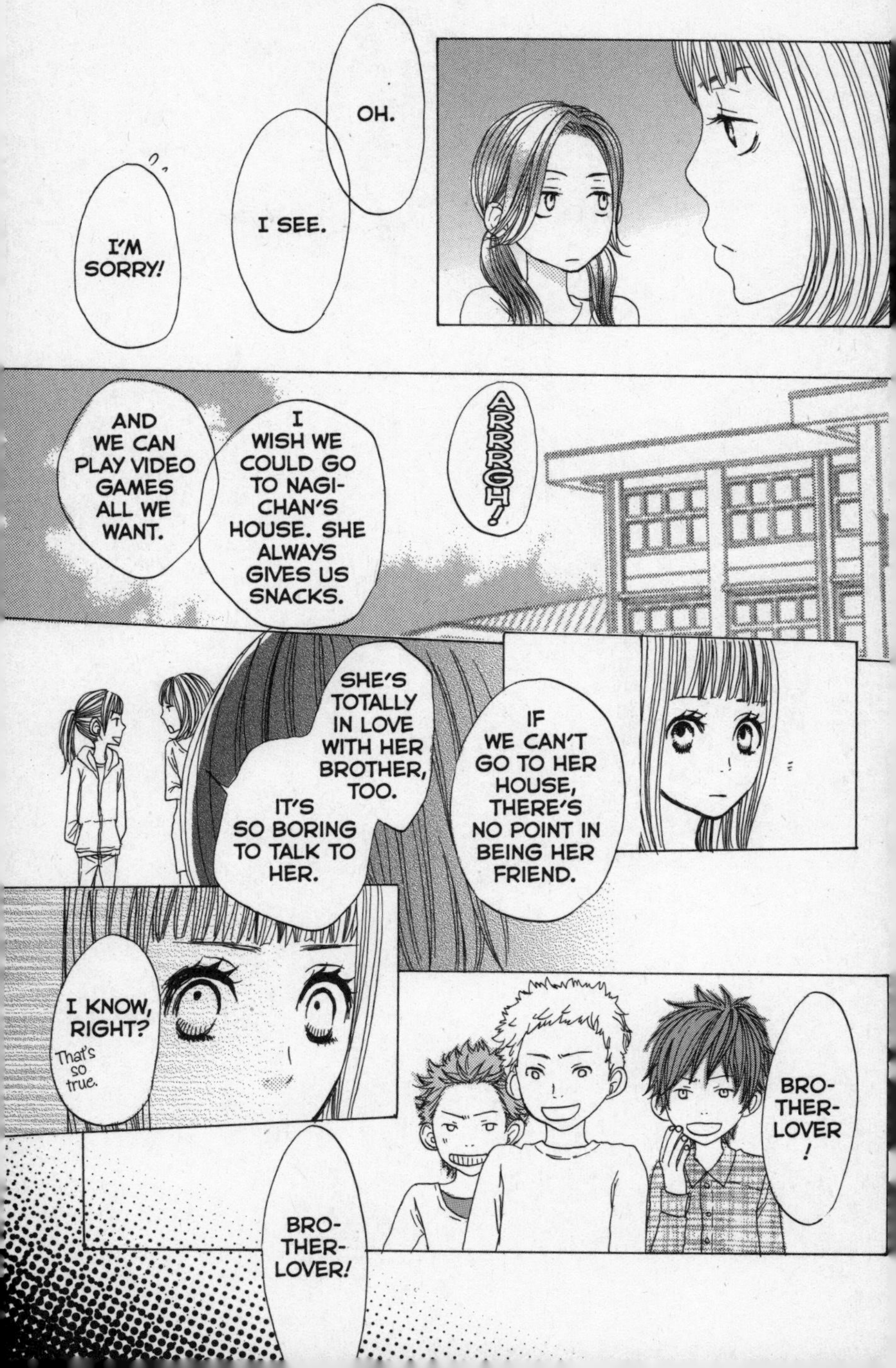

OH.
I SEE.
I'M SORRY!
ARRRGH!
I WISH WE COULD GO TO NAGI-CHAN'S HOUSE. SHE ALWAYS GIVES US SNACKS.
AND WE CAN PLAY VIDEO GAMES ALL WE WANT.
IF WE CAN'T GO TO HER HOUSE, THERE'S NO POINT IN BEING HER FRIEND.
SHE'S TOTALLY IN LOVE WITH HER BROTHER, TOO.
IT'S SO BORING TO TALK TO HER.
I KNOW, RIGHT?
That's so true.
BROTHER-LOVER!
BROTHER-LOVER!

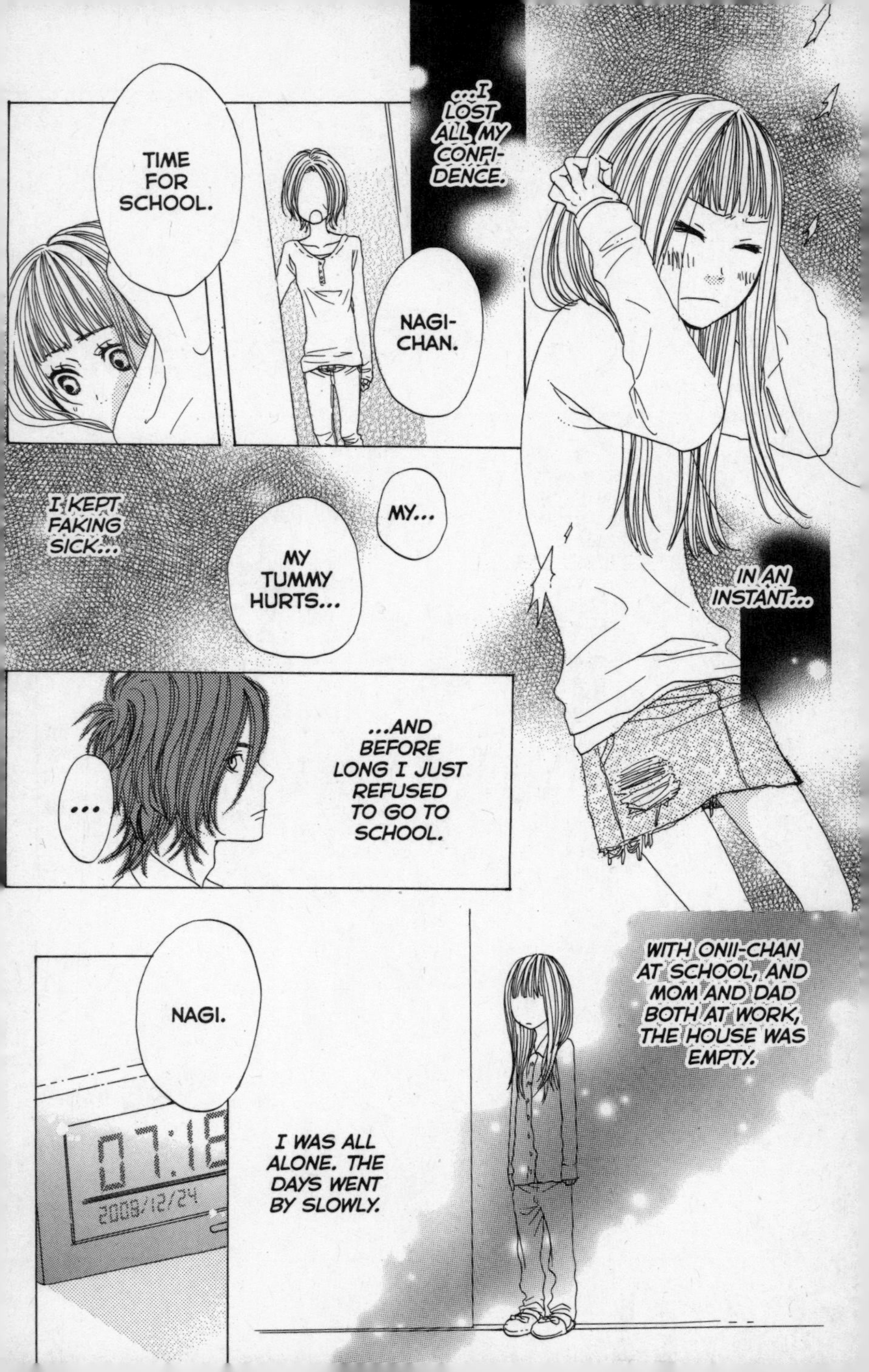
...I LOST ALL MY CONFIDENCE.
IN AN INSTANT...
NAGI-CHAN.
TIME FOR SCHOOL.
MY...
MY TUMMY HURTS...
I KEPT FAKING SICK...
...AND BEFORE LONG I JUST REFUSED TO GO TO SCHOOL.
...
WITH ONII-CHAN AT SCHOOL, AND MOM AND DAD BOTH AT WORK, THE HOUSE WAS EMPTY.
NAGI.
07:18
2009/12/24
I WAS ALL ALONE. THE DAYS WENT BY SLOWLY.

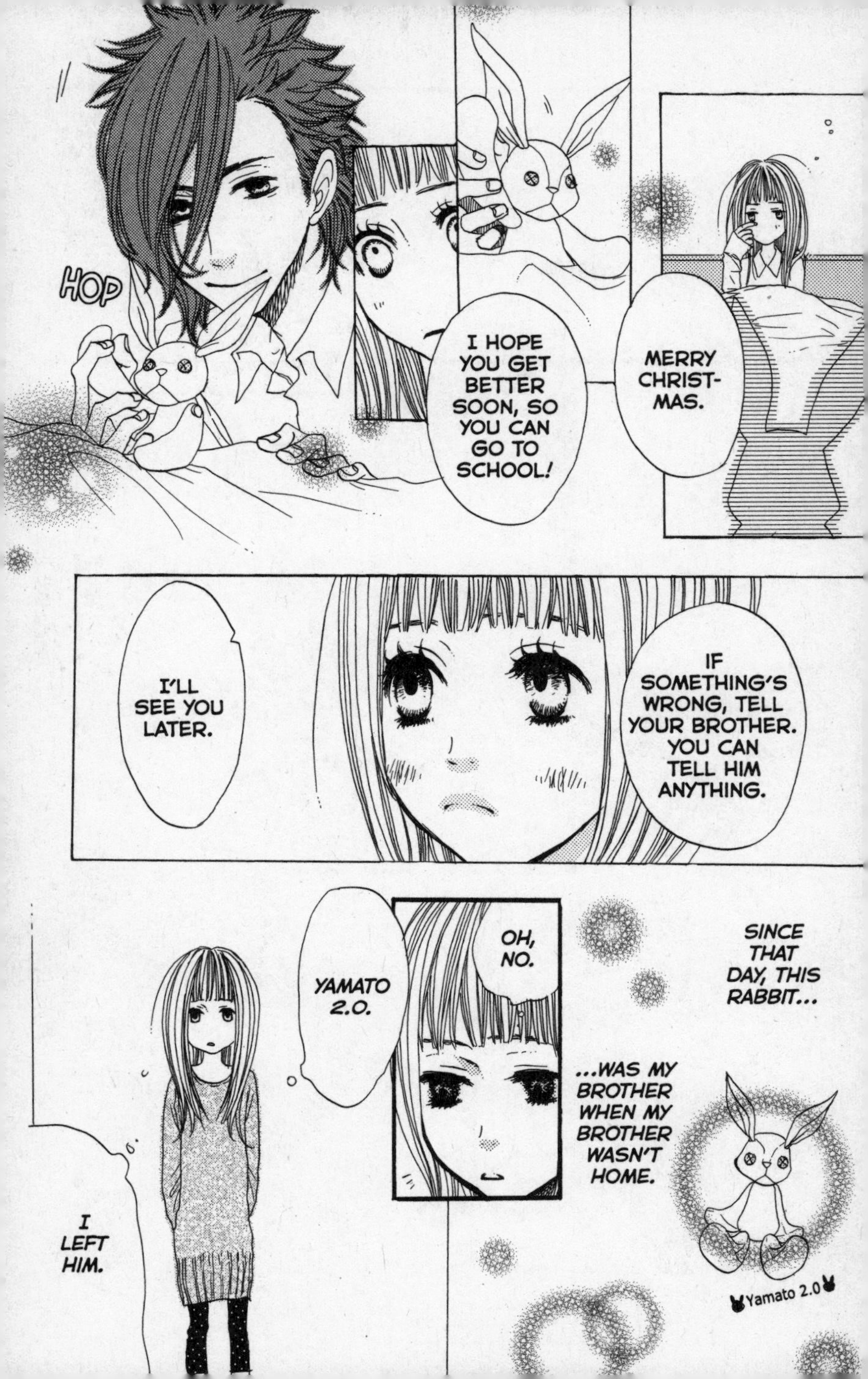
MERRY CHRIST-MAS.
I HOPE YOU GET BETTER SOON, SO YOU CAN GO TO SCHOOL!
HOP
IF SOMETHING'S WRONG, TELL YOUR BROTHER. YOU CAN TELL HIM ANYTHING.
I'LL SEE YOU LATER.
SINCE THAT DAY, THIS RABBIT...
...WAS MY BROTHER WHEN MY BROTHER WASN'T HOME.
Yamato 2.0
OH, NO.
YAMATO 2.0.
I LEFT HIM.

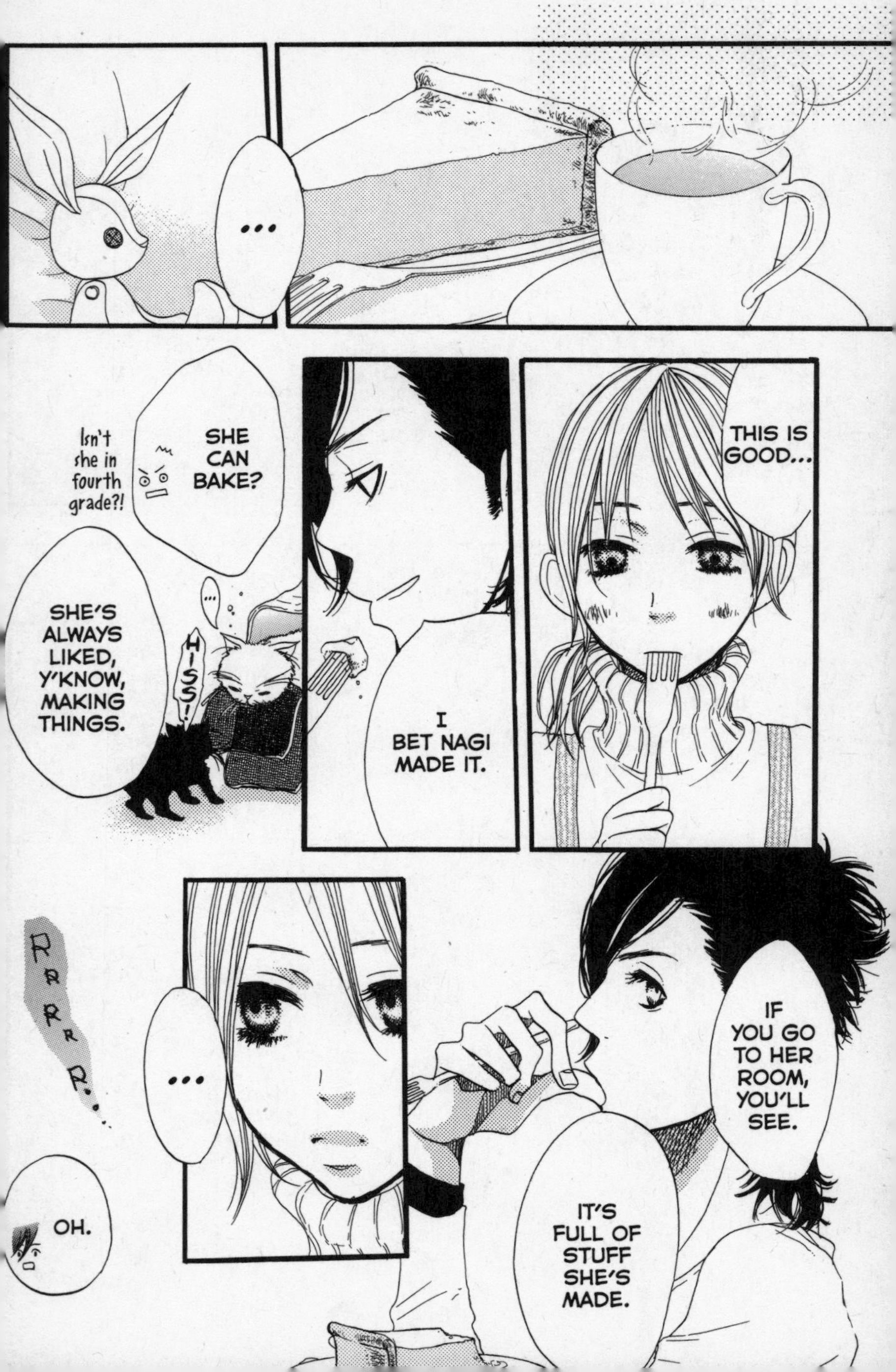
...
THIS IS GOOD...
I BET NAGI MADE IT.
SHE CAN BAKE?
Isn't she in fourth grade?!
SHE'S ALWAYS LIKED, Y'KNOW, MAKING THINGS.
...
HISS!
IF YOU GO TO HER ROOM, YOU'LL SEE.
IT'S FULL OF STUFF SHE'S MADE.
...
RRRRR...
OH.

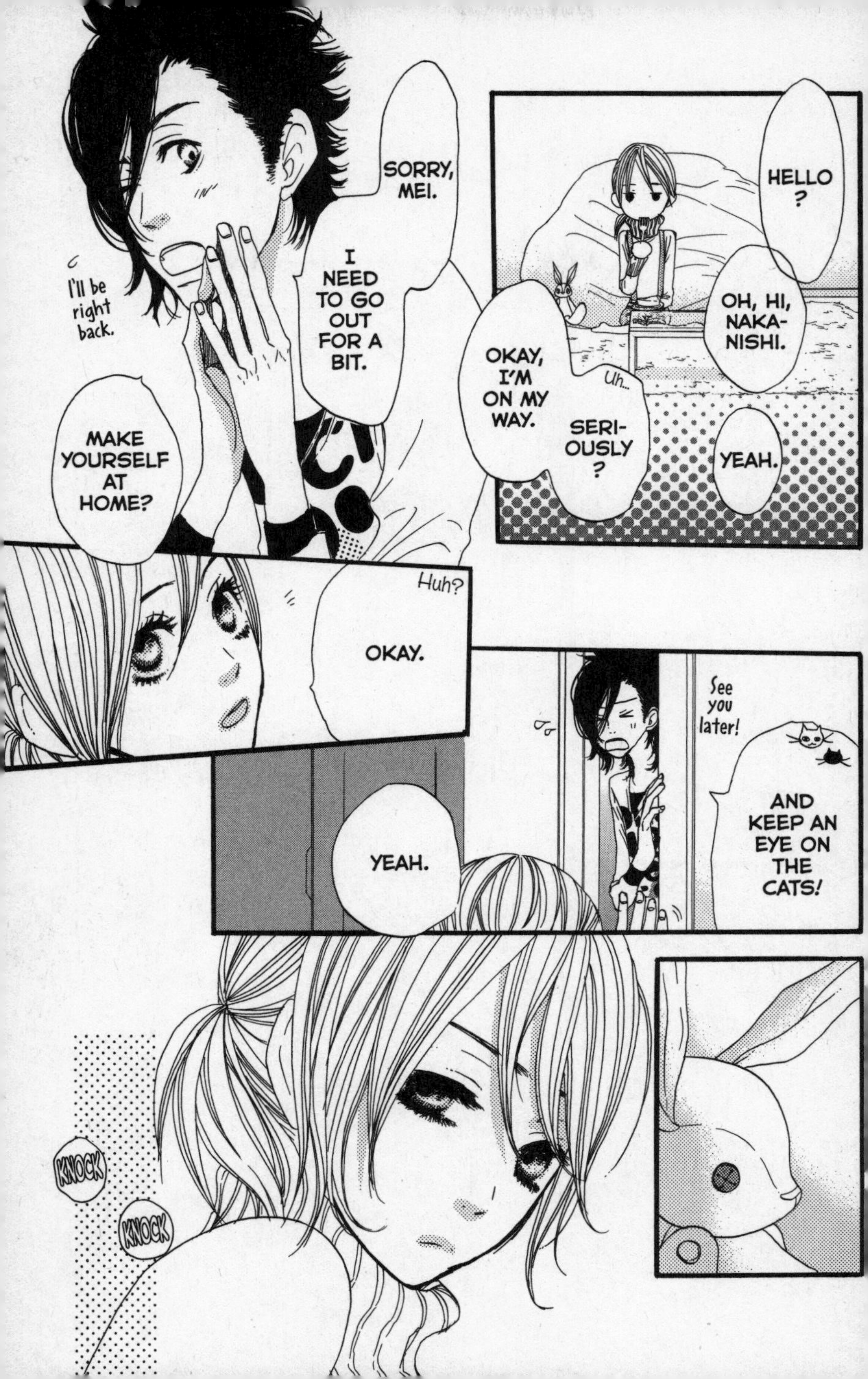
HELLO?
OH, HI, NAKANISHI.
YEAH.
Uh...
SERIOUSLY?
OKAY, I'M ON MY WAY.
SORRY, MEI.
I NEED TO GO OUT FOR A BIT.
I'll be right back.
MAKE YOURSELF AT HOME?
Huh?
OKAY.
See you later!
AND KEEP AN EYE ON THE CATS!
YEAH.
KNOCK
KNOCK

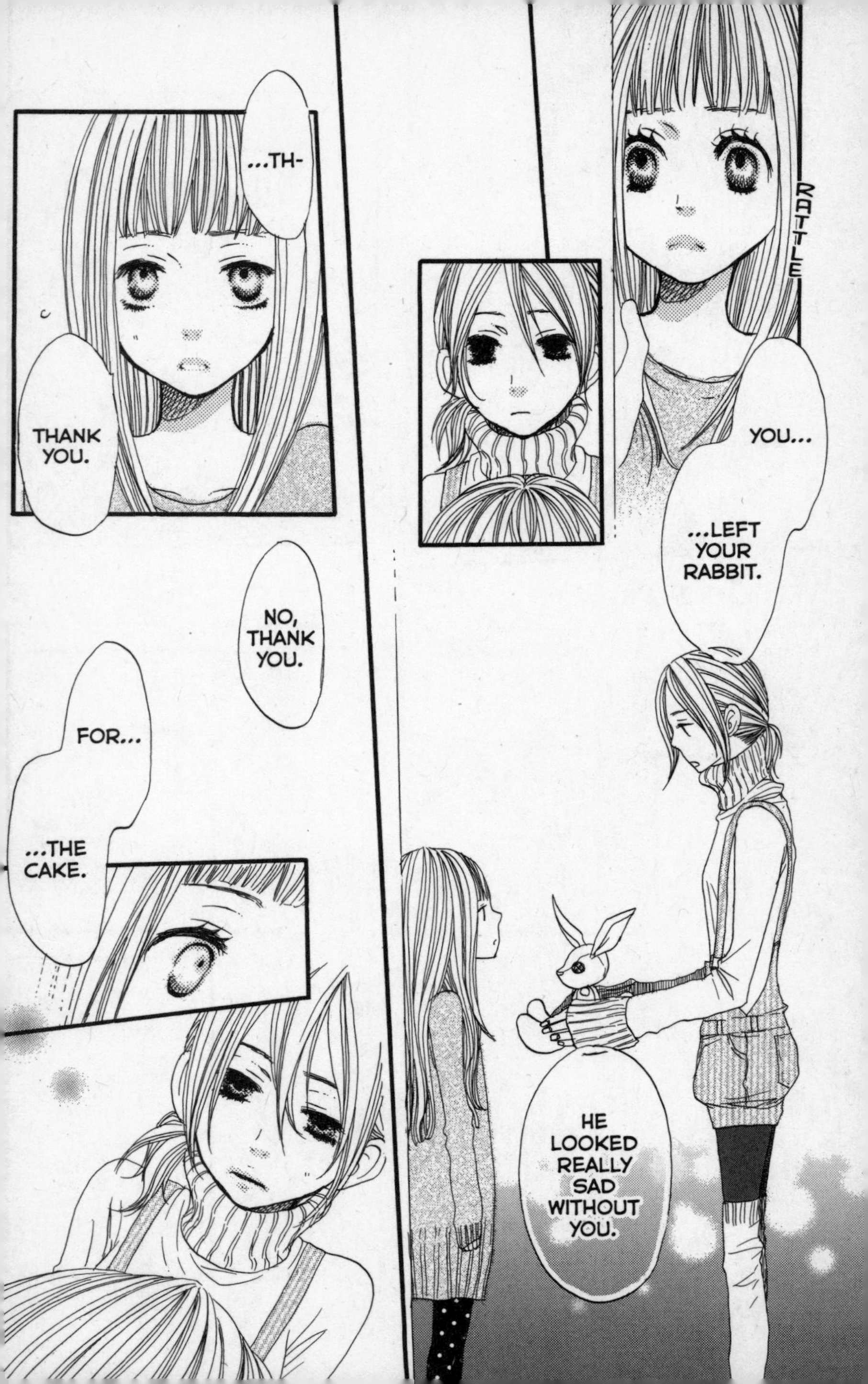
RATTLE
YOU...
...LEFT YOUR RABBIT.
HE LOOKED REALLY SAD WITHOUT YOU.
...TH-
THANK YOU.
NO, THANK YOU.
FOR...
...THE CAKE.

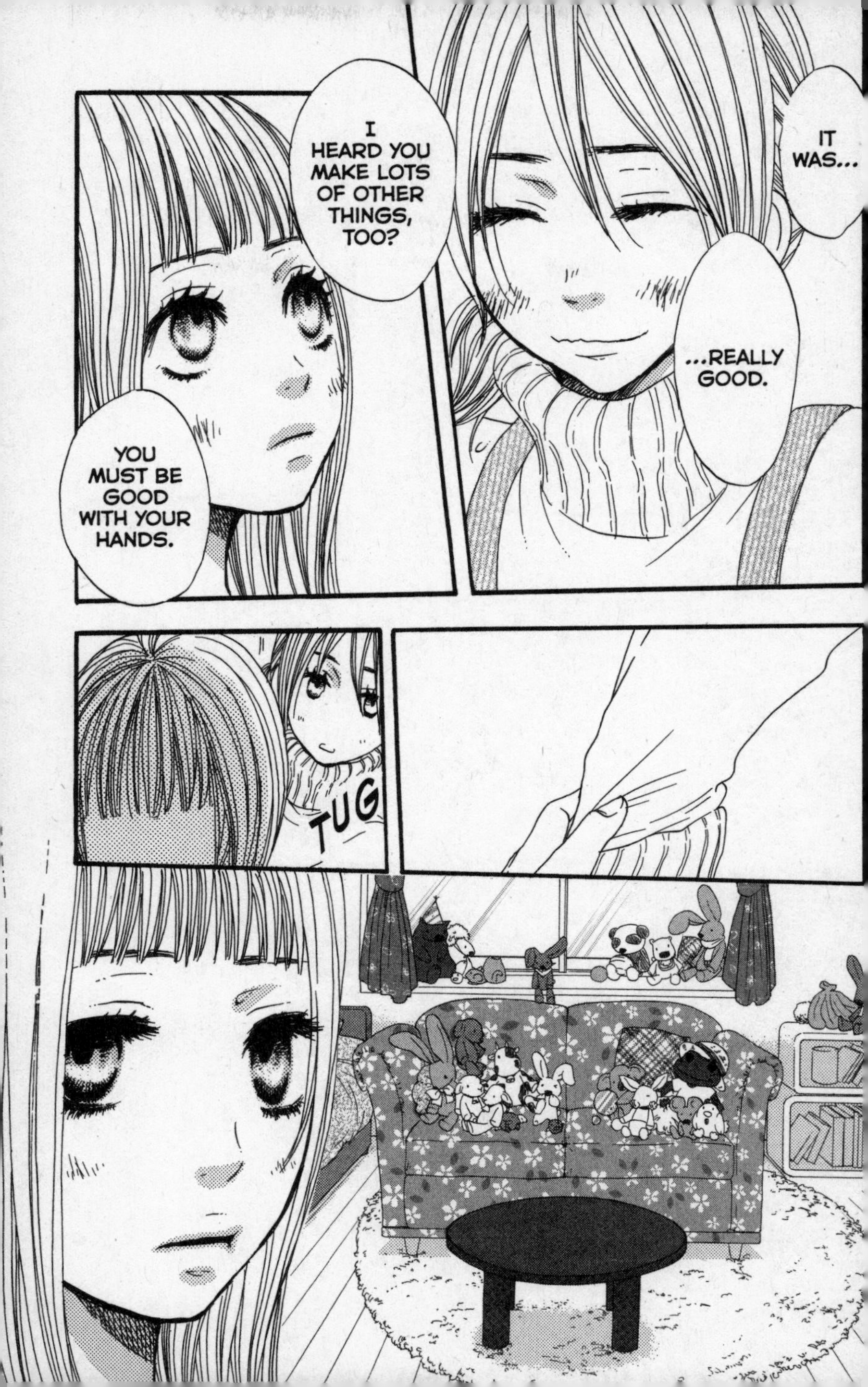
IT WAS...
...REALLY GOOD.
I HEARD YOU MAKE LOTS OF OTHER THINGS, TOO?
YOU MUST BE GOOD WITH YOUR HANDS.
TUG

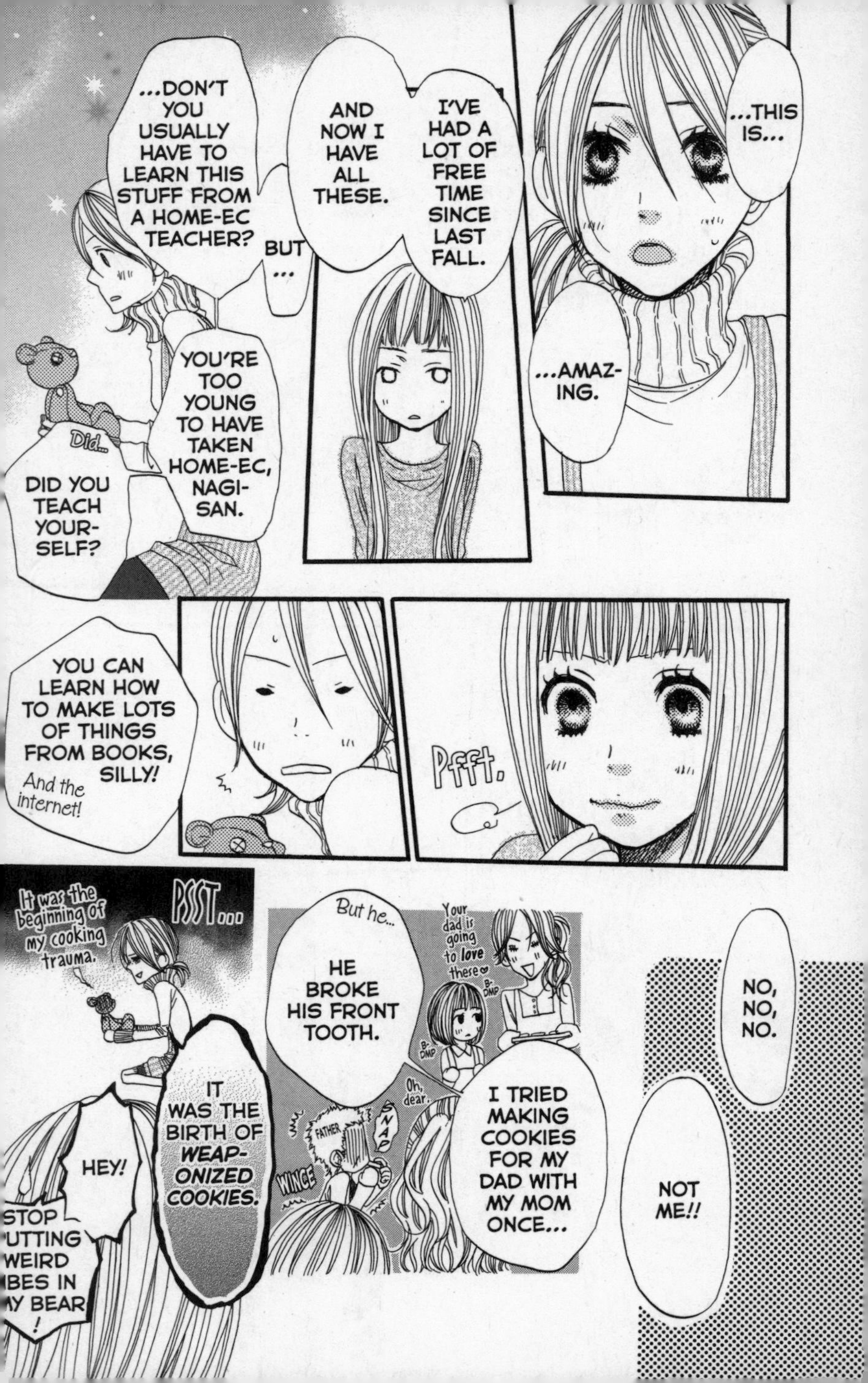
...THIS IS...
...AMAZ-ING.
I'VE HAD A LOT OF FREE TIME SINCE LAST FALL.
AND NOW I HAVE ALL THESE.
BUT ...
...DON'T YOU USUALLY HAVE TO LEARN THIS STUFF FROM A HOME-EC TEACHER?
YOU'RE TOO YOUNG TO HAVE TAKEN HOME-EC, NAGI-SAN.
Did...
DID YOU TEACH YOURSELF?
Pfft.
YOU CAN LEARN HOW TO MAKE LOTS OF THINGS FROM BOOKS, SILLY!
And the internet!
NO, NO, NO.
NOT ME!!
I TRIED MAKING COOKIES FOR MY DAD WITH MY MOM ONCE...
Your dad is going to love these
B-DMP
B-DMP
But he...
HE BROKE HIS FRONT TOOTH.
Oh, dear.
SNAP
FATHER
WINCE
PSST...
It was the beginning of my cooking trauma.
IT WAS THE BIRTH OF WEAPONIZED COOKIES.
HEY!
STOP UTTING WEIRD BES IN Y BEAR!

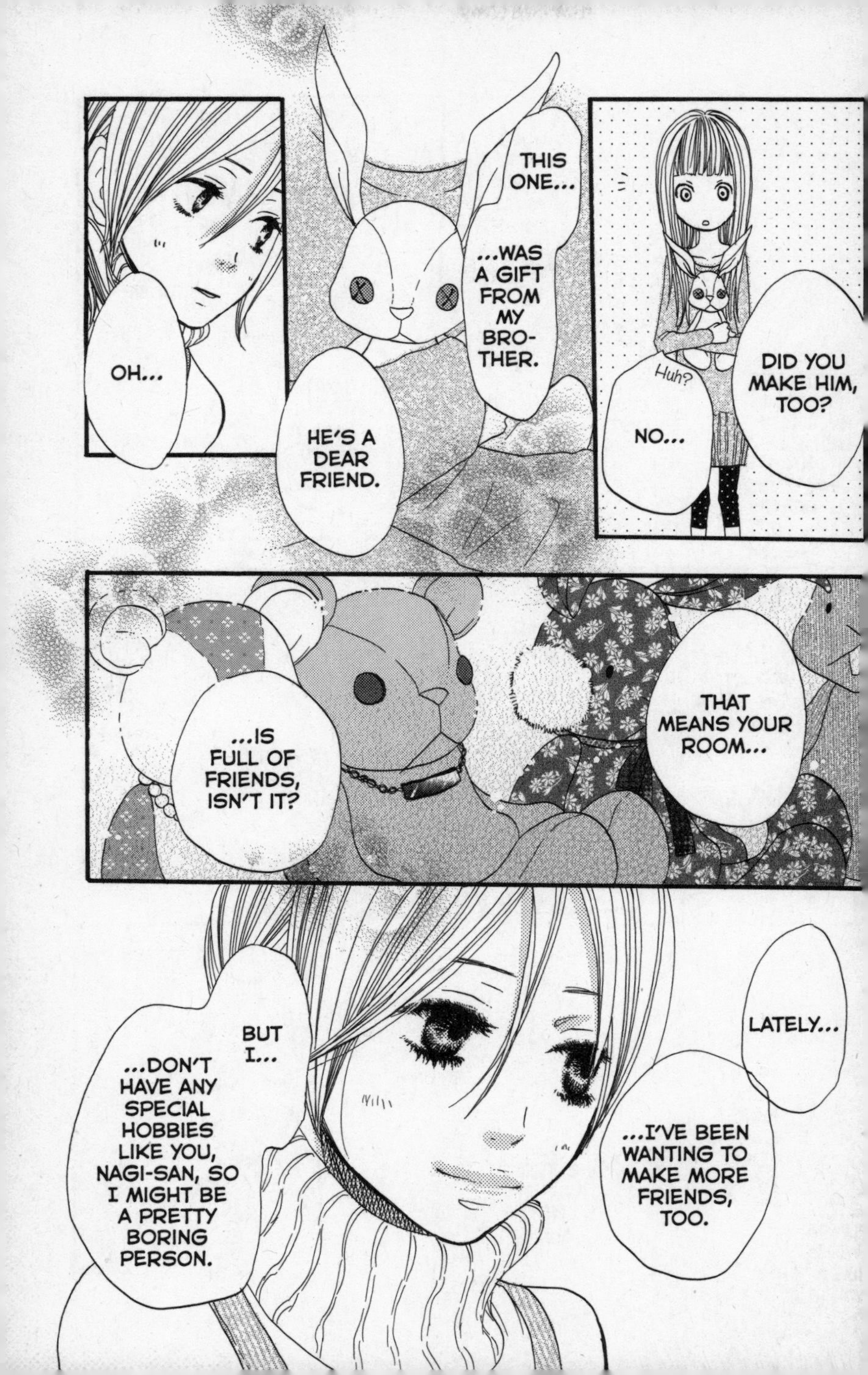
DID YOU MAKE HIM, TOO?
Huh?
NO...
THIS ONE...
...WAS A GIFT FROM MY BRO-THER.
HE'S A DEAR FRIEND.
OH...
THAT MEANS YOUR ROOM...
...IS FULL OF FRIENDS, ISN'T IT?
LATELY...
...I'VE BEEN WANTING TO MAKE MORE FRIENDS, TOO.
BUT I...
...DON'T HAVE ANY SPECIAL HOBBIES LIKE YOU, NAGI-SAN, SO I MIGHT BE A PRETTY BORING PERSON.

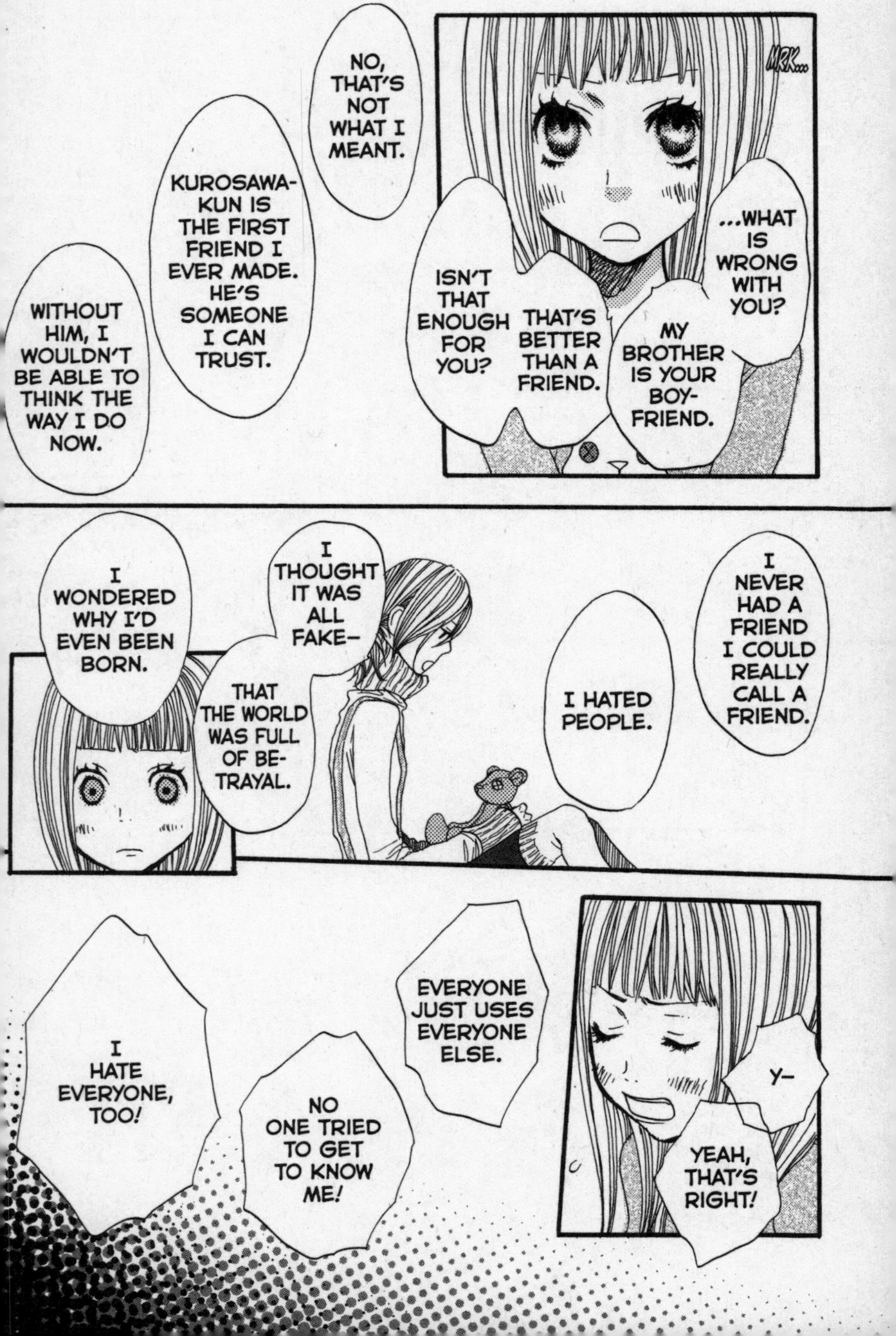
MRK...
...WHAT IS WRONG WITH YOU?
MY BROTHER IS YOUR BOY-FRIEND.
THAT'S BETTER THAN A FRIEND.
ISN'T THAT ENOUGH FOR YOU?
NO, THAT'S NOT WHAT I MEANT.
KUROSAWA-KUN IS THE FIRST FRIEND I EVER MADE. HE'S SOMEONE I CAN TRUST.
WITHOUT HIM, I WOULDN'T BE ABLE TO THINK THE WAY I DO NOW.
I NEVER HAD A FRIEND I COULD REALLY CALL A FRIEND.
I HATED PEOPLE.
I THOUGHT IT WAS ALL FAKE—
THAT THE WORLD WAS FULL OF BE-TRAYAL.
I WONDERED WHY I'D EVEN BEEN BORN.
Y—
YEAH, THAT'S RIGHT!
EVERYONE JUST USES EVERYONE ELSE.
NO ONE TRIED TO GET TO KNOW ME!
I HATE EVERYONE, TOO!

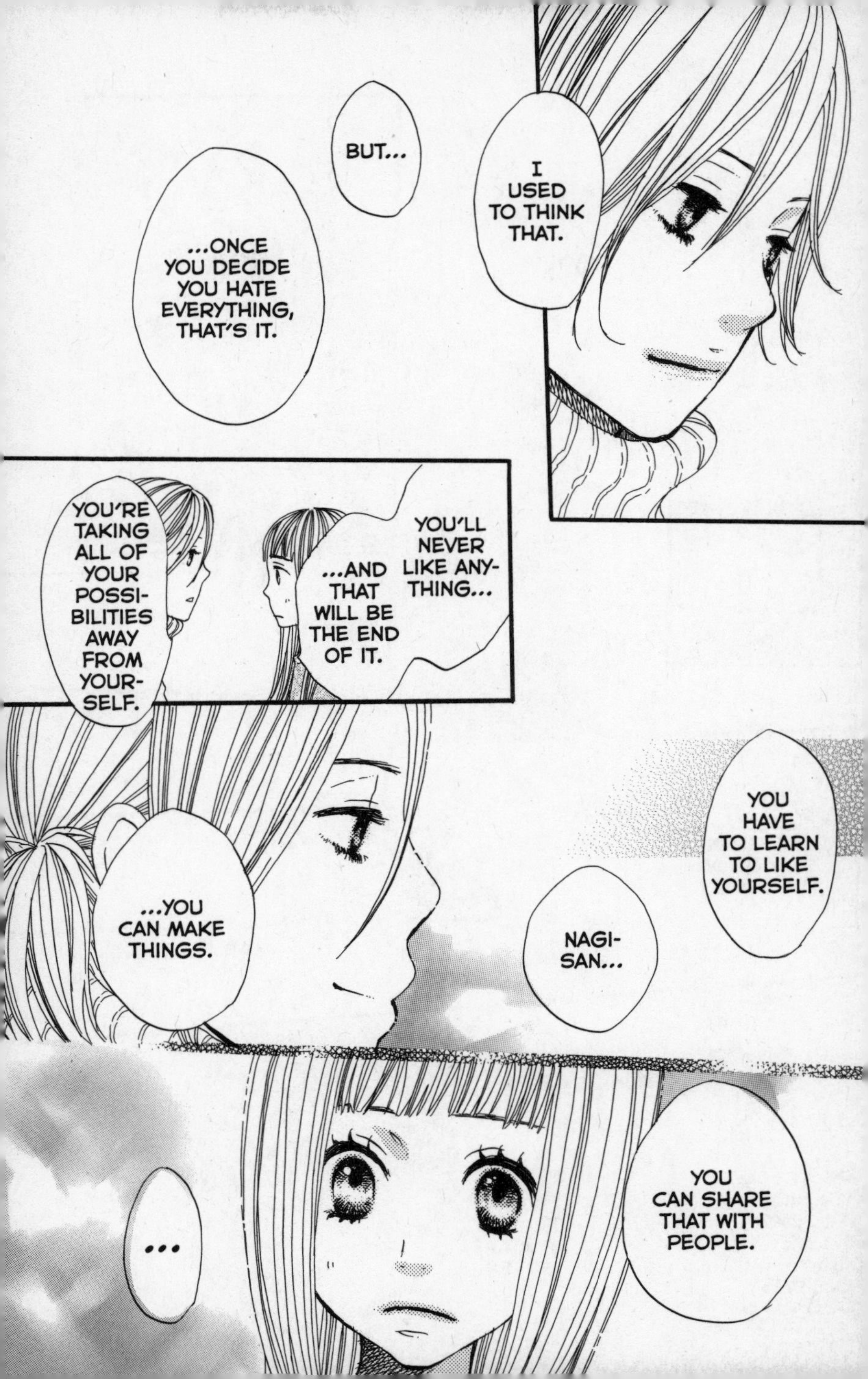
I USED TO THINK THAT.
BUT...
...ONCE YOU DECIDE YOU HATE EVERYTHING, THAT'S IT.
YOU'LL NEVER LIKE ANY-THING...
...AND THAT WILL BE THE END OF IT.
YOU'RE TAKING ALL OF YOUR POSSI-BILITIES AWAY FROM YOUR-SELF.
YOU HAVE TO LEARN TO LIKE YOURSELF.
NAGI-SAN...
...YOU CAN MAKE THINGS.
YOU CAN SHARE THAT WITH PEOPLE.
...

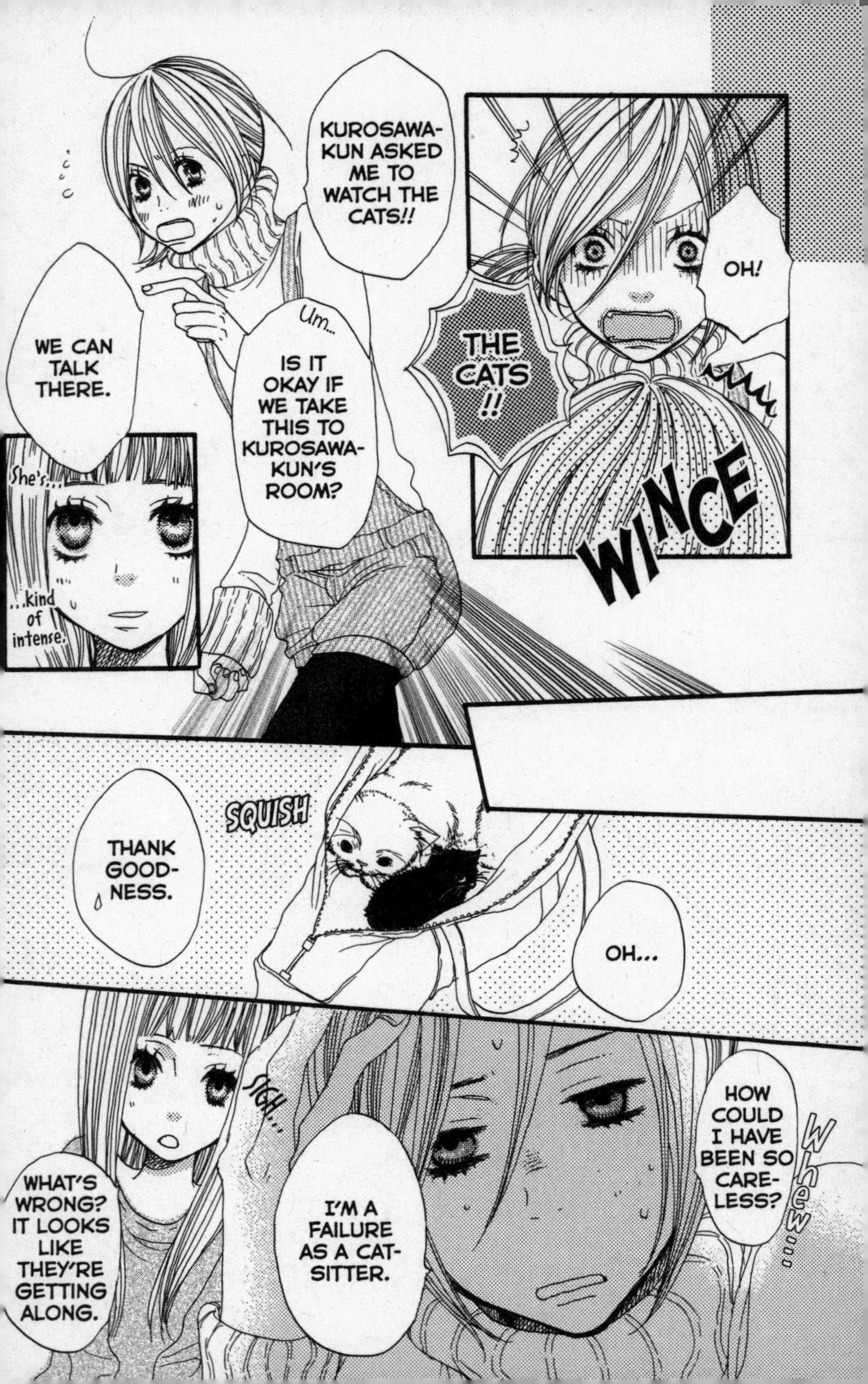
OH!
THE CATS!!
WINCE
KUROSAWA-KUN ASKED ME TO WATCH THE CATS!!
Um...
IS IT OKAY IF WE TAKE THIS TO KUROSAWA-KUN'S ROOM?
WE CAN TALK THERE.
She's...
...kind of intense.
OH...
SQUISH
THANK GOODNESS.
Whew...
HOW COULD I HAVE BEEN SO CARELESS?
SIGH...
I'M A FAILURE AS A CAT-SITTER.
WHAT'S WRONG? IT LOOKS LIKE THEY'RE GETTING ALONG.

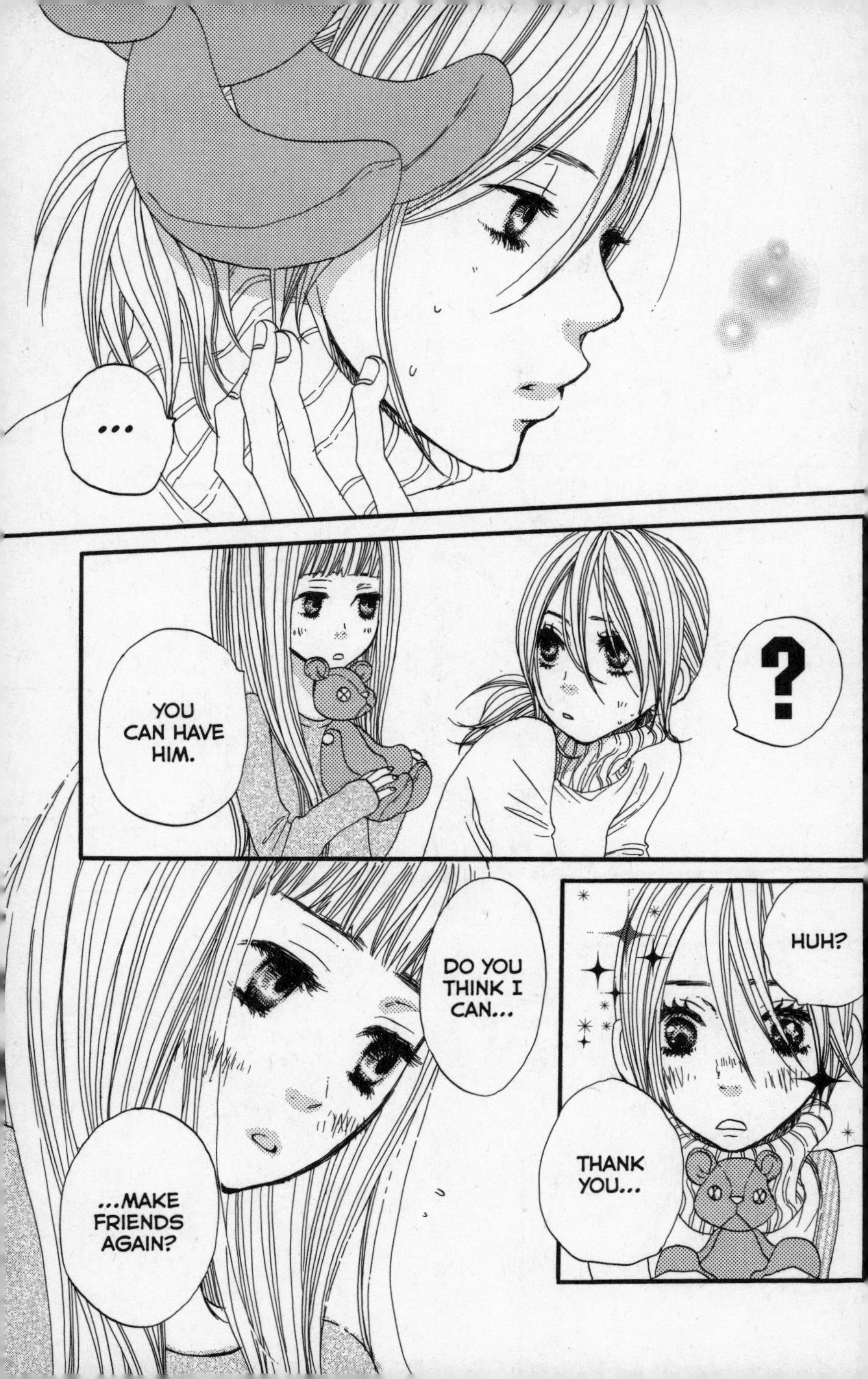
...
?
YOU CAN HAVE HIM.
HUH?
THANK YOU...
DO YOU THINK I CAN...
...MAKE FRIENDS AGAIN?

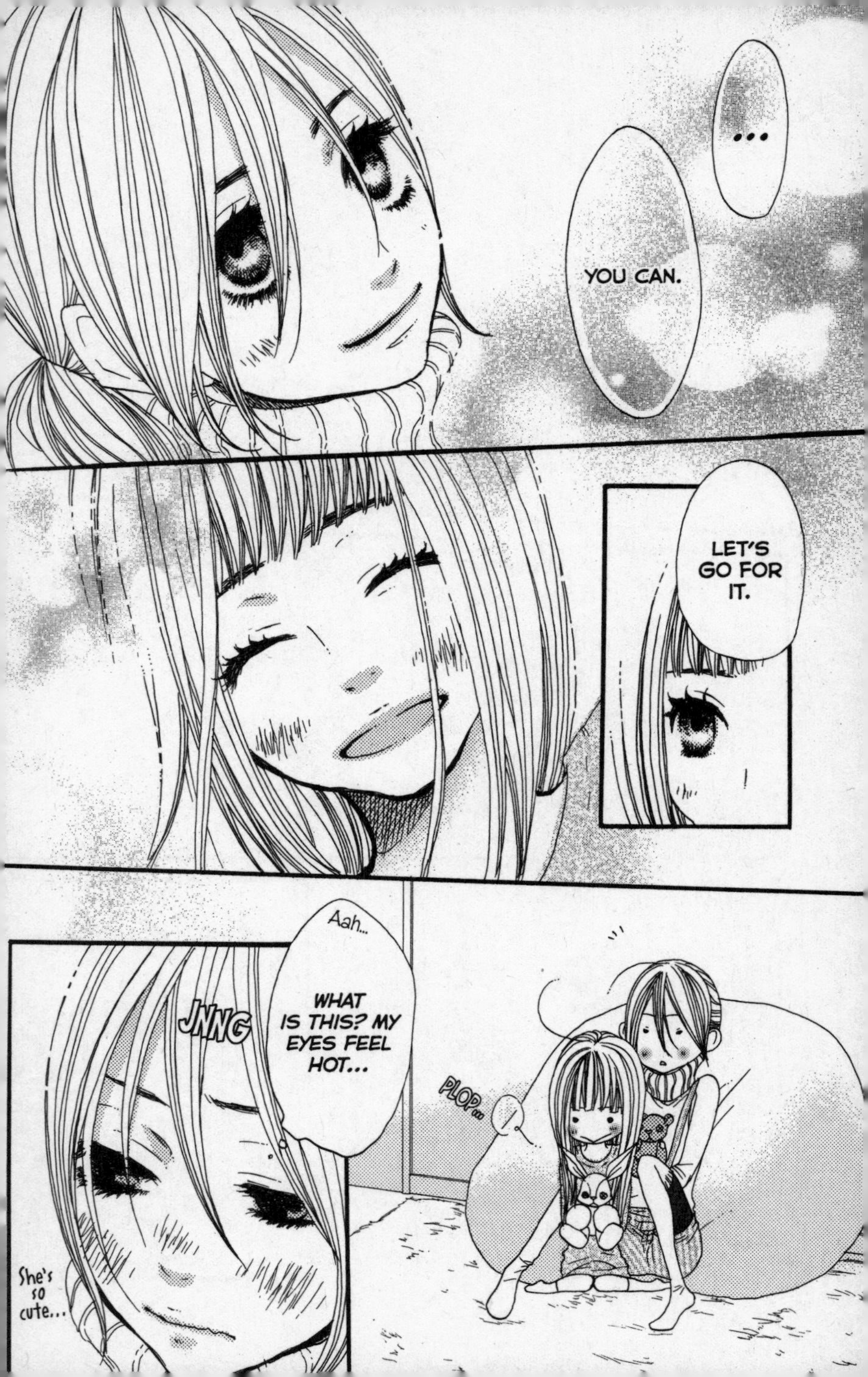
...
YOU CAN.
LET'S GO FOR IT.
PLOP...
Aah...
WHAT IS THIS? MY EYES FEEL HOT...
JNNG
She's so cute...

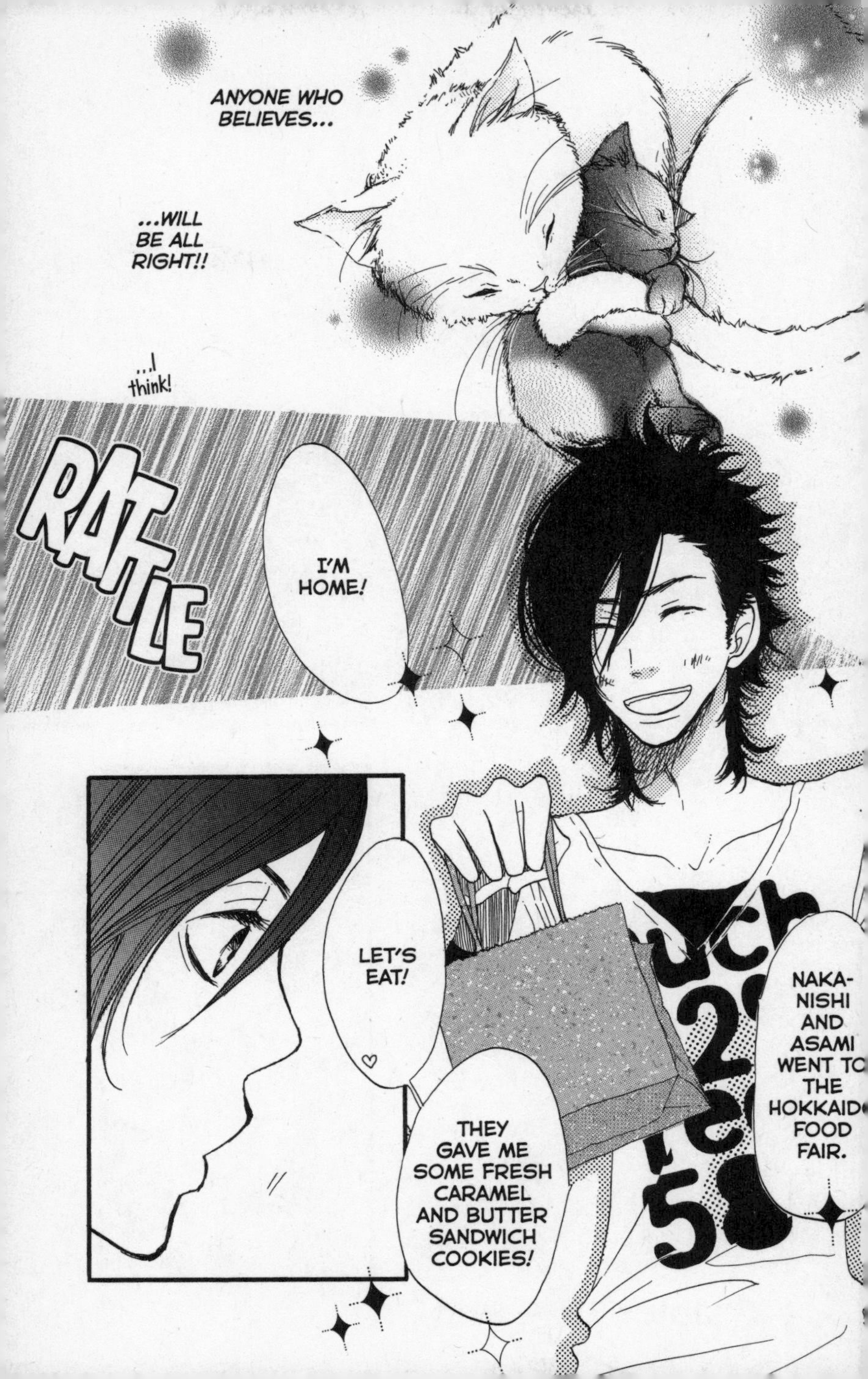
ANYONE WHO BELIEVES...
...WILL BE ALL RIGHT!!
...I think!
RATTLE
I'M HOME!
NAKA-NISHI AND ASAMI WENT TO THE HOKKAIDO FOOD FAIR.
THEY GAVE ME SOME FRESH CARAMEL AND BUTTER SANDWICH COOKIES!
LET'S EAT!

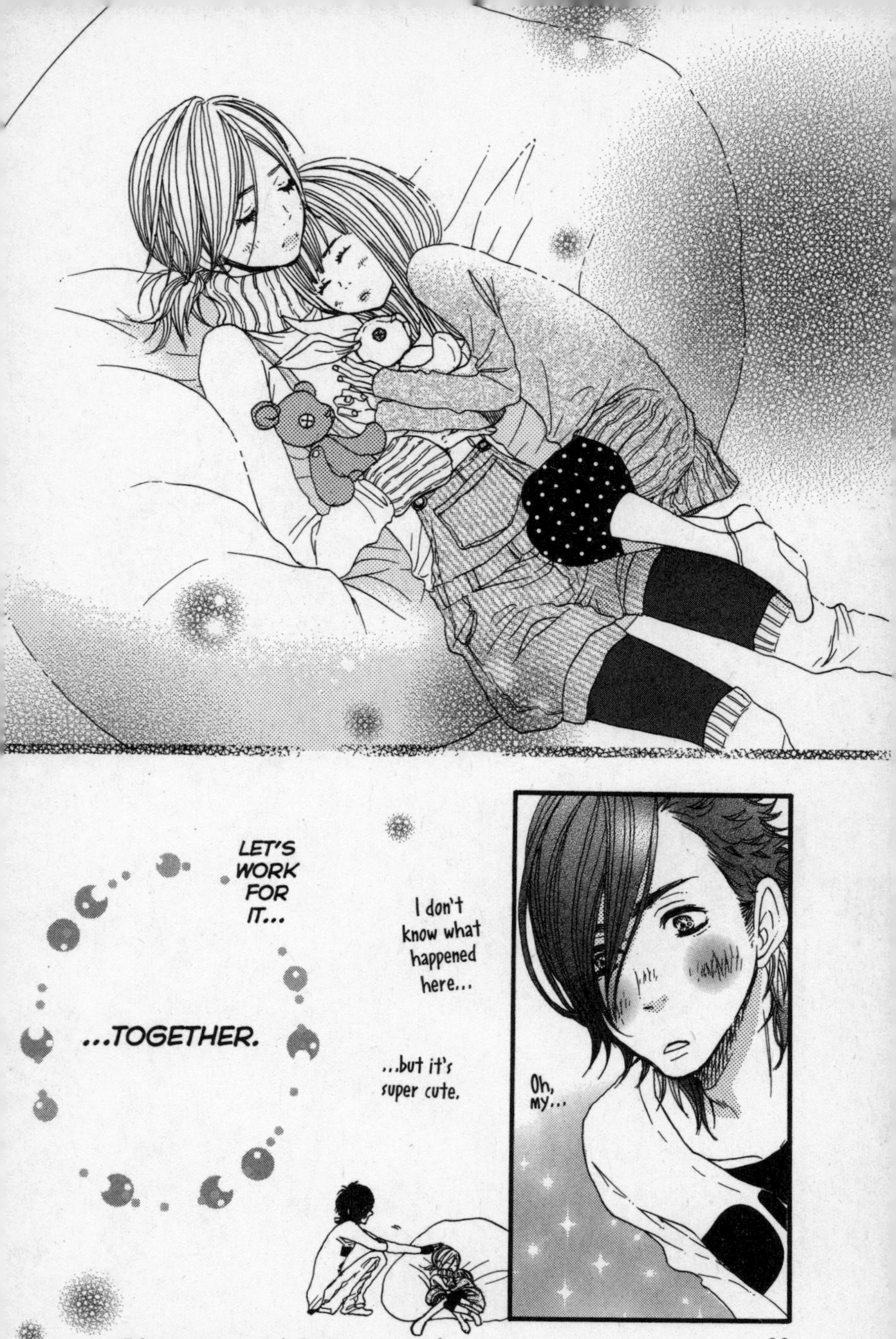
Oh, my...
I don't know what happened here...
...but it's super cute.
LET'S WORK FOR IT...
...TOGETHER.

Chapter 10 — end

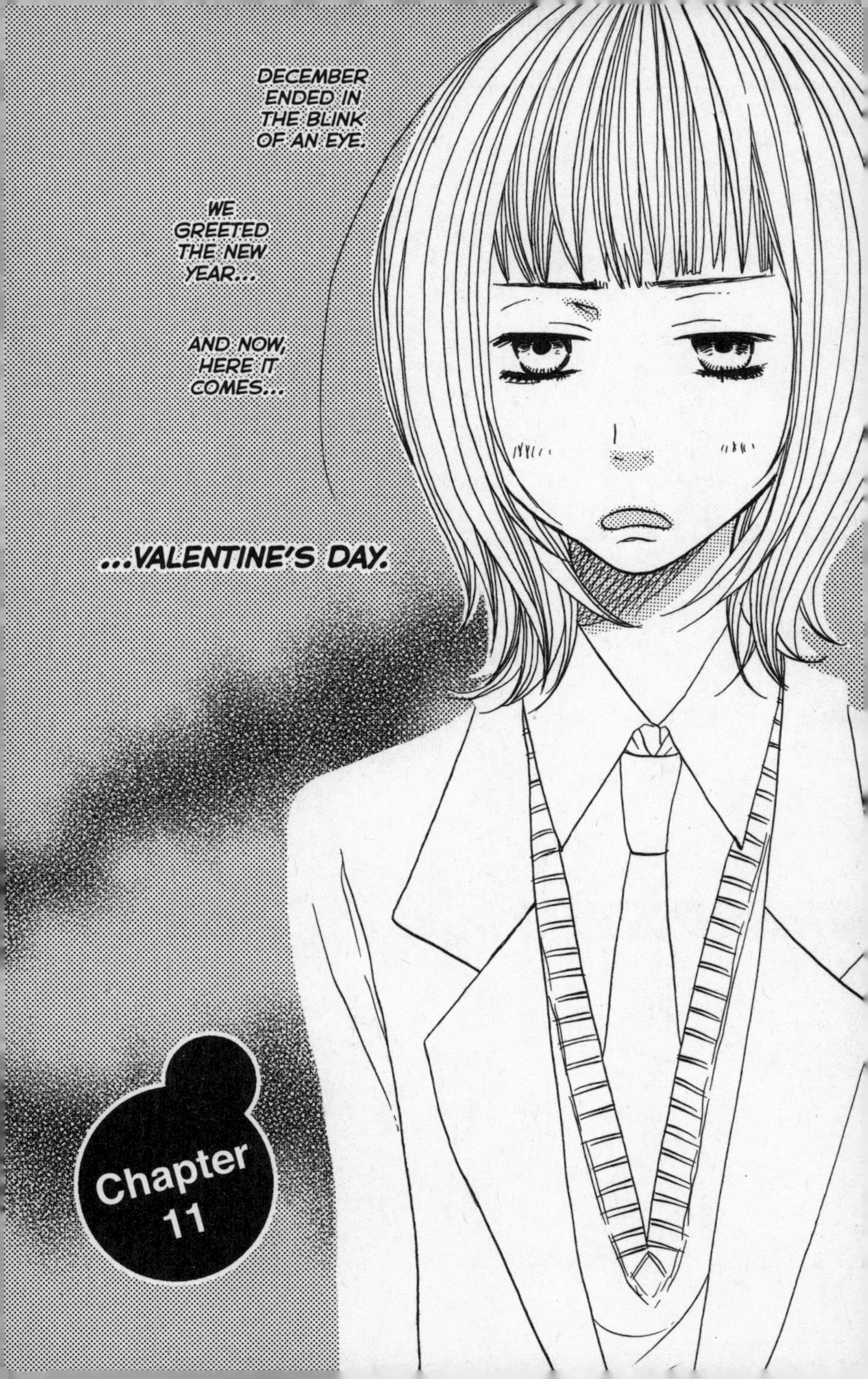
DECEMBER ENDED IN THE BLINK OF AN EYE.
WE GREETED THE NEW YEAR...
AND NOW, HERE IT COMES...
...VALENTINE'S DAY.
Chapter 11

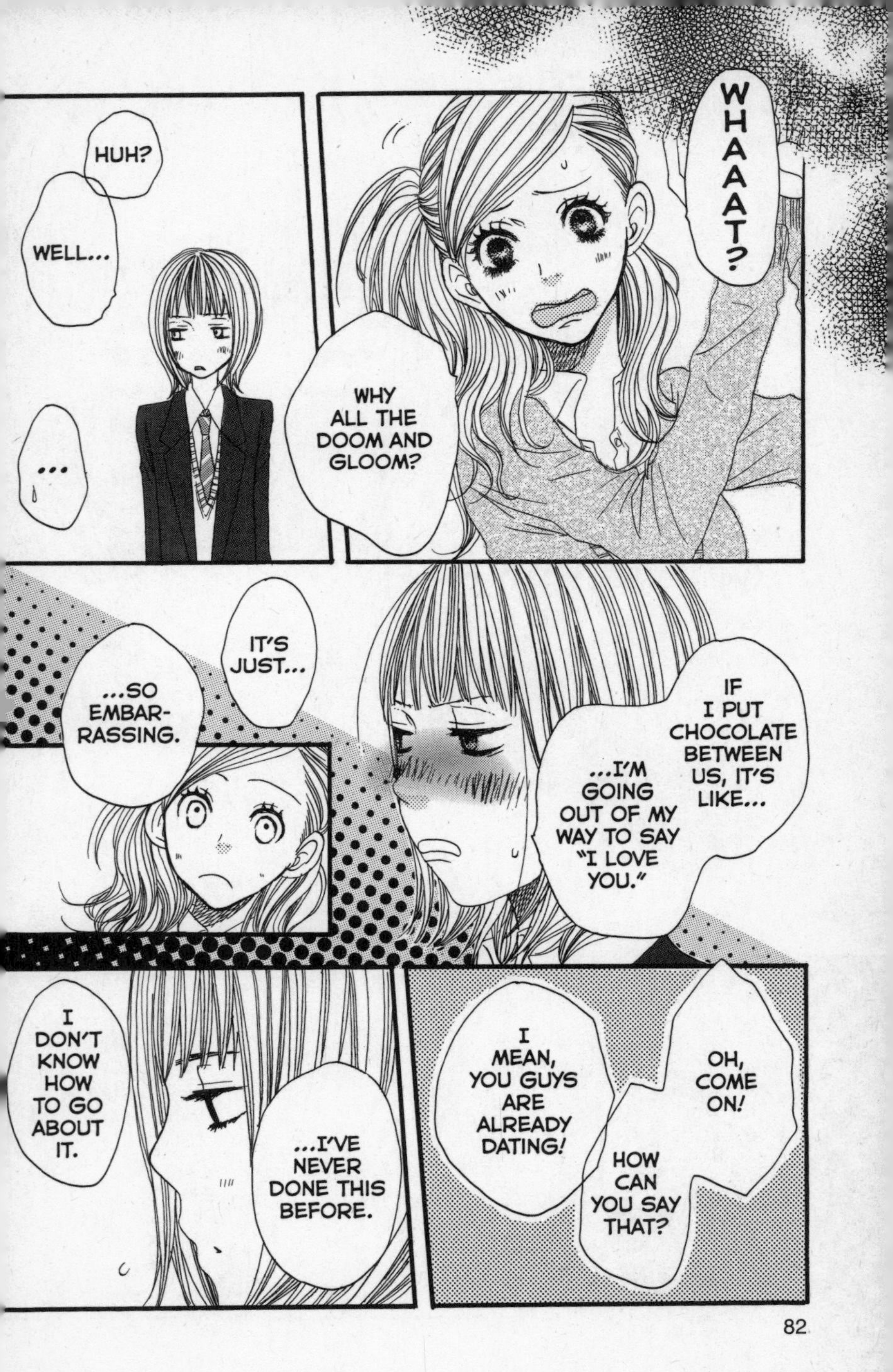
WHAAAT?
WHY ALL THE DOOM AND GLOOM?
HUH?
WELL...
...
IF I PUT CHOCOLATE BETWEEN US, IT'S LIKE...
...I'M GOING OUT OF MY WAY TO SAY "I LOVE YOU."
IT'S JUST...
...SO EMBARRASSING.
OH, COME ON!
HOW CAN YOU SAY THAT?
I MEAN, YOU GUYS ARE ALREADY DATING!
...I'VE NEVER DONE THIS BEFORE.
I DON'T KNOW HOW TO GO ABOUT IT.

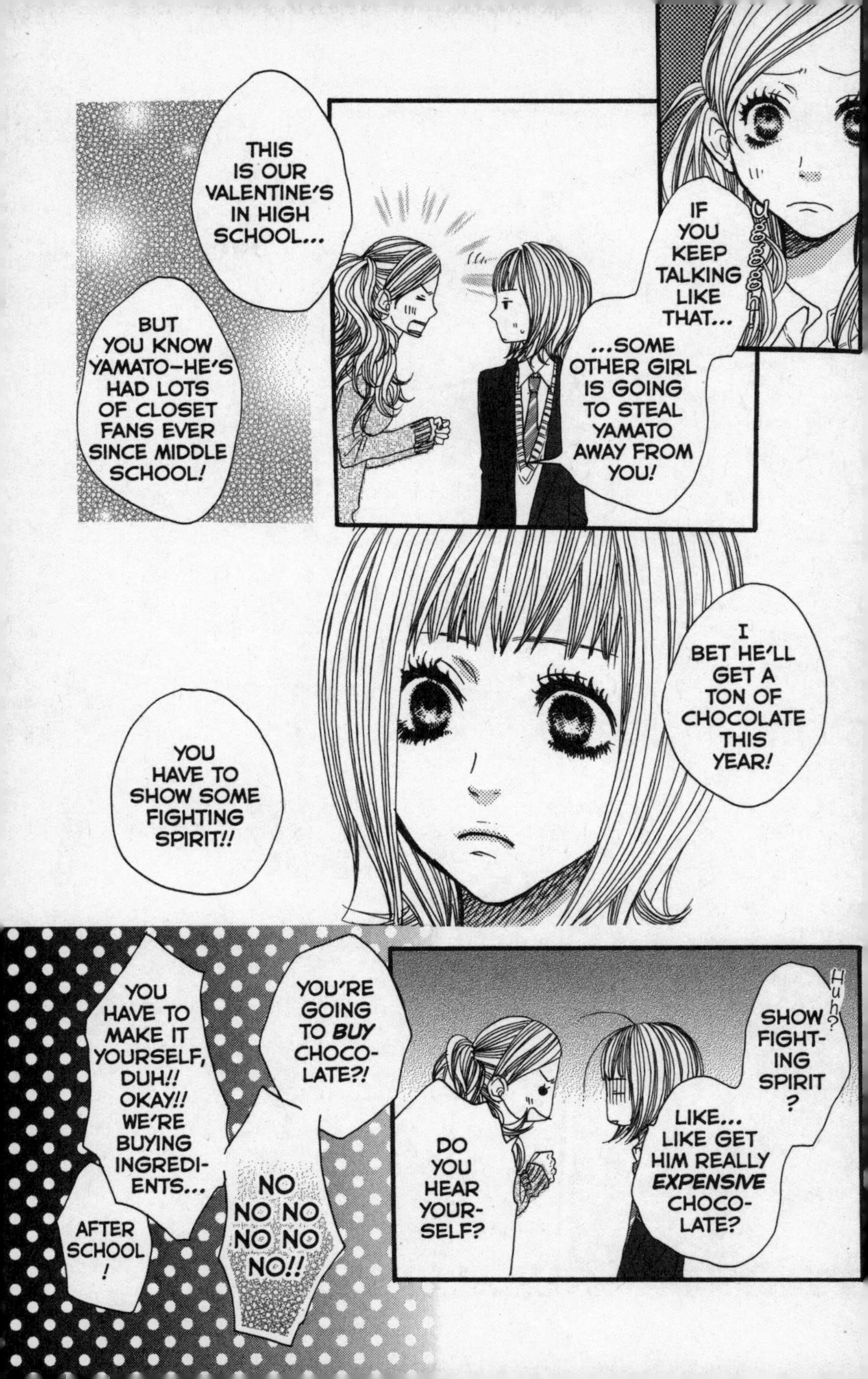
IF YOU KEEP TALKING LIKE THAT...
...SOME OTHER GIRL IS GOING TO STEAL YAMATO AWAY FROM YOU!
THIS IS OUR VALENTINE'S IN HIGH SCHOOL...
BUT YOU KNOW YAMATO—HE'S HAD LOTS OF CLOSET FANS EVER SINCE MIDDLE SCHOOL!
I BET HE'LL GET A TON OF CHOCOLATE THIS YEAR!
YOU HAVE TO SHOW SOME FIGHTING SPIRIT!!
Huh?
SHOW FIGHTING SPIRIT?
LIKE... LIKE GET HIM REALLY *EXPENSIVE* CHOCOLATE?
DO YOU HEAR YOURSELF?
YOU'RE GOING TO *BUY* CHOCOLATE?!
NO NO NO NO NO NO!!
YOU HAVE TO MAKE IT YOURSELF, DUH!! OKAY!! WE'RE BUYING INGREDIENTS...
AFTER SCHOOL!

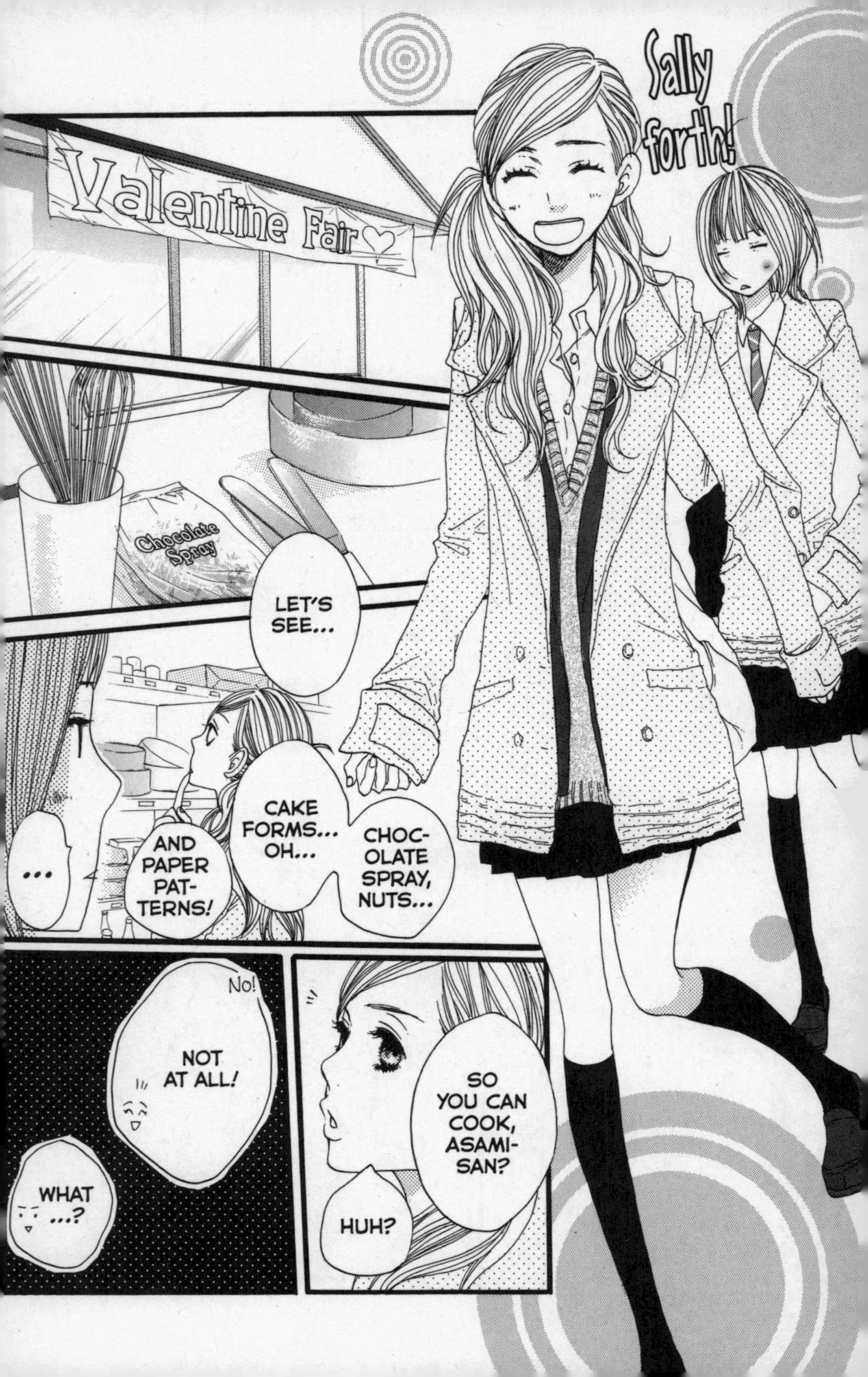
Sally forth!
Valentine Fair
Chocolate Spray
LET'S SEE...
CHOC-OLATE SPRAY, NUTS...
CAKE FORMS... OH...
AND PAPER PAT-TERNS!
...
SO YOU CAN COOK, ASAMI-SAN?
HUH?
No!
NOT AT ALL!
WHAT ...?

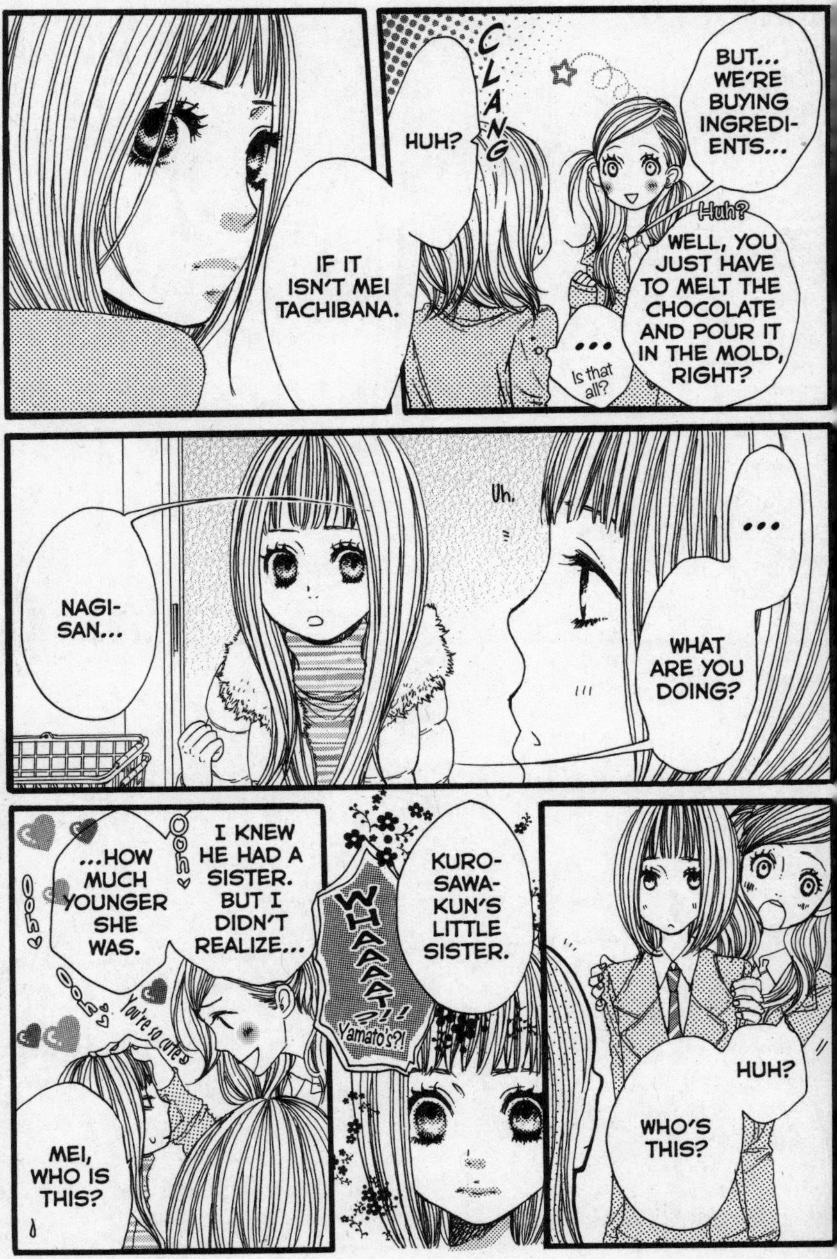
BUT... WE'RE BUYING INGREDI-ENTS...
Huh?
WELL, YOU JUST HAVE TO MELT THE CHOCOLATE AND POUR IT IN THE MOLD, RIGHT?
...
Is that all?
CLANG
HUH?
IF IT ISN'T MEI TACHIBANA.
...
WHAT ARE YOU DOING?
Uh.
NAGI-SAN...
HUH?
WHO'S THIS?
KURO-SAWA-KUN'S LITTLE SISTER.
WHAAAAAT?!!
Yamato's?!
I KNEW HE HAD A SISTER. BUT I DIDN'T REALIZE...
Ooh
...HOW MUCH YOUNGER SHE WAS.
Ooh
Ooh
You're so cute
MEI, WHO IS THIS?

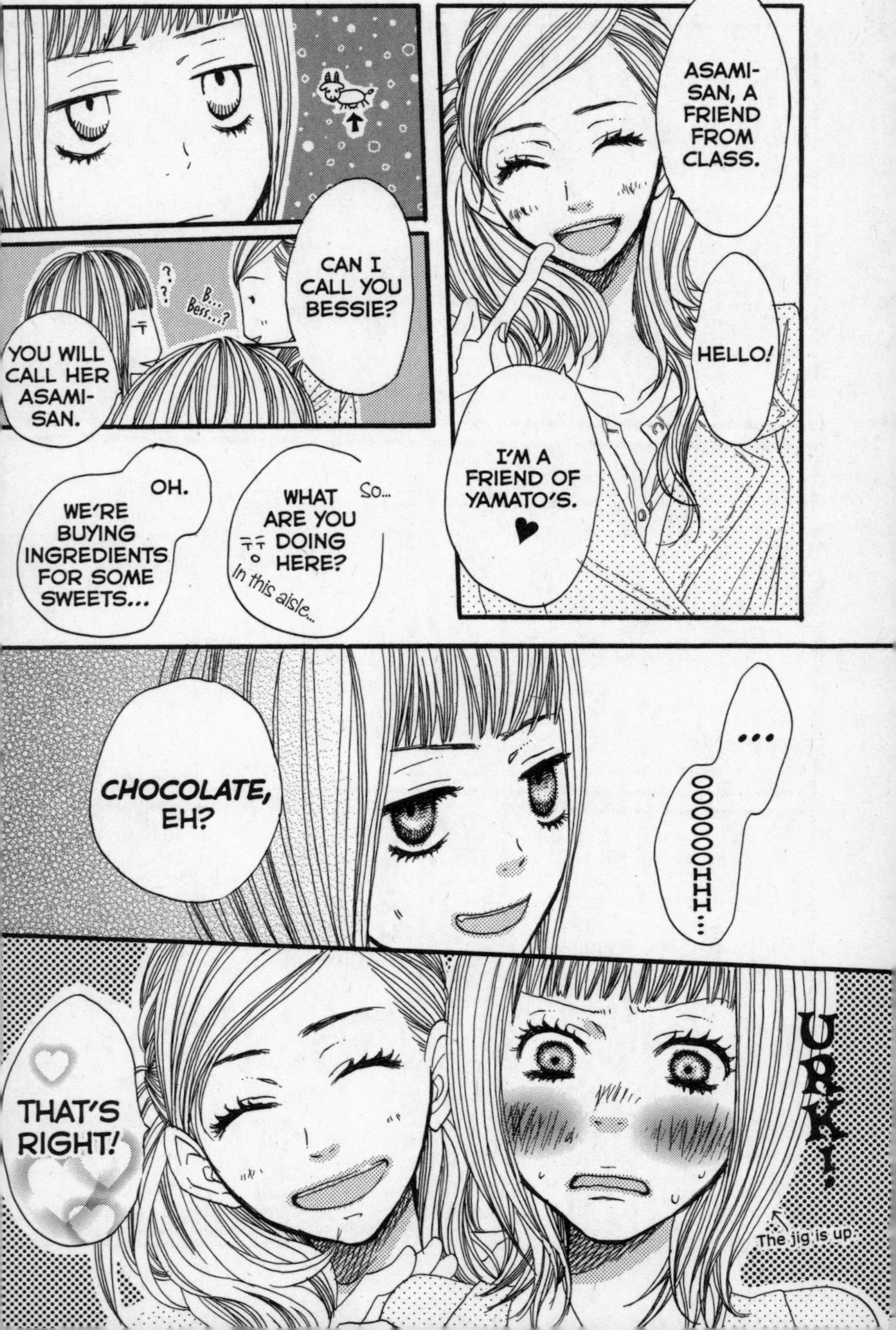
ASAMI-SAN, A FRIEND FROM CLASS.
HELLO!
I'M A FRIEND OF YAMATO'S. ♥
CAN I CALL YOU BESSIE?
B... Bess...?
YOU WILL CALL HER ASAMI-SAN.
So...
WHAT ARE YOU DOING HERE?
In this aisle...
OH. WE'RE BUYING INGREDIENTS FOR SOME SWEETS...
...OOOOOOHHH...
CHOCOLATE, EH?
URK!
The jig is up.
THAT'S RIGHT!

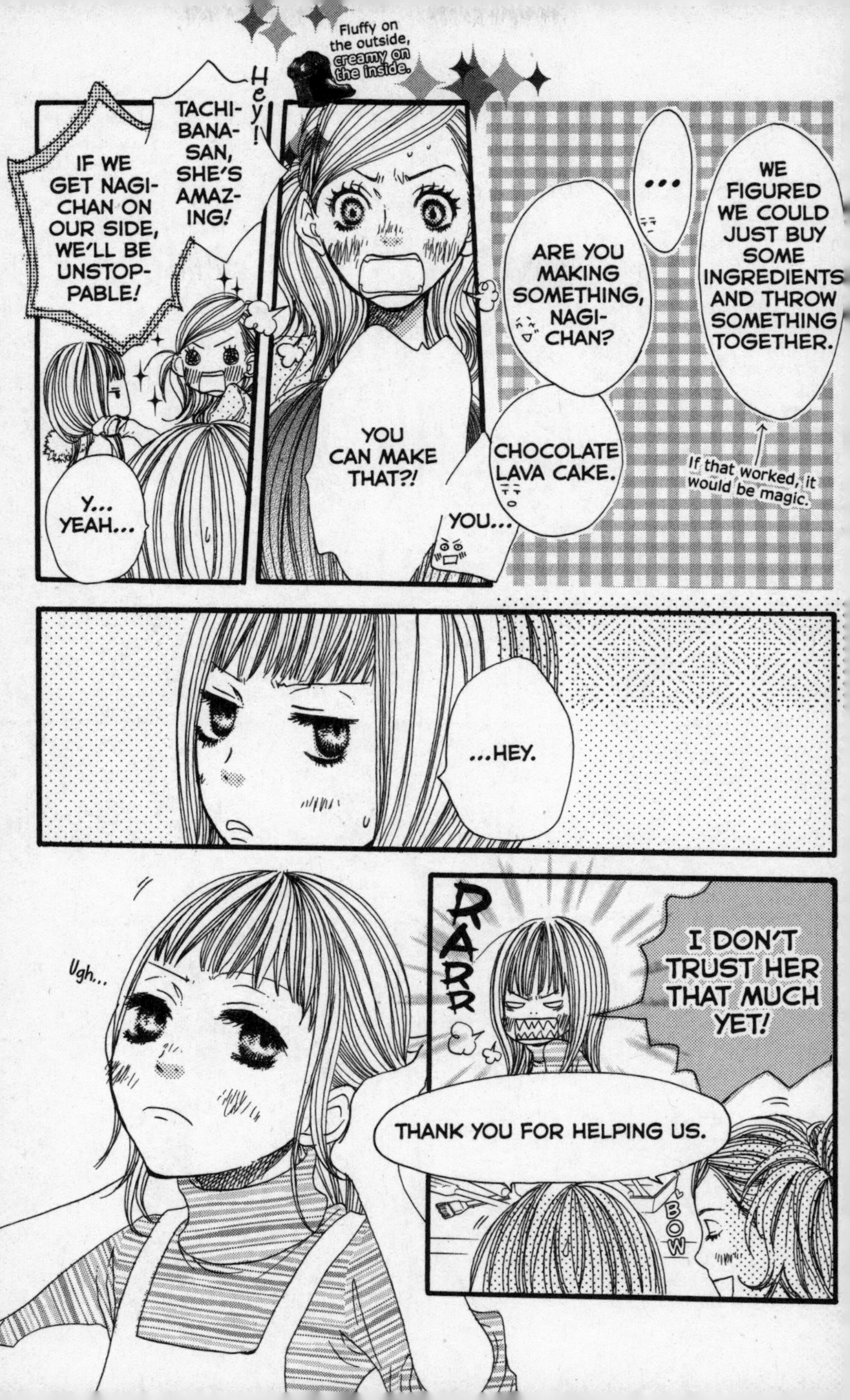
WE FIGURED WE COULD JUST BUY SOME INGREDIENTS AND THROW SOMETHING TOGETHER.
...
ARE YOU MAKING SOMETHING, NAGI-CHAN?
CHOCOLATE LAVA CAKE.
If that worked, it would be magic.
YOU...
YOU CAN MAKE THAT?!
Fluffy on the outside, creamy on the inside.
Hey!
TACHI-BANA-SAN, SHE'S AMAZ-ING!
IF WE GET NAGI-CHAN ON OUR SIDE, WE'LL BE UNSTOP-PABLE!
Y... YEAH...
...HEY.
THANK YOU FOR HELPING US.
BOW
RARR
I DON'T TRUST HER THAT MUCH YET!
Ugh...

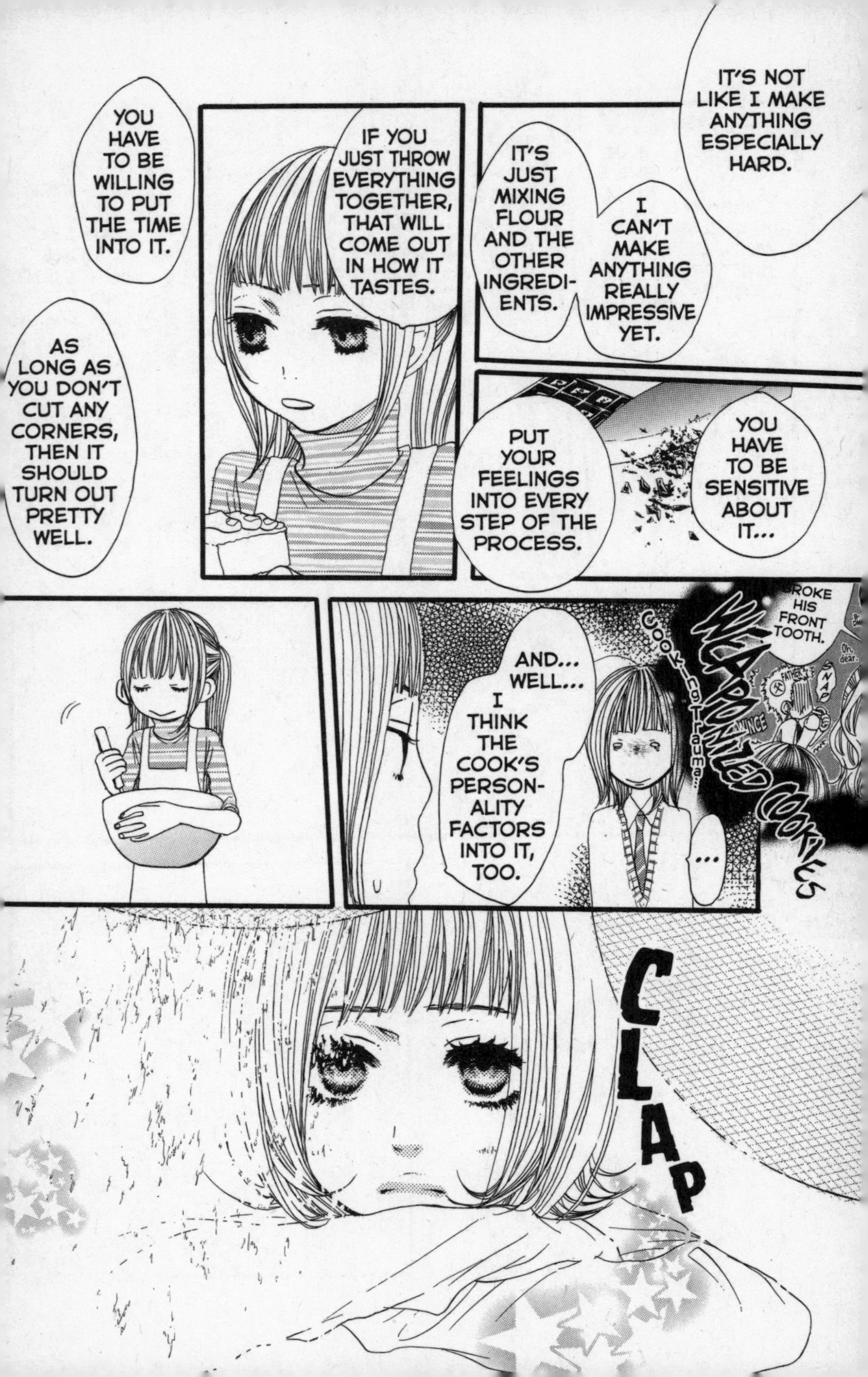
IT'S NOT LIKE I MAKE ANYTHING ESPECIALLY HARD.
I CAN'T MAKE ANYTHING REALLY IMPRESSIVE YET.
IT'S JUST MIXING FLOUR AND THE OTHER INGREDI-ENTS.
YOU HAVE TO BE SENSITIVE ABOUT IT...
PUT YOUR FEELINGS INTO EVERY STEP OF THE PROCESS.
IF YOU JUST THROW EVERYTHING TOGETHER, THAT WILL COME OUT IN HOW IT TASTES.
YOU HAVE TO BE WILLING TO PUT THE TIME INTO IT.
AS LONG AS YOU DON'T CUT ANY CORNERS, THEN IT SHOULD TURN OUT PRETTY WELL.
BROKE HIS FRONT TOOTH.
Oh, dear.
SNAP
FATHER
WINCE
WEAPONIZED COOKIES
Cooking Trauma...
...
AND... WELL... I THINK THE COOK'S PERSON-ALITY FACTORS INTO IT, TOO.
CLAP

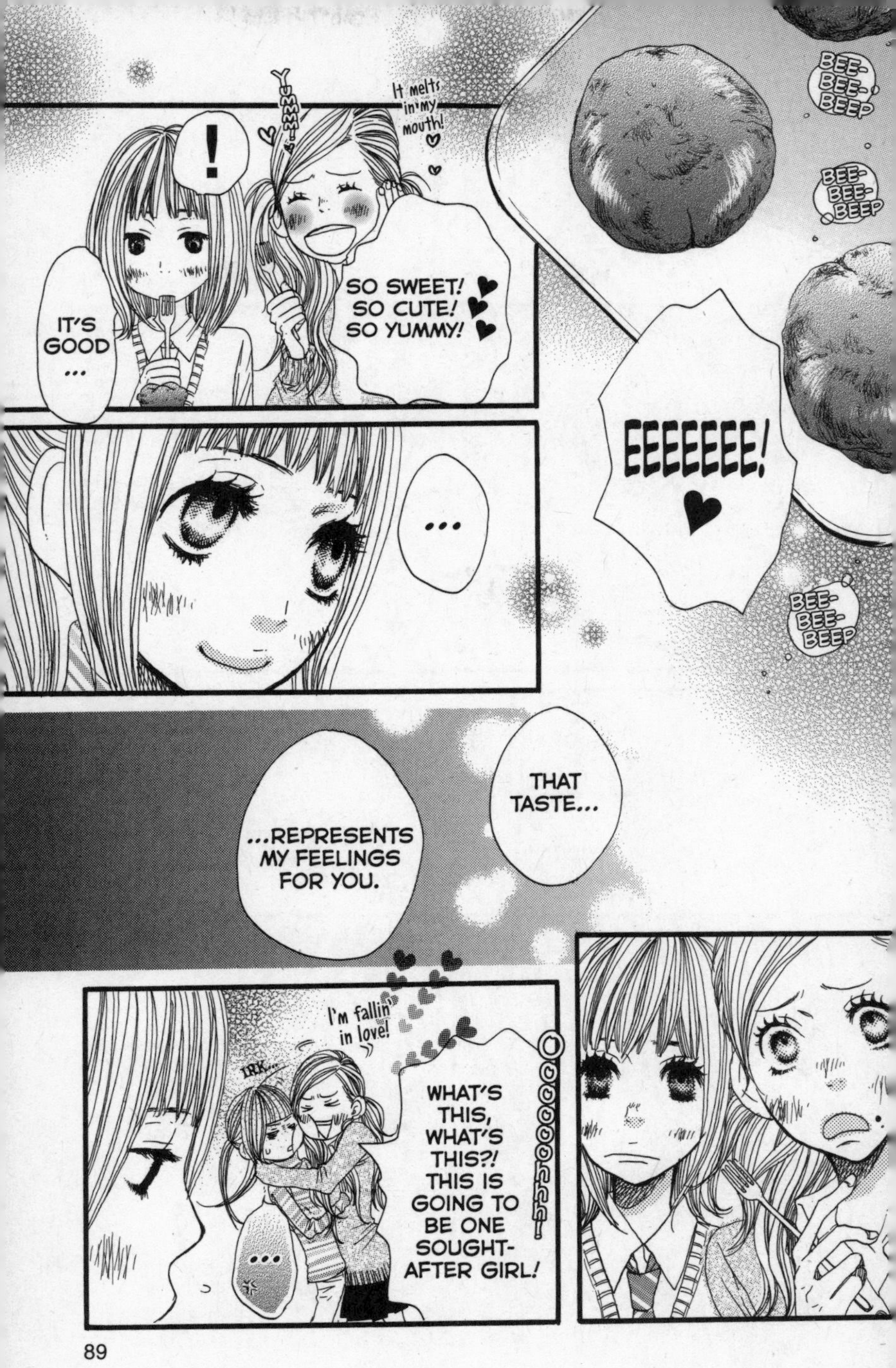

BEE-BEE-BEEP
BEE-BEE-BEEP
EEEEEEE!
BEE-BEE-BEEP
YUMMM!
It melts in my mouth!
SO SWEET! SO CUTE! SO YUMMY!
!
IT'S GOOD...
...
THAT TASTE...
...REPRESENTS MY FEELINGS FOR YOU.
OOOOOOhhh!
WHAT'S THIS, WHAT'S THIS?! THIS IS GOING TO BE ONE SOUGHT-AFTER GIRL!
I'm fallin' in love!
IRK...
...

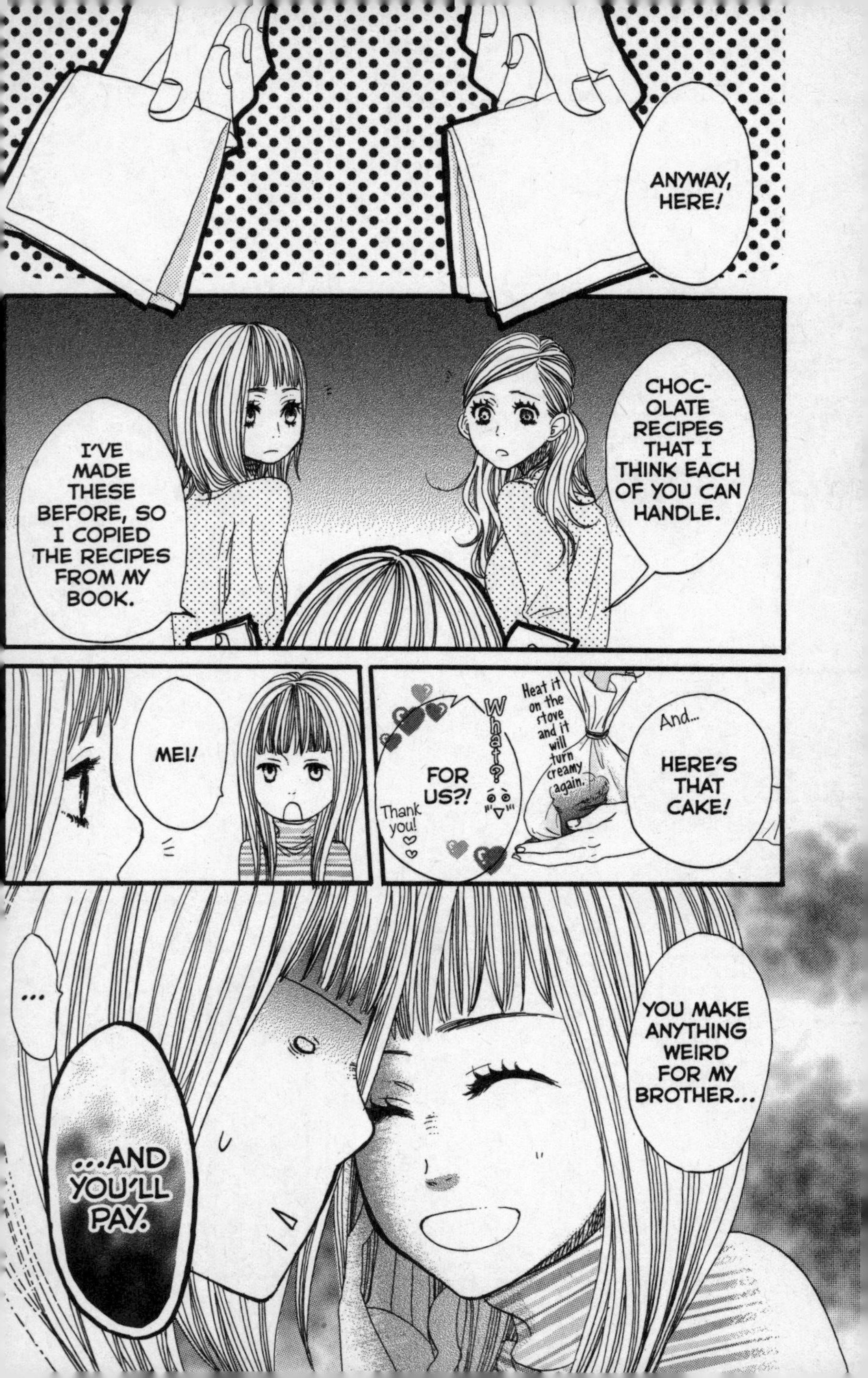
ANYWAY, HERE!
CHOC-OLATE RECIPES THAT I THINK EACH OF YOU CAN HANDLE.
I'VE MADE THESE BEFORE, SO I COPIED THE RECIPES FROM MY BOOK.
And... HERE'S THAT CAKE!
Heat it on the stove and it will turn creamy again.
What?
FOR US?!
Thank you!
MEI!
YOU MAKE ANYTHING WEIRD FOR MY BROTHER...
...
...AND YOU'LL PAY.

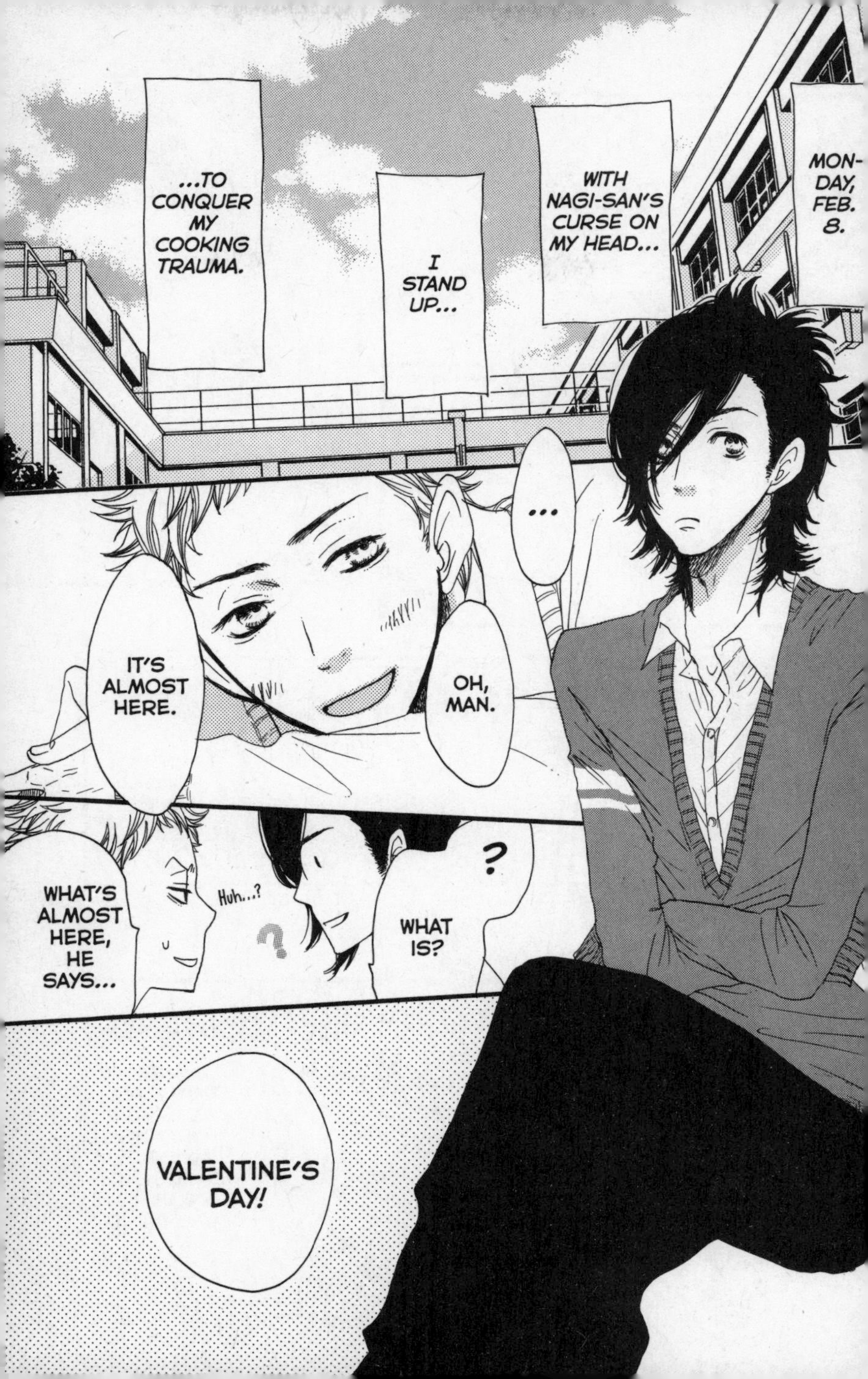
MONDAY, FEB. 8.
WITH NAGI-SAN'S CURSE ON MY HEAD...
I STAND UP...
...TO CONQUER MY COOKING TRAUMA.
...
OH, MAN.
IT'S ALMOST HERE.
?
WHAT IS?
Huh...?
WHAT'S ALMOST HERE, HE SAYS...
VALENTINE'S DAY!

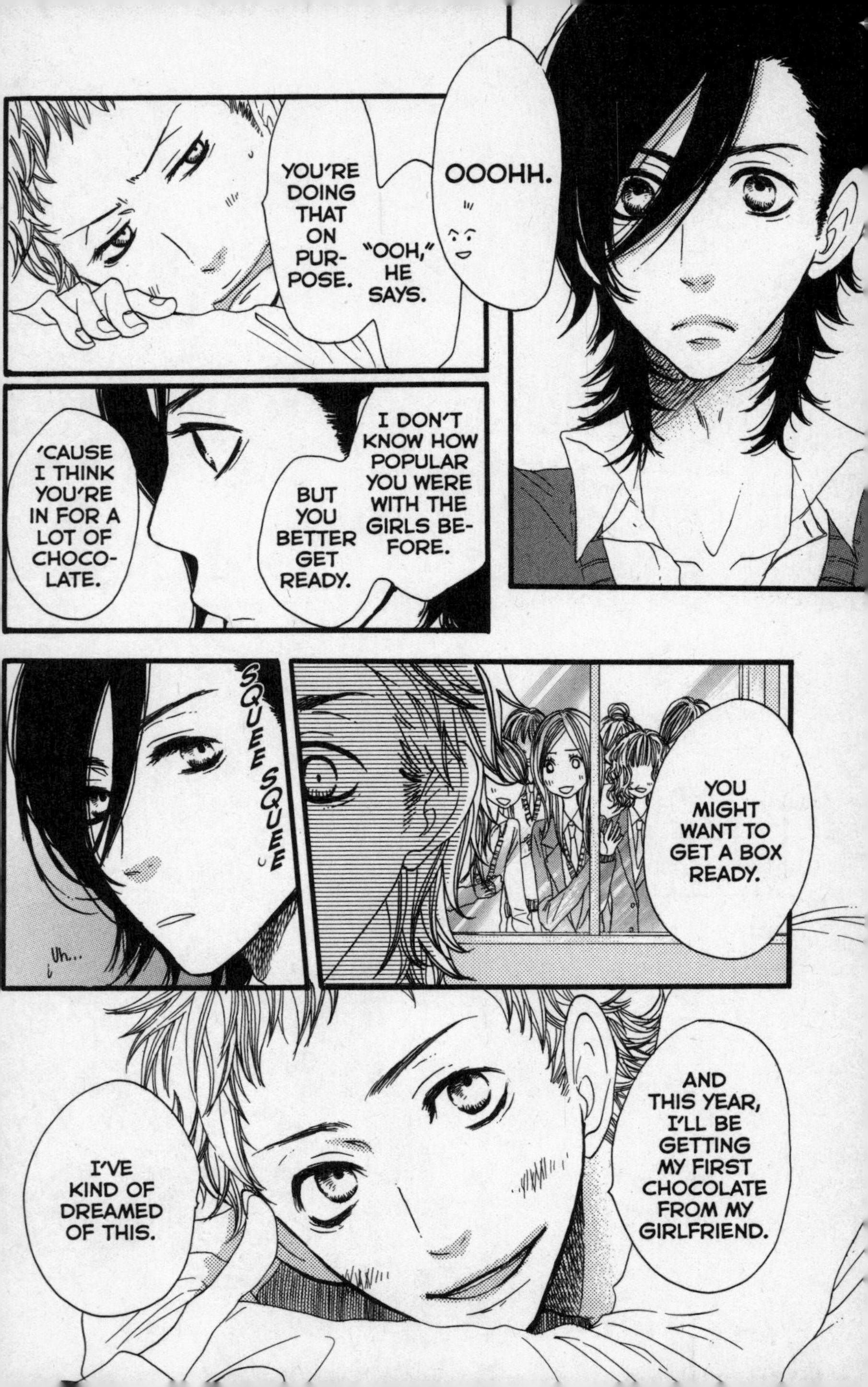
OOOHH.
"OOH," HE SAYS.
YOU'RE DOING THAT ON PUR-POSE.
I DON'T KNOW HOW POPULAR YOU WERE WITH THE GIRLS BE-FORE.
BUT YOU BETTER GET READY.
'CAUSE I THINK YOU'RE IN FOR A LOT OF CHOCO-LATE.
YOU MIGHT WANT TO GET A BOX READY.
SQUEE SQUEE SQUEE
Uh...
AND THIS YEAR, I'LL BE GETTING MY FIRST CHOCOLATE FROM MY GIRLFRIEND.
I'VE KIND OF DREAMED OF THIS.

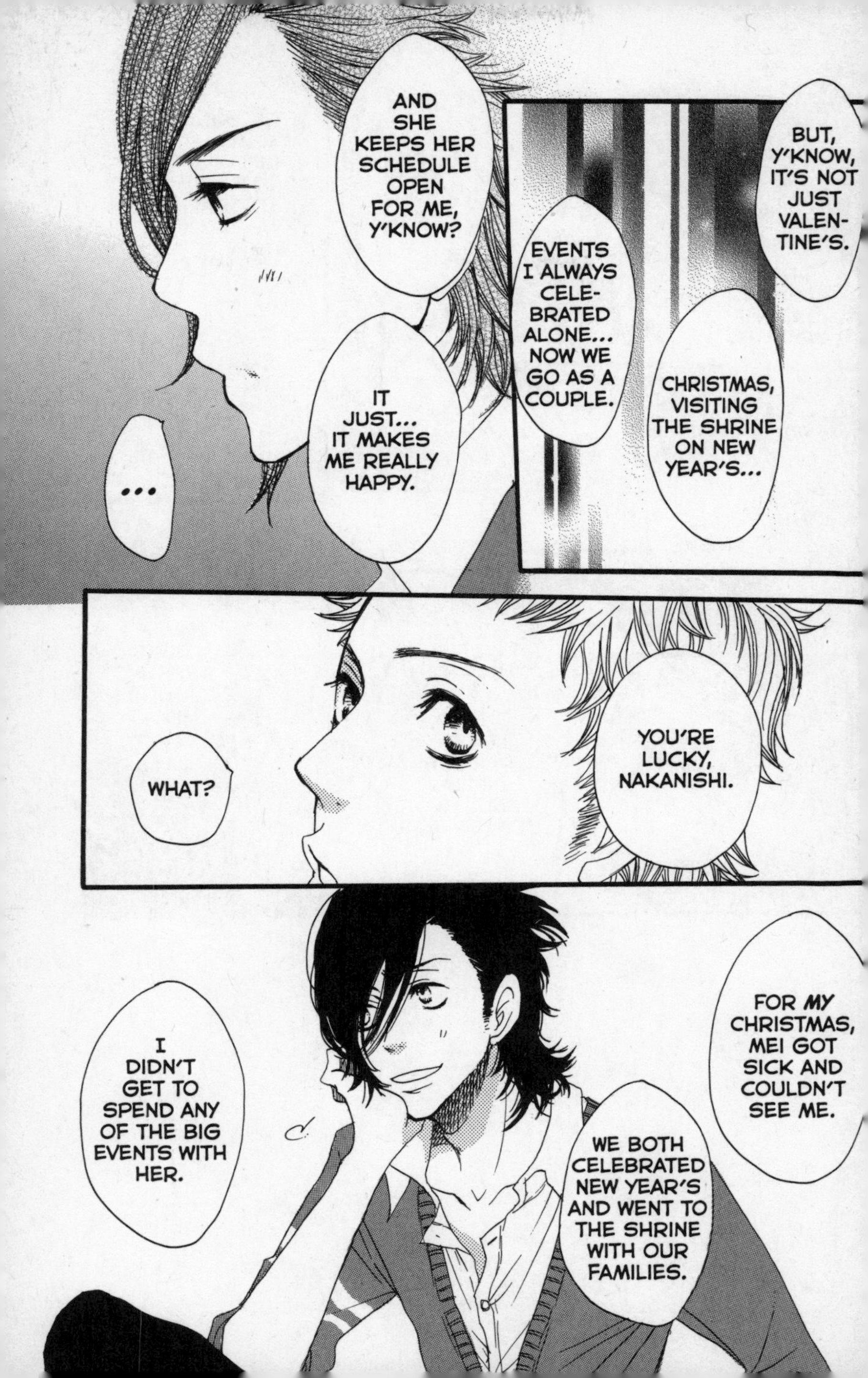
BUT, Y'KNOW, IT'S NOT JUST VALENTINE'S.
CHRISTMAS, VISITING THE SHRINE ON NEW YEAR'S...
EVENTS I ALWAYS CELEBRATED ALONE... NOW WE GO AS A COUPLE.
AND SHE KEEPS HER SCHEDULE OPEN FOR ME, Y'KNOW?
IT JUST... IT MAKES ME REALLY HAPPY.
...
YOU'RE LUCKY, NAKANISHI.
WHAT?
FOR *MY* CHRISTMAS, MEI GOT SICK AND COULDN'T SEE ME.
WE BOTH CELEBRATED NEW YEAR'S AND WENT TO THE SHRINE WITH OUR FAMILIES.
I DIDN'T GET TO SPEND ANY OF THE BIG EVENTS WITH HER.

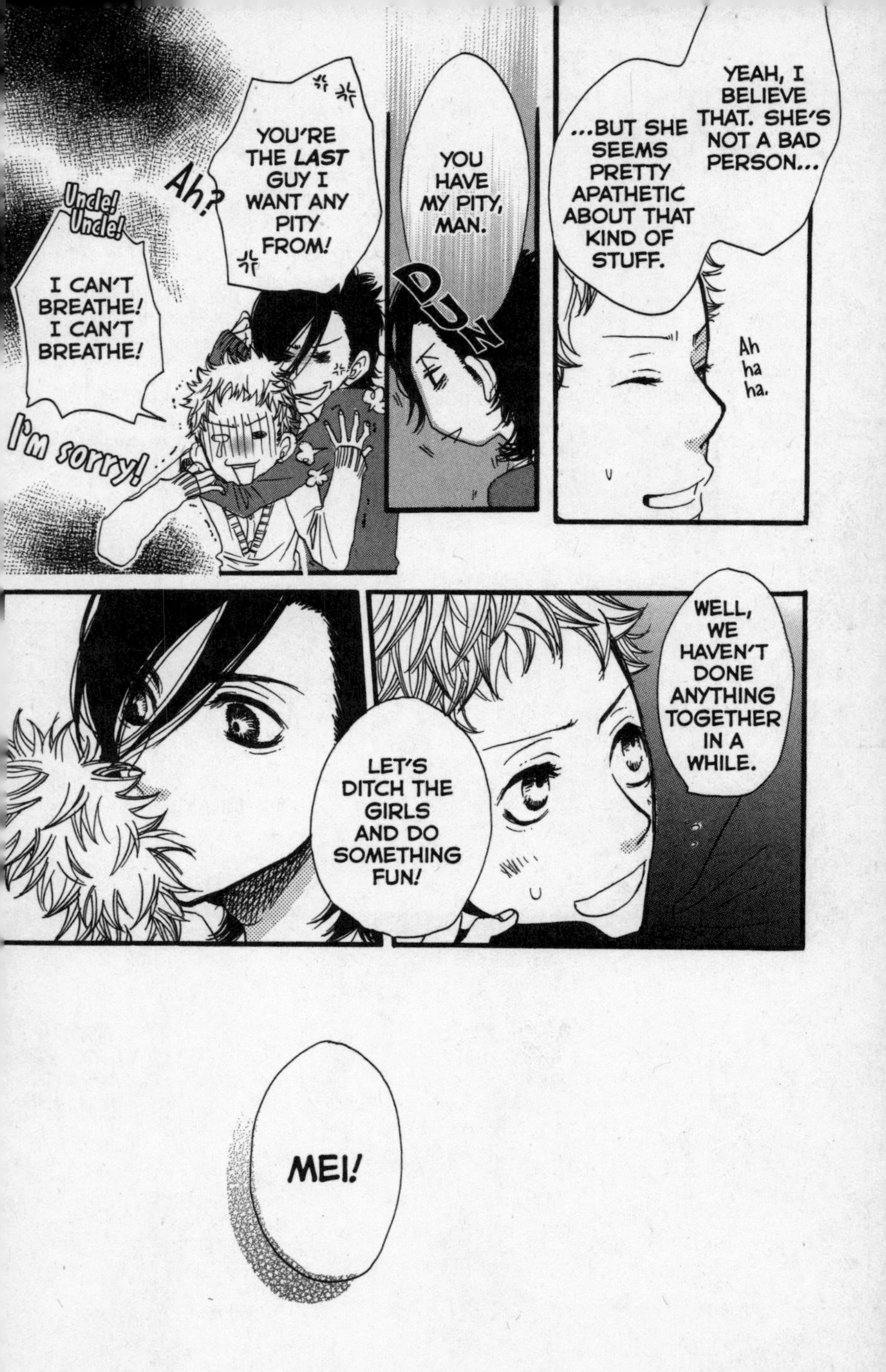
YEAH, I BELIEVE THAT. SHE'S NOT A BAD PERSON...
...BUT SHE SEEMS PRETTY APATHETIC ABOUT THAT KIND OF STUFF.
Ah ha ha.
YOU HAVE MY PITY, MAN.
DUN
YOU'RE THE *LAST* GUY I WANT ANY PITY FROM!
Ah?
Uncle! Uncle!
I CAN'T BREATHE! I CAN'T BREATHE!
I'm sorry!
WELL, WE HAVEN'T DONE ANYTHING TOGETHER IN A WHILE.
LET'S DITCH THE GIRLS AND DO SOMETHING FUN!
MEI!

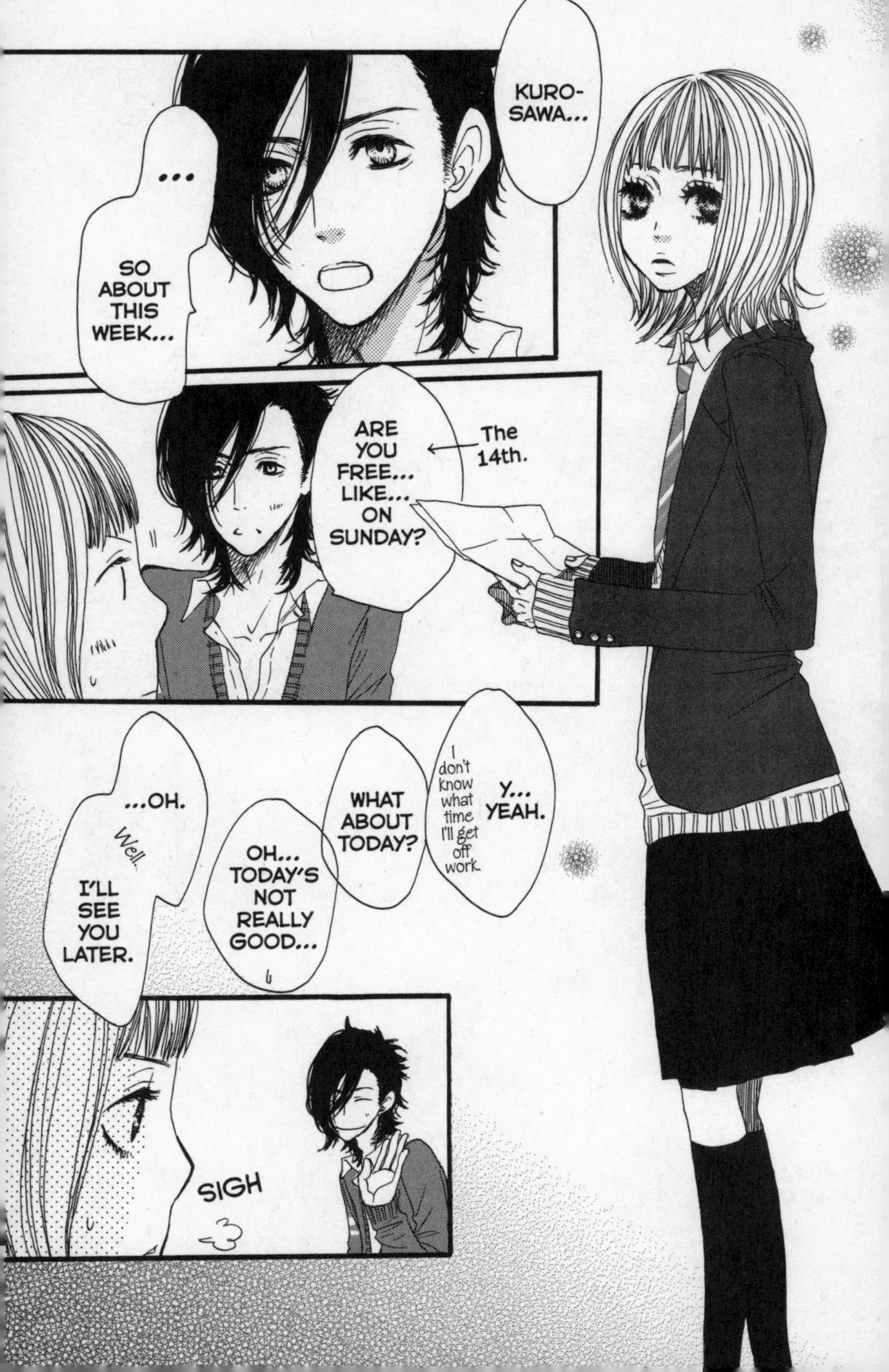

KURO-SAWA...
...
SO ABOUT THIS WEEK...
ARE YOU FREE... LIKE... ON SUNDAY?
The 14th.
Y... YEAH.
I don't know what time I'll get off work.
WHAT ABOUT TODAY?
OH... TODAY'S NOT REALLY GOOD...
...OH.
Well.
I'LL SEE YOU LATER.
SIGH

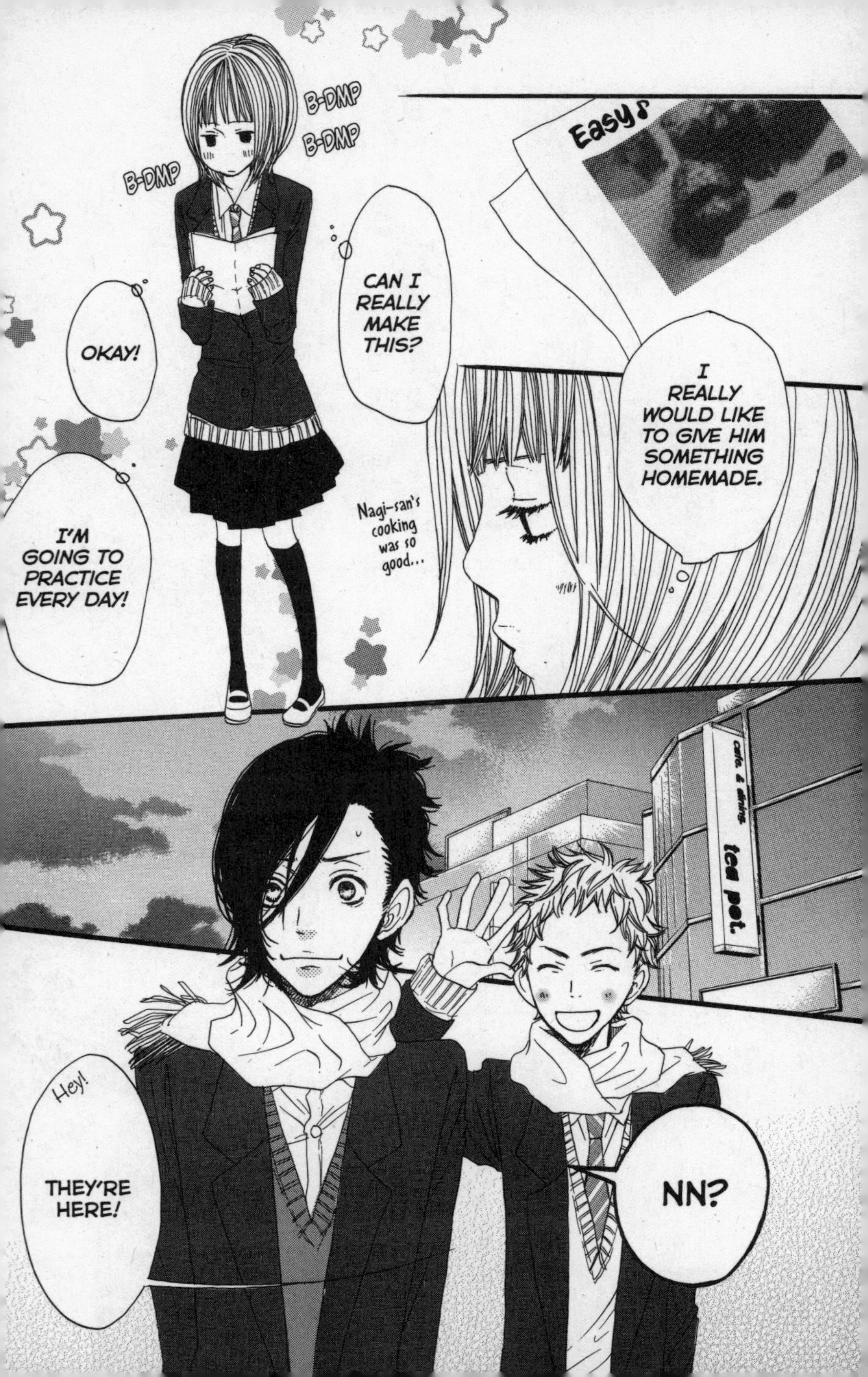

Easy
I REALLY WOULD LIKE TO GIVE HIM SOMETHING HOMEMADE.
Nagi-san's cooking was so good...
B-DMP
B-DMP
B-DMP
CAN I REALLY MAKE THIS?
OKAY!
I'M GOING TO PRACTICE EVERY DAY!
cafe & dining
tea pot.
Hey!
THEY'RE HERE!
NN?

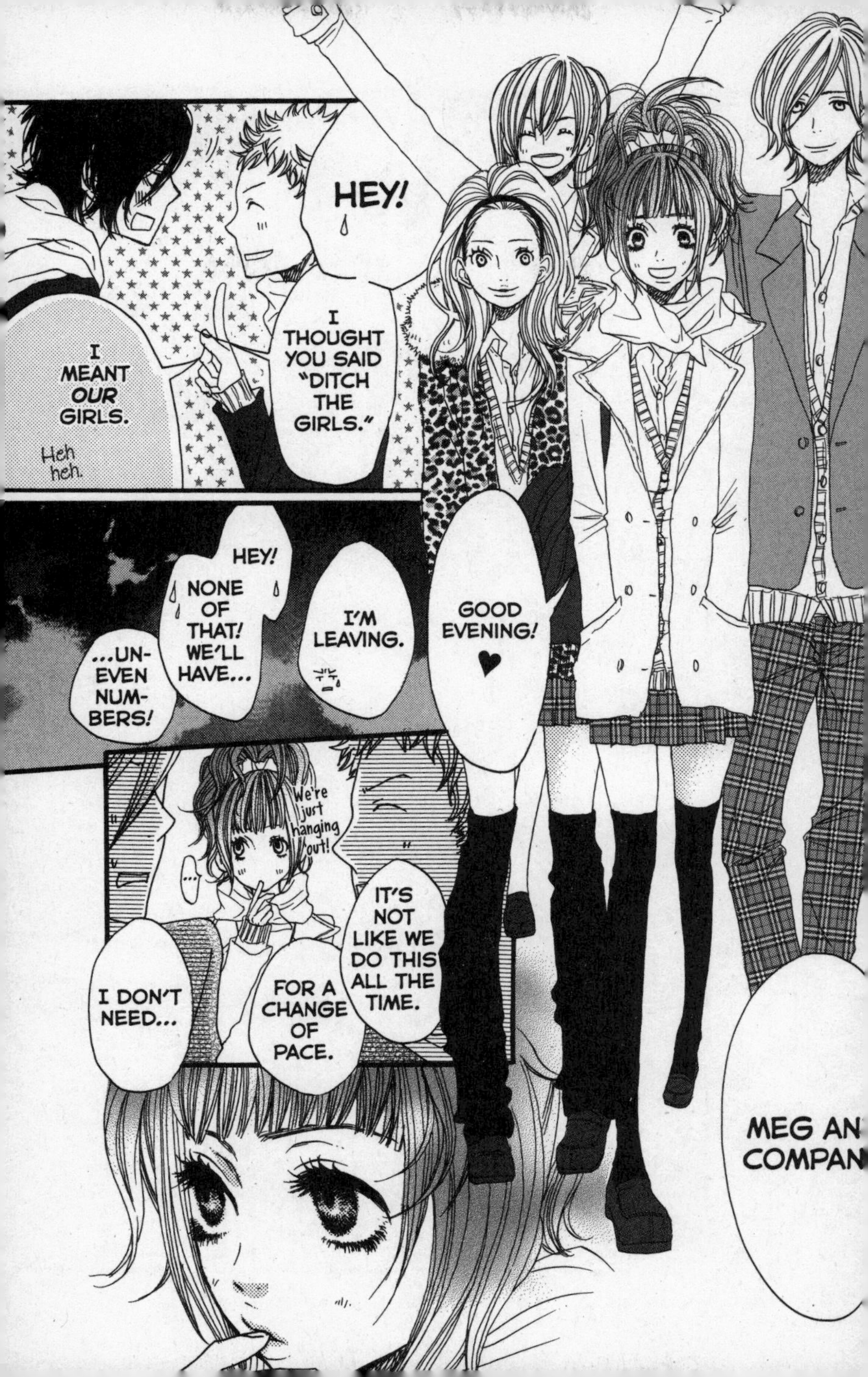
GOOD EVENING! ♥
MEG AN COMPAN
HEY!
I THOUGHT YOU SAID "DITCH THE GIRLS."
I MEANT OUR GIRLS.
Heh heh.
I'M LEAVING.
HEY! NONE OF THAT! WE'LL HAVE...
...UN-EVEN NUM-BERS!
IT'S NOT LIKE WE DO THIS ALL THE TIME.
FOR A CHANGE OF PACE.
We're just hanging out!
...
I DON'T NEED...

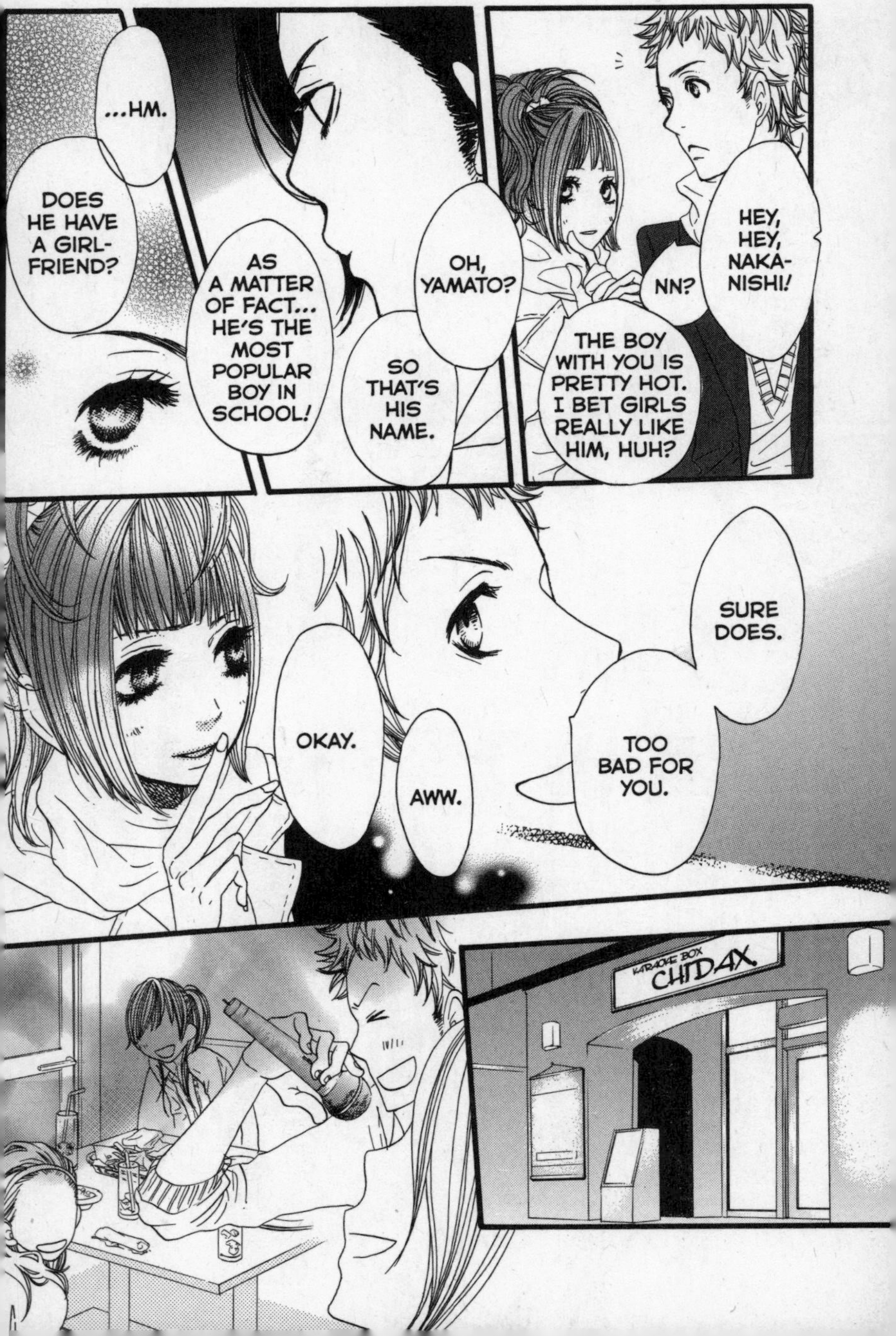
HEY, HEY, NAKA-NISHI!
NN?
THE BOY WITH YOU IS PRETTY HOT. I BET GIRLS REALLY LIKE HIM, HUH?
OH, YAMATO?
SO THAT'S HIS NAME.
AS A MATTER OF FACT... HE'S THE MOST POPULAR BOY IN SCHOOL!
...HM.
DOES HE HAVE A GIRL-FRIEND?
SURE DOES.
TOO BAD FOR YOU.
AWW.
OKAY.
KARAOKE BOX
CHIDAX.

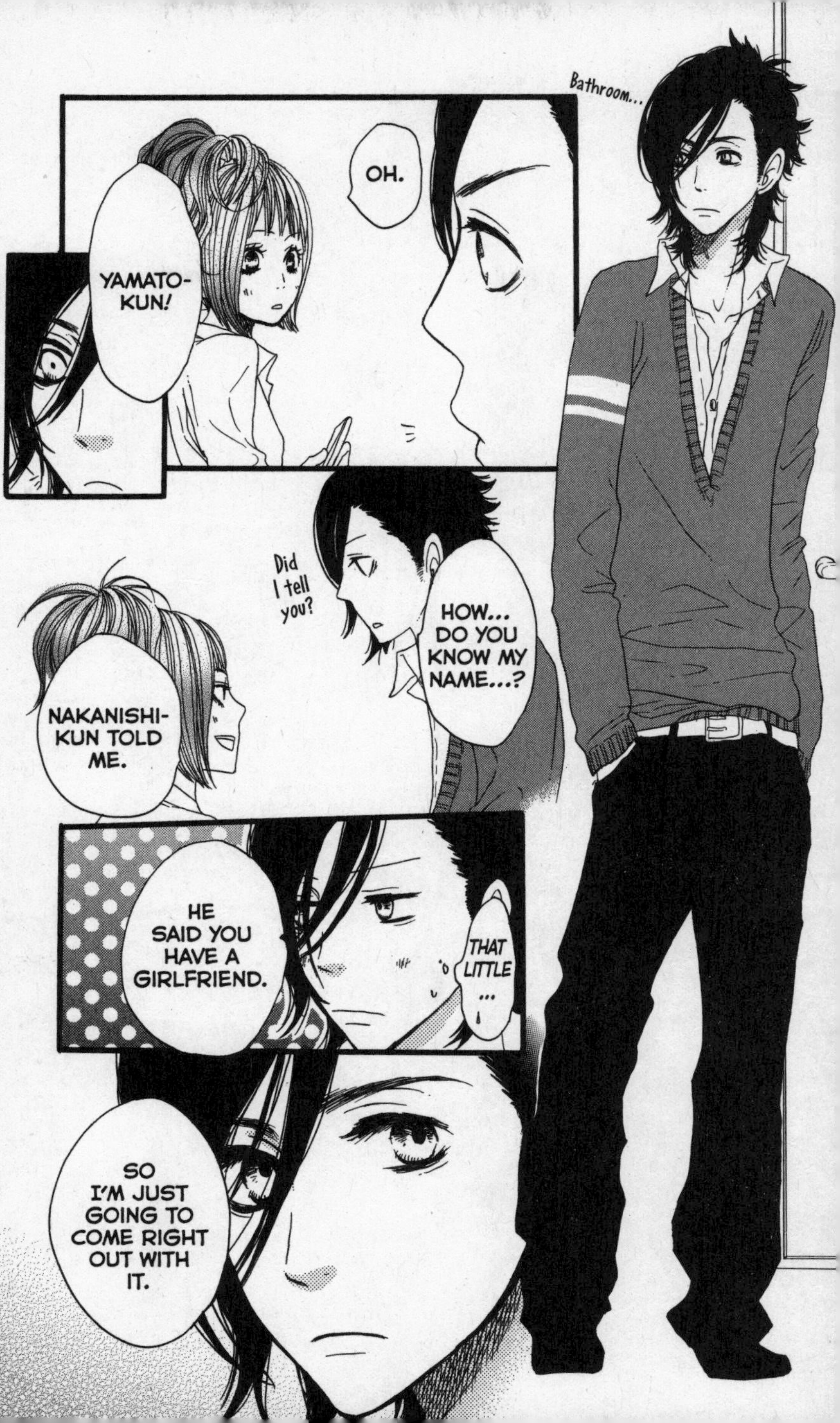
Bathroom...
OH.
YAMATO-KUN!
HOW... DO YOU KNOW MY NAME...?
Did I tell you?
NAKANISHI-KUN TOLD ME.
HE SAID YOU HAVE A GIRLFRIEND.
THAT LITTLE...
SO I'M JUST GOING TO COME RIGHT OUT WITH IT.

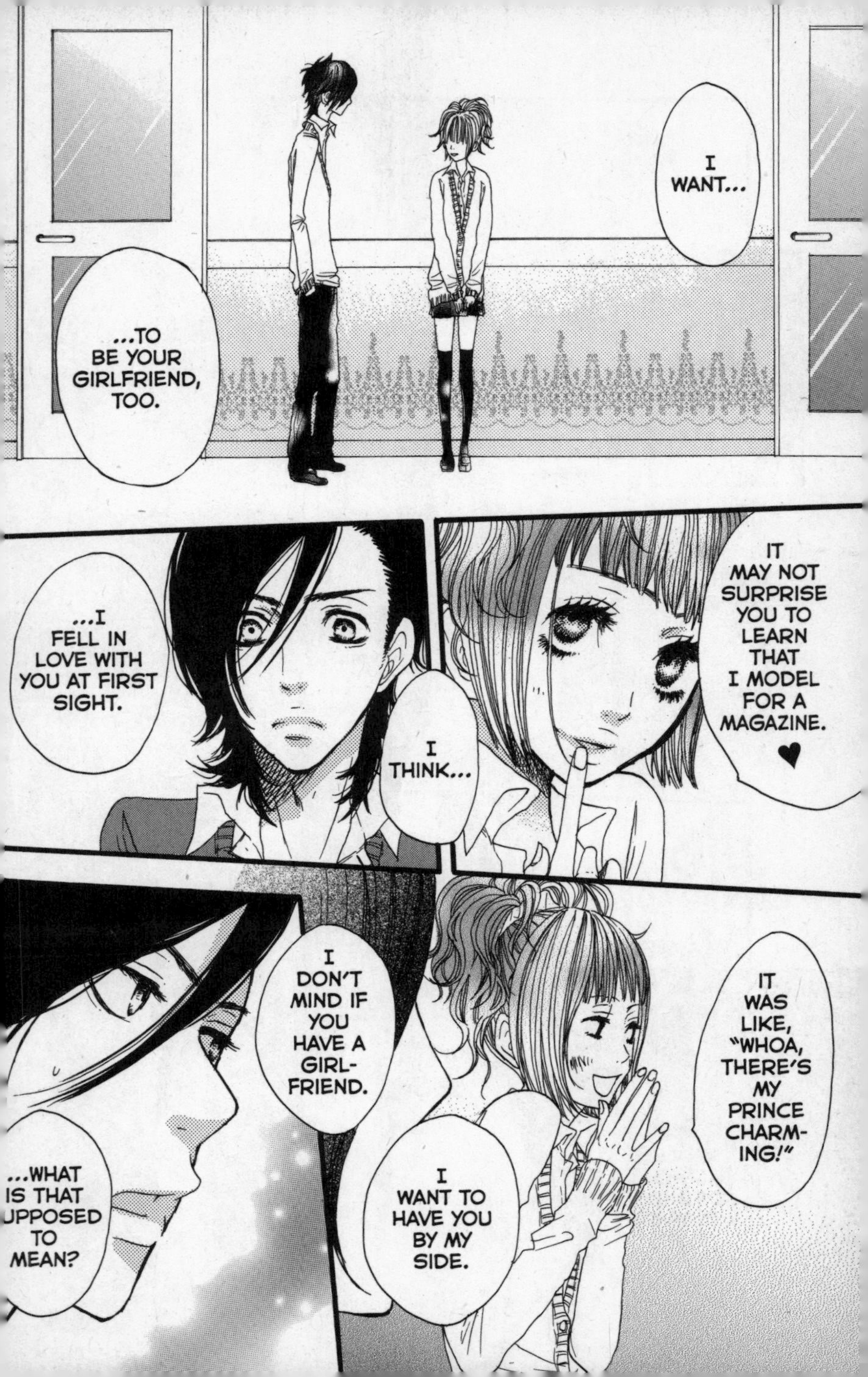
I WANT...
...TO BE YOUR GIRLFRIEND, TOO.
IT MAY NOT SURPRISE YOU TO LEARN THAT I MODEL FOR A MAGAZINE. ♥
I THINK...
...I FELL IN LOVE WITH YOU AT FIRST SIGHT.
IT WAS LIKE, "WHOA, THERE'S MY PRINCE CHARMING!"
I DON'T MIND IF YOU HAVE A GIRL-FRIEND.
I WANT TO HAVE YOU BY MY SIDE.
...WHAT IS THAT UPPOSED TO MEAN?

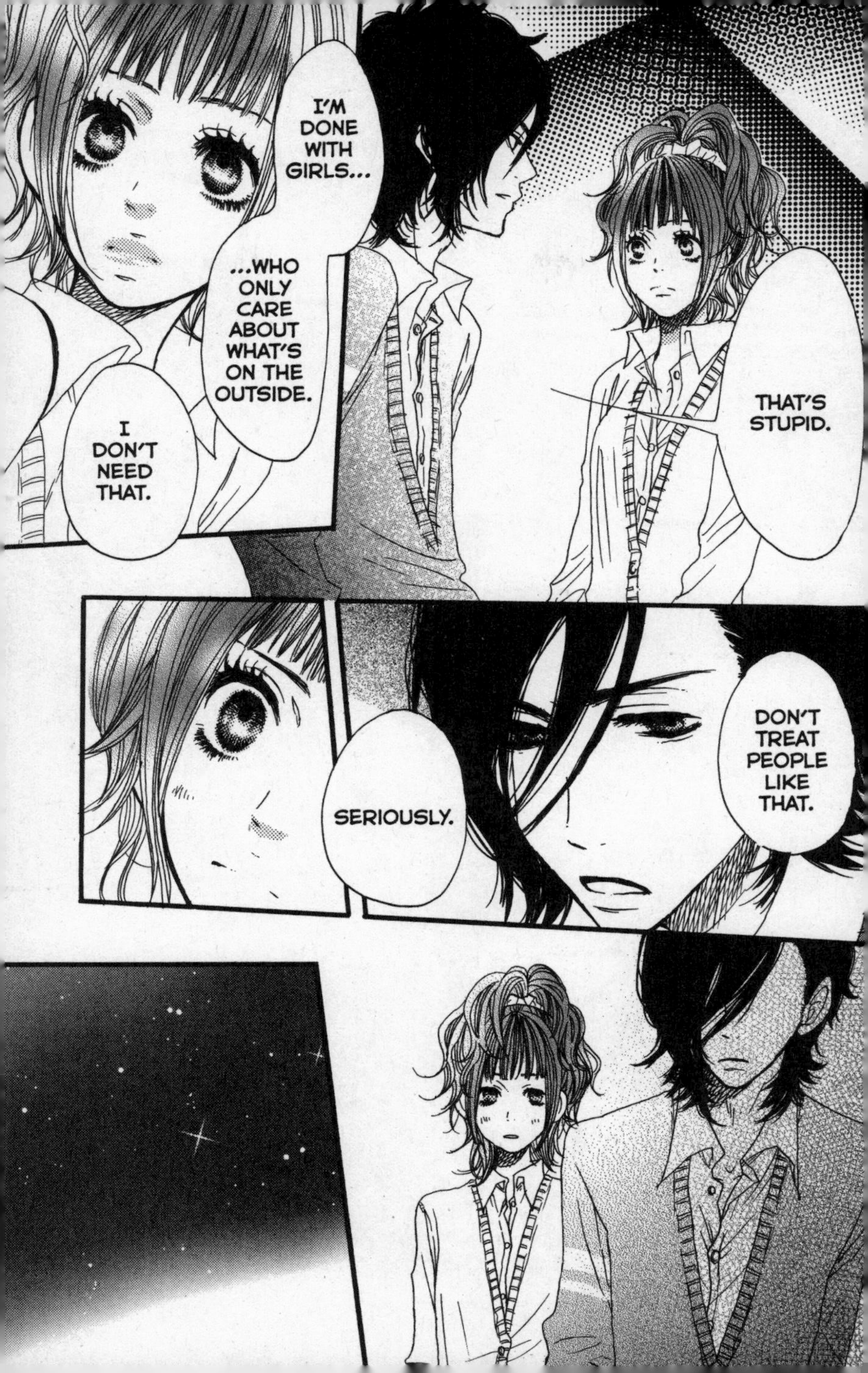
I'M DONE WITH GIRLS...
...WHO ONLY CARE ABOUT WHAT'S ON THE OUTSIDE.
I DON'T NEED THAT.
THAT'S STUPID.
DON'T TREAT PEOPLE LIKE THAT.
SERIOUSLY.

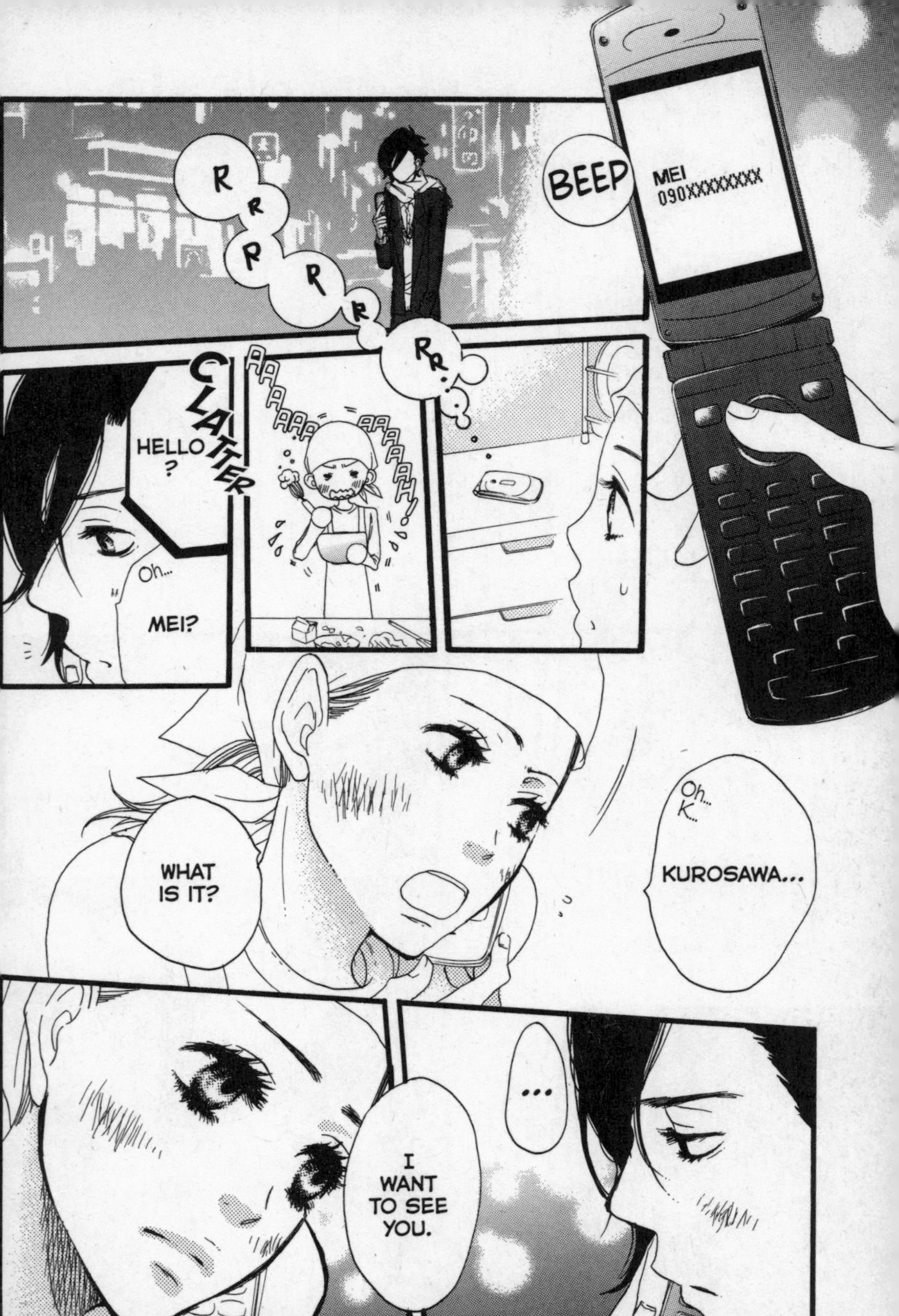
BEEP
MEI
090XXXXXXXX
RRRRRRR...
AAAAAA
AAAAAAH!
CLATTER
HELLO?
Oh...
MEI?
Oh... K...
KUROSAWA...
WHAT IS IT?
...
I WANT TO SEE YOU.

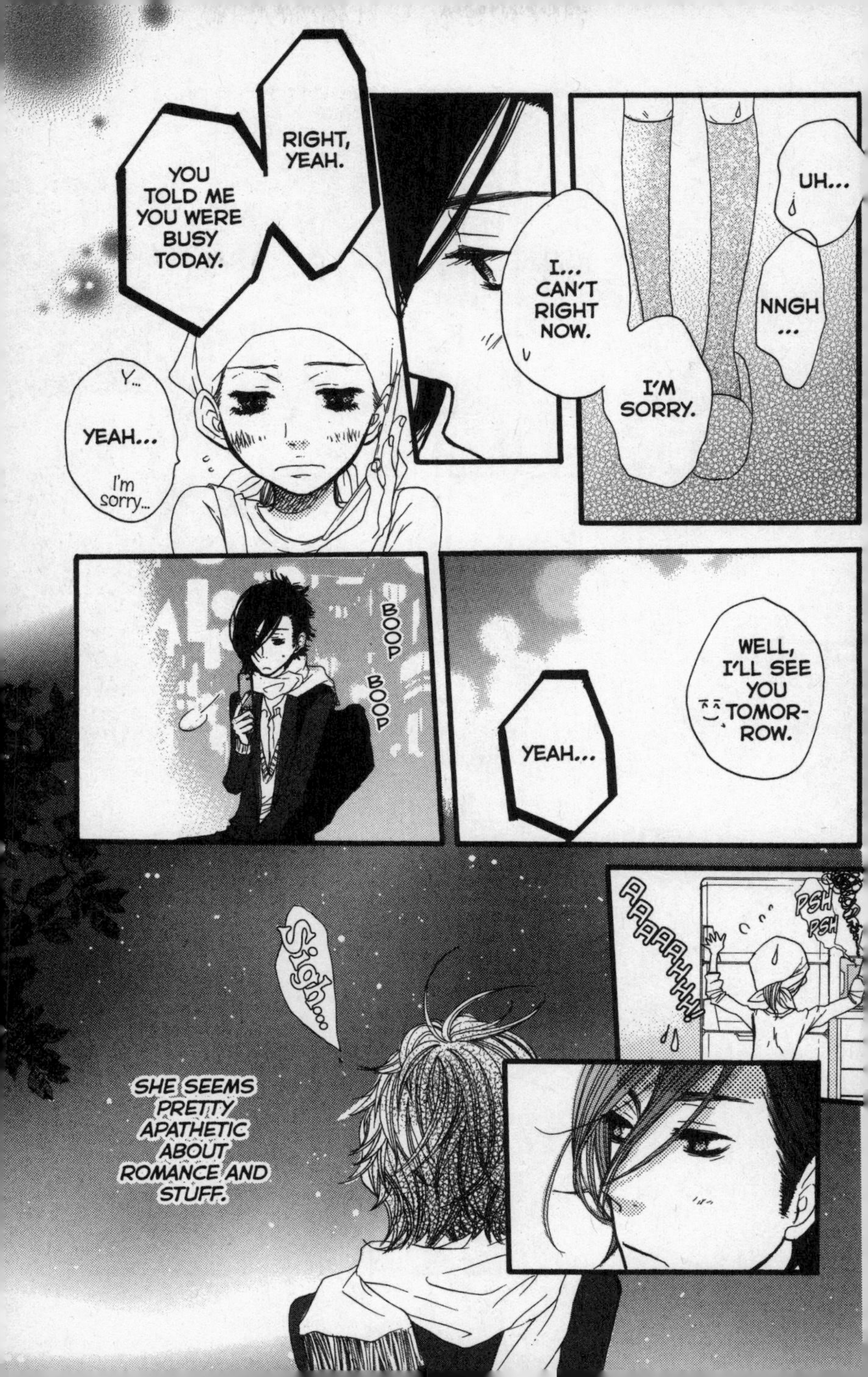
UH...
NNGH...
I... CAN'T RIGHT NOW.
I'M SORRY.
RIGHT, YEAH.
YOU TOLD ME YOU WERE BUSY TODAY.
Y... YEAH... I'm sorry...
WELL, I'LL SEE YOU TOMOR-ROW.
YEAH...
BOOP BOOP
AAAAHHH!
PSH PSH
Sigh...
SHE SEEMS PRETTY APATHETIC ABOUT ROMANCE AND STUFF.

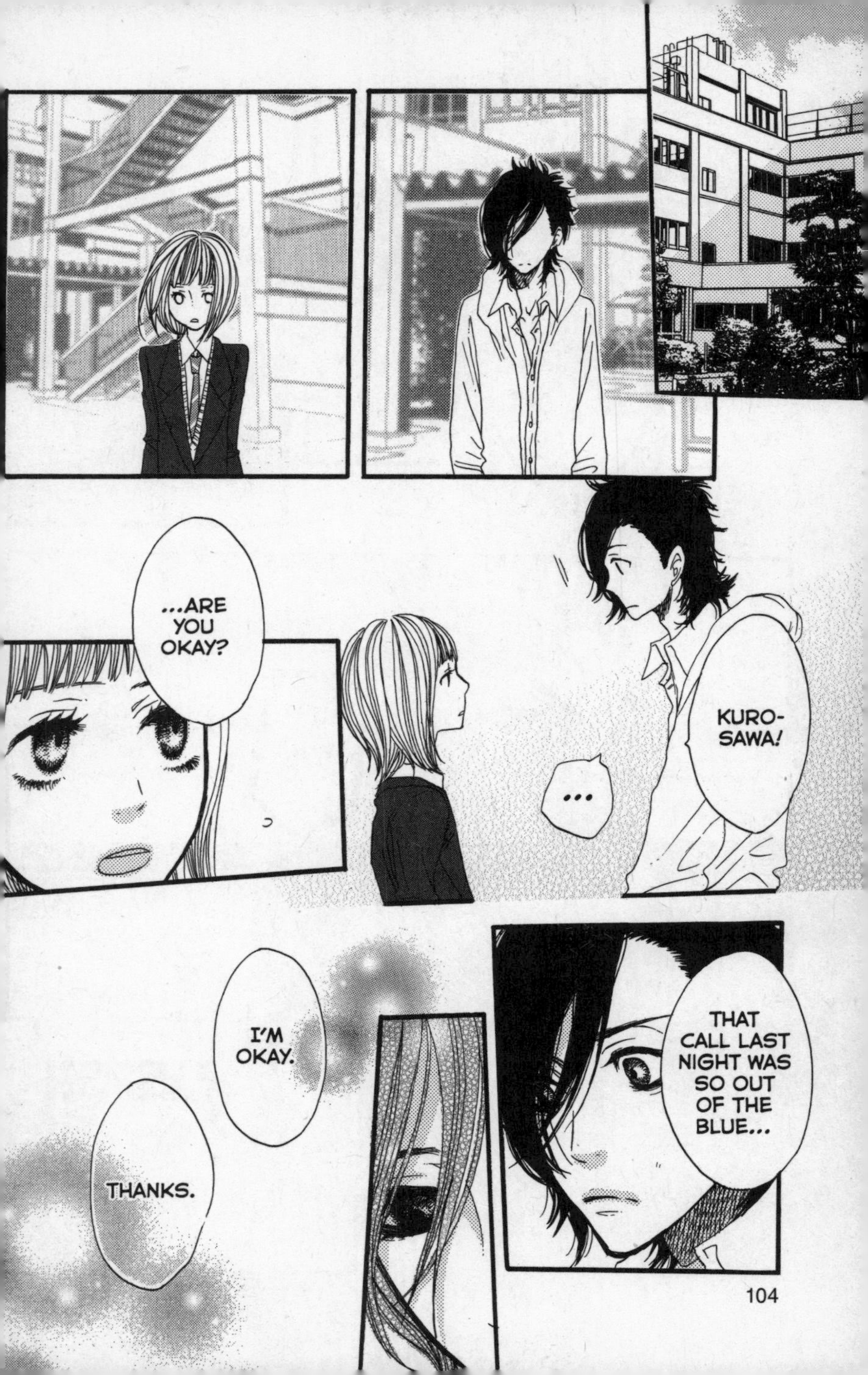
KURO-SAWA!
...
...ARE YOU OKAY?
THAT CALL LAST NIGHT WAS SO OUT OF THE BLUE...
I'M OKAY.
THANKS.

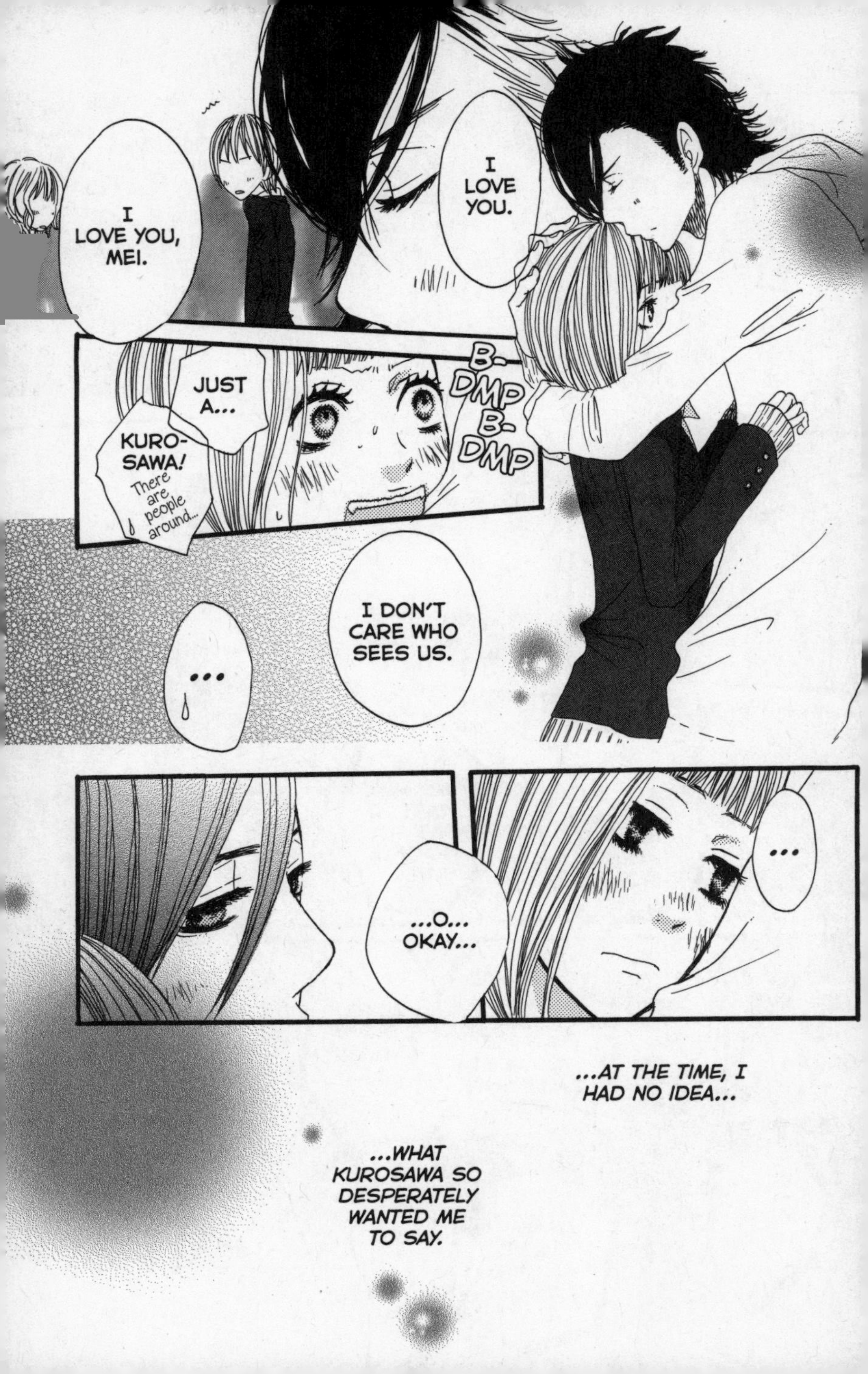
I LOVE YOU.
I LOVE YOU, MEI.
B-DMP B-DMP
JUST A...
KURO-SAWA! There are people around...
I DON'T CARE WHO SEES US.
...
...
...O... OKAY...
...AT THE TIME, I HAD NO IDEA...
...WHAT KUROSAWA SO DESPERATELY WANTED ME TO SAY.

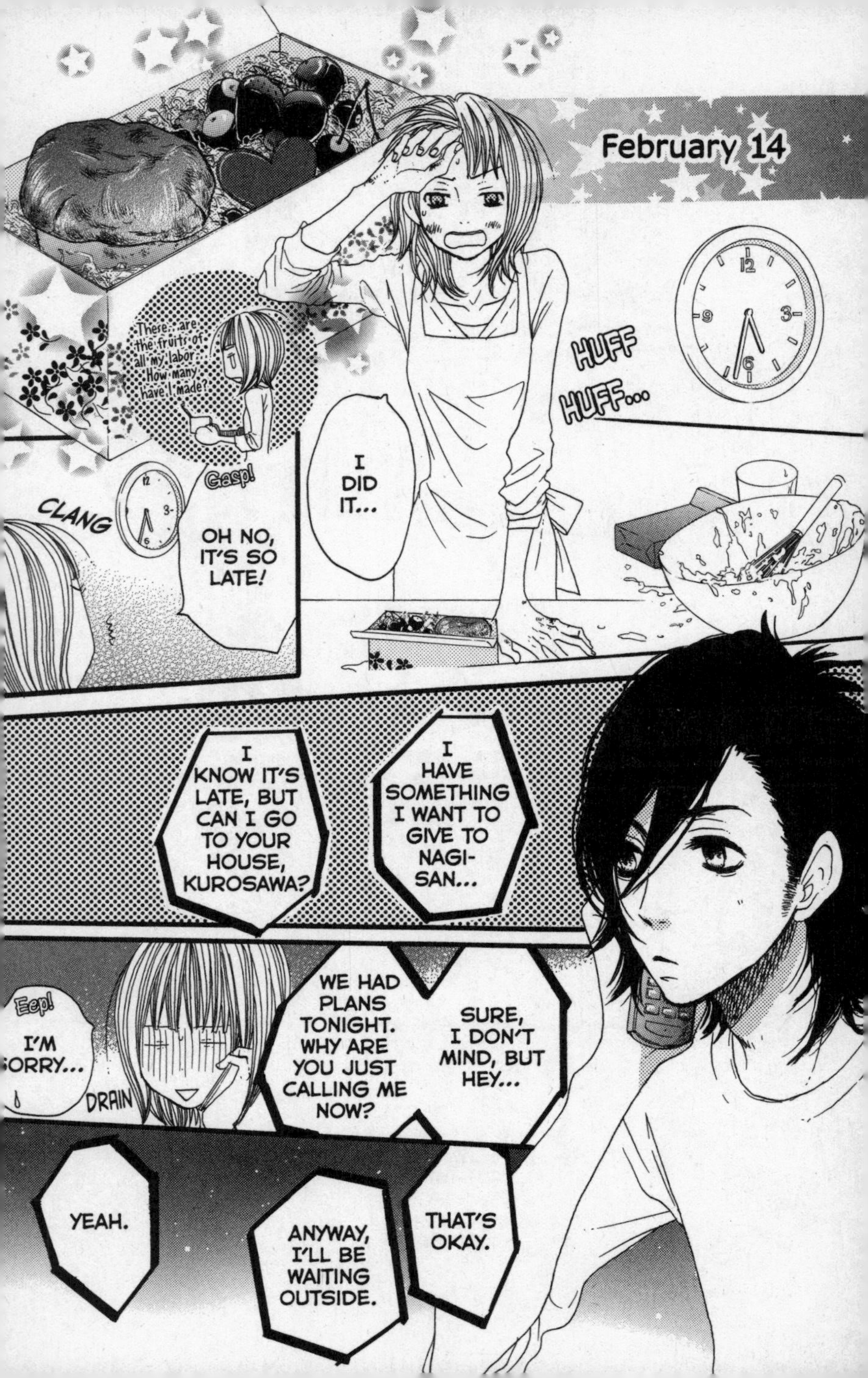
February 14
HUFF HUFF...
I DID IT...
There are the fruits of all my labor. How many have I made?
Gasp!
OH NO, IT'S SO LATE!
CLANG
I HAVE SOMETHING I WANT TO GIVE TO NAGI-SAN...
I KNOW IT'S LATE, BUT CAN I GO TO YOUR HOUSE, KUROSAWA?
SURE, I DON'T MIND, BUT HEY...
WE HAD PLANS TONIGHT. WHY ARE YOU JUST CALLING ME NOW?
Eep!
I'M SORRY...
DRAIN
THAT'S OKAY.
ANYWAY, I'LL BE WAITING OUTSIDE.
YEAH.

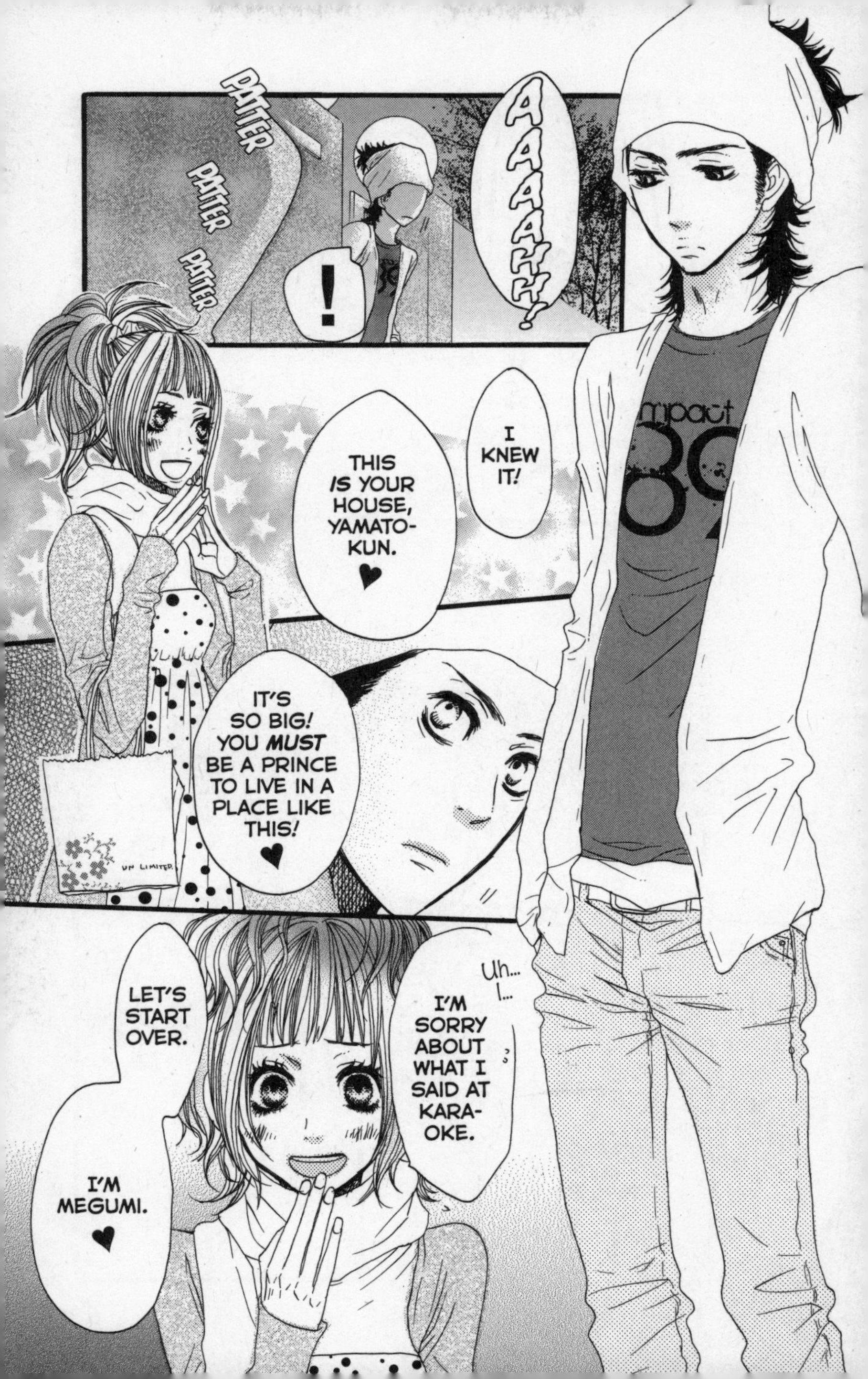
AAAAAH!
!
PATTER PATTER PATTER
I KNEW IT!
THIS *IS* YOUR HOUSE, YAMATO-KUN. ♥
IT'S SO BIG! YOU *MUST* BE A PRINCE TO LIVE IN A PLACE LIKE THIS! ♥
Uh... I...
I'M SORRY ABOUT WHAT I SAID AT KARAOKE.
LET'S START OVER.
I'M MEGUMI. ♥

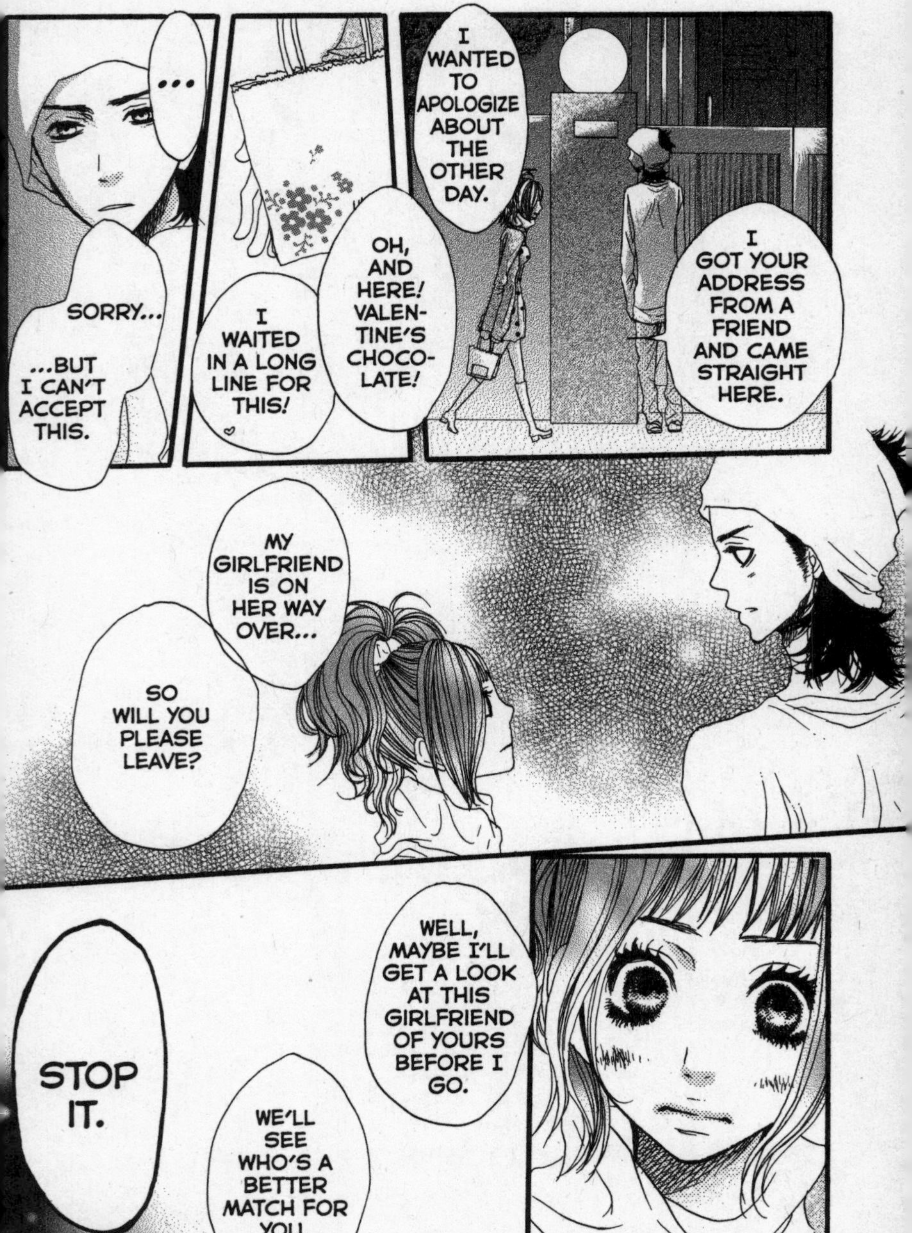
I GOT YOUR ADDRESS FROM A FRIEND AND CAME STRAIGHT HERE.
I WANTED TO APOLOGIZE ABOUT THE OTHER DAY.
OH, AND HERE! VALENTINE'S CHOCOLATE!
I WAITED IN A LONG LINE FOR THIS!
...
SORRY...
...BUT I CAN'T ACCEPT THIS.
MY GIRLFRIEND IS ON HER WAY OVER...
SO WILL YOU PLEASE LEAVE?
WELL, MAYBE I'LL GET A LOOK AT THIS GIRLFRIEND OF YOURS BEFORE I GO.
WE'LL SEE WHO'S A BETTER MATCH FOR YOU.
STOP IT.

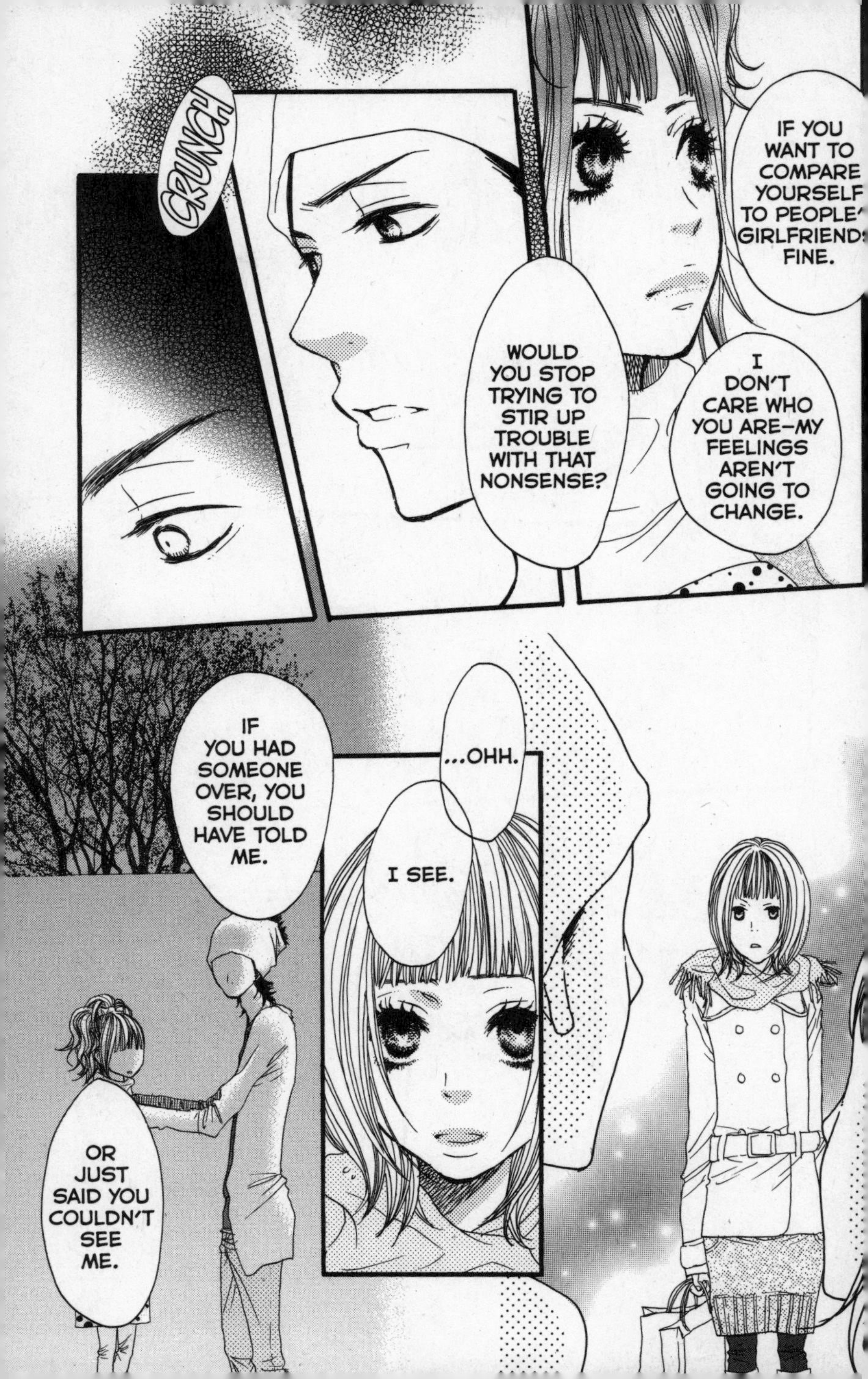
IF YOU WANT TO COMPARE YOURSELF TO PEOPLE' GIRLFRIEND FINE.
I DON'T CARE WHO YOU ARE—MY FEELINGS AREN'T GOING TO CHANGE.
WOULD YOU STOP TRYING TO STIR UP TROUBLE WITH THAT NONSENSE?
CRUNCH
...OHH.
I SEE.
IF YOU HAD SOMEONE OVER, YOU SHOULD HAVE TOLD ME.
OR JUST SAID YOU COULDN'T SEE ME.

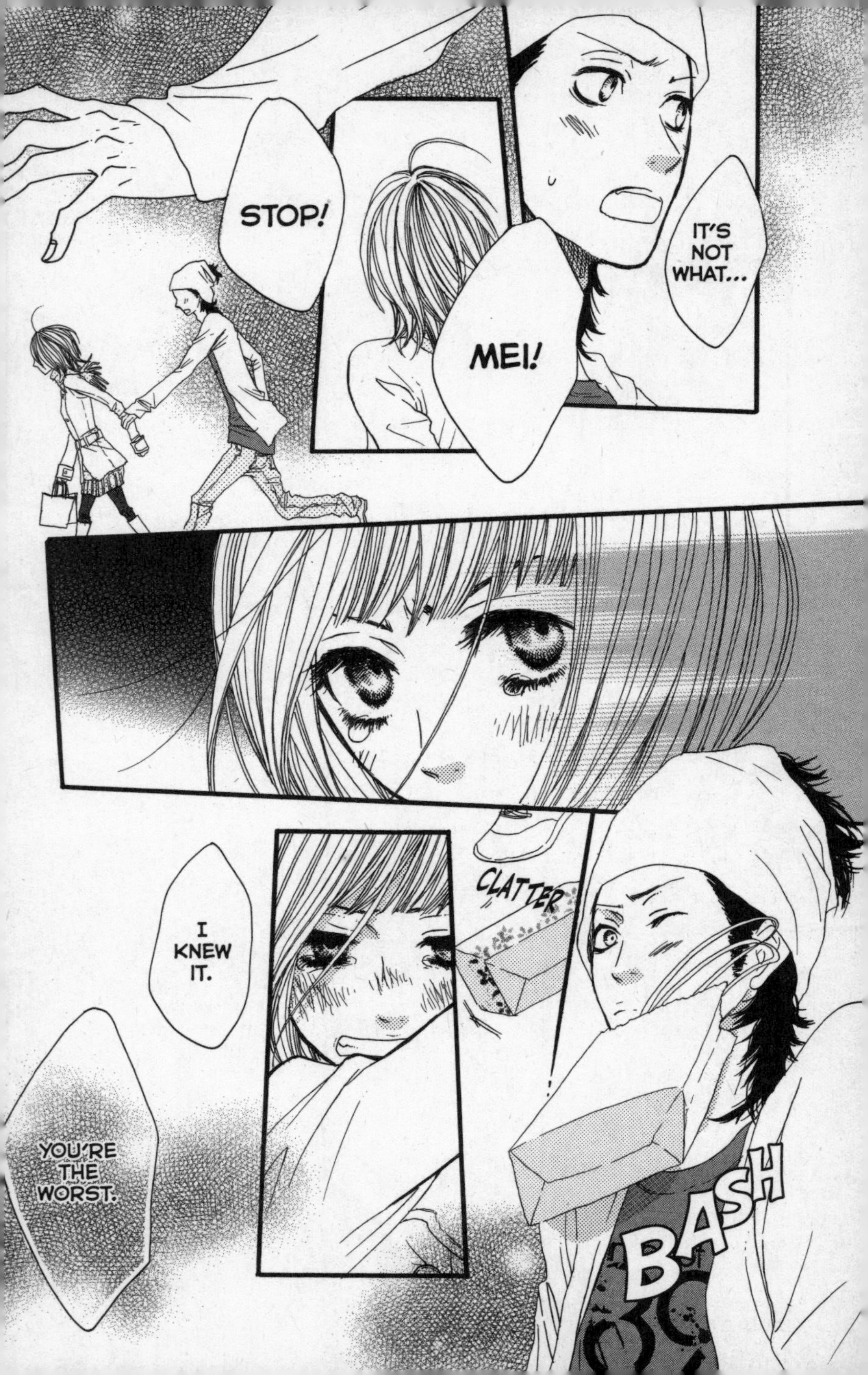
IT'S NOT WHAT...
MEI!
STOP!
CLATTER
BASH
I KNEW IT.
YOU'RE THE WORST.

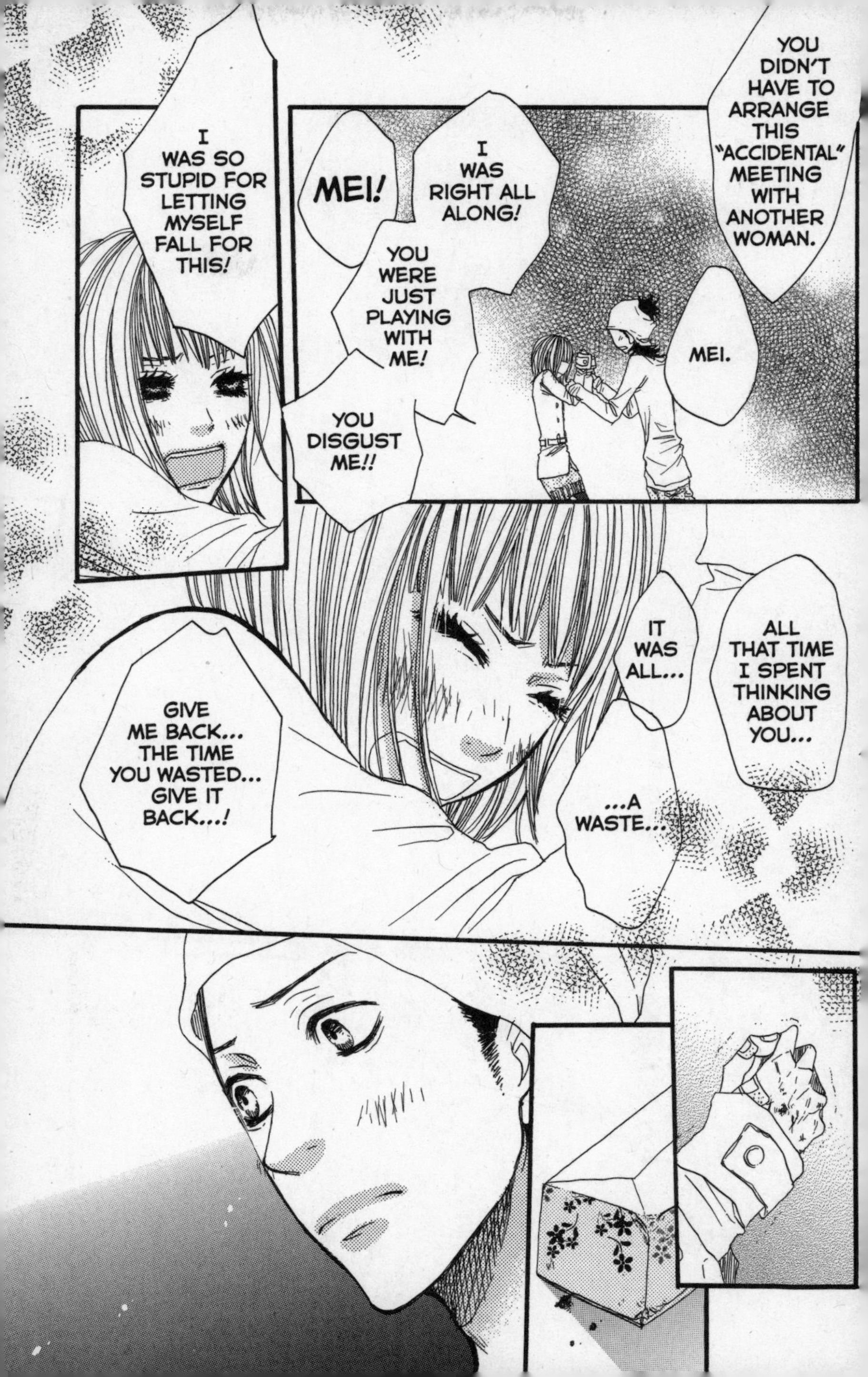
YOU DIDN'T HAVE TO ARRANGE THIS "ACCIDENTAL" MEETING WITH ANOTHER WOMAN.
MEI.
I WAS RIGHT ALL ALONG!
MEI!
YOU WERE JUST PLAYING WITH ME!
YOU DISGUST ME!!
I WAS SO STUPID FOR LETTING MYSELF FALL FOR THIS!
ALL THAT TIME I SPENT THINKING ABOUT YOU...
IT WAS ALL...
...A WASTE...
GIVE ME BACK... THE TIME YOU WASTED... GIVE IT BACK...!

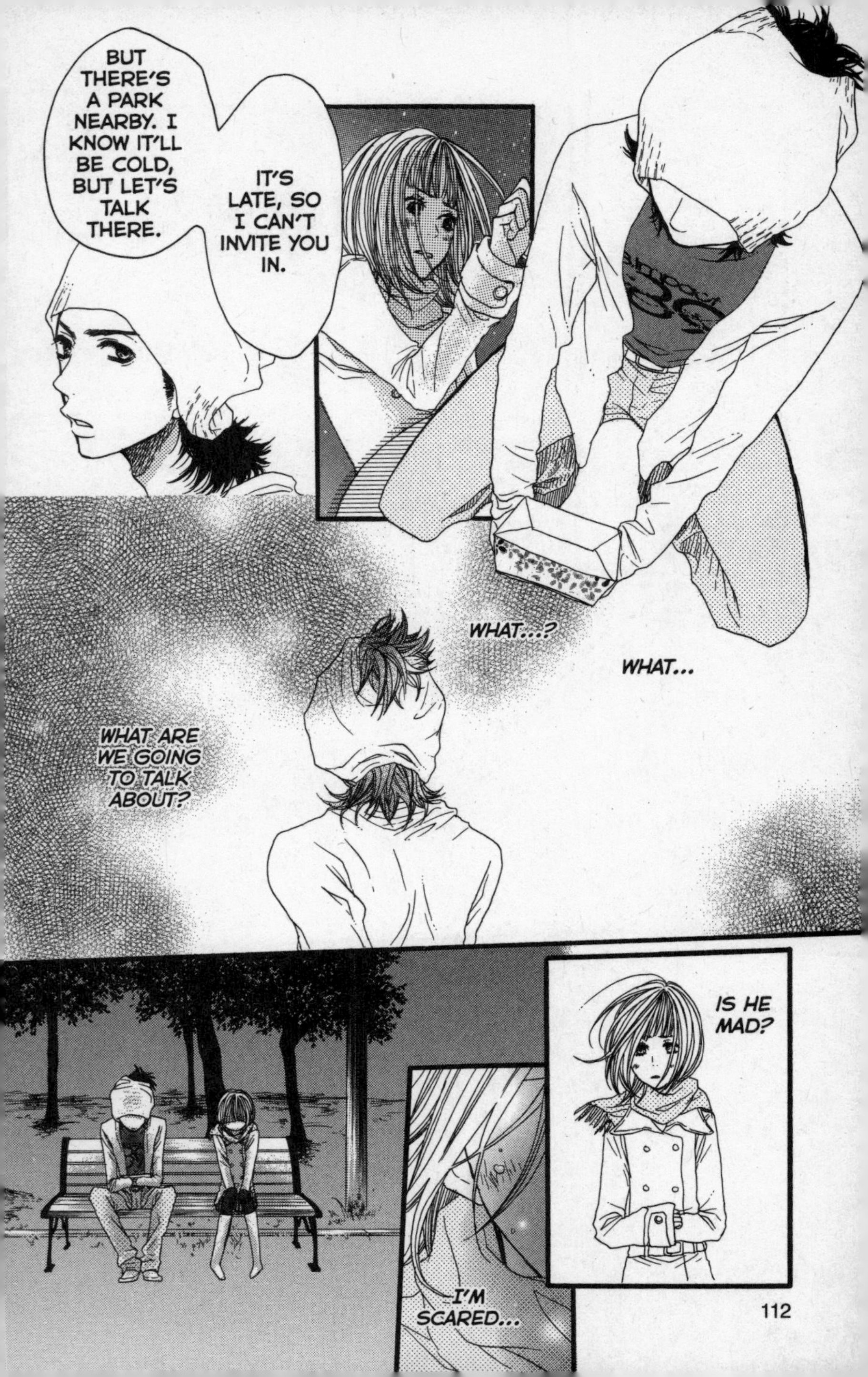
IT'S LATE, SO I CAN'T INVITE YOU IN.
BUT THERE'S A PARK NEARBY. I KNOW IT'LL BE COLD, BUT LET'S TALK THERE.
WHAT...
WHAT...?
WHAT ARE WE GOING TO TALK ABOUT?
IS HE MAD?
I'M SCARED...

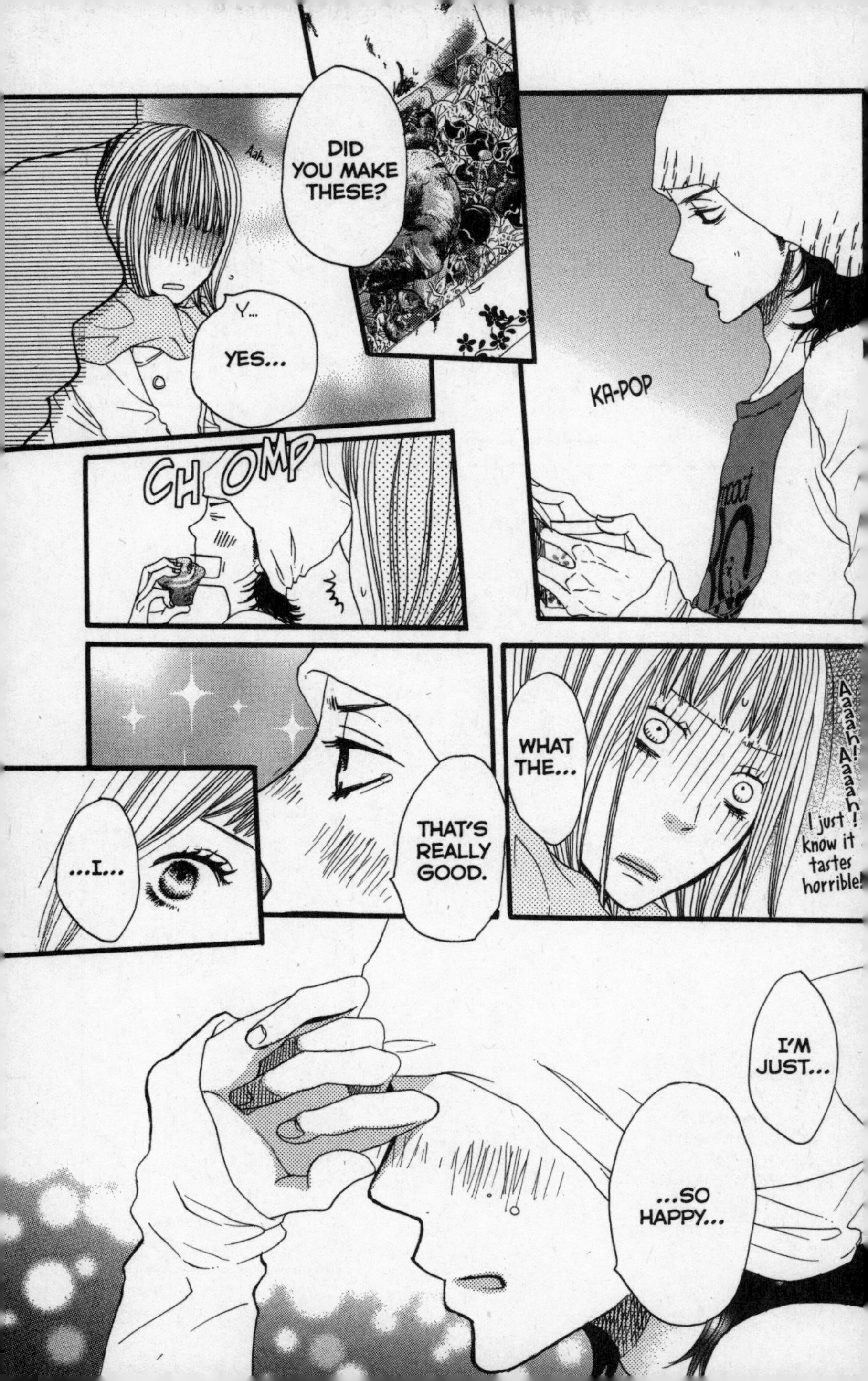

DID YOU MAKE THESE?
Aah...
Y...
YES...
KA-POP
CHOMP
WHAT THE...
Aaaah! Aaaah! I just know it tastes horrible!
THAT'S REALLY GOOD.
...I...
I'M JUST...
...SO HAPPY...

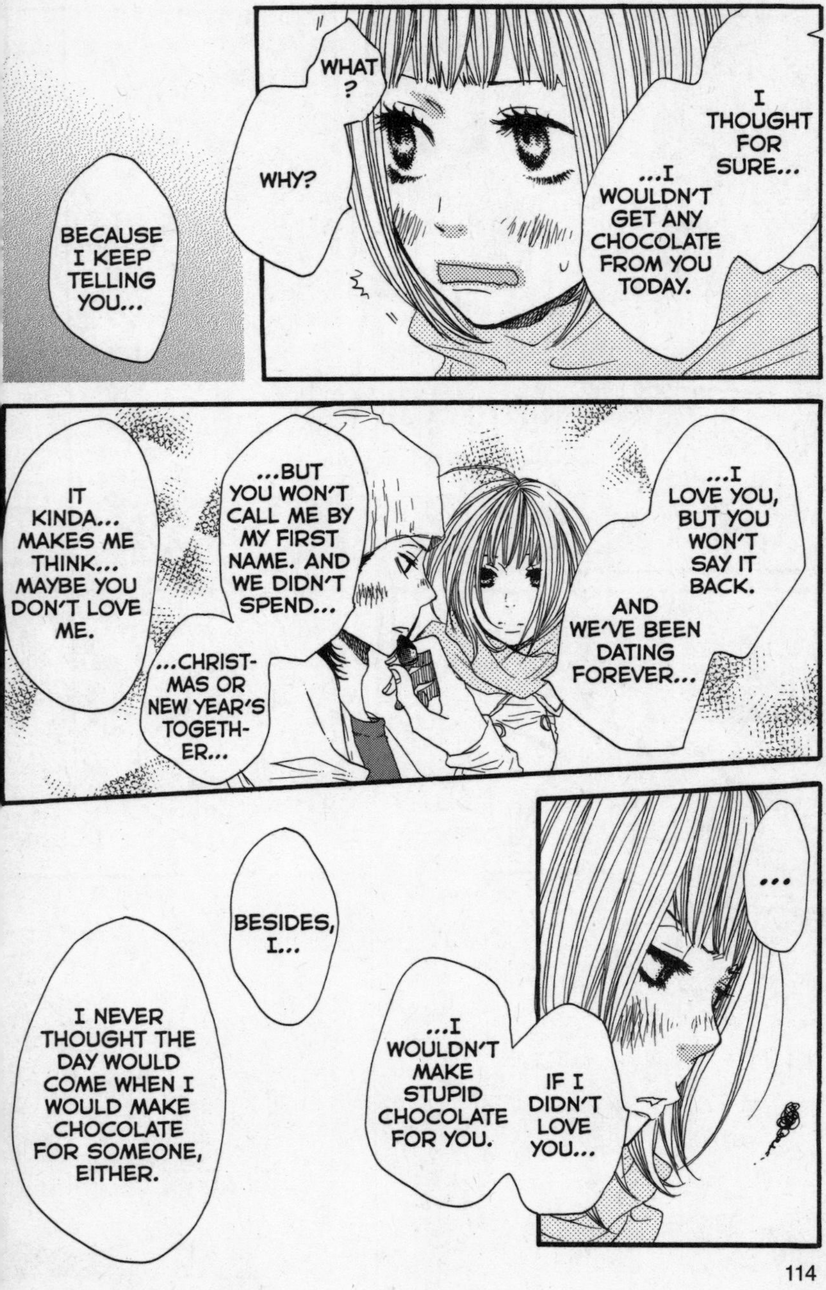
I THOUGHT FOR SURE...
...I WOULDN'T GET ANY CHOCOLATE FROM YOU TODAY.
WHAT?
WHY?
BECAUSE I KEEP TELLING YOU...
...I LOVE YOU, BUT YOU WON'T SAY IT BACK.
AND WE'VE BEEN DATING FOREVER...
...BUT YOU WON'T CALL ME BY MY FIRST NAME. AND WE DIDN'T SPEND...
...CHRIST-MAS OR NEW YEAR'S TOGETH-ER...
IT KINDA... MAKES ME THINK... MAYBE YOU DON'T LOVE ME.
...
IF I DIDN'T LOVE YOU...
...I WOULDN'T MAKE STUPID CHOCOLATE FOR YOU.
BESIDES, I...
I NEVER THOUGHT THE DAY WOULD COME WHEN I WOULD MAKE CHOCOLATE FOR SOMEONE, EITHER.

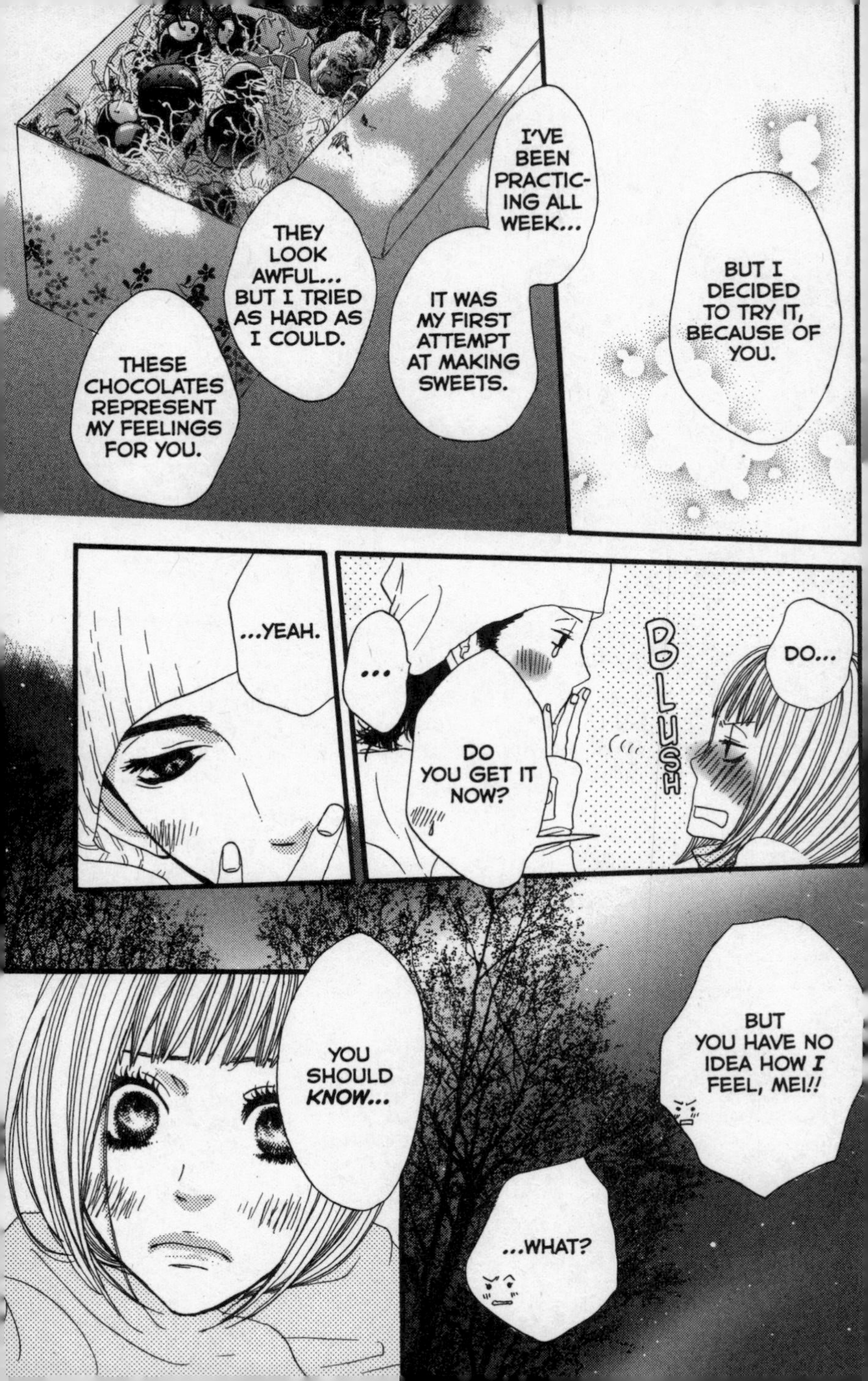
BUT I DECIDED TO TRY IT, BECAUSE OF YOU.
I'VE BEEN PRACTIC-ING ALL WEEK...
IT WAS MY FIRST ATTEMPT AT MAKING SWEETS.
THEY LOOK AWFUL... BUT I TRIED AS HARD AS I COULD.
THESE CHOCOLATES REPRESENT MY FEELINGS FOR YOU.
DO...
BLUSH
...
DO YOU GET IT NOW?
...YEAH.
BUT YOU HAVE NO IDEA HOW *I* FEEL, MEI!!
...WHAT?
YOU SHOULD *KNOW*...

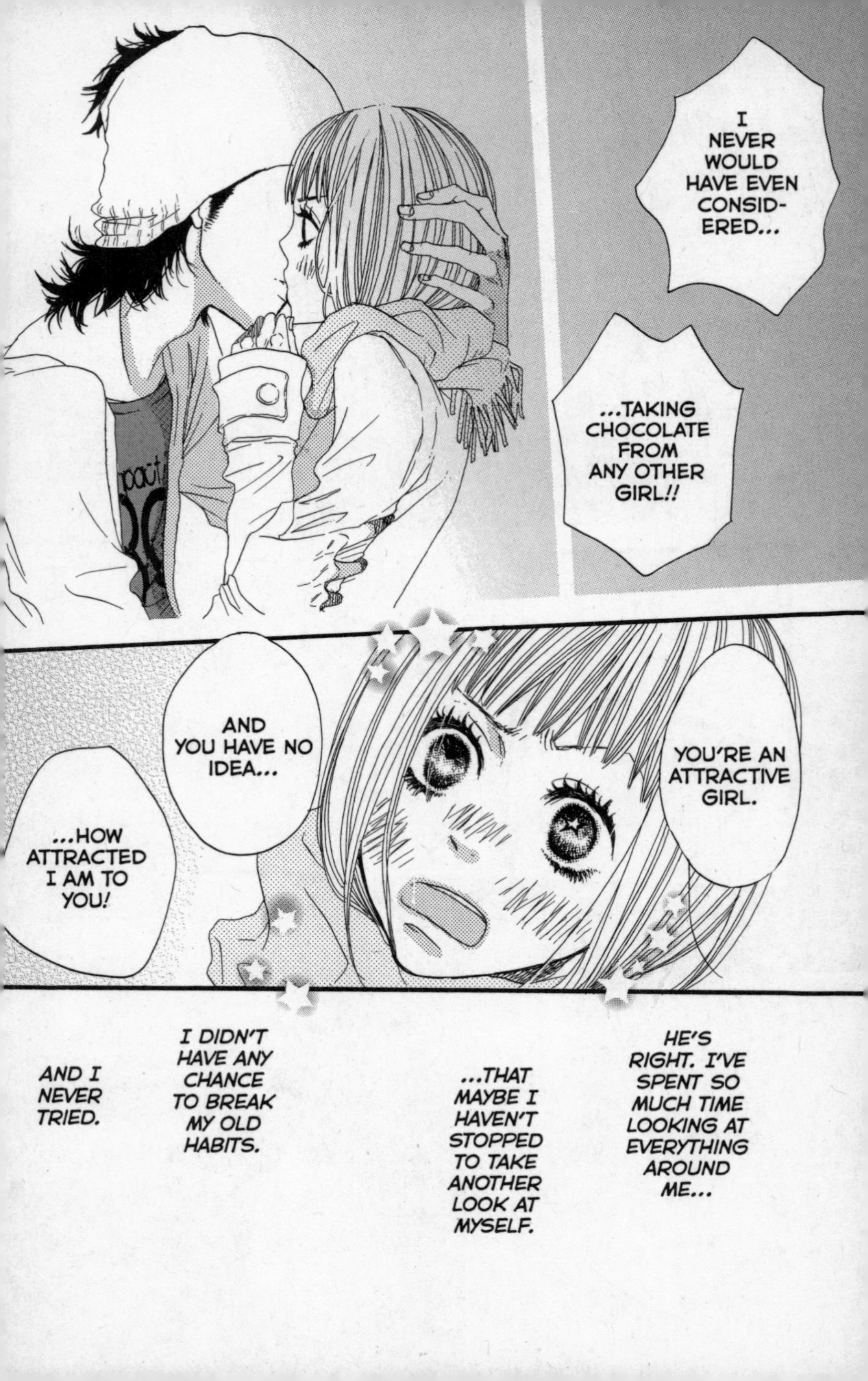

I NEVER WOULD HAVE EVEN CONSID- ERED...
...TAKING CHOCOLATE FROM ANY OTHER GIRL!!
YOU'RE AN ATTRACTIVE GIRL.
AND YOU HAVE NO IDEA...
...HOW ATTRACTED I AM TO YOU!
HE'S RIGHT. I'VE SPENT SO MUCH TIME LOOKING AT EVERYTHING AROUND ME...
...THAT MAYBE I HAVEN'T STOPPED TO TAKE ANOTHER LOOK AT MYSELF.
I DIDN'T HAVE ANY CHANCE TO BREAK MY OLD HABITS.
AND I NEVER TRIED.

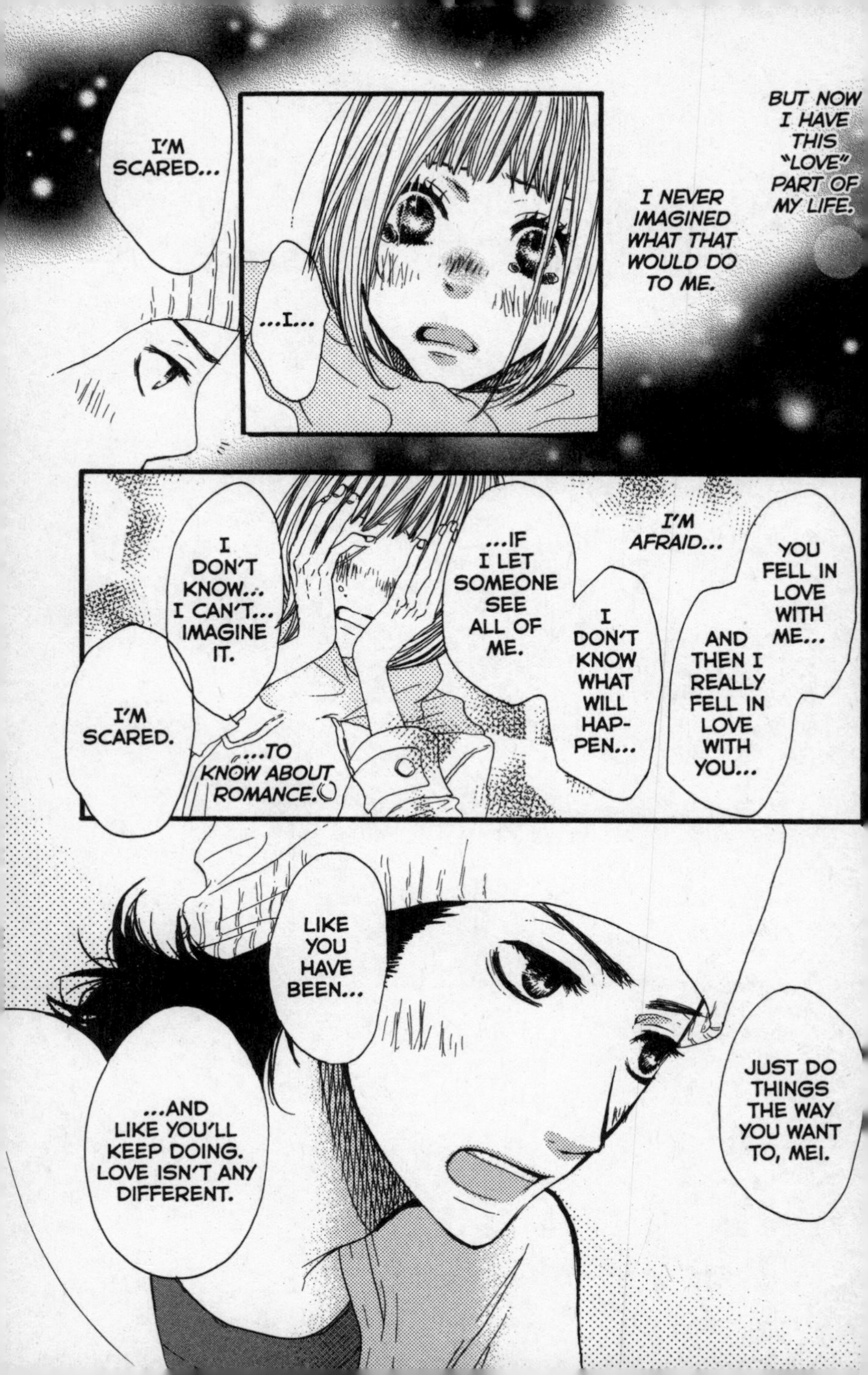
BUT NOW I HAVE THIS "LOVE" PART OF MY LIFE.
I NEVER IMAGINED WHAT THAT WOULD DO TO ME.
...I...
I'M SCARED...
YOU FELL IN LOVE WITH ME...
AND THEN I REALLY FELL IN LOVE WITH YOU...
I'M AFRAID...
I DON'T KNOW WHAT WILL HAP-PEN...
...IF I LET SOMEONE SEE ALL OF ME.
I DON'T KNOW... I CAN'T... IMAGINE IT.
...TO KNOW ABOUT ROMANCE.
I'M SCARED.
JUST DO THINGS THE WAY YOU WANT TO, MEI.
LIKE YOU HAVE BEEN...
...AND LIKE YOU'LL KEEP DOING. LOVE ISN'T ANY DIFFERENT.

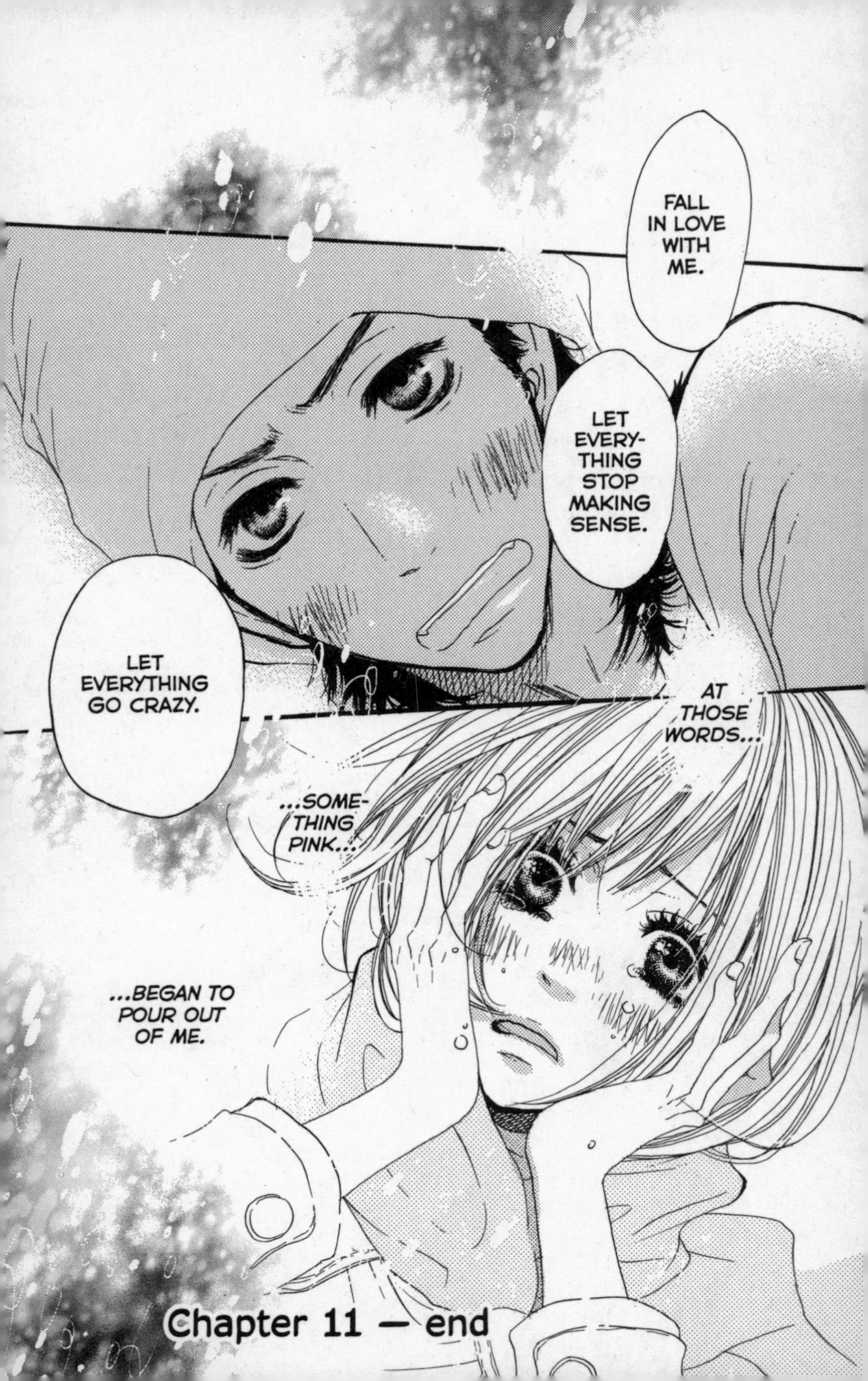
FALL IN LOVE WITH ME.
LET EVERY-THING STOP MAKING SENSE.
LET EVERYTHING GO CRAZY.
AT THOSE WORDS...
...SOME-THING PINK...
...BEGAN TO POUR OUT OF ME.
Chapter 11 — end

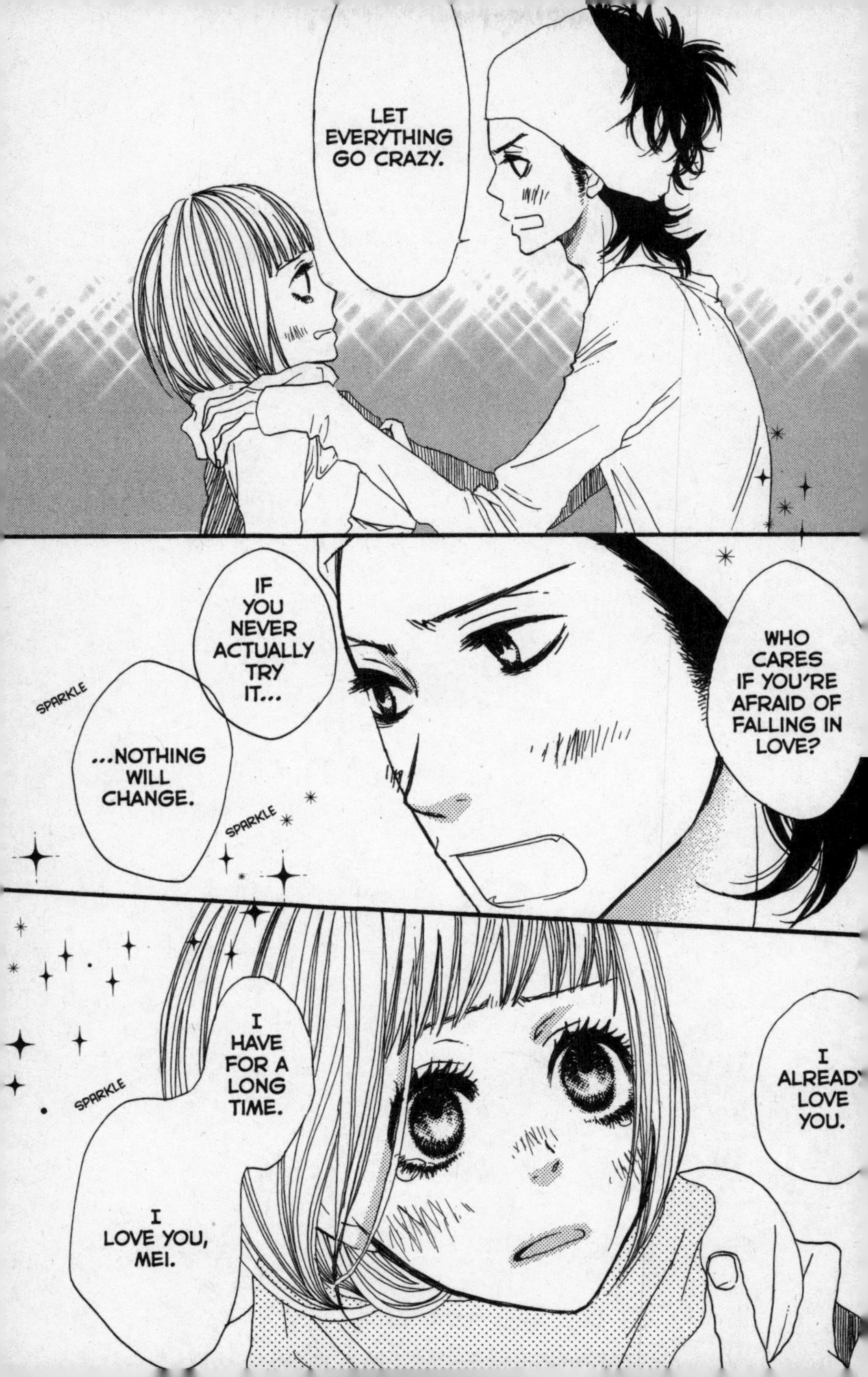
LET EVERYTHING GO CRAZY.
WHO CARES IF YOU'RE AFRAID OF FALLING IN LOVE?
IF YOU NEVER ACTUALLY TRY IT...
SPARKLE
...NOTHING WILL CHANGE.
SPARKLE
I ALREADY LOVE YOU.
I HAVE FOR A LONG TIME.
SPARKLE
I LOVE YOU, MEI.

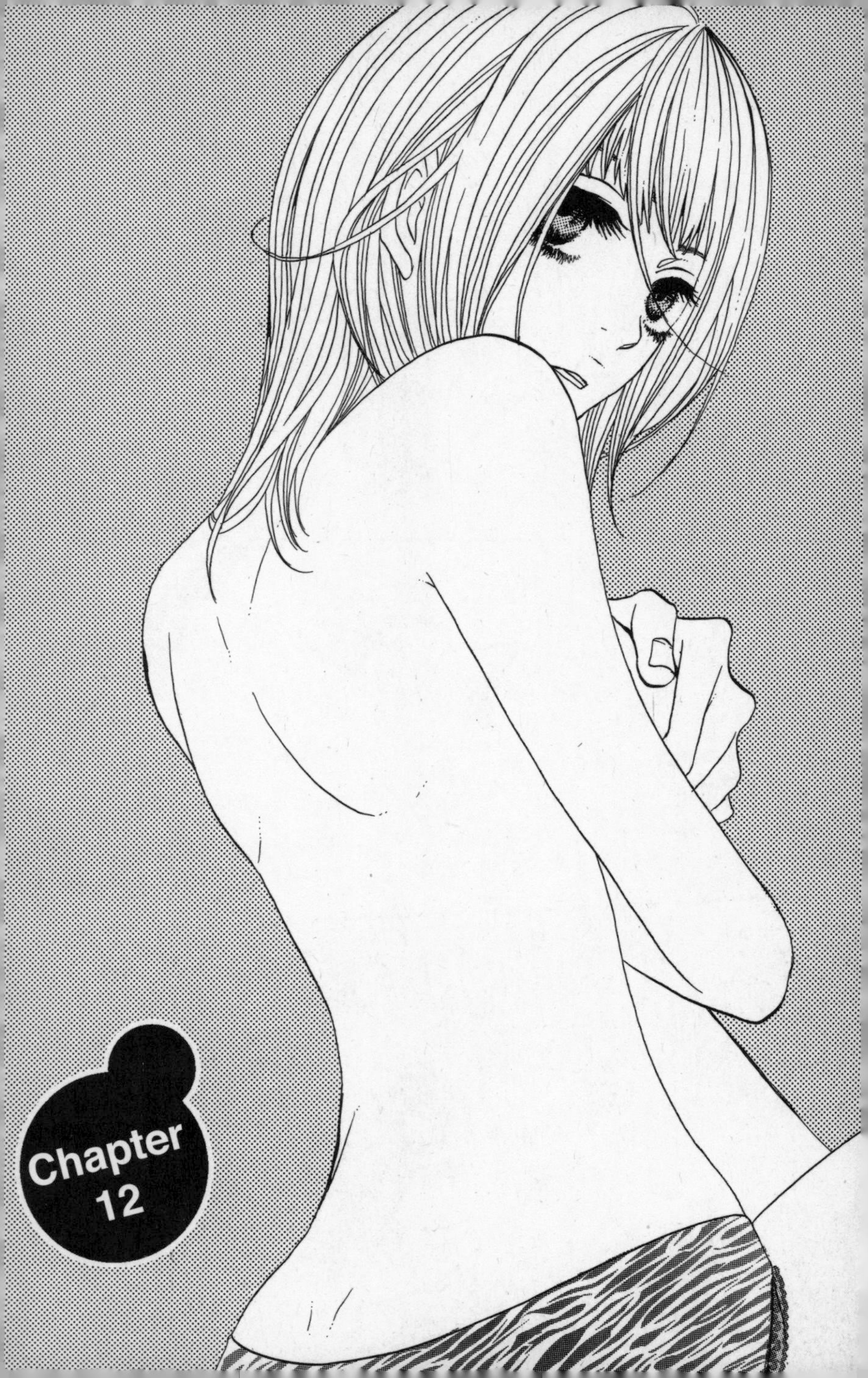
Chapter
12

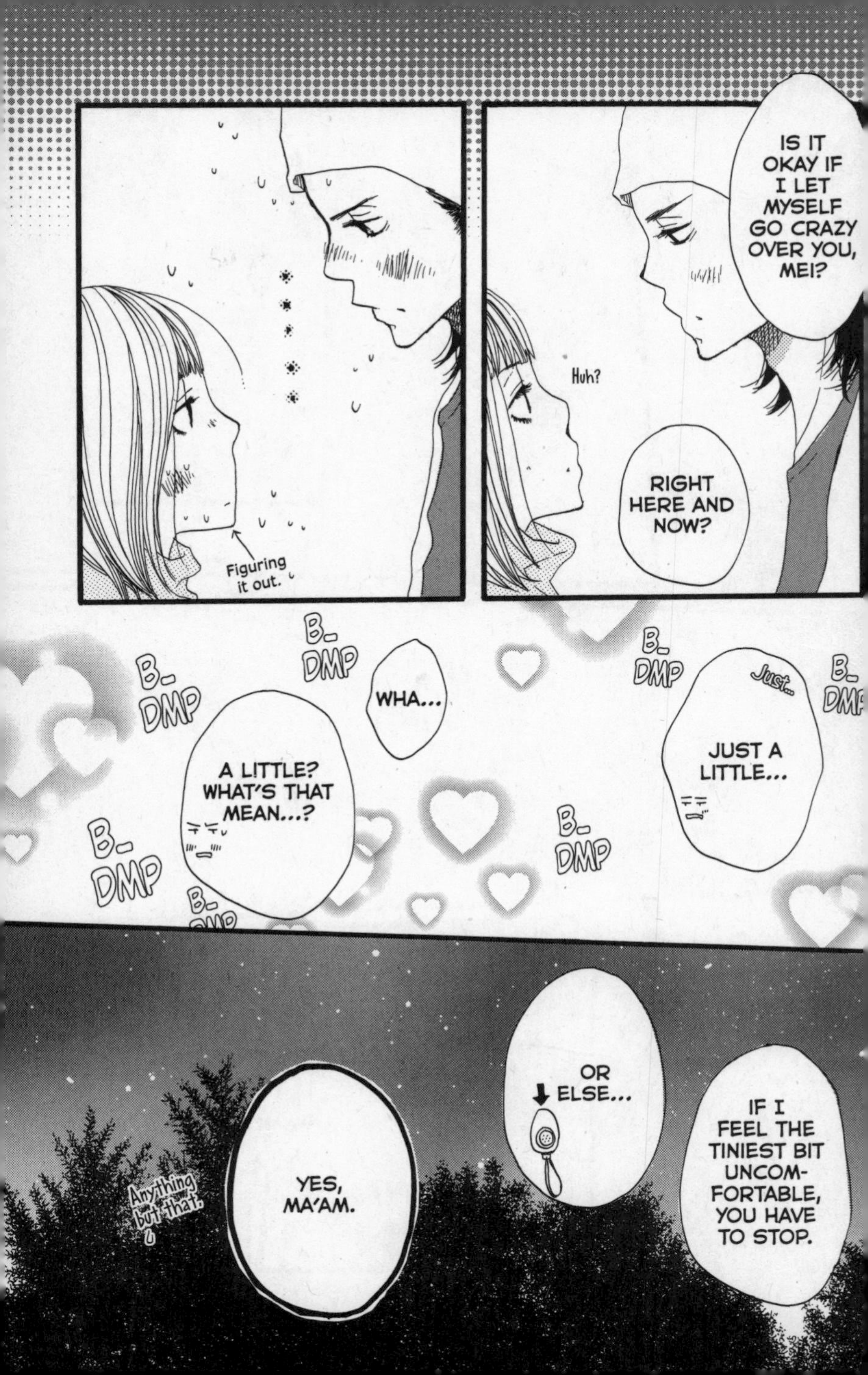
IS IT OKAY IF I LET MYSELF GO CRAZY OVER YOU, MEI?
Huh?
RIGHT HERE AND NOW?
Figuring it out.
B-DMP
Just...
JUST A LITTLE...
B-DMP
B-DMP
WHA...
B-DMP
B-DMP
A LITTLE? WHAT'S THAT MEAN...?
B-DMP
IF I FEEL THE TINIEST BIT UNCOM-FORTABLE, YOU HAVE TO STOP.
OR ELSE...
YES, MA'AM.
Anything but that.

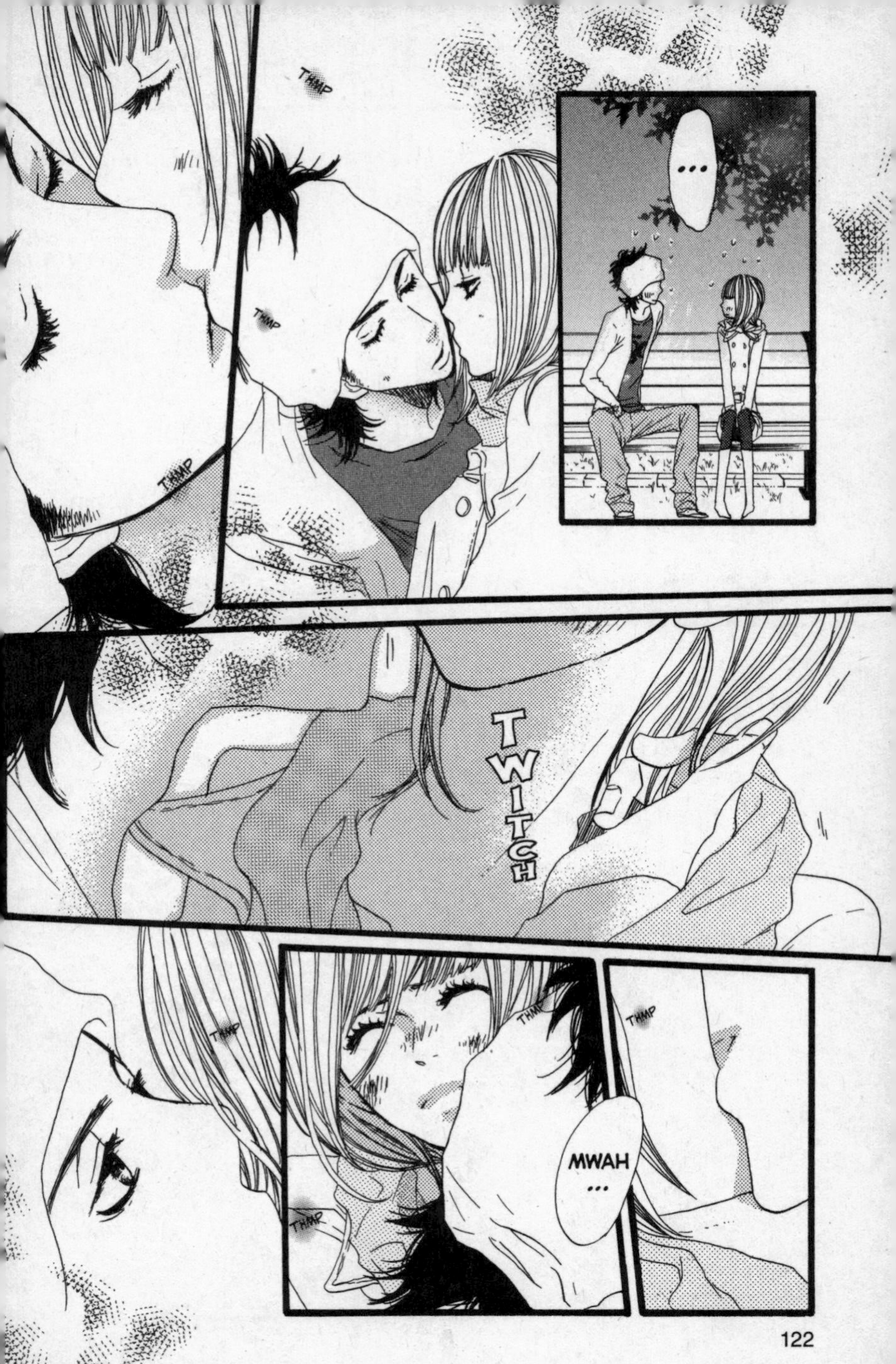
...
THMP
THMP
THMP
TWITCH
THMP
THMP
MWAH
...
THMP
THMP

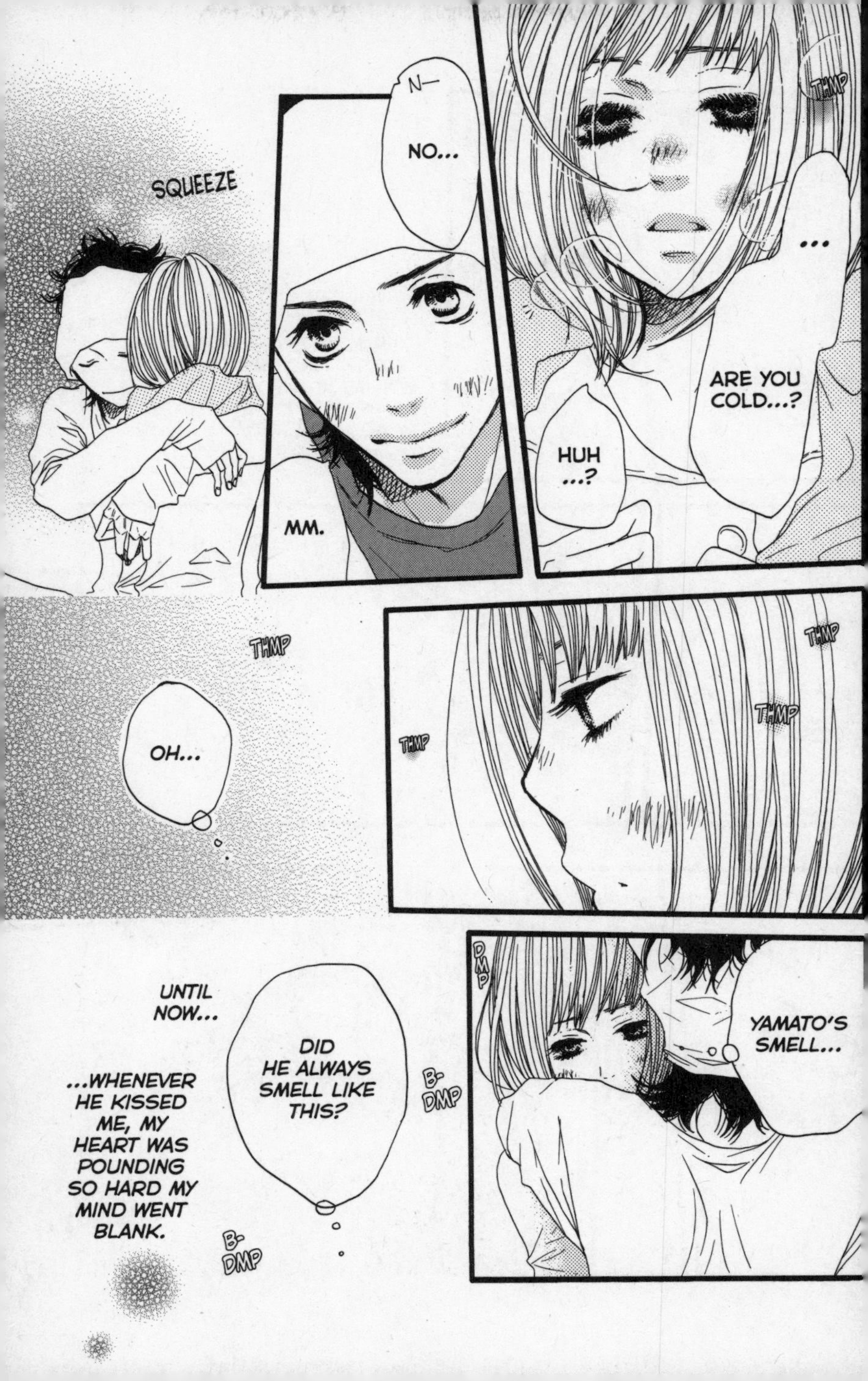
THMP
...
ARE YOU COLD...?
HUH ...?
N—
NO...
MM.
SQUEEZE
THMP
THMP
THMP
THMP
OH...
DMP
YAMATO'S SMELL...
B-DMP
DID HE ALWAYS SMELL LIKE THIS?
UNTIL NOW...
...WHENEVER HE KISSED ME, MY HEART WAS POUNDING SO HARD MY MIND WENT BLANK.
B-DMP

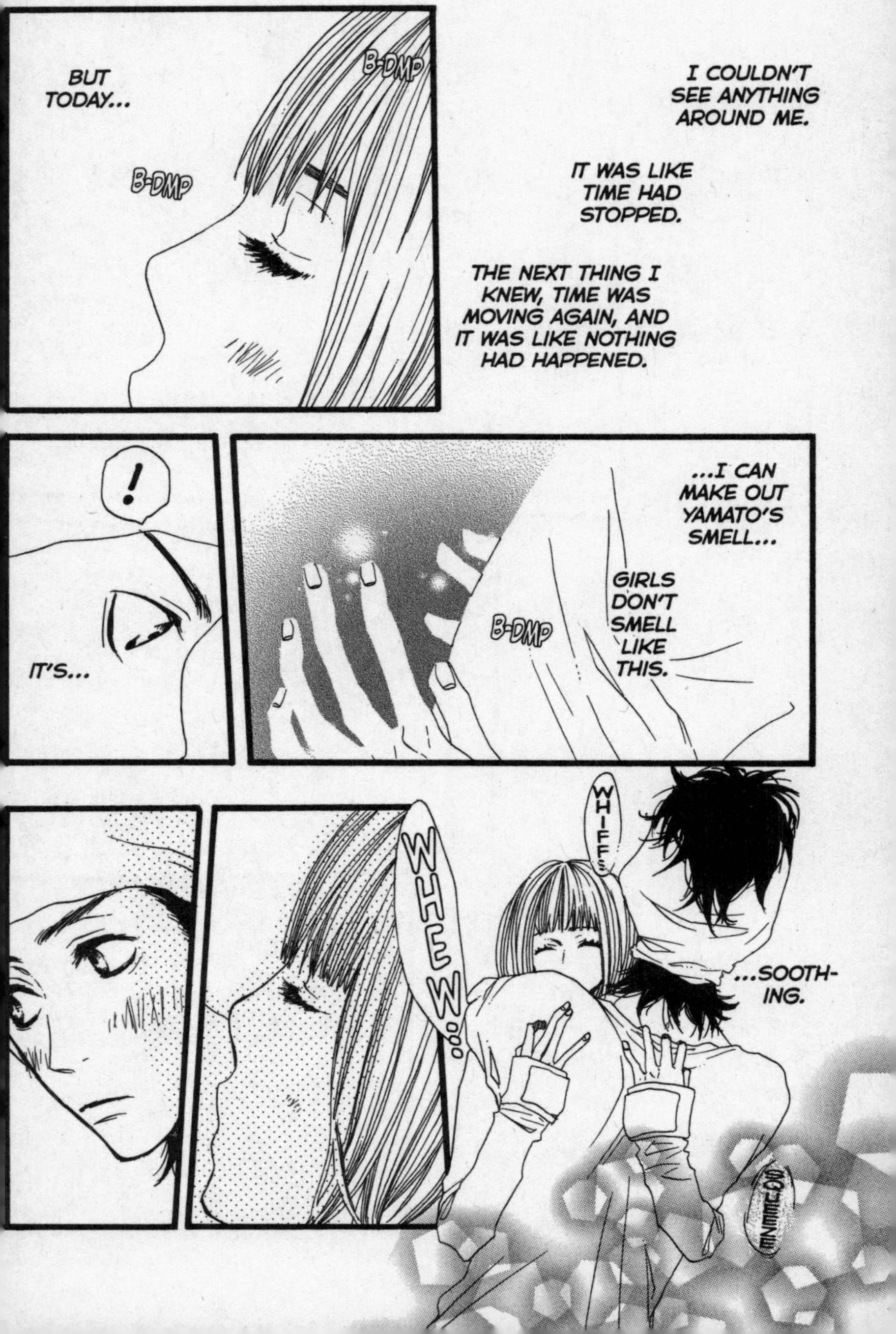
I COULDN'T SEE ANYTHING AROUND ME.
IT WAS LIKE TIME HAD STOPPED.
THE NEXT THING I KNEW, TIME WAS MOVING AGAIN, AND IT WAS LIKE NOTHING HAD HAPPENED.
B-DMP
BUT TODAY...
B-DMP
...I CAN MAKE OUT YAMATO'S SMELL...
GIRLS DON'T SMELL LIKE THIS.
B-DMP
!
IT'S...
WHIFF
...SOOTH-ING.
WHEW...

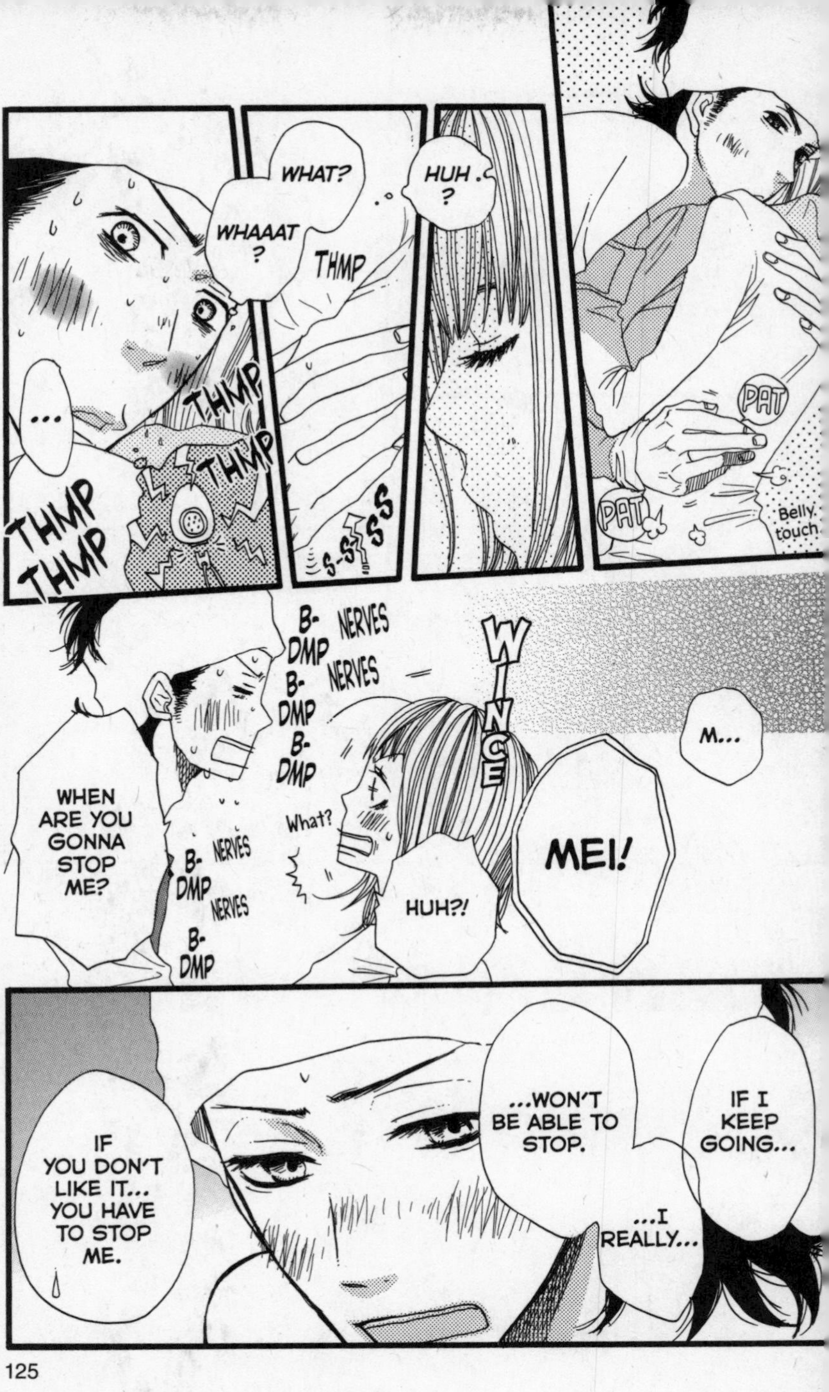
PAT
PAT
Belly touch
HUH ?
WHAT?
WHAAAT ?
THMP
S-S-S
...
THMP
THMP
THMP THMP
M...
MEI!
WINCE
HUH?!
What?
B- DMP
NERVES
B- DMP
NERVES
B- DMP
B- DMP
NERVES
B- DMP
NERVES
B- DMP
WHEN ARE YOU GONNA STOP ME?
IF I KEEP GOING...
...I REALLY...
...WON'T BE ABLE TO STOP.
IF YOU DON'T LIKE IT... YOU HAVE TO STOP ME.

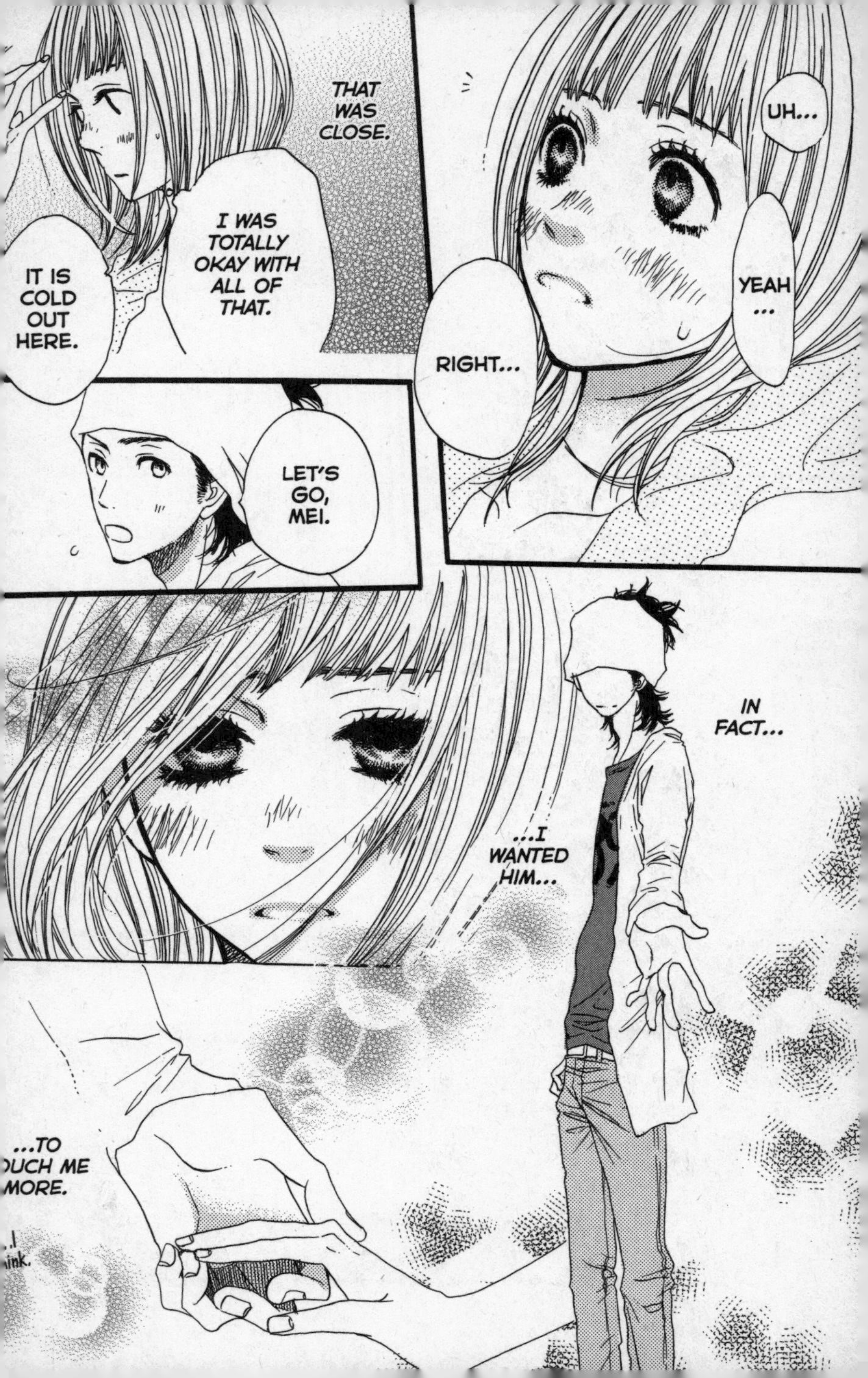
UH...
YEAH...
RIGHT...
THAT WAS CLOSE.
I WAS TOTALLY OKAY WITH ALL OF THAT.
IT IS COLD OUT HERE.
LET'S GO, MEI.
IN FACT...
...I WANTED HIM...
...TO
OUCH ME
MORE.
..I
hink.

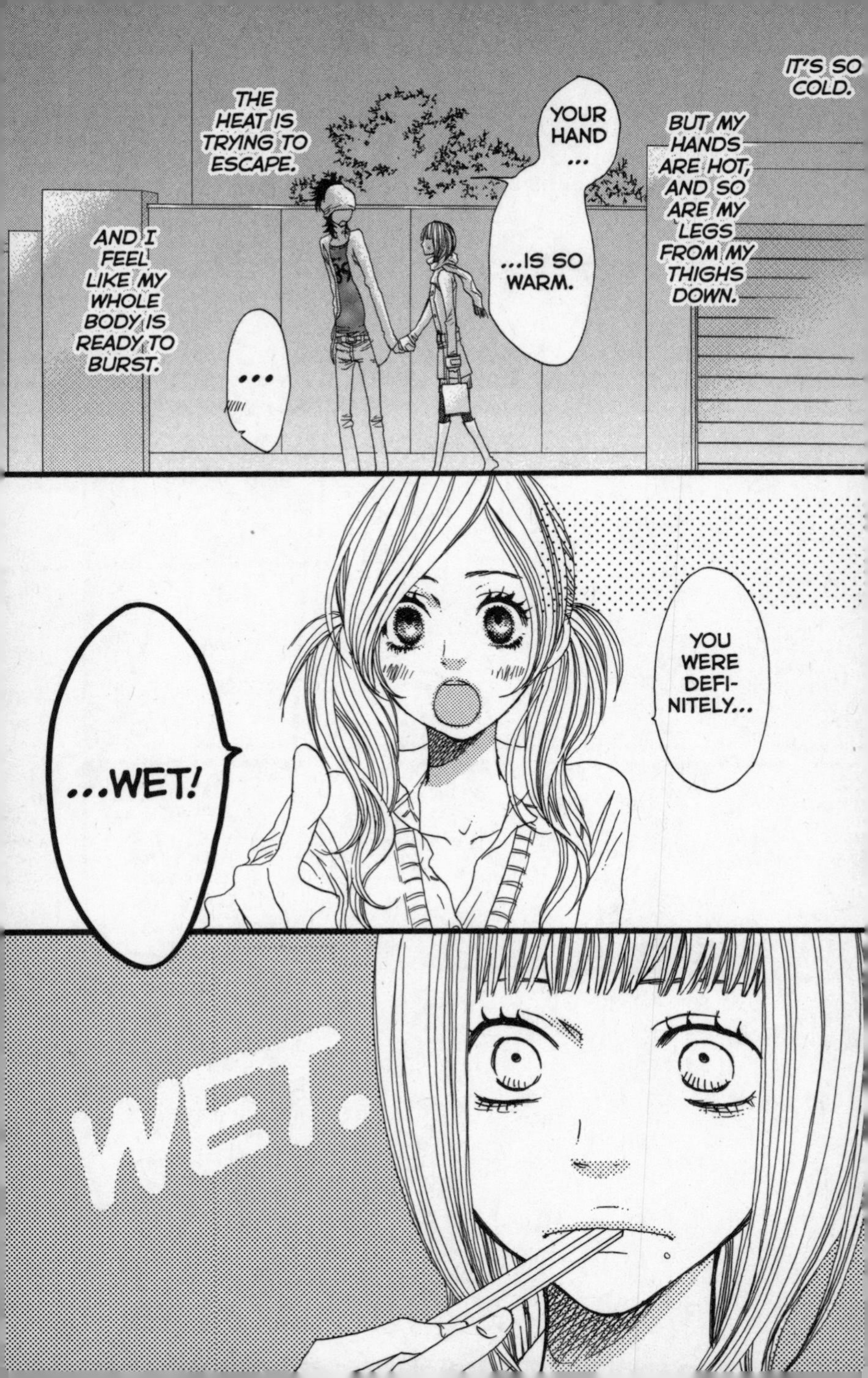
IT'S SO COLD.
BUT MY HANDS ARE HOT, AND SO ARE MY LEGS FROM MY THIGHS DOWN.
YOUR HAND...
...IS SO WARM.
THE HEAT IS TRYING TO ESCAPE.
...
AND I FEEL LIKE MY WHOLE BODY IS READY TO BURST.
YOU WERE DEFINITELY...
...WET!
WET.

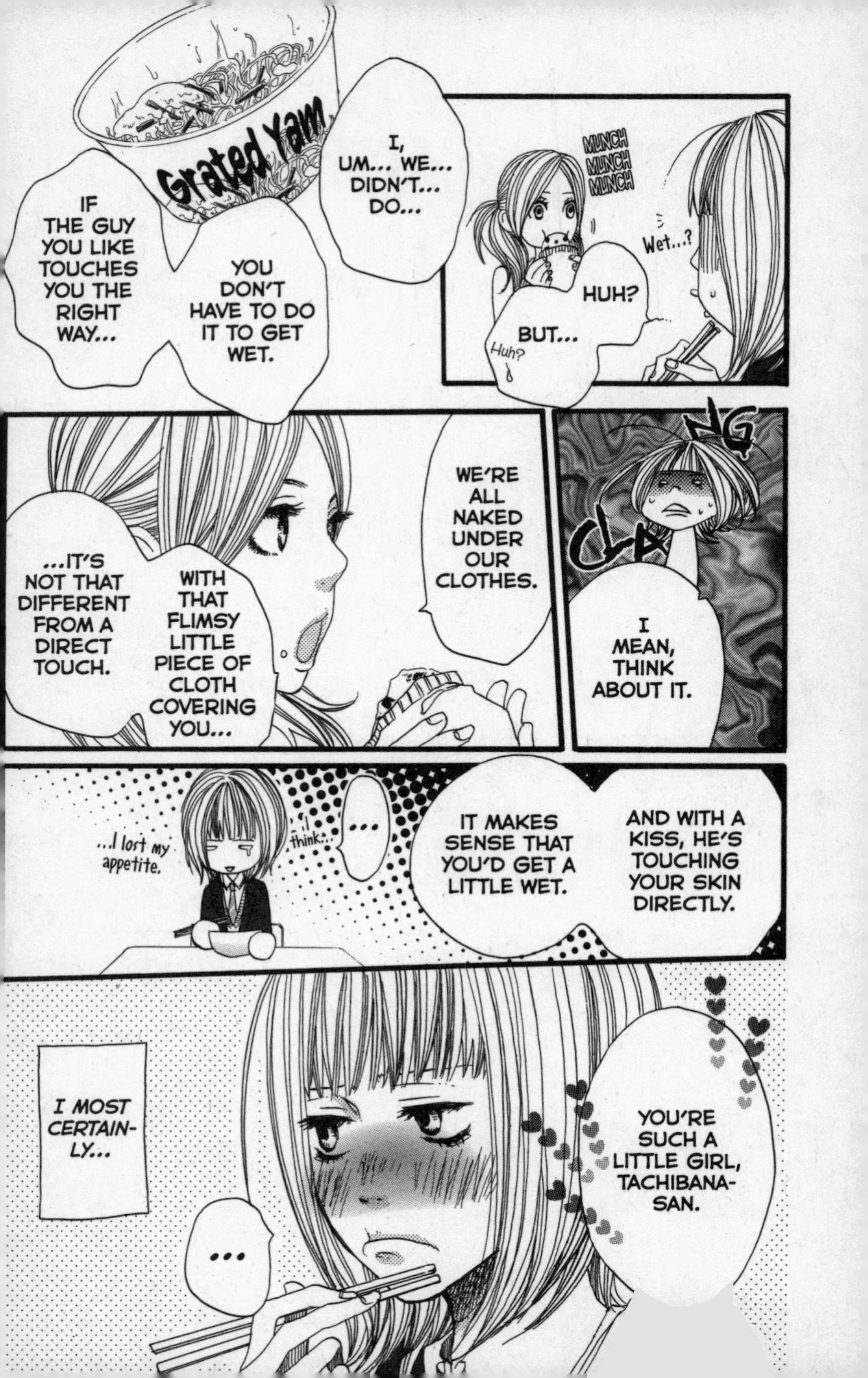
MUNCH MUNCH MUNCH
Wet...?
HUH?
BUT...
Huh?
I, UM... WE... DIDN'T... DO...
Grated Yam
IF THE GUY YOU LIKE TOUCHES YOU THE RIGHT WAY...
YOU DON'T HAVE TO DO IT TO GET WET.
CLANG
I MEAN, THINK ABOUT IT.
WE'RE ALL NAKED UNDER OUR CLOTHES.
WITH THAT FLIMSY LITTLE PIECE OF CLOTH COVERING YOU...
...IT'S NOT THAT DIFFERENT FROM A DIRECT TOUCH.
AND WITH A KISS, HE'S TOUCHING YOUR SKIN DIRECTLY.
IT MAKES SENSE THAT YOU'D GET A LITTLE WET.
...
I think...
...I lost my appetite.
YOU'RE SUCH A LITTLE GIRL, TACHIBANA-SAN.
...
I MOST CERTAIN-LY...

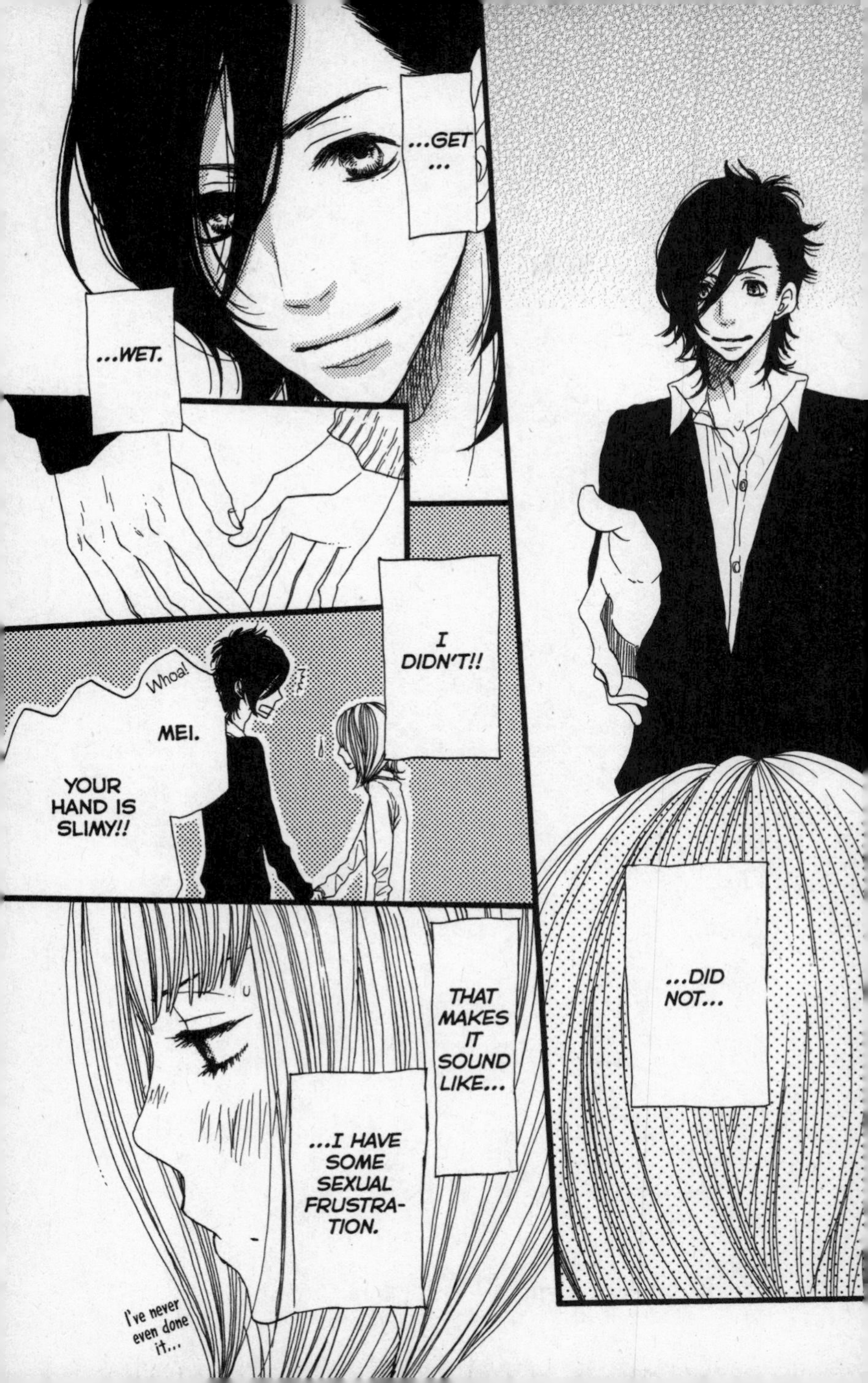
...DID NOT...
...GET...
...WET.
I DIDN'T!!
Whoa!
MEI.
YOUR HAND IS SLIMY!!
THAT MAKES IT SOUND LIKE...
...I HAVE SOME SEXUAL FRUSTRATION.
I've never even done it...

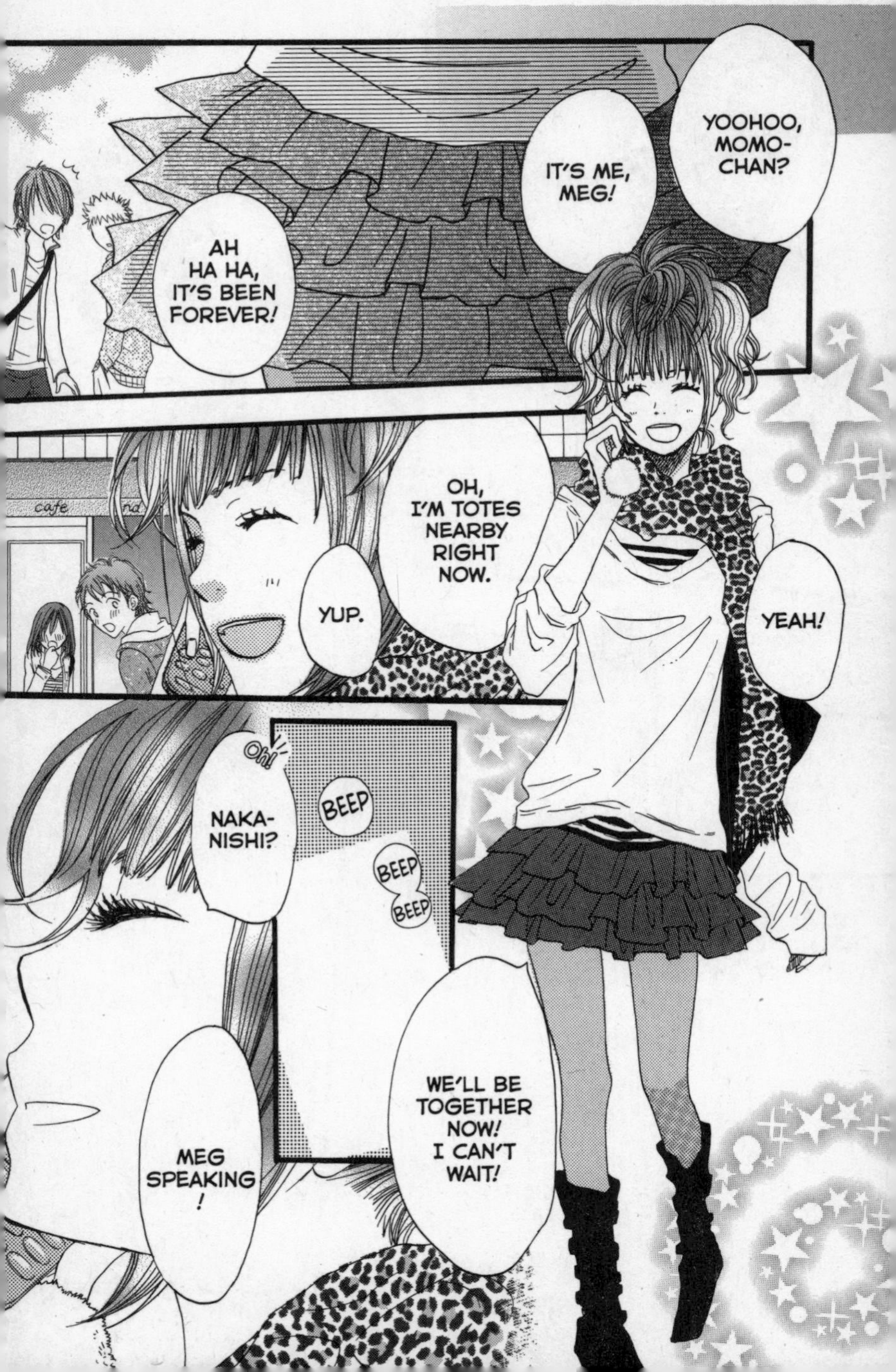
YOOHOO, MOMO-CHAN?
IT'S ME, MEG!
AH HA HA, IT'S BEEN FOREVER!
YEAH!
WE'LL BE TOGETHER NOW! I CAN'T WAIT!
OH, I'M TOTES NEARBY RIGHT NOW.
YUP.
BEEP
BEEP
BEEP
Oh!
NAKA-NISHI?
MEG SPEAKING!

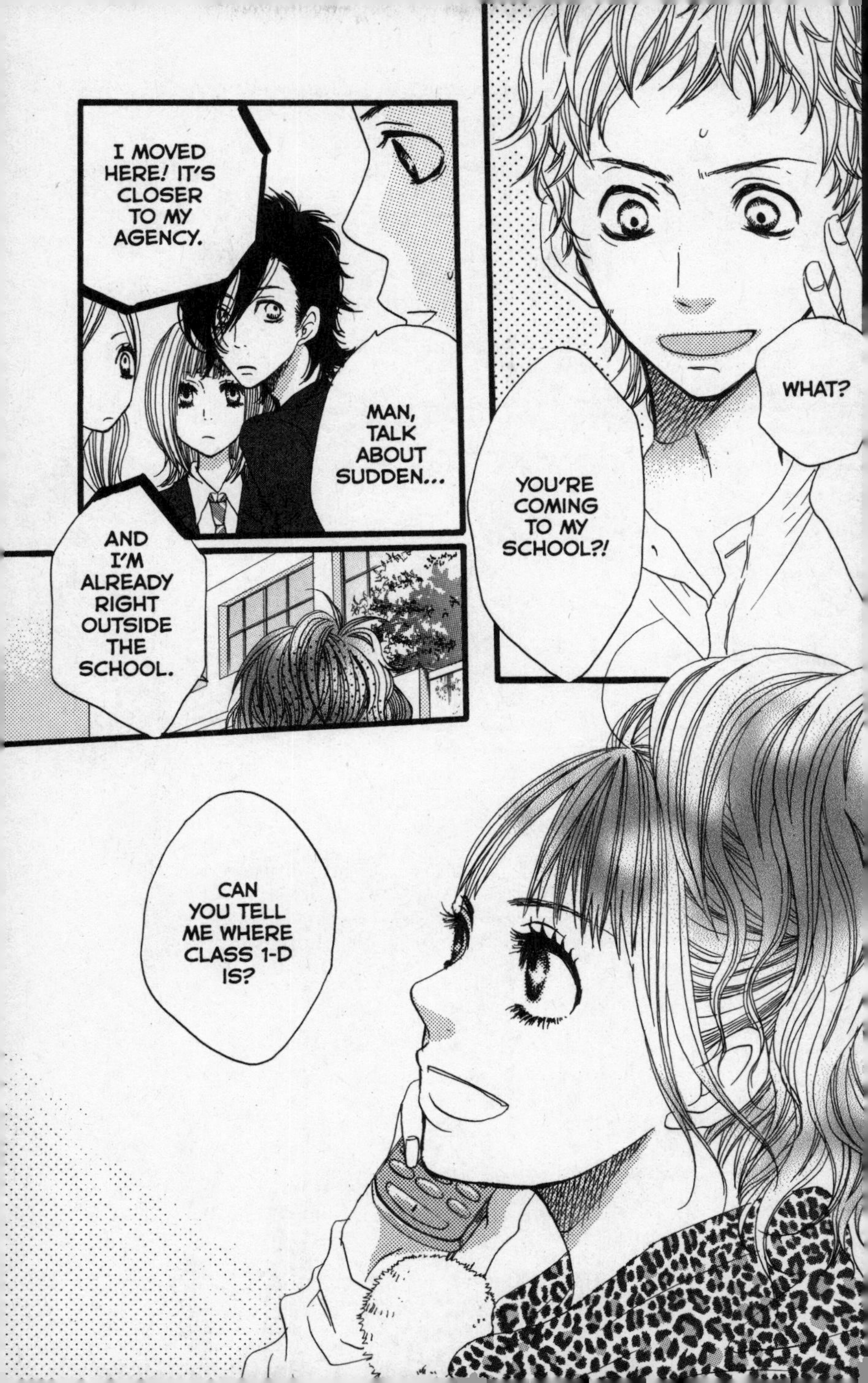
WHAT?
YOU'RE COMING TO MY SCHOOL?!
I MOVED HERE! IT'S CLOSER TO MY AGENCY.
MAN, TALK ABOUT SUDDEN...
AND I'M ALREADY RIGHT OUTSIDE THE SCHOOL.
CAN YOU TELL ME WHERE CLASS 1-D IS?

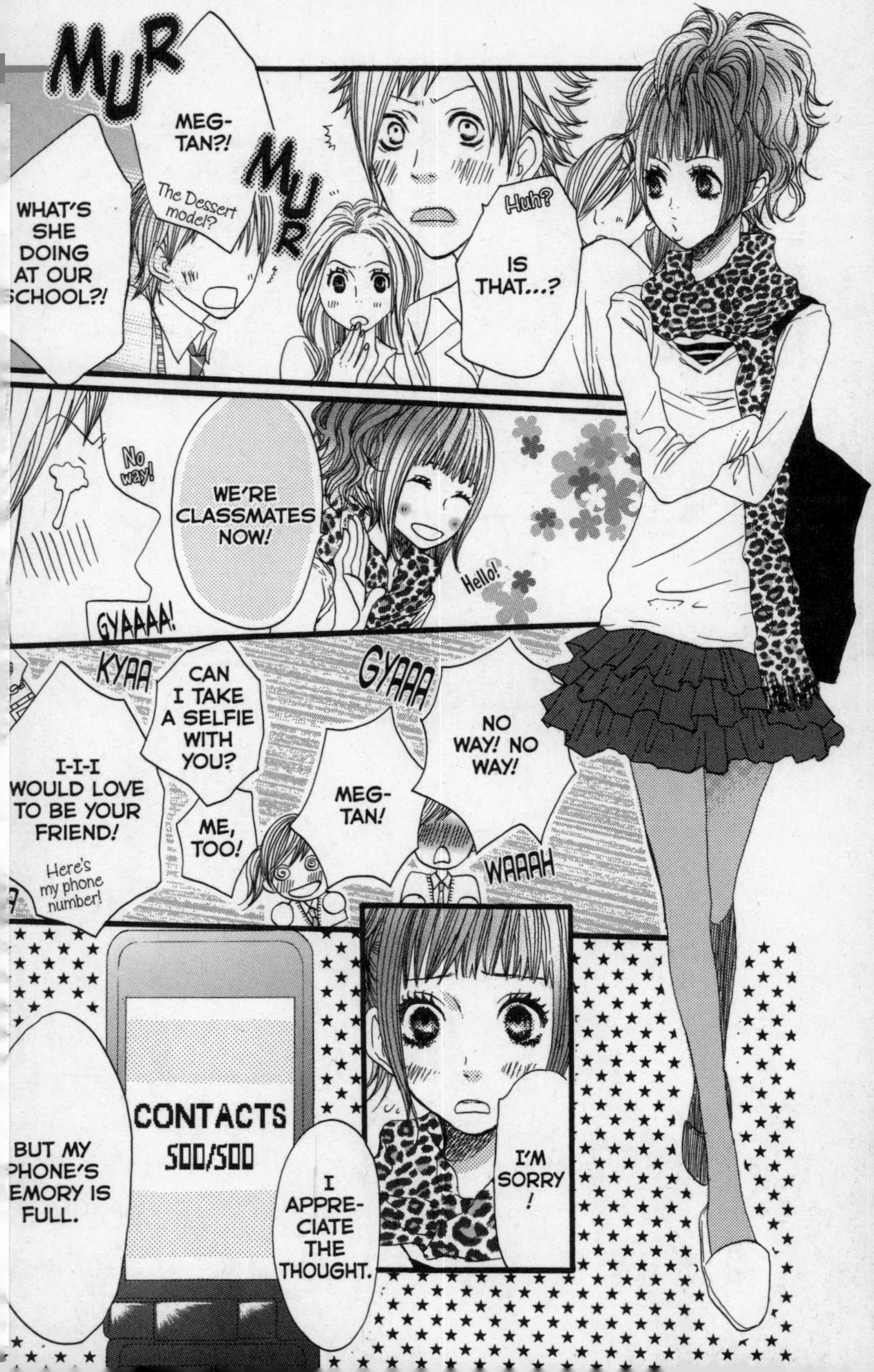
Huh?
IS THAT...?
MEG-TAN?!
The Dessert model!?
MUR
MUR
WHAT'S SHE DOING AT OUR SCHOOL?!
Hello!
WE'RE CLASSMATES NOW!
No way!
GYAAAA!
NO WAY! NO WAY!
WAAAH
GYAAA
MEG-TAN!
CAN I TAKE A SELFIE WITH YOU?
KYAA
ME, TOO!
I-I-I WOULD LOVE TO BE YOUR FRIEND!
Here's my phone number!
I'M SORRY!
I APPRECIATE THE THOUGHT.
CONTACTS
500/500
BUT MY PHONE'S EMORY IS FULL.

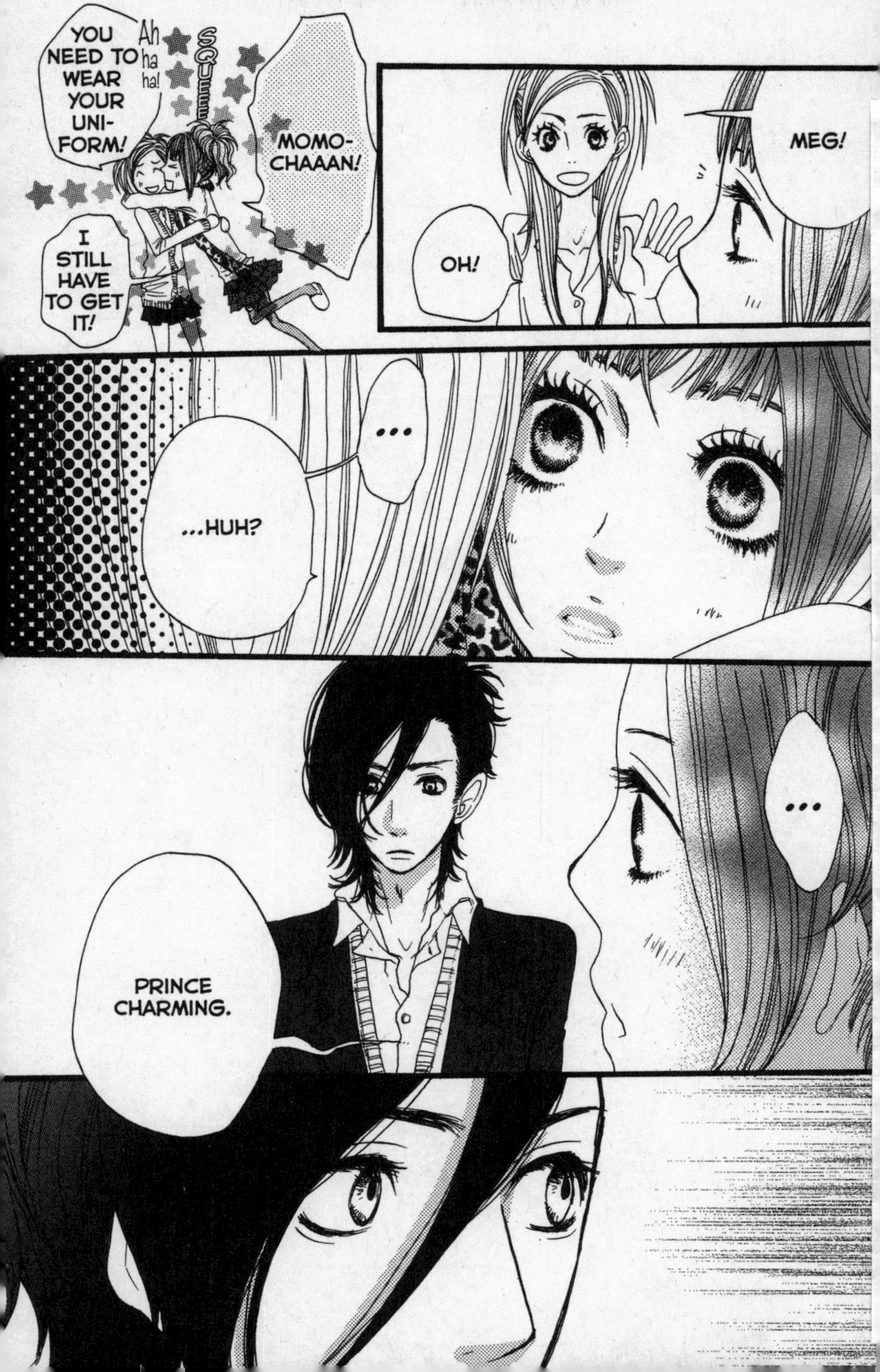
MEG!
OH!
MOMO-CHAAAN!
SQUEEE
Ah ha ha!
YOU NEED TO WEAR YOUR UNIFORM!
I STILL HAVE TO GET IT!
...
...HUH?
...
PRINCE CHARMING.

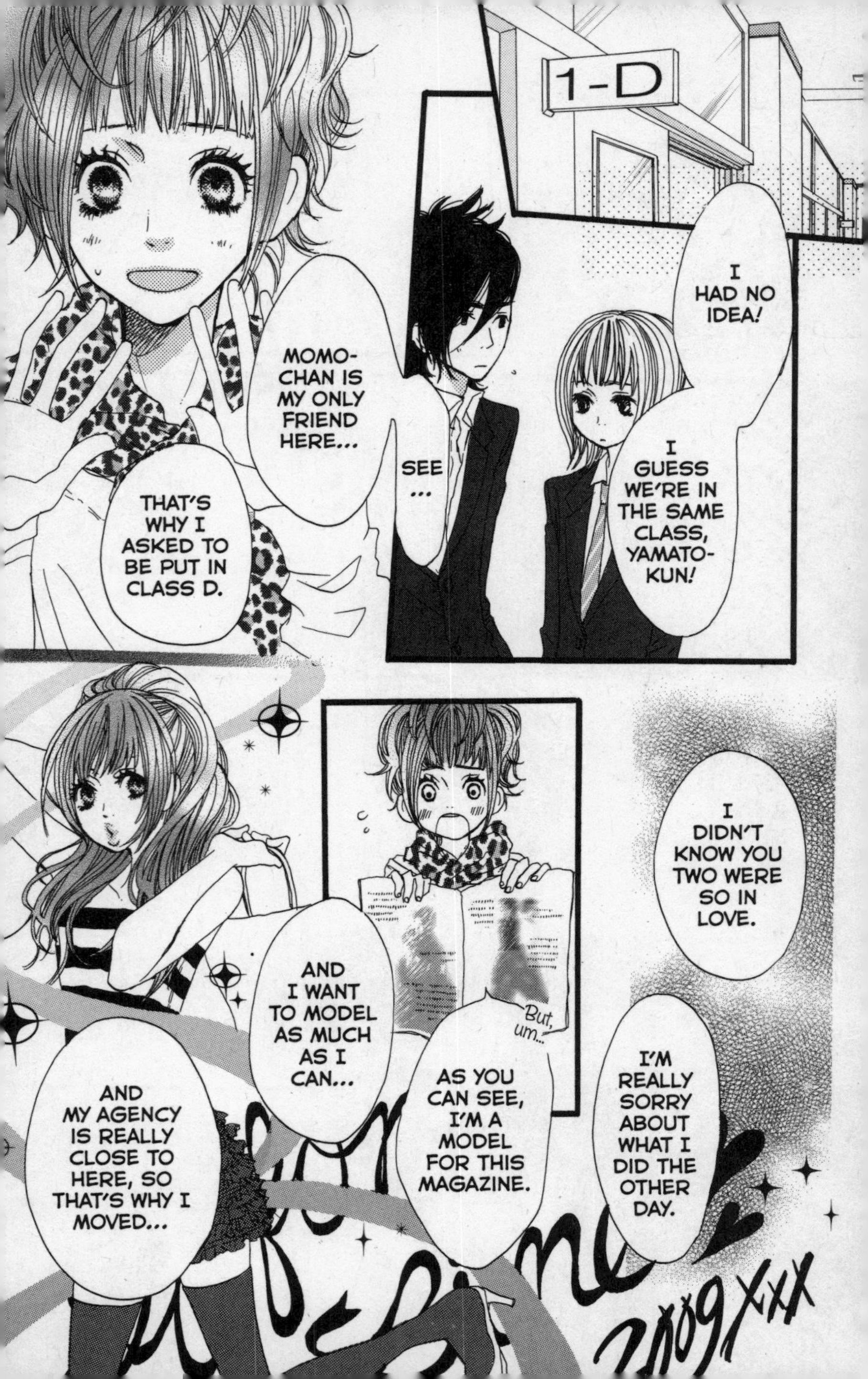
1-D
I HAD NO IDEA!
I GUESS WE'RE IN THE SAME CLASS, YAMATO-KUN!
SEE...
MOMO-CHAN IS MY ONLY FRIEND HERE...
THAT'S WHY I ASKED TO BE PUT IN CLASS D.
I DIDN'T KNOW YOU TWO WERE SO IN LOVE.
I'M REALLY SORRY ABOUT WHAT I DID THE OTHER DAY.
But, um...
AS YOU CAN SEE, I'M A MODEL FOR THIS MAGAZINE.
AND I WANT TO MODEL AS MUCH AS I CAN...
AND MY AGENCY IS REALLY CLOSE TO HERE, SO THAT'S WHY I MOVED...

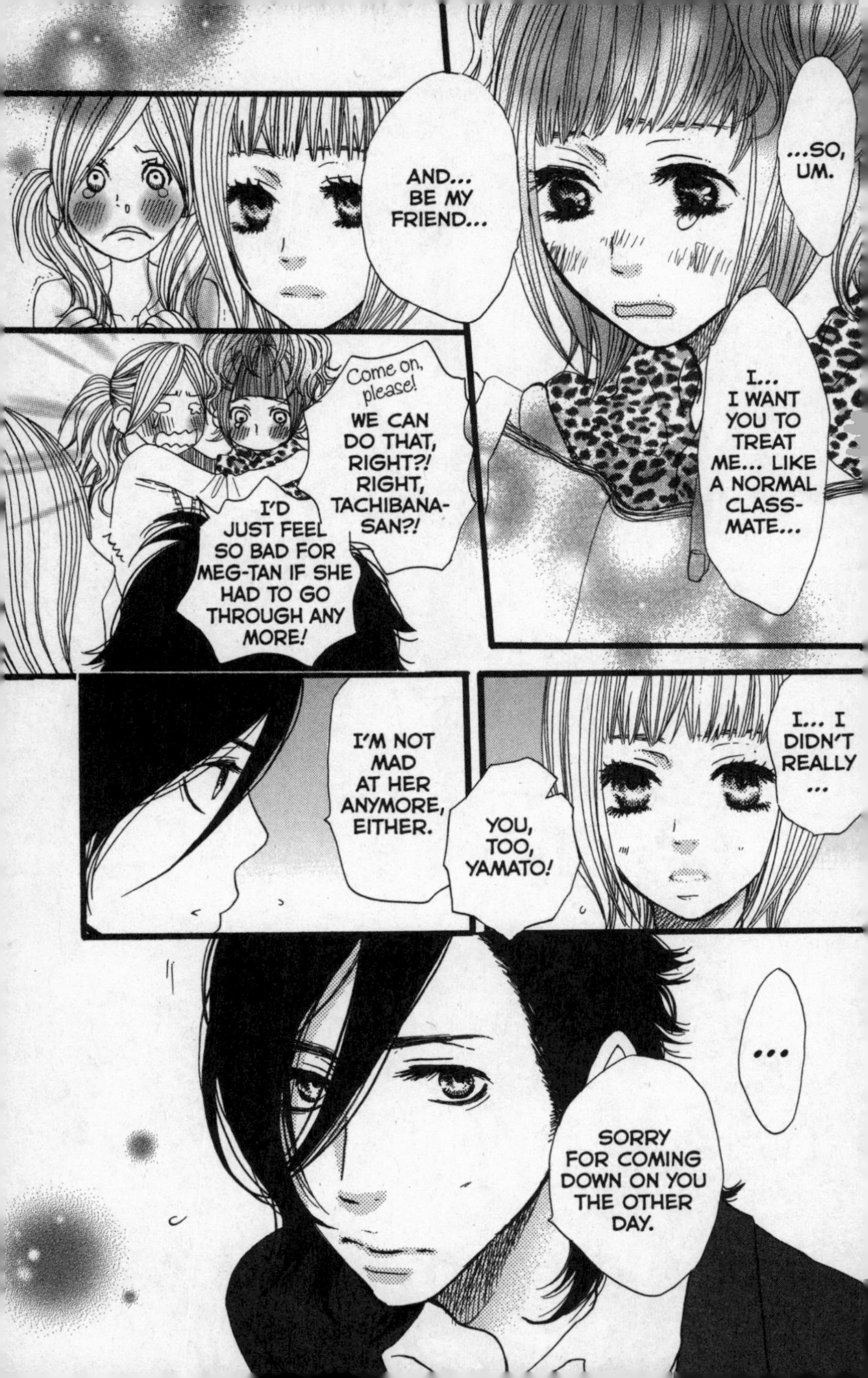
...SO, UM.
AND... BE MY FRIEND...
I... I WANT YOU TO TREAT ME... LIKE A NORMAL CLASS-MATE...
Come on, please!
WE CAN DO THAT, RIGHT?! RIGHT, TACHIBANA-SAN?!
I'D JUST FEEL SO BAD FOR MEG-TAN IF SHE HAD TO GO THROUGH ANY MORE!
I... I DIDN'T REALLY ...
YOU, TOO, YAMATO!
I'M NOT MAD AT HER ANYMORE, EITHER.
...
SORRY FOR COMING DOWN ON YOU THE OTHER DAY.

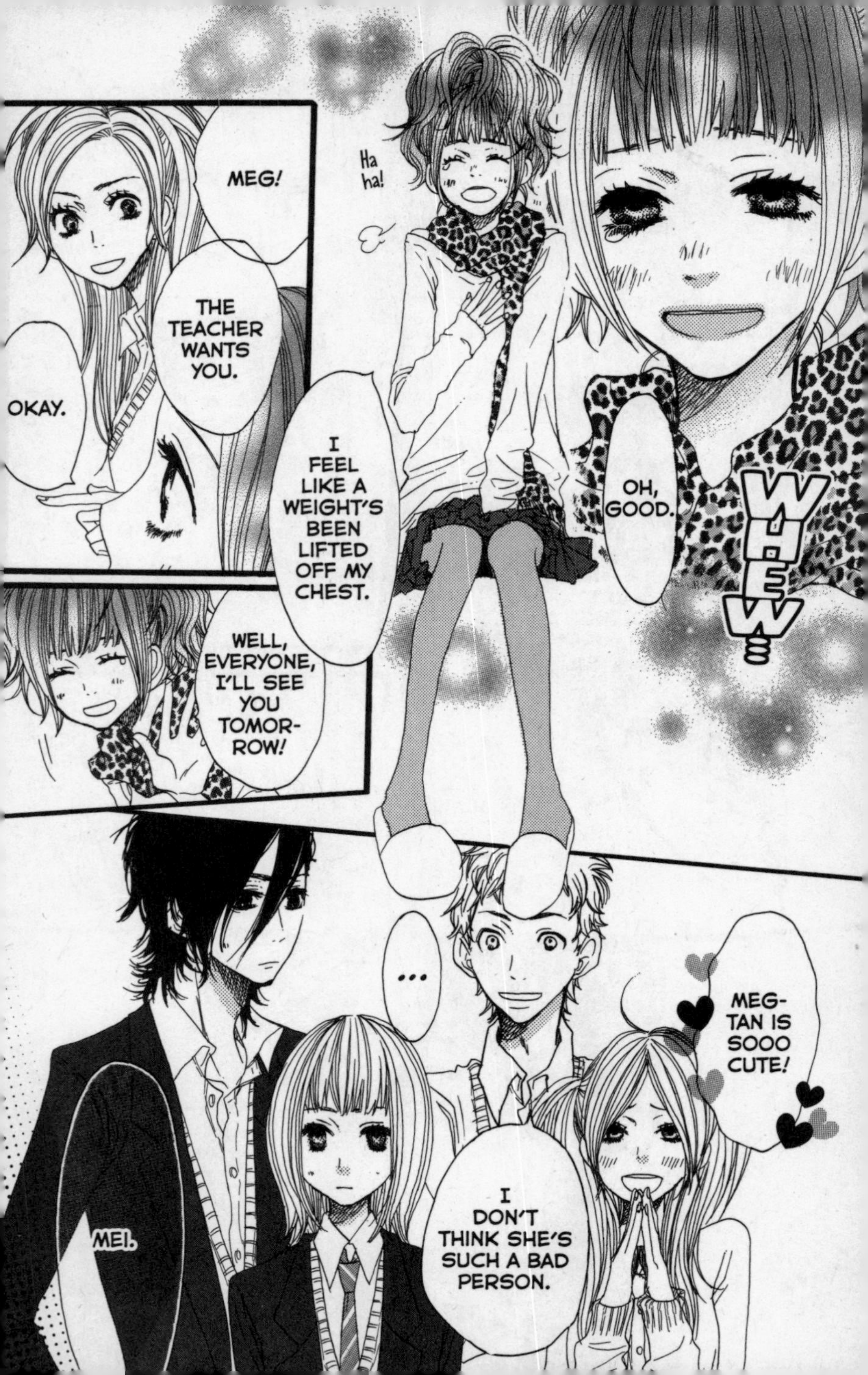

Ha ha!
OH, GOOD.
WHEW
I FEEL LIKE A WEIGHT'S BEEN LIFTED OFF MY CHEST.
MEG!
THE TEACHER WANTS YOU.
OKAY.
WELL, EVERYONE, I'LL SEE YOU TOMORROW!
MEG-TAN IS SOOO CUTE!
...
I DON'T THINK SHE'S SUCH A BAD PERSON.
MEI.

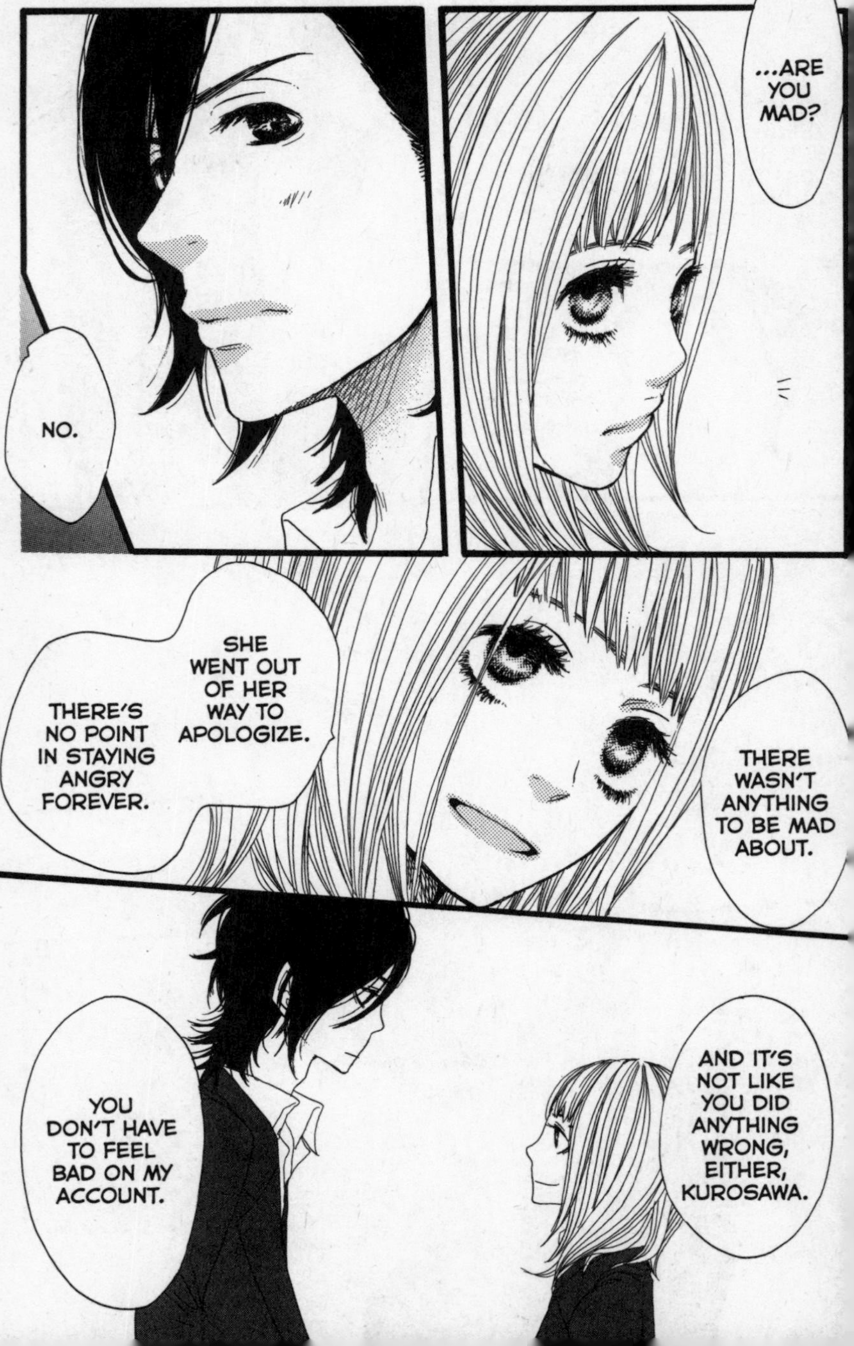
...ARE YOU MAD?
NO.
THERE WASN'T ANYTHING TO BE MAD ABOUT.
SHE WENT OUT OF HER WAY TO APOLOGIZE.
THERE'S NO POINT IN STAYING ANGRY FOREVER.
AND IT'S NOT LIKE YOU DID ANYTHING WRONG, EITHER, KUROSAWA.
YOU DON'T HAVE TO FEEL BAD ON MY ACCOUNT.

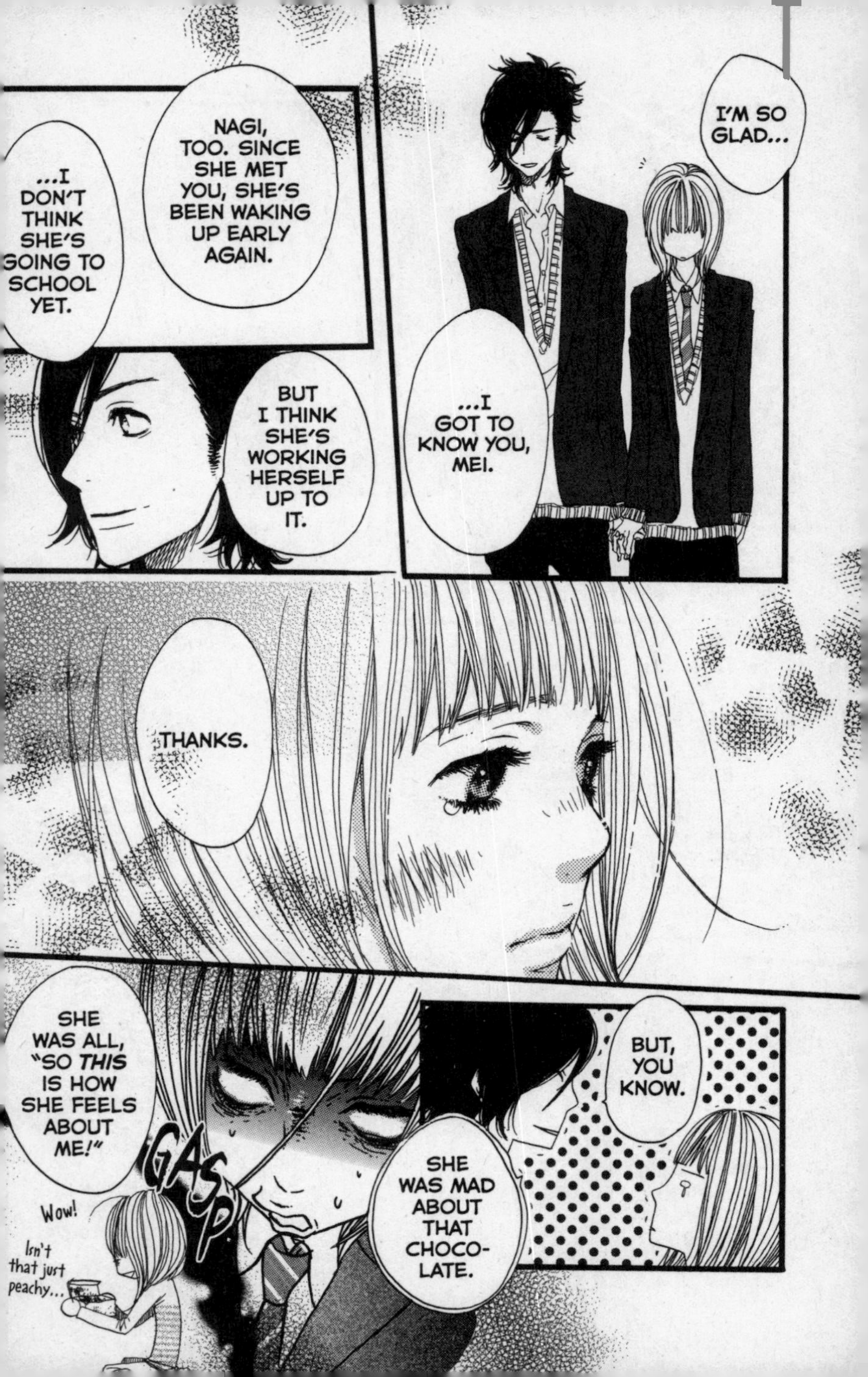
I'M SO GLAD...
...I GOT TO KNOW YOU, MEI.
NAGI, TOO. SINCE SHE MET YOU, SHE'S BEEN WAKING UP EARLY AGAIN.
...I DON'T THINK SHE'S GOING TO SCHOOL YET.
BUT I THINK SHE'S WORKING HERSELF UP TO IT.
THANKS.
BUT, YOU KNOW.
SHE WAS MAD ABOUT THAT CHOCOLATE.
SHE WAS ALL, "SO THIS IS HOW SHE FEELS ABOUT ME!"
GASP
Wow!
Isn't that just peachy...

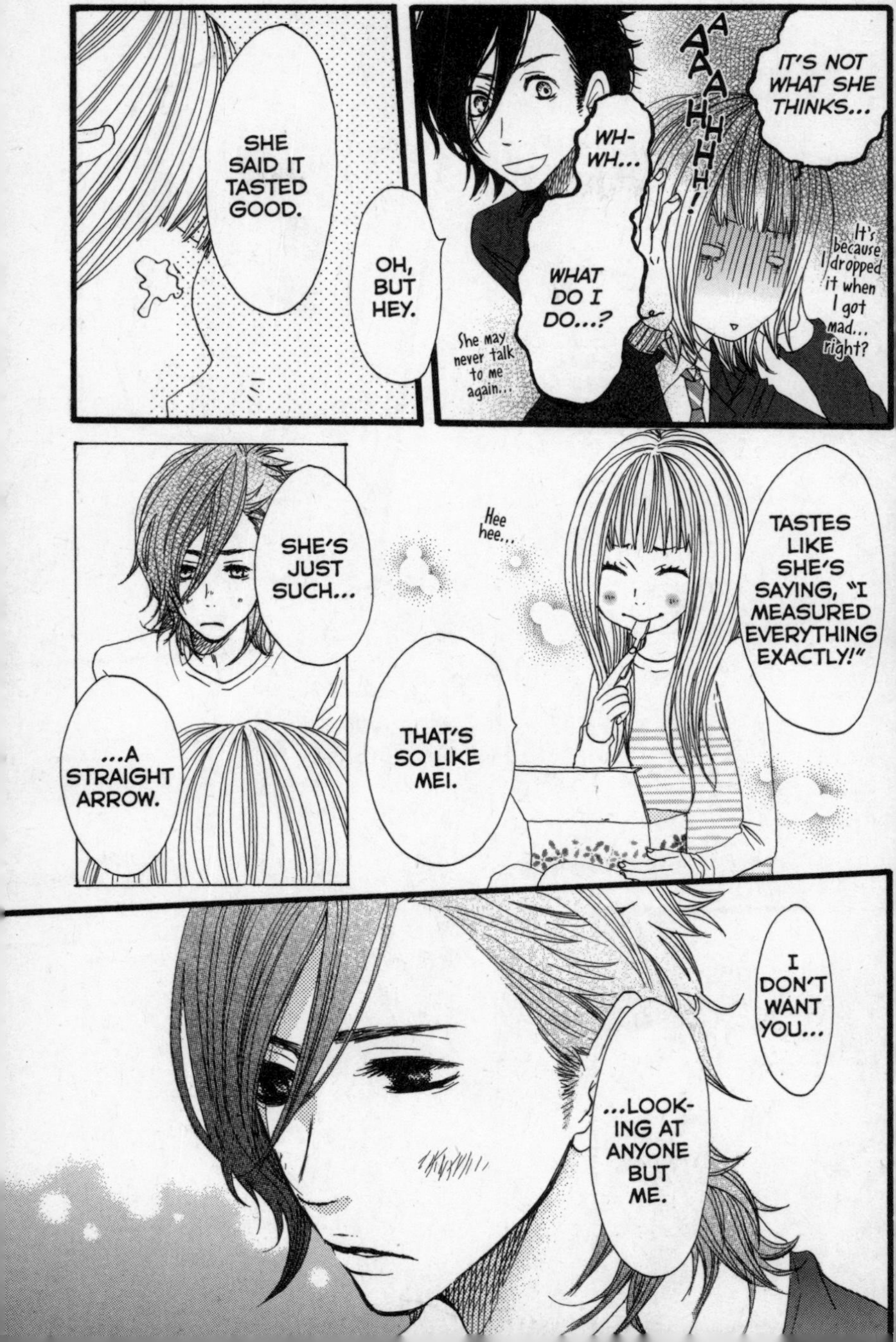
AAAHHHH!
IT'S NOT WHAT SHE THINKS...
It's because I dropped it when I got mad... right?
WH- WH...
WHAT DO I DO...?
She may never talk to me again...
OH, BUT HEY.
SHE SAID IT TASTED GOOD.
TASTES LIKE SHE'S SAYING, "I MEASURED EVERYTHING EXACTLY!"
Hee hee...
THAT'S SO LIKE MEI.
SHE'S JUST SUCH...
...A STRAIGHT ARROW.
I DON'T WANT YOU...
...LOOKING AT ANYONE BUT ME.

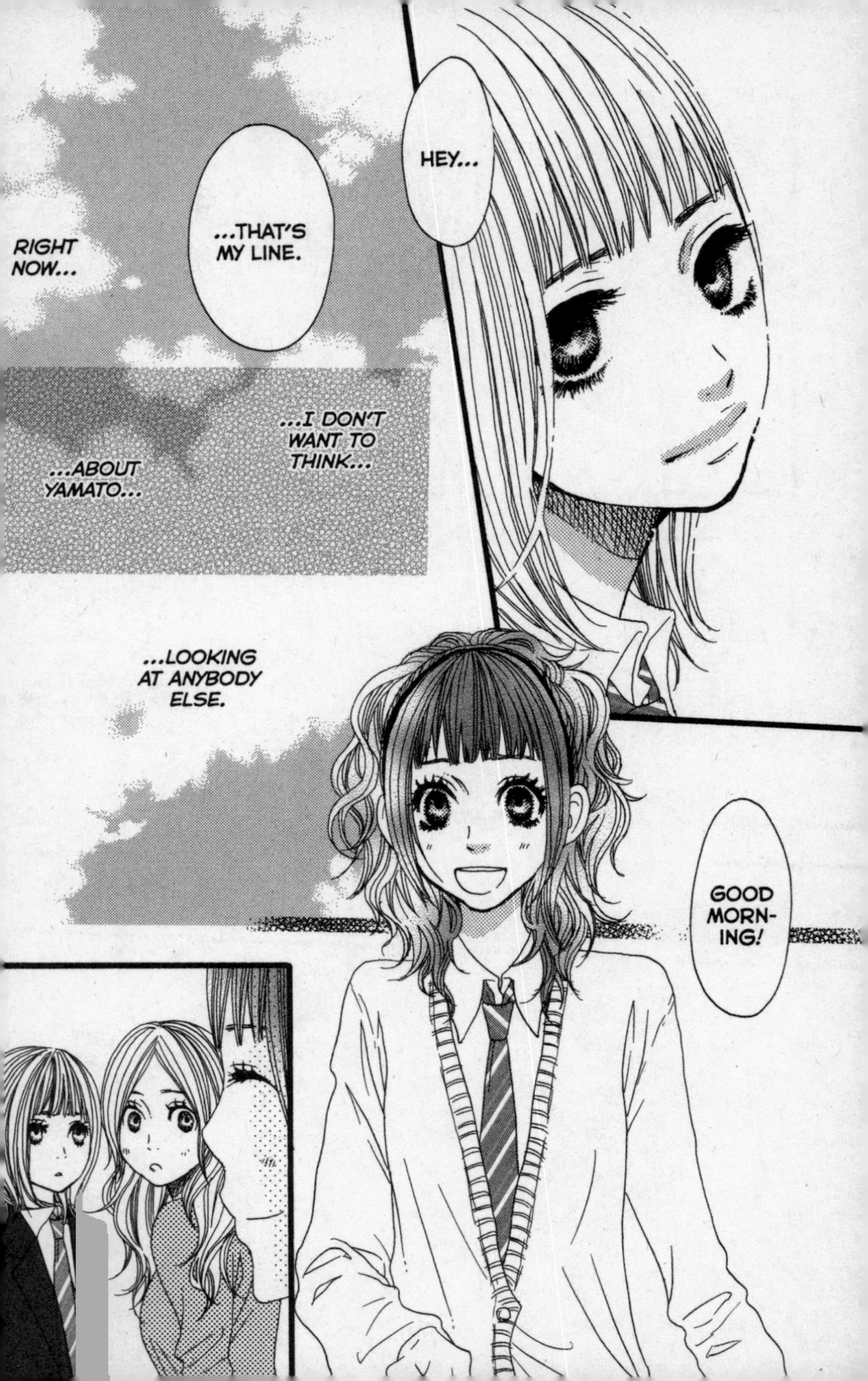
HEY...
...THAT'S MY LINE.
RIGHT NOW...
...I DON'T WANT TO THINK...
...ABOUT YAMATO...
...LOOKING AT ANYBODY ELSE.
GOOD MORN-ING!

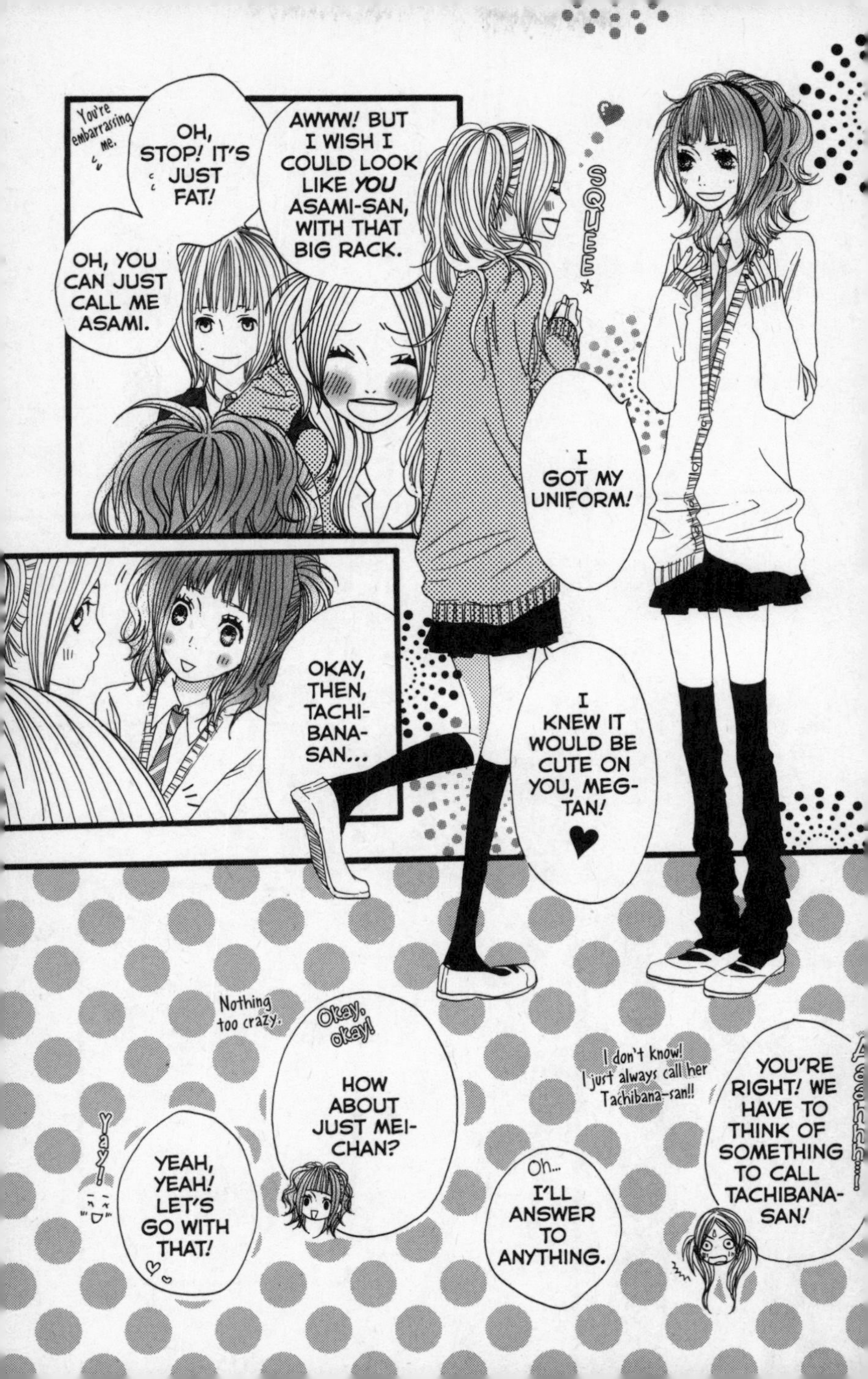

SQUEE
I GOT MY UNIFORM!
I KNEW IT WOULD BE CUTE ON YOU, MEG-TAN!
AWWW! BUT I WISH I COULD LOOK LIKE *YOU* ASAMI-SAN, WITH THAT BIG RACK.
OH, STOP! IT'S JUST FAT!
You're embarrassing me.
OH, YOU CAN JUST CALL ME ASAMI.
OKAY, THEN, TACHIBANA-SAN...
YOU'RE RIGHT! WE HAVE TO THINK OF SOMETHING TO CALL TACHIBANA-SAN!
I don't know! I just always call her Tachibana-san!!
Oh... I'LL ANSWER TO ANYTHING.
Okay, okay!
HOW ABOUT JUST MEI-CHAN?
Nothing too crazy.
YEAH, YEAH! LET'S GO WITH THAT!
Yay!

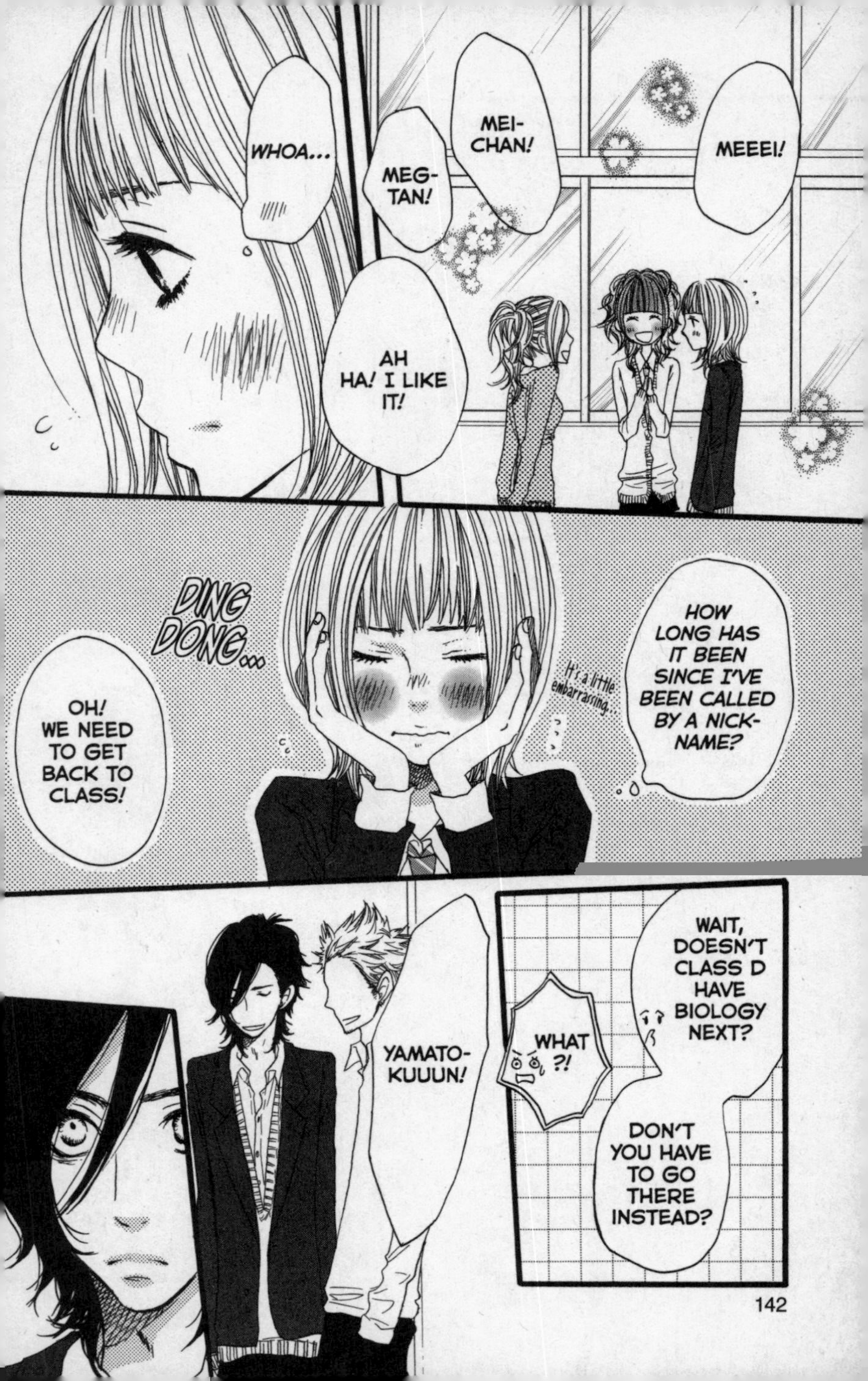
MEEEI!
MEI-CHAN!
MEG-TAN!
AH HA! I LIKE IT!
WHOA...
HOW LONG HAS IT BEEN SINCE I'VE BEEN CALLED BY A NICK-NAME?
It's a little embarrassing...
DING DONG...
OH! WE NEED TO GET BACK TO CLASS!
WAIT, DOESN'T CLASS D HAVE BIOLOGY NEXT?
WHAT?!
DON'T YOU HAVE TO GO THERE INSTEAD?
YAMATO-KUUUN!

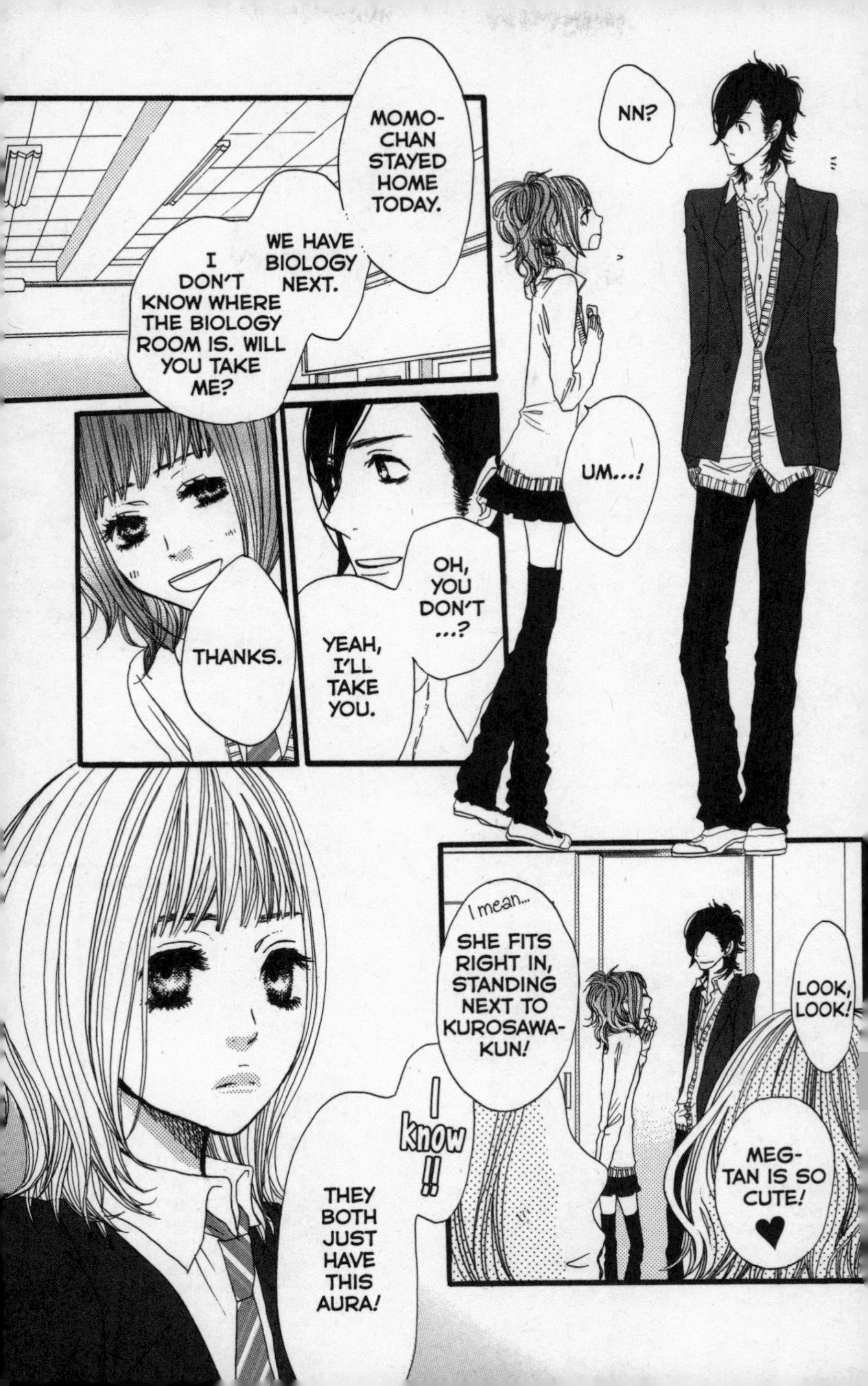
UM...!
NN?
MOMO-CHAN STAYED HOME TODAY.
WE HAVE BIOLOGY NEXT.
I DON'T KNOW WHERE THE BIOLOGY ROOM IS. WILL YOU TAKE ME?
OH, YOU DON'T ...?
YEAH, I'LL TAKE YOU.
THANKS.
LOOK, LOOK!
MEG-TAN IS SO CUTE! ♥
I mean...
SHE FITS RIGHT IN, STANDING NEXT TO KUROSAWA-KUN!
I know!!
THEY BOTH JUST HAVE THIS AURA!

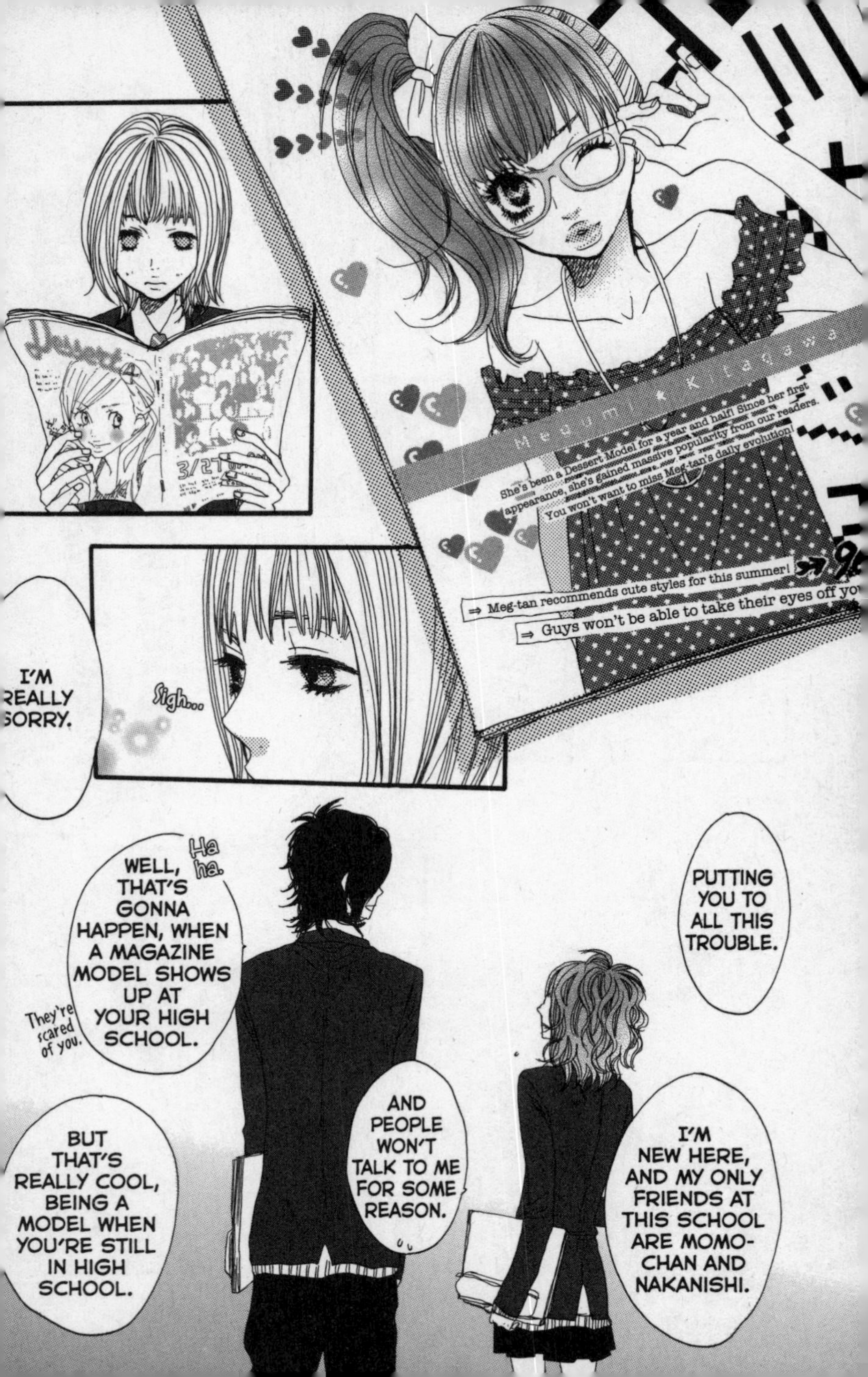
Megumi Kitagawa
She's been a Dessert Model for a year and half! Since her first appearance, she's gained massive popularity from our readers.
You won't want to miss Meg-tan's daily evolution!
⇒ Meg-tan recommends cute styles for this summer!
⇒ Guys won't be able to take their eyes off yo
Dessert
3/27
Sigh...
I'M REALLY SORRY.
PUTTING YOU TO ALL THIS TROUBLE.
Ha ha.
WELL, THAT'S GONNA HAPPEN, WHEN A MAGAZINE MODEL SHOWS UP AT YOUR HIGH SCHOOL.
They're scared of you.
I'M NEW HERE, AND MY ONLY FRIENDS AT THIS SCHOOL ARE MOMO-CHAN AND NAKANISHI.
AND PEOPLE WON'T TALK TO ME FOR SOME REASON.
BUT THAT'S REALLY COOL, BEING A MODEL WHEN YOU'RE STILL IN HIGH SCHOOL.

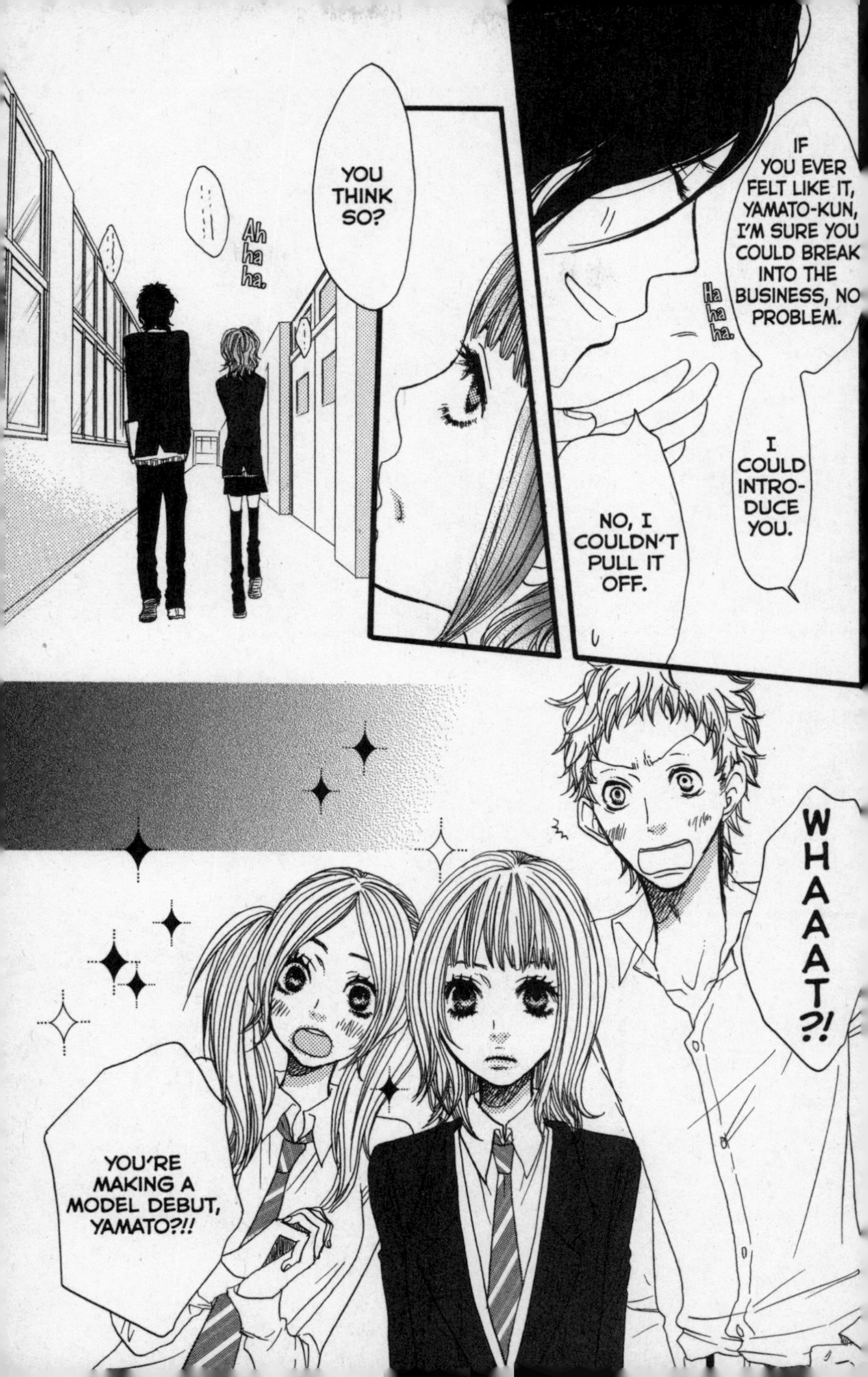
IF YOU EVER FELT LIKE IT, YAMATO-KUN, I'M SURE YOU COULD BREAK INTO THE BUSINESS, NO PROBLEM.
Ha ha ha.
I COULD INTRO-DUCE YOU.
NO, I COULDN'T PULL IT OFF.
YOU THINK SO?
Ah ha ha.
WHAAAT?!
YOU'RE MAKING A MODEL DEBUT, YAMATO?!!

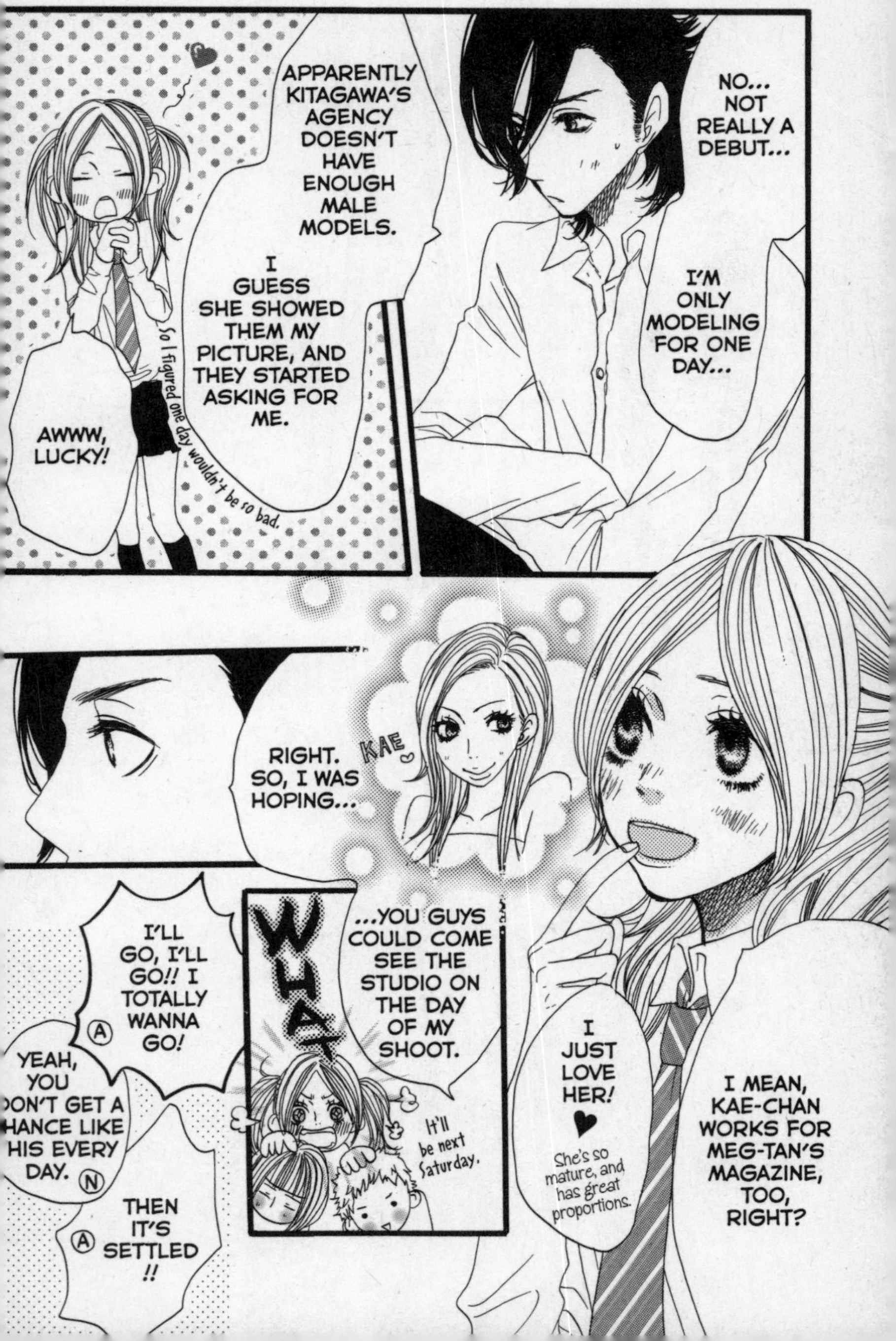

NO... NOT REALLY A DEBUT...
I'M ONLY MODELING FOR ONE DAY...
APPARENTLY KITAGAWA'S AGENCY DOESN'T HAVE ENOUGH MALE MODELS.
I GUESS SHE SHOWED THEM MY PICTURE, AND THEY STARTED ASKING FOR ME.
So I figured one day wouldn't be so bad.
AWWW, LUCKY!
I MEAN, KAE-CHAN WORKS FOR MEG-TAN'S MAGAZINE, TOO, RIGHT?
I JUST LOVE HER!
She's so mature, and has great proportions.
KAE
RIGHT. SO, I WAS HOPING...
...YOU GUYS COULD COME SEE THE STUDIO ON THE DAY OF MY SHOOT.
It'll be next Saturday.
WHAT
I'LL GO, I'LL GO!! I TOTALLY WANNA GO!
YEAH, YOU ON'T GET A HANCE LIKE HIS EVERY DAY.
THEN IT'S SETTLED !!

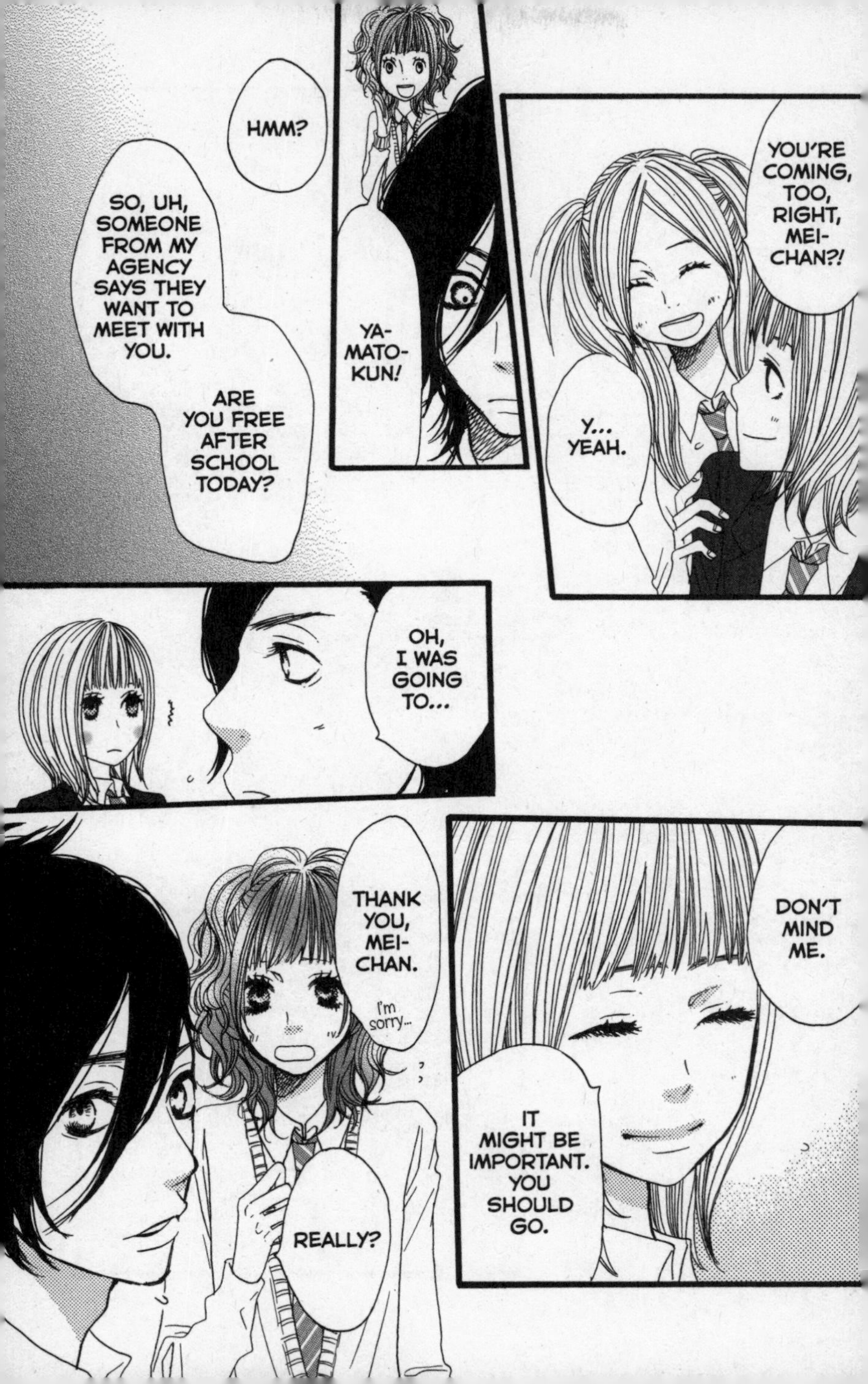
YOU'RE COMING, TOO, RIGHT, MEI-CHAN?!
Y... YEAH.
YA-MATO-KUN!
HMM?
SO, UH, SOMEONE FROM MY AGENCY SAYS THEY WANT TO MEET WITH YOU.
ARE YOU FREE AFTER SCHOOL TODAY?
OH, I WAS GOING TO...
DON'T MIND ME.
IT MIGHT BE IMPORTANT. YOU SHOULD GO.
THANK YOU, MEI-CHAN.
I'm sorry...
REALLY?

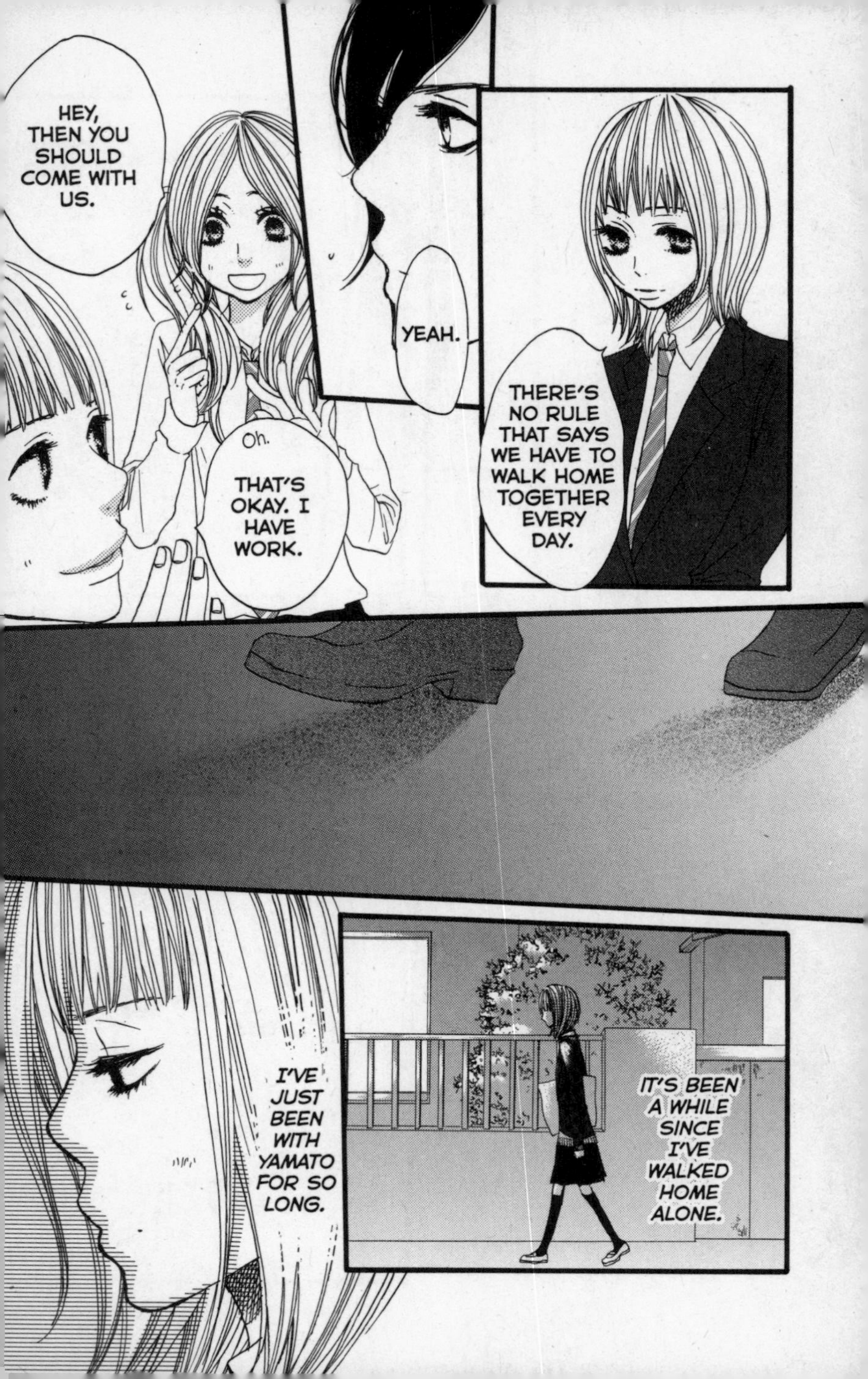
THERE'S NO RULE THAT SAYS WE HAVE TO WALK HOME TOGETHER EVERY DAY.
YEAH.
HEY, THEN YOU SHOULD COME WITH US.
Oh.
THAT'S OKAY. I HAVE WORK.
IT'S BEEN A WHILE SINCE I'VE WALKED HOME ALONE.
I'VE JUST BEEN WITH YAMATO FOR SO LONG.

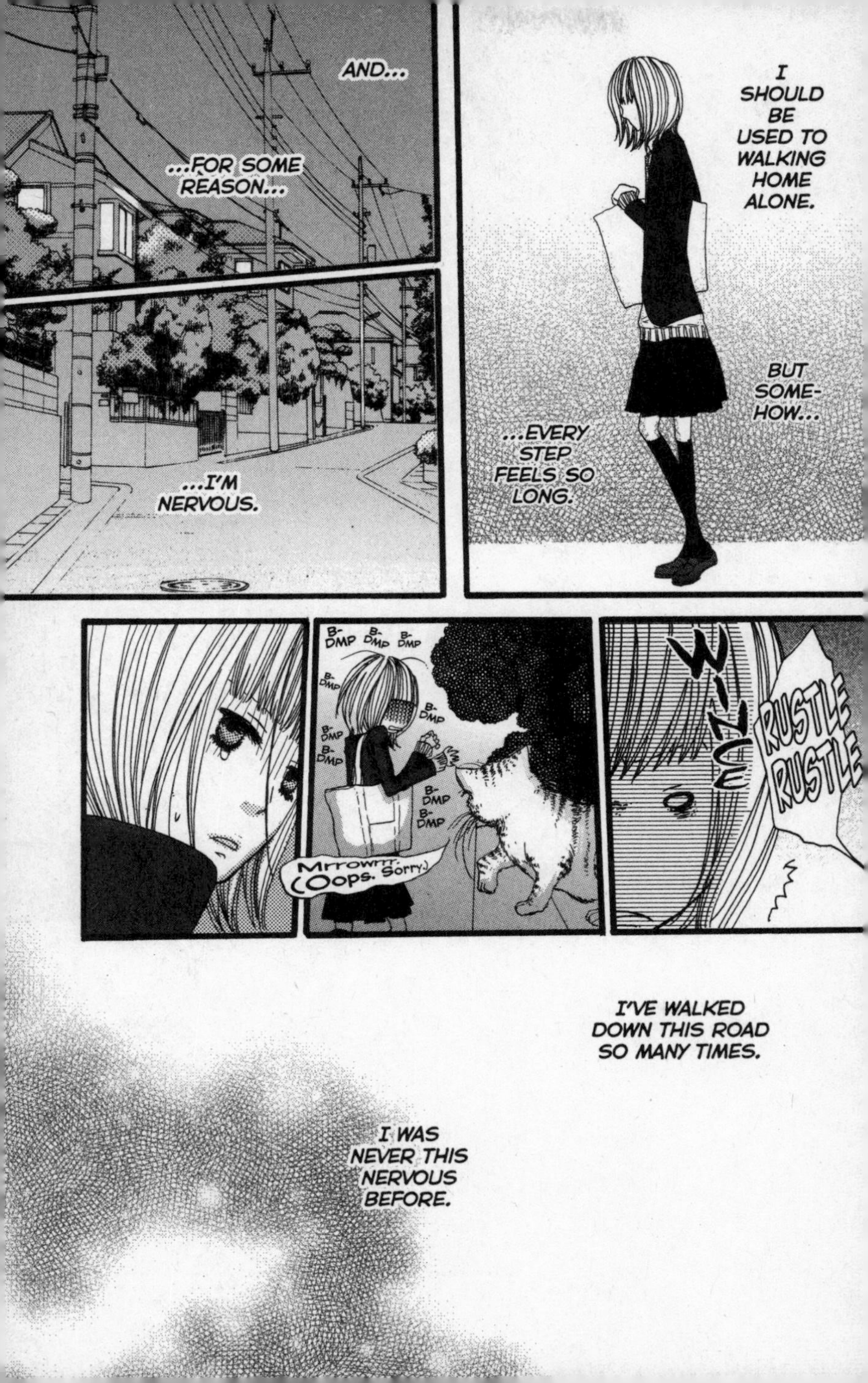
I SHOULD BE USED TO WALKING HOME ALONE.
BUT SOME-HOW...
...EVERY STEP FEELS SO LONG.
AND...
...FOR SOME REASON...
...I'M NERVOUS.
W-I-N-C-E
RUSTLE RUSTLE
B-DMP B-DMP B-DMP B-DMP B-DMP B-DMP B-DMP B-DMP B-DMP
Mrrowrrr. (Oops. Sorry.)
I'VE WALKED DOWN THIS ROAD SO MANY TIMES.
I WAS NEVER THIS NERVOUS BEFORE.

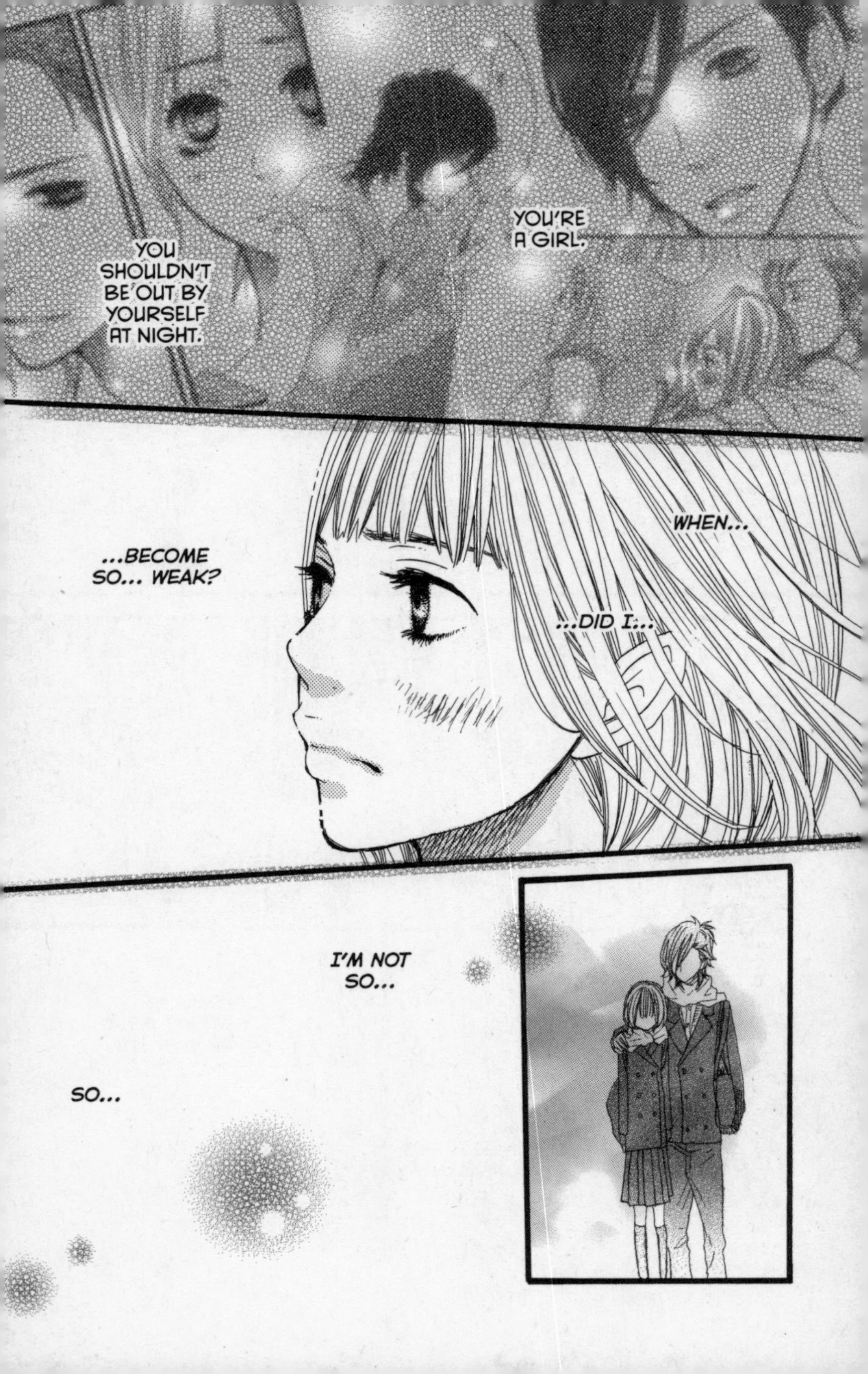
YOU'RE A GIRL.
YOU SHOULDN'T BE OUT BY YOURSELF AT NIGHT.
WHEN...
...DID I...
...BECOME SO... WEAK?
I'M NOT SO...
SO...

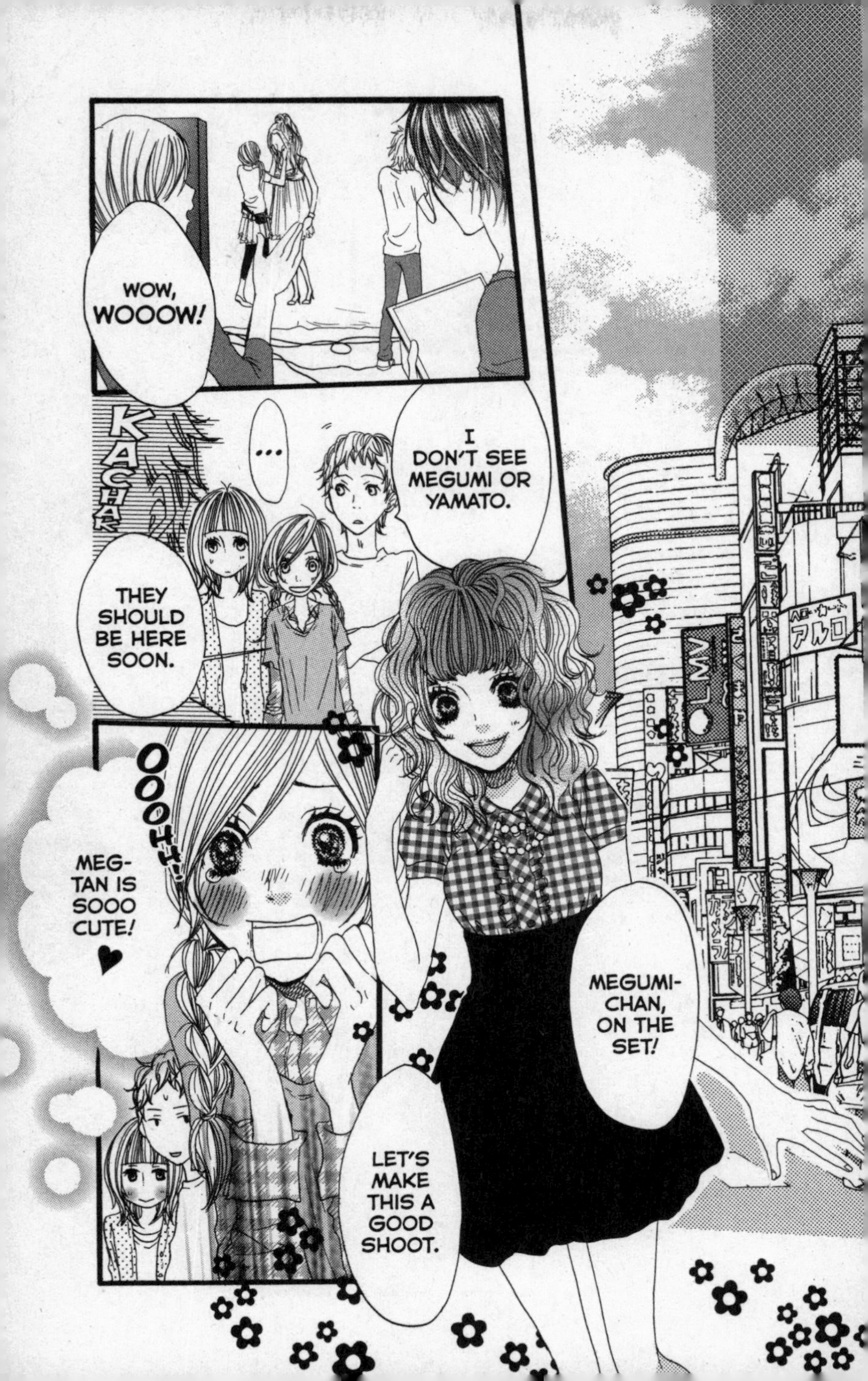
WOW, WOOOW!
KACHAK
...
I DON'T SEE MEGUMI OR YAMATO.
THEY SHOULD BE HERE SOON.
MEGUMI-CHAN, ON THE SET!
LET'S MAKE THIS A GOOD SHOOT.
OOOOHH!
MEG-TAN IS SOOO CUTE! ♥

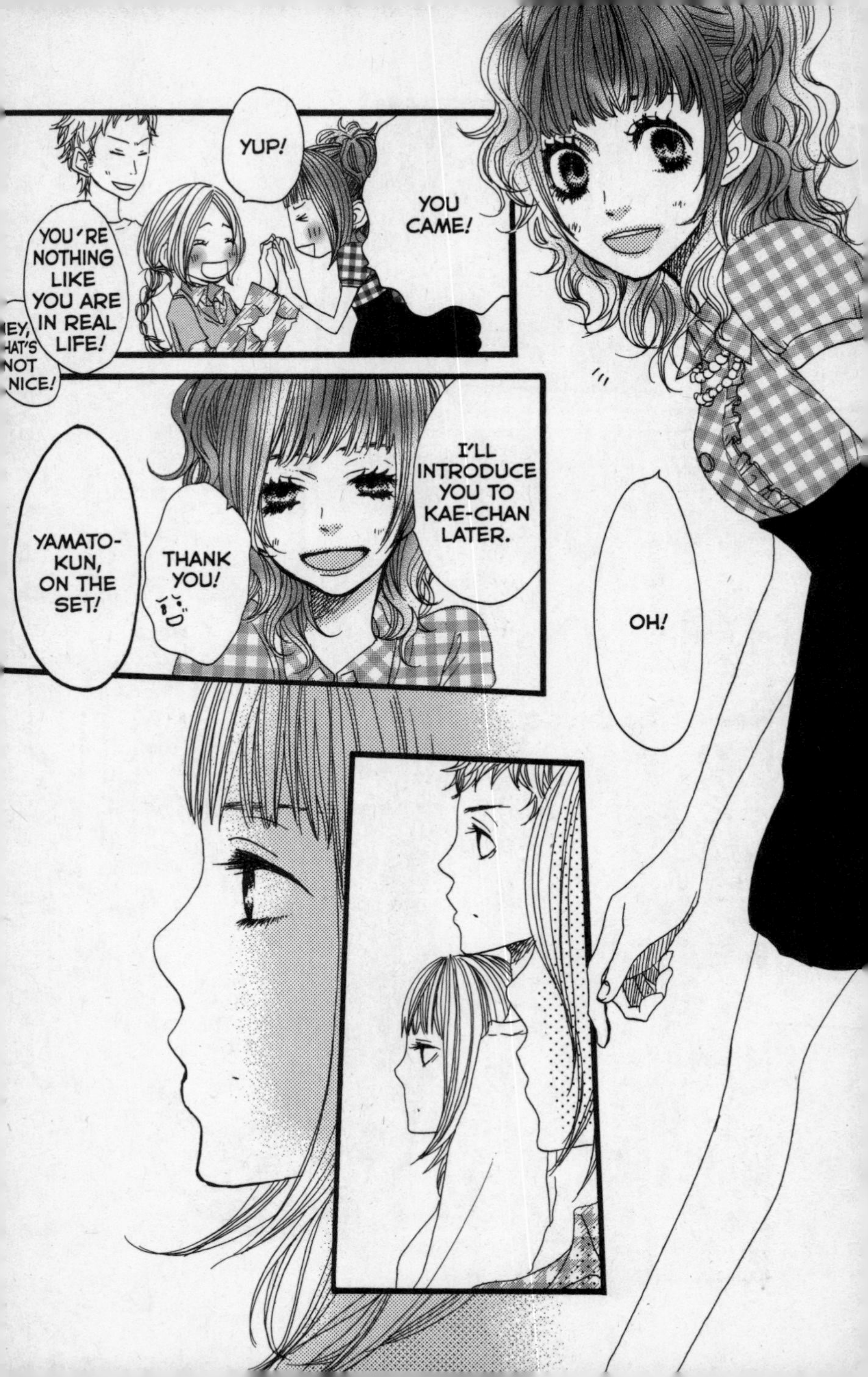
YOU CAME!
YUP!
YOU'RE NOTHING LIKE YOU ARE IN REAL LIFE!
EY, HAT'S NOT NICE!
I'LL INTRODUCE YOU TO KAE-CHAN LATER.
THANK YOU!
YAMATO-KUN, ON THE SET!
OH!

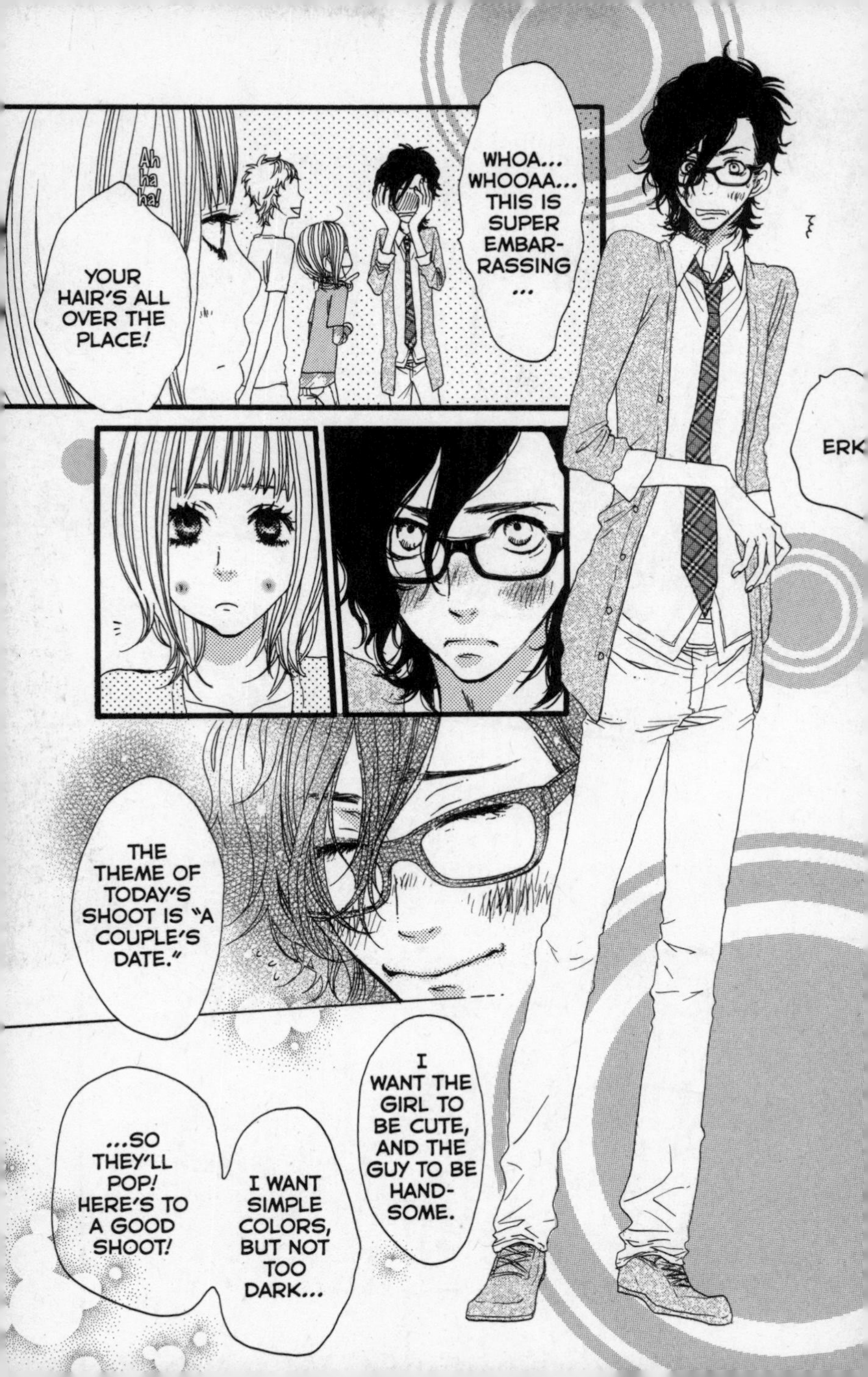
WHOA... WHOOAA... THIS IS SUPER EMBARRASSING...
ERK
Ah ha ha!
YOUR HAIR'S ALL OVER THE PLACE!
THE THEME OF TODAY'S SHOOT IS "A COUPLE'S DATE."
I WANT THE GIRL TO BE CUTE, AND THE GUY TO BE HANDSOME.
I WANT SIMPLE COLORS, BUT NOT TOO DARK...
...SO THEY'LL POP! HERE'S TO A GOOD SHOOT!

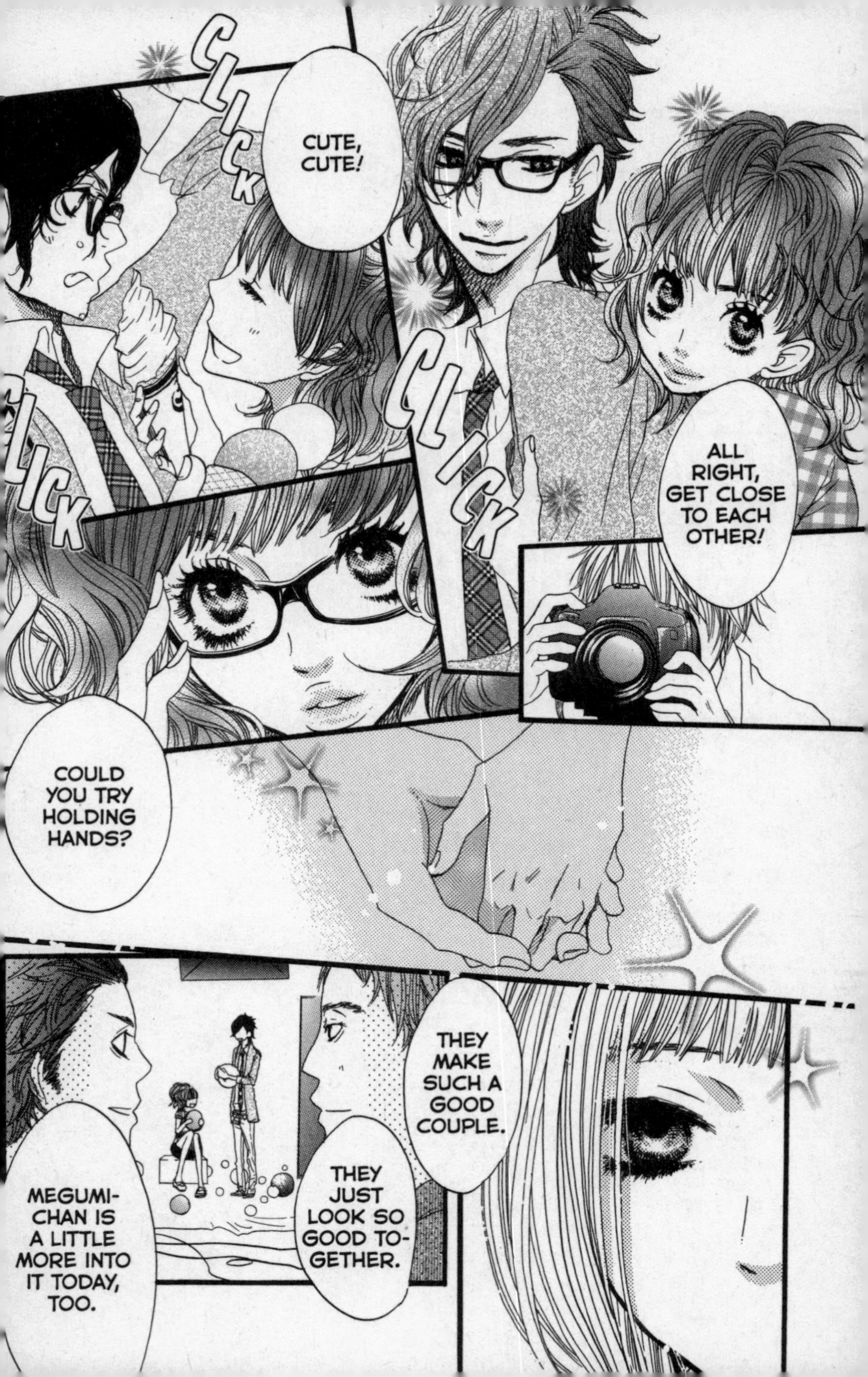
CLICK
CUTE, CUTE!
CLICK
CLICK
ALL RIGHT, GET CLOSE TO EACH OTHER!
COULD YOU TRY HOLDING HANDS?
THEY MAKE SUCH A GOOD COUPLE.
THEY JUST LOOK SO GOOD TO-GETHER.
MEGUMI-CHAN IS A LITTLE MORE INTO IT TODAY, TOO.

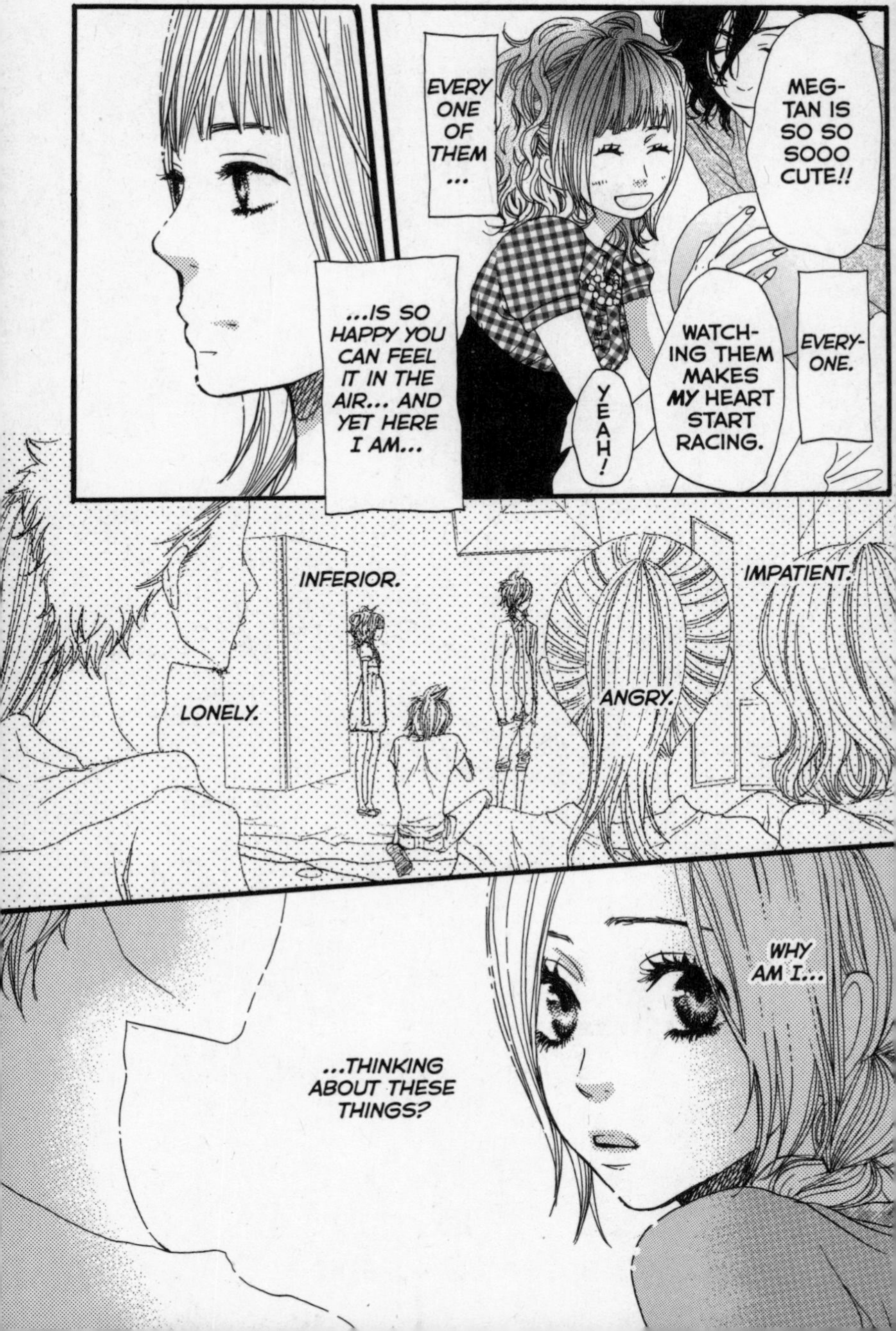
MEG-TAN IS SO SO SOOO CUTE!!
EVERY ONE OF THEM ...
EVERYONE.
WATCHING THEM MAKES MY HEART START RACING.
YEAH!
...IS SO HAPPY YOU CAN FEEL IT IN THE AIR... AND YET HERE I AM...
IMPATIENT.
ANGRY.
INFERIOR.
LONELY.
WHY AM I...
...THINKING ABOUT THESE THINGS?

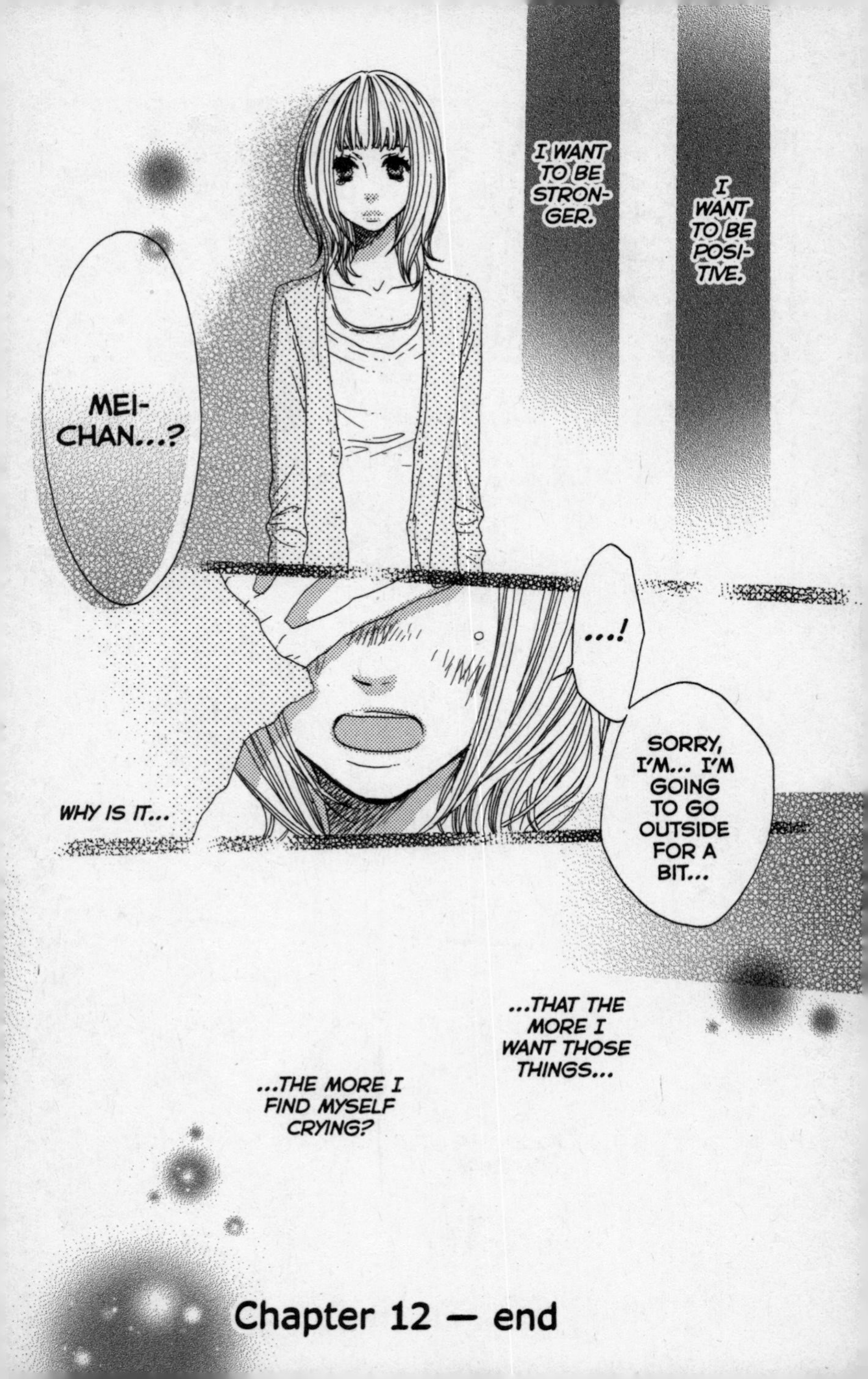
I WANT TO BE POSI-TIVE.
I WANT TO BE STRON-GER.
MEI-CHAN...?
...!
SORRY, I'M... I'M GOING TO GO OUTSIDE FOR A BIT...
WHY IS IT...
...THAT THE MORE I WANT THOSE THINGS...
...THE MORE I FIND MYSELF CRYING?
Chapter 12 — end

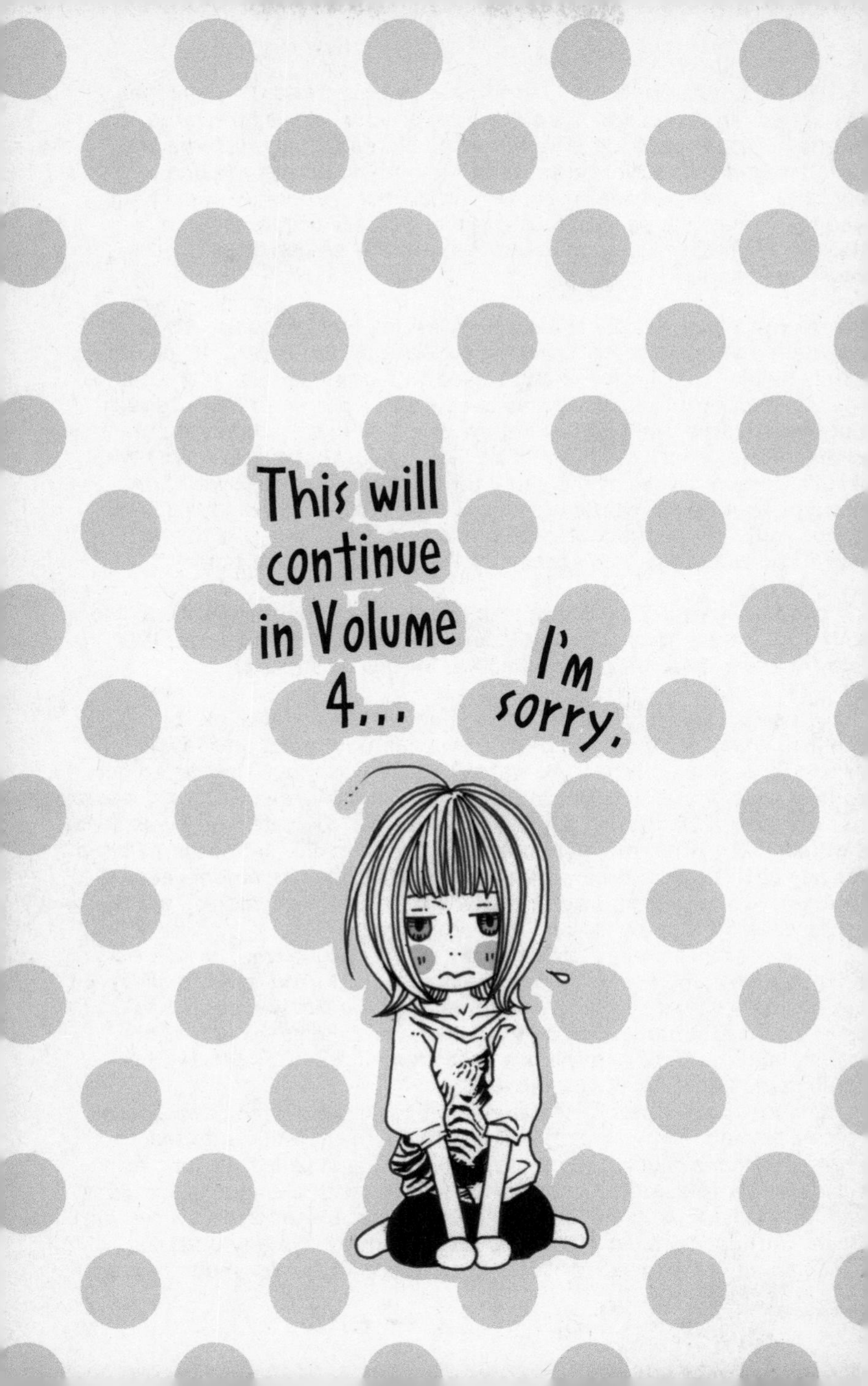
This will continue in Volume 4...
I'm sorry.

Hello, I'm Kanae Hazuki, and this is volume three. I've matched my series-length record. Thank you all for your very appreciated words in response to my afterwords in volume one and volume two.

"I'm going through the same thing, but you helped me find courage," "Your personality comes out in your manga" — everything you say makes me so happy, and you're actually supporting me, helping me feel really good about drawing this series. Thank you so much for reading.

As for a life update... It's nothing special, but I'm happy. No, maybe it's because there's nothing special that I'm happy. At any rate, I fully believe that I have been blessed with good people all around me. Maybe I'm just realizing this because I've gotten to be my age, but I was a little more selfish before. Everything was all about me... If someone was short with me, I'd be like, "Heh, what's with them? What a rude person!" while at the same time, I wanted to be loved. I only thought about what worked for me. I tried asking myself, "Well, what about you? Do you think of everyone around you, and love them?"... and I realized that I didn't really. That's just the type of person I used to be.

Now, everyone I associate with is very important to me. I want to know all of their strengths and failings, and love them for all of it. I want them to always be happy, and to always be smiling.

When I tried to figure out what changed the way I think, I realized it was my mother's death. I was an only child, and I was raised by a single mother. We weren't really close, but I expected her to take care of me, even when I got older, and all I ever did was cause her problems. I was such a hopeless, hopeless daughter. So I was sure I wouldn't cry when my mom died, but then she did, and while I waited for her at the crematorium, I was hit by a huge sense of loneliness. I realized, "I'm all alone. I don't even have my mom anymore," and the tears wouldn't stop coming.

Then, with tears in their eyes, my friends said to me, "If there's anything we can do to help, don't hesitate to ask. You're not alone. We'll always be here for you." And then, the funeral was supposed to be a closed funeral, with only relatives, so I didn't tell any of my friends about it until right before it happened, and they jumped back at me with, "Why didn't you tell us?!"

Maybe that's when it started—when I started thinking that I want to do anything for these people. I started actively wanting to talk to more and more people, and to deepen my relationships. As long as I live, I want to use that limited time to talk about all kinds of things with all kinds of people—I want to love people. I want to do everything I can. But just because I think that doesn't mean I'm any better at associating with people. I think that all depends on how much I work on it.

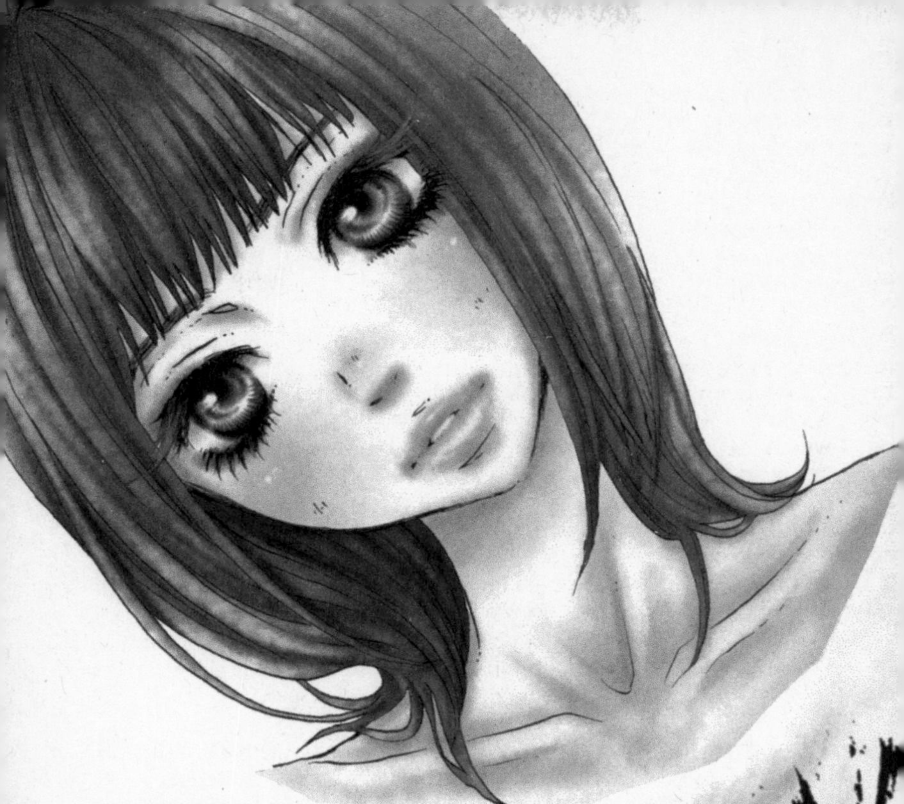

But even after I've talked to a lot of people, I still feel the same. I think that it's not just about other people—you have to make your own happiness. It's not going to come to you if you just sit around waiting. Happiness comes as a result of effort.

People tend to say, "Whatever you're thinking about them, they're probably thinking the same thing," and I think that might be truer than it sounds. But only as long as the other person isn't too self-centered (ha ha).

If you only think about yourself, then that's as far as your happiness goes. If you get involved with—and think about—other people, then it will naturally make everyone happy—not just the other person, but you too.

Then you're both happy! How awesome it that? I want to keep pressing forward with this belief. Because I want to always be smiling. Well, I'll see you in volume four.

Kanae Hazuki
July 2009

A Kodansha Comics Trade Paperback Original
Say I Love You. volume 3 copyright © 2009 Kanae Hazuki
English translation copyright © 2014 Kanae Hazuki

All rights reserved.

Published in the United States by Kodansha Comics, an imprint of
Kodansha USA Publishing, LLC, New York.

Publication rights for this English edition arranged through
Kodansha Ltd, Tokyo.

First published in Japan in 2009 by Kodansha Ltd., Tokyo
as *Sukitte iinayo.* volume 3.

ISBN 978-1-61262-604-8

Printed in the United States of America.

www.kodanshacomics.com

9 8 7 6 5 4 3 2 1
Translation: Alethea and Athena Nibley
Lettering: John Clark
Editing: Ben Applegate